Greener Purchasing
Opportunities and Innovations

Edited by Trevor Russel

Greener
Purchasing

OPPORTUNITIES AND INNOVATIONS

EDITED BY TREVOR RUSSEL

Greenleaf **Publishing**
1998

© 1998 Greenleaf Publishing unless otherwise stated.

Published by _Greenleaf_ Publishing

Greenleaf Publishing is an imprint of
Interleaf Productions Limited
Broom Hall
Sheffield S10 2DR
England

Typeset by Interleaf Productions Limited and printed on
environmentally friendly, acid-free paper from managed forests by
The Cromwell Press, Trowbridge, Wiltshire.

British Library Cataloguing in Publication Data:
Greener purchasing : opportunities and innovations
   1. Industrial procurement - Environmental aspects
   2. Government purchasing - Environmental aspects
   3. Industrial procurement - Case studies   4. Industrial
procurement - Government policy   5. Environmental protection,
- Government policy
I. Russel, Trevor
658.4'08

ISBN 1 874719 04 7

Contents

Foreword

President, World Business Council for Sustainable Development

BUSINESS IS MAKING considerable progress in responding to the sustainable development challenge, and the drive by a growing number of companies towards more eco-efficient practices is one encouraging feature of what has been, and is being, accomplished.

To date, the focus of most companies' actions has been on the production side of the equation. But this is changing. Increasing attention is now being paid to the consumption side—and this is certainly an area where the WBCSD is actively engaged: for example, through its ongoing work on 'Sustainability in the Market'.

Rightly so: companies aiming for eco-efficiency must also take a hard look at their supply chain arrangements. What materials and products they buy and use will be important to them achieving their goal of reducing environmental impact at every stage of their operations—while, as consumers themselves, they can exercise substantial leverage and influence over other producers (their suppliers) and the products and services they provide.

Of course, the path to 'greener purchasing' is strewn with many practical issues— starting with what is a 'green' or 'greener' product, and continuing through to the criteria for judging and selecting 'green' suppliers. But the general thesis that companies should, wherever possible, choose the most environmentally acceptable or preferable products and services is right, and should become a guiding principle within business.

And I believe that the multiplier effect of companies managing their supply chains along such lines can be another significant driver to promoting and cascading the philosophy and practice of eco-efficiency more widely in industry, in particular to smaller enterprises.

This book is timely because it appears when more and more companies are seeing the business and environmental benefits of adopting eco-efficiency, and when they are also understanding that their internal actions towards eco-efficiency should include changing their consumption, as well as production, patterns.

It provides a very comprehensive examination of the key issues around the topic of 'greener purchasing'. However, it also sets out the nuts and bolts, the 'how to', of developing 'greener' supply chain management policies and implementing them, and showing how several major companies have done this, and what the results have been. These sections will be important reading for all purchasing officers.

But, of course, it is the senior management—starting with the CEO—that sets a company on course to eco-efficiency. Given the importance of integrating 'greener' supply chain management into the overall actions toward achieving eco-efficiency, this book is also essential reading for top-level management.

Introduction

Trevor Russel

||| *A Driver for Greener Products and Services*

Buying (and selling) goods and services *per se* is, of course, fundamental to sustaining economic growth. **Greener** purchasing can become a vital tool for achieving **sustainable** development.

Every organisation, public and private—indeed, just about every person on earth—buys something and, by doing so, greases and turns the wheels of every economy. Moreover, those with major purchasing power—notably big companies and the whole public sector—exert considerable economic influence throughout the supply chain over the quality and price of what is produced, sold and bought.

Greener purchasing—**the integration of environmental considerations into purchasing policies, programmes and actions**—is the means for those with buying clout to use their power to drive, faster and further, the whole process of producing greener products and services—from manufacture, through sales and distribution, to final disposal.

Ordinary consumers can do this on one level by demanding, then buying, for example, organic produce or recycled toilet rolls. But, much more significantly, corporate buyers—both private and public sector—can quicken progress towards sustainability by preferring goods and services that are themselves environmentally friendlier than alternatives, or have been produced in a more environmentally friendly way, or both. It is on the public and private sectors that this book concentrates.

And we need to be clear that greener purchasing is not simply about a company (or public-sector authority) buying recycled stationery, or energy-efficient light bulbs, or replacing its fleet of company cars and/or delivery trucks with more environmentally friendly vehicles, nor even buying the right raw materials. This is important—but not enough. **Greener purchasing is also about using suppliers who themselves meet strict environmental standards, so that greening the supply chain is an integral part of the greener purchasing process.**

The potential of greener purchasing is therefore very considerable. One organisation or company can use thousands of immediate suppliers who, in turn, have their own suppliers, so the trickle-down effect of an initiative started at the top of the supply chain can have a transformative effect on the environmental awareness (and performance) of a whole industry. It can contribute to a further significant greening of big business and the public sector. It can even be argued that greener purchasing also does more to green the smaller enterprise sector than dozens of new rules and regulations.

In addition to its potential to drive changes in supplier performance, purchasing also represents a major environmental impact for any company or organisation. Take retailing. If a major supermarket or DIY store were to address on-site issues such as energy efficiency or out-of town developments but ignored the environmental impacts of the thousands of product lines on its shelves, it could not be considered to have an effective environmental management system. Every paint pot, toilet roll or sandwich roll has an environmental impact and, consequently, so too does every contract signed by the buyers in a given company or organisation. With financial capacity comes environmental responsibility. Consequently, the potential and importance of purchasing requires that it is placed at the heart of an environmental management policy.

Given this, where then does greener purchasing rank on the environmental action checklist? Surely, at a time when the environment is increasingly centre-stage, becoming an integral part of everyday management responsibilities, and having a growing impact on most corporate functions (whether in a company or in a central or local government department), greener purchasing is now becoming mainstream to doing business?

Unfortunately, it is not.

III *The Cinderella of Corporate Environmentalism?*

In many cases, greener purchasing has appeared to be the 'Cinderella' of environmental management. Many companies continue to underplay the environmental consequences of their consumption patterns even while they are paying increasing attention to their production patterns. A Business in the Environment (BiE) survey of the top 100 companies in the UK (BiE 1993) found that 'the biggest gap to close is in the creation of environmental programmes with suppliers'. These firms are not environmental laggards, with BiE commending them on activities such as cutting down on emissions and waste, and moving towards eco-efficient production. Yet, to date, they have not put the same effort behind greener purchasing.

If we regard these UK companies as representative of corporate attitudes and behaviour generally, the conclusion must be that the role of greener purchasing in improving environmental performance is widely under-prioritised in business generally. Why is this?

One reason must be the flood of environmental legislation over the last few years which has concentrated the minds of managers on reducing the environmental impacts of production: air and water quality, waste management and so on. A second reason is that environmental purchasing initiatives are just plain difficult to put in place—difficult to promote internally, difficult to start, difficult to manage and difficult to maintain. They are difficult to promote internally because legislation does not demand action, but rather an enlightened recognition of the benefits and opportunities coming from beyond-compliance environmental performance. It is difficult to know where to start because suppliers are numerous, product lines more numerous, and their environmental impacts more numerous still. Greener purchasing initiatives are also difficult to manage because they involve delicate, 'political' negotiations with external organisations and companies. Finally, they are difficult to maintain because they can generate so much information!

This book aims to be the glass slipper for greener purchasing. By providing examples of greener purchasing in practice we aim to help the reader overcome the difficult challenges and implement successful initiatives. The contributors to this volume provide evidence that many major companies *are* now greening their purchasing activities—putting greener purchasing firmly alongside price, quality, delivery, security of supply and other issues critical to their business success. They are buying green goods, and also greening their supply chains by requiring suppliers to meet certain environmental criteria.

Some firms—such as in the detergent industry—have been successfully doing this for a number of years. The forest products industry is another sector where environmental issues shape every stage of the product chain, and greener purchasing initiatives are now rife. Gronow, Pento and Rajotte (Chapter 6), Murphy and Bendell (Chapter 9) and Humphrey (Chapter 24) outline some of the major developments in this industry, while Polonsky *at al.* (Chapter 11) examine the purchase of recycled paper by Western Australian organisations.

Also, public procurement, as the OECD has noted (OECD 1997), *is* going greener. Pento (Chapter 1), van der Grijp (Chapter 4), Environment Canada (Chapter 2), Sanders (Chapter 3) and Wescott (Chapter 5) examine some examples, at local as well as central government level. And, as the public sector progressively greens its purchasing activities, this will have far-reaching ramifications for thousands of companies who are contractors to public bodies.

‖ *The Business Reasons for Greener Purchasing*

Still, this is hardly a ringing endorsement of business awareness and action in exploiting the potential and opportunities of greener purchasing. Just as the best companies have realised there are powerful *business* reasons—quite separate and distinct from compliance obligations—for improving environmental performance, the very best have recognised that these reasons apply equally to greening their purchasing actions. Examples are given by McIntyre (Chapter 20), Sarkis, Liffers and Malette (Chapter 21) and Shimp and Henau (Chapter 22).

Most firms, however, are clearly yet to grasp this, and their short-sightedness is disappointing. Consider, as one example, the **benefit versus cost** issue. What a company spends on buying goods and services represents a major share of its total operating costs. Companies have moved away from choosing suppliers only on the basis of price; **the quality of supply affects profits too**. Companies have for years invested in improving the quality of both their own and their suppliers' operations, thereby improving the performance of their own organisation. The same logic applies to investment in the environmental management of the supply chain— not because of legislative requirements but because companies see **the business case** for doing so.

Working with greener suppliers can **reduce a company's costs**. There is little argument now that improvements, for instance, in waste disposal, energy consumption and material usage actually save money. If suppliers make improvements in these areas, their customers—big companies—will almost certainly ensure some of those savings are passed on to them. They have the leverage to do so—but first they have to use their leverage to insist that suppliers green *their* operations.

Another reason for companies to involve themselves in upgrading their suppliers' environmental performance is **security of supply**: to avert any risk that *their* ability to deliver to customers will be interrupted through a supplier failing to supply specified goods because it falls foul of environmental regulations.

Also, **the way in which companies are judged by customers and investors is undergoing a sea change**. Customers once cared only about the price and quality of products, and the financial community only about profitability. Today, businesses are measured increasingly by the quality of their management, and by the soundness of their environmental practices—with the latter being one of the benchmarks for assessing the former. A greener purchasing policy is a further important opportunity for a company to demonstrate it has quality management committed to improved environmental practice in all areas it can control and/or influence, i.e. including its suppliers. It also avoids the possibility that a company may be tainted by its suppliers' poor environmental performance.

So there are compelling business reasons (never mind any others) for the major companies—who will mainly drive progress to greener purchasing in the private sector—to put environmental considerations at the heart of their purchasing and supply policies. With private consumption responsible for 50%–60% of GDP expenditures in the OECD countries (OECD 1997), it is vital that the private sector adopts greener purchasing as a core management philosophy.

▌ *Greener Public Procurement*

In the next few years, the public sector will also be a key player in pushing greener purchasing higher up the agenda. In the OECD countries, 'government-driven consumption' of products and services accounts for 10%–15% of total GDP spending—which added up to US$1.87–2.81 trillion in 1996 (OECD 1997). Public bodies are definitely big customers—even for the largest multinationals—and governments, central and local, are major players when they come to decide what they buy, and who they buy from.

There is **a growing momentum for greener public procurement**. According to the OECD, initiatives are 'mushrooming'—though, interestingly enough, these are mainly at the local authority level, and 'only a handful of governments have developed or are developing comprehensive national strategies' (OECD 1997). Some examples of central government initiatives include:

▶ **Denmark**—which has an Action Plan for Sustainable Public Procurement policy covering all public purchasing activities, but focusing in particular on ten types of product, including office machinery equipment and supplies, electrical and electronic goods and cars.

▶ **Germany**—which requires all federal institutions to buy products that avoid or reduce waste, use secondary materials, have greater durability, and are either recyclable or can be repaired.

▶ **Japan**—which has an Action Plan for Greening Government Operations: a framework for the selection of environmentally preferable goods.

▶ **United States**—where there is a wide array of programmes and initiatives aimed at encouraging the Federal government to buy 'green'. Many of them target a specific attribute, such as recycled content or energy efficiency.

▶ **UK**—where the Department of Environment, Transport and the Regions has issued a 'Guide for Choosing Environmentally Preferable IT Equipment'. However, it has no statutory force, and there is no commitment by government ministries to follow it—although they 'are looking at greening the whole purchasing chain'.

The European Union is also taking some preliminary steps. In November 1997, the European Parliament urged the European Commission to develop a public procurement policy that promotes sustainability and the integration of environmental considerations into purchasing decisions.

▐ *The Potential Barriers to Progress*

So, there is a growing groundswell of activity on greener purchasing in both the private and public sectors. The Green Purchasing Network in Japan and the new European Green Purchasing Network could provide an important boost to greening purchasing procedures, as Sato (Chapter 14) and van Ermen and Mielisch (Chapter 15) explain. Yet, while the environmental *and* economic case for greener purchasing is indisputable, it has to be pointed out that there are a number of issues to be addressed, some of which could potentially prove a barrier to faster progress.

Identifying green products is a crucial factor—arguably the most important one—in the greener purchasing equation: obviously, the whole notion of buying green falls flat if purchasers do not know which products and services are environmentally preferable. The key to identification is bringing together verifiable information about the effects that products (and services) may have on the environment. Energy efficiency and, more so, minimum recycled content are the two most widely used criteria for judging environmentally preferred products. If a product passes muster on one or both of these, it is often accepted to be a 'greener' product.

Yet, while environmental criteria clearly must underpin greener purchasing decisions, there are snags to relying on 'single-issue' criteria, such as energy efficiency or recycled content, because they do have a number of limitations. A serious one, from an environmental standpoint, is that they could substitute one undesirable impact for another. If, for instance, energy efficiency is based on increased insulation, this may cause problems in the waste phase. Similarly, recycling may not always represent the best environmental option, so minimum recycled content requirements can raise new environmental concerns.

Current greener purchasing initiatives have developed mainly on the basis of single-issue criteria, but their drawbacks are recognised. This explains the drive behind the development of **life-cycle assessments** and **life-cycle approaches**. The first applies to the efforts to develop a tool for the objective assessment of the environmental effects of products and processes through the entire 'cradle-to-grave' lifetime of products. The second covers approaches aimed at encompassing the scientific method and the social, political and economic dimensions of products' environmental effects. A lot of effort is being put into developing the science of life-cycle assessment (LCA), but it is still evolving and maturing and, as things stand, it is being severely questioned whether LCA can be the sole basis for deciding what products are 'best' for the environment.

Eco-labelling schemes, which select products according to multiple environmental criteria, seem a better option, and enjoy growing popularity and support—for example, in Canada, France, Germany, South Korea, the Nordic countries, Japan, the United States and the European Union. Michael Jones discusses their potential in Chapter 17. Despite their popularity, the impact of eco-labels remains fairly marginal. The problem is that they have had little effect on consumer behaviour, except in countries where consumers are strongly environmentally motivated—and, more importantly, there is also no evidence that companies do or would take them into account in their purchasing decisions. Indeed, most of business opposes eco-labelling.

One of the biggest problems encountered at all levels of the purchasing process is the **lack of available and reliable information** about the environmental characteristics of goods and services. This situation is improving as companies put into place environmental management systems (EMSs) to strengthen their capacity to track and record environmental data—and, in turn, to better assess their suppliers' environmental effects vis-à-vis their own products. But the information issue—including the cost of information—remains an obstacle, not least because it inhibits more rapid development of multi-criteria specification of products' environmental characteristics. Julie Haines (Chapter 13) reports interesting findings in the opinions of leading US companies on ISO 14001 and the supply chain.

The role of **technical specifications and standards** is still evolving, but will assume a growing importance, certainly in greener public procurement procedures. There is, says the OECD, a marked preference for performance over design standards, and for international over firm-specific or national standards (OECD 1997).

In addition, 'selecting greener suppliers rather than greener products is a very attractive option' since 'it may enlarge the scope of greener purchasing by rewarding companies that are making the greatest efforts' and hence, 'environmental preferability would be linked to a comprehensive improvement, and not merely to a firm's product' (OECD 1997). While the OECD is referring to the public sector, the same principle can be applied to the private sector—and raises some interesting possibilities.

The link between greener purchasing, particularly by public authorities, and trade is an altogether different issue. The international community still has to work out how to reconcile the potential for conflict between trade rules and environmental regulations—and greener purchasing policies represent one of the pieces of this jigsaw, because there is a very real risk that greener public procurement programmes could be (at least, could be claimed to be) barriers to international trade. Sørensen and Russel discuss this problem in Chapter 7.

Thus, **the path to greener purchasing is strewn with many potential obstacles**. Yet many companies and public-sector bodies have shown that it pays off. And if it works for them, it can—and will—work for others. But how do they green their purchasing procedures and supply chains? Pento (Chapter 1), Cannon (Chapter 19) and Birett (Chapter 8) set out various guidelines for companies and public authorities to follow.

▌ *Following the Innovators*

Of course, purchasing officers aiming to green their purchasing policies can do no better than follow the example of those companies that have led the way. A study by General Motors and the Business for Social Responsibility Education Fund (Calahan Klein *et al.* 1997) examined twenty companies with sales of over $US100 million who source products from US and international suppliers. It identified three models of environmental supply chain management:

▶ A **comprehensive integrated approach** marked by extensive vendor selection and performance evaluation processes, as well as an expectation that suppliers will go beyond compliance to tackle LCA, green design and eco-efficiency.

▶ A **targeted supplier effort**, emphasising supplier compliance with existing environmental laws and regulations.

▶ An **industry standard approach**, asking suppliers to conform to the industry's environmental code of conduct.

The study also identified nine key characteristics of leaders in this area:

1. Strong, high-level corporate commitment to environmental stewardship

2. Desire to lead industry efforts to improve suppliers' environmental performance

3. Integration of environmental goals and staff members into core business functions involving suppliers

4. Clear internal communication on environmental issues and the value of good environmental performance to the company

5. Clear, two-way communication about environmental issues with suppliers

6. Targeted supplier effort

7. Supplier solicitation, selection and monitoring processes that incorporate environmental performance

8. Ongoing supplier education

9. Feedback mechanisms to improve suppliers' environmental management programme

In the UK, Business in the Environment (BiE) has identified seven key steps towards adopting and implementing a greener purchasing policy (BiE 1993). They apply to big companies working with small suppliers—and cover some of the areas mentioned by Baylis, Connell and Flynn in Chapter 10 on the implications of greener purchasing for small and medium-sized enterprises—an absolutely crucial issue.

The first, and this is crucial, is to **understand the business reasons**: companies need to be—and in many cases, probably will be—convinced by the business arguments. But step two, **understanding the environmental reasons** for greener purchasing, is also essential because such initiatives must make environmental as well as economic sense, especially if we are to pre-judge developments in this area.

The third step is that companies must **understand their supply chain**. Major firms have hundreds, even thousands of suppliers; therefore, says BiE, they must prioritise them, deciding which suppliers are linked, through the products/services they provide, to the environmental issues of most importance to the firm, including any question of environmental risk. Ranking suppliers in this area is, inevitably, a crude process, and will largely depend on purchasing officers' judgement. Key or strategic suppliers—for example, those who can bring the firm's business to a halt—will certainly be included. But other suppliers need to be examined too: for instance, those where environmental issues can still be significant, even though they supply only small quantities of materials.

The fourth step is to **adopt a partnership style**. The partnership concept is already a firmly established part of purchasing supply in many organisations, and now, says BiE, needs to be extended to cover greener purchasing. It should involve formal partnership arrangements to share information and work together on environmental improvements. This approach has proved successful in the timber trade, as described by Murphy and Bendell in Chapter 9., Hutchison (Chapter 12) underlines the need to motivate suppliers.

Firms should recognise the information management implications of a greener purchasing initiative and not bombard their suppliers with indiscriminate requests for large amounts of information—the fifth step. Instead, **collect only the information needed**. Key indicators of supplier performance could include: management commitment to environmental improvement; environmental policy; environmental management system; defined targets; and progress towards targets, for example on product composition, processes and environmental management performance.

Step six—obviously critical—is to **validate suppliers' environmental performance**. The mode of validation will largely depend on the type of information collected from the previous stage. It could include reviewing suppliers' internal documents, visiting their sites and auditing their process inputs and outputs, or the processes themselves. There are a number of independent bodies that undertake validation to predetermined performance or systems standards, such as SGS (see Murphy and Bendell, Chapter 9). BiE makes the point that, where suppliers have not undertaken their own environmental review or established an environmental policy, they can actually benefit from being audited, then advised on what improvements to make. Whitaker (Chapter 23) also points out that companies need to measure their performance in managing their supply chains.

The seventh and final of BiE's steps is to **set a timetable for performance improvement**—with clear targets for improvement and an action plan for achieving them. Targets also form the basis of performance measurement.

BiE also stresses that introducing greener purchasing policies is dependent on training—for both suppliers and company (or public authority) purchasing officers. The latter clearly need to know in particular why the environment is important to their company and, especially, to purchasing; what are the company's key environmental issues and improvement targets areas; and how to rate suppliers' environmental credentials.

What happens after corporate purchasing departments have completed all seven steps? Says BiE:

> When the dust has settled, there will be suppliers with whom you are working closely towards common environmental goals and commercial advantage. With others, you will have developed action plans to bring their product or operating procedures up to the required standards. There will, of course, be some who you feel you cannot continue to do business with in the short term (BiE 1993).

Ⅲ *An Outline of the Book*

The book has four parts, covering: public procurement, private purchasing, innovations in greener purchasing and, in the final section, case histories from companies that have successfully 'greened' their purchasing operations. The flow is designed to examine the issues—sometimes different—in the public and private sectors, present some important initiatives to promote greener purchasing in both sectors and, finally, to demonstrate the benefits of greener purchasing in practice.

Tapio Pento (Chapter 1) sets the scene by looking at the three key factors in greener public procurement programmes: who purchases, and when and how are such activities organised; how can a buyer incorporate environmental criteria into purchasing; and how do different types of organisation manage and control their programmes? In Chapters 2 and 3, Environment Canada and Sanders, of the US EPA, explain the policies and practices of their organisations—both of them not only major purchasers, but also important influencers. Van der Grijp (Chapter 4) describes the development and application of environment-oriented public procurement in the Netherlands, including its relevance as an instrument of environmental policy. In Chapter 5, Wescott focuses on the role that local governments have in fostering sustainable communities, including leveraging their power as major purchasers of goods and services locally. The initiatives and programmes being implemented by Finland, Norway and Sweden to green their procurement of paper are reported by Pento, Gronow and Rajotte (Chapter 6), with a useful comparison between the Nordic approach and the practices and guidelines of other OECD countries. Finally, Sørensen and Russel (Chapter 7) draw attention to a key emerging issue: the relationship between greener public procurement initiatives and international trade rules—are they in conflict; will each impede the other?

Section 2 is opened by Birett (Chapter 8) who bridges the public and private sectors by describing how one Canadian municipality has spurred greener purchasing among local businesses. Another partnership initiative—between DIY retailers in the UK and the WWF to source wood products from well-managed products—is described by Murphy and Bendell (Chapter 9). Baylis, Connell and Flynn (Chapter 10) draw on the results of their research among large and small companies in South Wales to explore the implications of greener purchasing on small and medium-sized enterprises (SMEs): those companies most likely to struggle to improve environmental performance, yet which are crucially important to every economy. In Chapter 11,

Polonsky *et al.* look at the role of purchasing agents, the importance they attach to environmental factors, and their relationship with companies marketing environmentally preferable products. Hutchison (Chapter 12) explores the factors motivating companies to integrate environmental criteria into purchasing and supply decisions, and in particular examines the value perceptions from applying or receiving supply chain pressure. Finally, in this section, Haines (Chapter 13) confirms that greening the supply chain is gaining momentum, and in doing so is reinforcing the role of large multinationals in promoting certain behaviours in the marketplace.

The Japanese Green Purchasing Network and its recently launched European counterpart are important innovations in pushing greener purchasing along faster. Sato (Chapter 14) and van Ermen and Mielisch (Chapter 15) respectively explain how their organisations work, and what their objectives are. Sutton (Chapter 16) notes that, as corporate environmentalism takes off in leaps and bounds, there is a tendency to overlook the effects on biodiversity: he provides a methodology to assist companies to take nature into account in developing greener purchasing policies and practices. Jones (Chapter 17) describes the potential role of eco-labelling in the greener purchasing equation. But greener purchasing is only another step along the road to sustainable development, and in Chapter 18 Godfrey sets out a forward-looking agenda for moving the supply chain beyond purely environmental issues.

The case histories in the fourth section are diverse. Cannon (Chapter 19) looks at the problems associated with the cost of purchasing recycled products, with specific attention to examples in Washington State, USA. In Chapter 20, McIntyre assesses some of the issues around the measurement of environmental performance in supply chains as experienced by Xerox Ltd. Sarkis, Liffers and Malette (Chapter 21) investigate the purchasing relationships between Digital Corporation's demanufacturing operation, its customers and suppliers, drawing conclusions that, while specific to this example, have general application in industry. In explaining the approach by one of the world's leading consumer products companies, Shimp and Henau (Chapter 22) stress the need for interaction between all partners—within the company and between them and suppliers—to make greener purchasing work. Whitaker (Chapter 23) draws on his former experiences with IBM to describe the What, Why and How of greener purchasing, while, finally, Humphrey (Chapter 24) takes a detailed look at supply chain management at one of the UK's leading DIY retailers.

III *Not the Final Step*

It is clear that greener purchasing has a considerable amount of ground to cover before it becomes an established business orthodoxy in either the private or public sector. This book attempts to highlight its importance to the goal of improving the environment through improved environmental performance, at every level.

However, environmental improvement is not by itself sustainable development—only a component. Companies and public authorities will need to go much further in their activities and actions (and philosophies) to help achieve that goal. Godfrey (Chapter 18) positions greener purchasing in this wider framework and, in doing so, raises some thought-provoking questions and issues. Nor should we overlook the effects of purchasing on biodiversity: Sutton (Chapter 16) presents a detailed methodology for enabling companies to take this issue into account. In the near future, greener purchasing may become an integral part of the standard ethical sourcing policies of all organisations—in which case, now is the time to act.

But those considerations are a little further down the track. For the moment, the need is to get greener purchasing accepted, adopted and implemented as a central tenet of environmental management; for the public sector to make it the key criterion for deciding what they buy and from whom; for the private sector to afford it the same priority as cleaning up their production operations.

There has been, and continues to be, progress. But much more needs to be done.

I warmly thank all contributors for their enthusiasm for and participation in this book, and for sharing the fruits of their knowledge and experience. I am also extremely grateful to John Stuart at Greenleaf Publishing for all his unflagging encouragement and support, and enviable professionalism.

Section I

Public Purchasing

I

Implementation of Public Green Procurement Programmes

Tapio Pento

EMPIRICAL EVIDENCE suggests that many environmentally oriented public procurement programmes have underachieved because of less than optimal implementation. The failure to take into account existing procurement practices, purchase authority delegation, and oversights in programme management, organisation and motivation are among the reasons for poor results. This chapter illustrates three factors that play an important role in the implementation of green public procurement programmes:

1. Who purchases; and when and how are procurement activities organised?

2. How can a buyer decide that a product is environmentally preferable?

3. How is the green procurement programme managed and controlled across different types of organisation?

The chapter is based on an earlier study made by the author for the OECD (Pento 1997) and a new collection of empirical data on the procurement of goods and adoption of environmental programmes in public organisations in Finland.

III *Decision-Making Units and Procurement Inertia*

A government's policy decision to purchase only environmentally preferable goods does not guarantee that the current direction of procurement will be changed. The decision-making units (DMUs) that are authorised to make purchasing decisions are independent and may not follow the adopted policy. A DMU may consist of only one person, as is the case when a department secretary orders more copying paper. Multiple-person DMUs are common when the purchase is of a higher value or when a product is purchased either for the first time or for a longer time-period. A large DMU may consist of buyers, managers responsible for budgets, users of the product, experts on purchasing and contracts, technical specialists, and nowadays also environmental experts. All members of the DMU may have disincentives—imagined or real—against choosing green products.

The functionality of green products may be a concern. For example, the decision to buy recycled copying paper may raise difficulties with the members of the

DMU if the new paper does not perform as well as the old paper. Some recycled paper has generated negative user experience, because it causes dust to collect in high-speed copying machines, or jams laser printers. If it is likely or even possible that the members of the DMU will be criticised for their selection of a green product, it is easier for them to continue to purchase the same product as before.

Secondly, existing user preferences and habits work against switching to green products. An air-blower in a toilet may be better for the environment than paper towels, but if the users strongly voice their preference for towels, a DMU minimises its own risks by continuing to order towels. Changing user preferences on environmental grounds will not always be easy, unless a green product is clearly less expensive.

A DMU may also perceive the principles of a green procurement programme as an encroachment on their purchasing authority, especially if their opinions are not taken into account. An example of this is a city bus depot, whose purchasing decision-makers were pushed by the managers of a green procurement programme to make certain changes toward greener products. The depot people did not react well to the imposition, and were not happy about being forced to choose products with which they were not familiar, while supposedly retaining all operative and budget responsibilities. Such resistance is enhanced by strong user preferences for existing products.

The running-in of new green products without the acceptance of—or, in some cases, with strong resistance from—most or all members of each DMU cannot be made and should not be attempted in public procurement. Users must have their say, because they can create operative problems if they do not like the product that has been chosen for them. A green procurement programme falters when the operators of copying machines refuse to run the machines with recycled paper. Buyers can slow down the order–delivery process if they consider that their expertise has not been heard. Managers responsible for budgets cannot be bypassed, especially if the green products will cost more than the least-cost alternative. Technical specialists, such as healthcare authorities or managers of public archives, have their own product requirements. Lack of consideration may put any of these parties into a defensive or hostile position, which may totally scupper the implementation of green purchasing for extended periods of time.

Organisational inertia will delay implementation, as will the existence of long procurement cycles. Acceptance by the DMU does not imply that a green product will be bought immediately. Many products are purchased with long-term contracts, which are changed periodically when products and suppliers are under review. Further delays can be expected when a selection of a particular product or an operating system in the past has locked in future choices for long time-periods. A clinical laboratory reagent system based totally on throw-away consumables is not environmentally friendly, but cannot be easily changed, because it is part of a much larger system which involves operating practices across the hospital and the processing of patient information.

II| *The Organisation of the Procurement Function*

The magnitude of the management task in the implementation of a green procurement programme depends largely on how the public purchasing function is organised. If the organisation has only a few decision-making units, a green procurement programme is easy to communicate to the decision-makers, and product and brand recommendations and choices can be managed with relatively small amounts of resources.

Some governments and cities have centralised all of their purchasing to a government supply organisation, which makes the product choices for all public organisations and is the sole source from which they can order goods. In some countries, government supply houses are organised geographically or functionally so that schools, hospitals, universities, postal services, etc. each have their own centralised supply. A supply house may stock the goods, or may have the suppliers make direct deliveries.

In centralised procurement, the decision about which brands will be available is made by the decision-making units of a governmental supply organisation (see Fig. 1). Each DMU is made up of experts from the supply organisation and from other government organisations, possibly augmented with users' representatives. The DMU selects the brands that will be available from the supply for a given time-period, and reviews this decision before the end of the period.

The communication of a green procurement programme to the relatively few DMUs in a centralised procurement system is straightforward. The aims of the programme, product recommendations and other information can be communicated directly to the DMUs and the managers of the supply house. The choice of an environmentally preferable brand by the DMU changes all purchasing by all governmental units, because all must order through the central supply. In this system, green procurement programmes can be implemented, managed and controlled by a few individuals who participate in the work of the DMUs.

The switch to environmentally preferable products in this system is also slowed down by procurement inertia and users' habits. The members of the centralised DMUs may hesitate in changing products and brands because they are open to criticisms from very many directions inside government organisations and from suppliers and distributors. Any objective or subjective failure of a new product may damage the position and the reputation of the employees of the government supply house. The adoption of multi-lining, i.e. the introduction of environmentally preferable products as one choice among the available product lines reduces this risk.

Centralised government procurement is becoming rare because many governments have decided to purchase on the open market. For example, Finland, the Netherlands and the United States have made this change in the last few years.[1] All purchasing tasks in an open procurement organisation are delegated to cost centres,

---

1. The Government Service Authority of the United States lost its central supply role with the Federal Acquisition Streamlining Act of 1995, and the Finnish Government Procurement Centre VHK was privatised in the beginning of the same year. Both the GSA and the successor to the VHK now act as government-owned distributors, which do not have the position of sole suppliers, and which have lost much of their earlier share of public purchases.

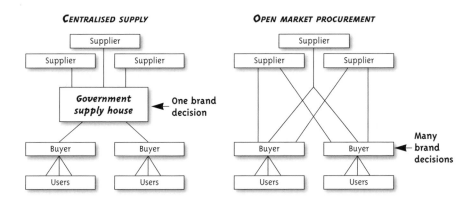

Figure 1: Centralised Supply and Open-Market Procurement

i.e. to operative units in central or local government. These have their own budgets and are responsible for their costs. The cost centres are free to make their product and brand choices within the limits of their own budgets without interference from above. Each cost centre has its own decision-making units, which select products and make contracts with suppliers and distributors as they see best.

The number of decision-making units in open-market procurement can be very large. There will be tens of thousands of individuals who make product and brand decisions in smaller countries, and millions in large ones, all of whom have their own product and brand preferences and attitudes toward environmental procurement. This organisational format makes the task of implementing environmentally preferable procurement (EPP) programmes similar to convincing all consumers to use environmentally better products. Extensive resources and long time-periods are required in implementing a programme, and emphasis will be shifted toward communication and education of the buyers to increase their motivation for using green products. The implementation of a green procurement programme is hampered by the lack of direct communication to the buyers, who are not readily identified (e.g. 'Who buys copying paper in this office?'). In addition, the cost centres' budget independence limits the role of a centralised green procurement programme in making recommendations about product and brand choices.

Many governments have combined open-market purchasing with a frame agreement system, in which a central procurement organisation negotiates discounts with suppliers, and acts as an adviser to the buyers about available products, brands and prices. The logic of these arrangements is that the size of the total volume that is purchased by the public organisations as a whole will facilitate a strong negotiation position and thus lower prices. The central organisation studies available products and suppliers, prices and delivery conditions, technical merits of products in different applications, and selects the products and suppliers that it considers the best, negotiates a frame agreement with the suppliers that specifies prices or, more commonly, discounts, which are given to governmental buyers. It produces lists of products and suppliers and the agreed frame prices or discounts and delivers the lists to the buyers to use, typically at an interval of six to twelve months.

The buyers may opt to use the frame agreement in their purchasing, or may try to improve the terms of the frame by renegotiating with the specified suppliers, or may use other suppliers or products if they so wish. Interviews conducted in Finland and Norway indicate that the small-quantity users tend to adhere to the frame, because separate negotiations for them are not economically or organisationally productive, and their lack of purchasing volume prevents them from gaining terms better than they get with the frame. Larger buyers, who can use their own volume as a leverage, and buyers in remote or other special locations, are prone to making less use of the frame, and renegotiate directly with suppliers.

The existence of frame organisations offers a possibility for the managers of an EPP programme to make sure that green products and brands are at least offered and recommended to the buyers. The central frame organisation also provides a good communication channel, because it is in touch with most of the buyers through its activities. The regular flows of information from the frame organisation to the buyers and users about the newest frame agreement conditions may serve as a channel for environmental messages. It is worth noting that not all government organisations do make use of the frame agreements: some have their own DMUs, and not all consumption can be affected through the frames because the final choice is with the local buyers and users.

Some government supply houses have been privatised and have become, in essence, private distributors, which compete with other suppliers for the custom of organisations of central and local governments. These tend to concentrate on governmental buyers, and some have retained large market shares in this segment.

Government-owned distributors operate on the principles of open markets and have several distribution methods. Some may work extensively with their own frame agreements, which they negotiate directly with manufacturers and other local distributors, normally without any formal governmental decision-making unit. Under these agreements, small-volume buyers can use the credit cards or credit lines issued by the distributor to make their purchases at the specified retailers or other supply houses at current frame prices or discounts. Larger buyers can specify their product preferences to some extent, and order goods in bulk from the distributors' warehouses. Largest users decide their product choices and negotiate their prices and terms periodically, taking deliveries either from the warehouses of the distributors or as drop-shipments directly from the manufacturers.

The distributors offer a communication channel through which a section of governmental buyers can be reached. They know their customers, and often have regular mailings or campaigns, which can be used as channels of information concerning green procurement news. The decision-making power of a government-owned distributor concerning product choices is reduced almost to that of a normal wholesaler or office supply house, who will mostly concentrate on goods that are the easiest to sell and offer the best margins. The distributor is in competition with other suppliers, and will offer its customers the products they prefer. It can be persuaded to make available products from green lists, but the distributor is not always capable or willing to influence excessively the customers' product decisions. The commercial interest of the firm is to attract the customer's business via a certain product, not to increase costs by educating the customer on which product to choose.

Managers of green procurement programmes have little sway over the free-market distributors. They can wish for and, in the case of a government-owned distributor, can point out to the existence of a new procurement programme, but the decision of what products are offered and how they are promoted is in the hands of the distributors. Permanent changes in procurement patterns can be accomplished only through educating public buyers and users to demand green products from their suppliers.

The basic organisational structures described above relate to government units. Procurement programmes may also embrace non-governmental purchasing, when the government requires that its outside suppliers, or organisations otherwise financed by the government, must comply with set procurement rules. For example, the Finnish Law on Public Procurement 1505/92 (*Laki julkisista hankinnoista*, §6) specifies that the law also applies to purchases made by private firms, but which receive more than 50% of their financing from the government. A government may also require, like the US Environmental Protection Agency, that important suppliers follow the procurement rules set by the government unit. However, the running-in and control of non-governmental purchases by outside organisations may not be easy to accomplish, because of the lack of information and monitoring facilities.

▓ *Operationalisation of Procurement Criteria*

Public purchasing is controlled by laws and directives that are usually geared toward directing the purchaser to the lowest-cost option. Finnish law on public procurement (*Laki julkisista hankinnoista*) is typical in this respect, stating that, of all competitive offers, the one that is accepted must be lowest in price or lowest in total costs. A total cost calculation can be invoked when the costs of products vary over their economic life-cycles.

Environmental criteria, as set forth by the LCA approach, are only a subset of the criteria to be considered in public procurement. The main criteria specify products that give the best economic value, in terms of quality, delivery, after-sales service, operating costs and so on. The law is currently under revision, and the new version is expected to recognise explicitly the existence of environmental motives.

Under such legislation, it is possible to have a sequential procurement rule, in which regular purchasing criteria are first applied to find a set of products that are identical or nearly identical in price or total cost. Environmental characteristics of the products would then be taken into account at this point, and the final selection must be made between products that are still identical after this evaluation.

Another approach is to select the most important characteristics of the product and to specify 'hurdles' that have to be satisfied. This procedure is common in the European Union and the hurdle values are published in tenders. According to the new Green Paper on Public Procurement, the characteristics may include environmental considerations but, during the contract award phase, environmental factors could only play a part in identifying the most economically advantageous tender (CEC 1996b: 41).

In practice, purchasing officers and buyers have considerable leeway in their application of the rules. Hurdles can be set at levels that can be met by a number of products, and the final decision will then often be made using informal rules, such as relationships with existing suppliers, nationality or locality of the supplier, and so on. This latitude may facilitate the practice of environmental procurement informally, even when formal rules either do not recognise it or prohibit it. The introduction of environmental criteria informally, especially when undertaken by a purchasing officer, offers almost the same environmental potential as a formal programme.

III *Management of an Environmentally Preferable Procurement Programme*

The key issue in the management of environmentally preferable procurement is actually getting the members of governmental decision-making units to adopt purchasing practices that favour the environmental products and to persuade manufacturers to supply them at a competitive price. Skills in marketing the environmental agenda are needed in both tasks. Good programme management practice calls for an analysis of the present situation, the identification of people who are responsible for the programme, the setting of goals, prioritisation of project tasks and actions, and monitoring of the programme's effects.[2]

Defining the target members of staff is the first task of an internal environmental procurement marketing plan. The type of procurement system that is in place defines the number and the locations of the DMUs and their relative autonomy. As mentioned above, a concerted action on environmentally sound purchasing practices is not feasible without considerable networking and discussions with concerned individuals. The establishment of effective multi-stakeholder task forces to work on the development of suitable purchase criteria and procedures requires the deployment of resources. Optimal focusing of resources necessitates a prioritisation of products and targets. A selection of a narrower target could be based, for example, on some organisational units only, on high-volume buyers, or on a geographical area. Selections of products involve quantity criteria, and an analysis of the environmental improvements that can be accomplished by changed procurement practices. Another consideration is to prioritise those products for which the likelihood of adoption by governmental buyers and users is highest.

The marketing of a programme requires that the DMUs switch to using the products on the green lists, possibly even at the expense of other performance attributes and possibly even at a slightly higher price. One of the oldest buyer behaviour models, the AIDA, states that this can be accomplished by changing peoples' attitudes so that they become interested enough to make the desired purchase decisions. The attitudes of government employees can be expected not to deviate significantly from those of the general population. Attitude studies have shown that the majority of people are not against environmentally better products, but are conservative in their product choices, are afraid of getting products that are second-rate in performance, and are generally unlikely to forego their personal convenience or pay more for green products.

2. The Norwegian governmental Green Programme Paper also stresses the prioritisation of inputs and support programmes at all organisational levels (MiljøKompetans 1994: 30-53).

Information about an EPP programme and its goals, as well as detailed facts and training in the use of the new product choices are the main tools in changing attitudes and raising the interest of users and buyers. Information and training are needed because organisational buyers, just like consumers, cannot internalise external costs easily, and are hesitant of making changes because of lack of reliable information (Kaas 1992). The marketing experience of some EPP programmes has shown that a couple of meetings with departmental managers and a few half-hearted mailing campaigns plus a story in some employee magazines are not sufficient to produce the desired results. Suitable green promotional campaigns, backed by the decision and continuous support of the highest government authorities are the main tools for an attitude-changing programme. The implementation of internal green marketing programmes has been the subject of increasing research in recent years, and tools for such programmes are available.[3]

Standard project management tools can also be employed in managing EPP programmes, especially until the programmes have become established organisational practice. The objectives of the project are defined; the personnel and the main goals are specified; the target personnel in government organisations and in supply firms are selected; the promotional, educational and training tools are chosen; action plans and time schedules are produced; and monitoring procedures for the success of the programme and the direction and amount of necessary additional action are designed and put into place. The literature on change management in organisations points out that people are inclined to resist altering their behavioural patterns and decisions, and effecting change may take a long time, especially if there is no emergency to justify it. Involving people makes the process faster and easier for everyone. Changing the attitudes of government employees at all levels towards a more favourable view of environmental products, and raising their active interest to a level where they will spontaneously include environmental considerations in decision-making will (together with organisational inertia) prolong the schedules of EPP programmes.

The key problem in managing an EPP programme is the interface between manufacturers and suppliers/distributors and the volume of 'green' goods required. Suppliers perceive volumes that are too small to be of economic interest, and buyers perceive an insufficient number of goods and suppliers. The legal requirement for government procurement programmes to seek tenders from several suppliers exacerbates this problem. It is not economical to launch a new type of paper by initially manufacturing small quantities, because the scale of current industry practice requires that tens or hundreds of thousands of tons of annual demand must exist before a new grade is introduced. In addition, new organisational procedures in government, with the delegation of purchasing authority, reduce the possibility of making volume guarantees. Yet assurances of sufficient volumes could be a decisive tool in providing manufacturers with the incentive to invest in environmentally more benign products and processes. For example, if a large country could guarantee the continuous purchase of 300,000 tons of a sandwich paper annually at a given price, one can surmise that several manufacturers would seriously consider making the necessary investment.

---

3. See, e.g., Cahill (1996) on internal marketing, and Meffert and Kirchgeorg (1993) or Peattie (1995) on green marketing.

The management of an EPP programme also involves co-ordination with other environmental policies, strategies, programmes and rules. Several dimensions are of interest here, beginning with the alignment of paper procurement with programmes of which it is a part, with the running-in and improvement of internal distribution practices in public organisations, efficiencies in consumption, and the co-ordination of the programme with command-and-control regulations and other general environmental programmes.

The effects of a paper procurement programme are enhanced by the simultaneous implementation of other practices. Reduction of consumption can be attempted by introducing two-sided copying, use of the smaller A4R size instead of A3 when possible, economy drives on hygiene paper, minimising the length of reports and the efficient use of electronic mail. The co-ordination and marketing of procurement preferences and related practices can feasibly be integrated under the same project management.

Management of the interface between the organisation and paper suppliers requires first of all an understanding of the economic principles and priorities of manufacturers. Proponents of environmental programmes appear to be more likely to believe in win–win situations, in which an environmentally better product or production also makes economic sense for the manufacturers.[4] When this is not the case, its introduction into discussions is not amenable to improving relations or getting the manufacturers to respond in an optimal way.

---

4. For a discussion of the prevalence of win–win possibilities in heavy industries, see Walley and Whitehead (1995) and *Harvard Business Review* (1994).

2 *Towards Greener Government Procurement*
An Environment Canada Case Study

Environment Canada, Corporate Services,
Administration Directorate

GREENER GOVERNMENT PURCHASING is an important component of the Government of Canada's larger strategy to advance sound environmental management for government policies and operations. Like many federal departments, Environment Canada is working to promote greener procurement through the effective management of its own operations. It is also working informally with industry and other governments to advance greener government procurement both nationally and internationally in a similar fashion.

▌ *The Government of Canada's Purchasing Power*

The Government of Canada, through its purchasing practices, can have a significant impact on the national economy and on the goods and services made available in the marketplace. This impact is articulated in different ways. First, spending by the Government of Canada is highly visible and is frequently scrutinised by the media and general public. This public scrutiny provides the federal government with both the opportunity and the obligation to lead by example in demonstrating its environmental commitment through greener purchasing practices. This issue of environmental leadership is particularly relevant for Environment Canada as a congruence between its policies and actions is needed for the department to be credible nationally and internationally.

Second, as the largest single buyer and property manager in Canada, the federal government has an opportunity to harness its spending power. A 1996 report by Price Waterhouse (Price Waterhouse 1996) determined that the Government of Canada spends $11.6 billion annually on products and services, and manages approximately 64,000 buildings throughout Canada. In some areas, such as the environmental industry sector, computer purchases and defence and security products, the federal government is among the largest buyers due to the dollar value of purchases made and its unique procurement requirements. In these areas, government procurement has the potential to be an important driver for the supply of environmentally preferable products and services.

Ⅲ *Benefits of Greener Government Procurement*

Greener government procurement can result in many environmental, economic and social benefits. Some of the environmental and economic advantages of purchasing environmentally friendly products and services include (Government of Canada 1996; NRTEE 1998):

▶ Increased savings from buying goods that can be re-used or remanufactured

▶ Lower costs due to efficient waste and hazardous materials management

▶ Cost savings from employing energy-, water- and fuel-conserving devices

▶ Lower health costs related to exposure to toxics

▶ Reduced demand for landfill space

These savings are particularly attractive given the fiscal restraint that the federal government has imposed on its internal operations.

Greener government procurement also supports Environment Canada's mandate to promote pollution prevention, and the use of environmental management systems and life-cycle management. A recent Canadian study found that federal government procurement has the potential broadly to stimulate manufacturers and suppliers to upgrade their processes, implement cleaner production techniques and change the way in which their services are delivered (NRTEE 1997). In this way, greener federal procurement is an important complement to a broad mix of policy tools such as voluntary programmes, economic instruments and reporting mechanisms that seek to influence industry through non-legislative means.

Effective use of federal spending power also helps to strengthen market demand for environmental goods, services and technologies, thus supporting growth and innovation in Canada's environmental industry. The environmental industries sector in Canada is large and growing. It is composed of 4,500 firms employing 150,000 workers with annual sales of $16 billion (Statistics Canada 1995). Canada's environmental industry is largely an enabling sector that provides expertise, technologies and services to meet the environmental needs of traditional industrial sectors. While strong environmental regulations are one of the most important drivers for the demand of environmental services, federal spending can at the very least add to overall market demand for these services.

Finally, the process of implementing a greener government procurement strategy is an effective means of fostering positive cultural change and improving employee commitment within individual departments. This is due to the fact that greener government action plans and training programmes engage employees in the change process, increase organisational awareness and encourage personal responsibility for the environment.

Ⅲ *The Government of Canada's Framework for Sustainable Development*

The goal of greener government procurement fits within the Government of Canada's broader effort to integrate environmental and sustainable development considerations into the day-to-day decision-making of managers and employees at all levels. To this end, a broad framework has been established. In 1995, legislation was passed requiring federal government departments and agencies to table sustainable development strategies in Parliament by December 1997. Sustainable development strategies include action plans to address some of the economic, environmental and social impacts of departmental policies, programmes and operations. To ensure momentum is maintained, departments must publicly report their progress in achieving their targets annually and update their strategies every three years. A Commissioner of the Environment and Sustainable Development was also mandated[1] to monitor how departments have implemented their action plans and to determine whether they have met the objectives of their sustainable development strategies.

In an effort to guide the sustainable development work of departments, the Government of Canada endorsed two key policies in 1995. *A Guide to Green Government* (Government of Canada 1995a) outlines the federal government's commitment to integrate sustainable development into the way government defines its business and makes its decisions. The *Directions on Greening Government Operations* (Government of Canada 1995b) policy directs departments to implement environmental management systems (EMSs) and identifies greener procurement as a key environmental issue to be addressed by departments. Because individual departments have flexibility and discretion in managing their environmental risks and opportunities, they are at different stages of EMS implementation. Many departments are working to implement greener purchasing strategies as part of their overall EMS strategies.

To provide guidance on the specific issue of greener government procurement, the Government of Canada has included environmental requirements in its *Material Management Policy*. This policy indicates that managers are required to 'include environmental considerations in all aspects of managing material from the planning phase through acquisition, use and disposal of material' (Treasury Board of Canada Secretariat 1995: Ch. 1-1). Direction is provided to apply the four Rs (reduce, re-use, recycle and recover) throughout the materiel life-cycle, which is composed of the planning, acquisition, maintenance/operations, and disposal phases.

The *Material Management Policy* is important as it outlines the broad goal for which federal departments must strive. However, because each department must establish its own path for implementation, little guidance has been given to assist federal departments in the operationalisation of this policy. This absence of procurement targets, monitoring and reporting requirements, and high-level 'signalling' regarding the importance of greener procurement poses challenges. As a result, efforts to employ a co-ordinated approach across federal departments have been unfocused and limited to date.

||| *Challenges to Greener Government Procurement*

In addition to the absence of centralised direction, federal departments face many other challenges in increasing the quantity of greener goods and services purchased. One is the increasingly decentralised manner in which purchasing is carried out in

---

1. Amendments to the Government of Canada's *Auditor General Act,* 1995.

federal departments. The procurement process has dramatically changed in recent years due to a reduced reliance on central purchasing agents and a corresponding increase in the number of managers and employees who have purchasing authority through non-electronic purchasing instruments such as credit cards. Within Environment Canada, procurement decisions were previously co-ordinated by a small group of professional procurement officers. Today, however, more than 25% of employees have the authority to make purchases of goods and services valued up to $5,000 (Janhager 1995). These purchases, in terms of actual transactions, account for the majority of Environment Canada acquisitions. This trend will only grow in time as purchasing authority is expected to increase to up to $25,000 in the coming years.

Decentralisation and the reliance on non-electronic purchasing instruments make it difficult for departments to measure accurately and monitor the purchasing practices of its employees, particularly for those items under $5,000. As a result, departments often do not have the necessary information to quantify the percentage of greener purchases made, to develop concrete procurement targets and to measure the effectiveness of greener procurement action plans. Preliminary work by departments to find solutions to this problem indicates that there are few measures that could be easily put into place without significant system and labour costs.

Limited time and financial resources also pose challenges to increasing greener government procurement. There is a frequently held misconception that environmentally preferable products cost more and perform less well than their alternatives (NRTEE 1997). As a result, ongoing and punctual educational efforts are needed to change these negative biases.

There are cases where the original acquisition costs of greener goods are indeed higher. However, the economic benefits for these greener goods can often be demonstrated when the costs associated with the product's full life-cycle are factored into the buying decision. Unfortunately, managers typically do not have the capacity nor time to calculate the life-cycle costs and benefits of their procurement decisions. This is particularly the case for goods such as computer or laboratory equipment that experience a high rate of technological change. Moreover, most if not all of the secondary costs do not represent a charge against manager budgets. As a result, procurement decisions are all too often based on perceptions of product quality and original acquisition costs.

Limited resources pose a special concern for managers responsible for the environmental management of the internal operations of departments. They typically employ a risk management approach to prioritise the use of funds for internal environmental activities. Because internal environmental initiatives related to health and safety and legal compliance are given greatest priority, internal greener procurement initiatives often do not receive adequate attention or resources.

Another complicating factor for government departments is the need to reconcile the goal of greener purchasing with competing priorities, as government procurement is often employed to advance a range of policy objectives. Managers must therefore evaluate other considerations, including competitive pricing, job creation, reduction of regional disparities and the promotion of employment equity. One example is the federal *Procurement Strategy for Aboriginal Business* (PSAB) (Treasury Board of Canada Secretariat 1996). The purpose of this strategy is to increase representation of aboriginal business in federal government contract awards and sub-contracts. All federal departments and agencies with contracting budgets in excess of $1 million must develop and report on multi-year performance objectives, such as the estimated number and dollar value of contracts awarded to aboriginal businesses. As a result of these different procurement priorities, win–win solutions are not always possible.

International trade agreements also complicate the government procurement process. Government of Canada departments are subject to various trade agreements including the 1996 World Trade Organisation Agreement on Government Procurement and the 1992 North American Free Trade Agreement (NAFTA). These agreements have been endorsed to eliminate barriers to trade and to facilitate the cross-border movement of goods and services between signatory countries. As a result, enterprises of signatory countries can bid for contracts that exceed the thresholds of the varying agreements. For example, Government of Canada contracts must be open to the United States for goods valued CDN$34,100 or greater; while the threshold for services for both the United States and Mexico is approximately CDN$72,000.

In some cases, these trade agreements can hinder greener government purchasing as contracts can only specify greener performance criteria and cannot, for example, specify 'national' eco-labelling trademarks. That said, these agreements recognise the need for the protection of essential security interests and, as a result, some contract categories are excluded. These exceptions enable departments, such as Environment Canada, to be more prescriptive for contracts in areas such as research and development, utilities and weather reporting and observation services.[2]

❘❘❘ Defining 'Greener' Goods and Services

Given these challenges, departments require simple, easy-to-use tools to inform and guide employee procurement decisions. However, managers responsible for the development of simple tools face challenges in determining what constitutes a greener product or service. This process can often be both intimidating and value-laden, as it is difficult to weigh environmental merits across different product categories and attributes. For example, how does one evaluate the merits of wool versus synthetic carpeting made from recycled pop bottles; or the merits of processes that emphasise toxic reduction versus energy efficiency? In an effort to select greener goods and services, departments are trying to employ a multi-faceted approach that includes the use of national eco-labelling programmes, the incorporation of environmental specifications in government tenders and life-cycle analysis. That said, greener procurement strategies have relied most heavily on national eco-labelling programmes, with the most influential being Canada's Environmental Choice Program (ECP).

Environment Canada established the ECP in 1988 to guide consumers in making environmentally sound purchasing decisions and to encourage the commercial development of less harmful products. The ECP, currently managed by TerraChoice

---

2. North American Free Trade Agreement between the Government of Canada, the United Mexican States and the United States of America, 1992, Annex 1001.1b-1.

Environmental Services Inc., was the second such programme to be developed in the world. The ECP awards the official 'Environmental Choice' logo certification mark to products or services that meet environmental criteria established in co-operation with industry, government and public interest groups. Certification may be awarded for those products that have been re-used, or are made in a way that improves energy efficiency, reduces hazardous by-products or uses recycled materials. In some ECP guidelines, supplier production processes are considered for goods such as paints, printers, adhesives and engine coolants. While the ECP does not currently require companies to have an operating EMS or to carry out environmental audits, its certification process recognises companies that are ISO 14004 certified.

The ECP enjoys international credibility due to a comprehensive third-party certification process that includes a review of product and process information; an examination of quality assurance/control measures; and an audit of the company's facilities and processes relevant to the product being certified. The programme has guidelines for over fifty products and services. In addition, there are currently over 165 companies licensed to use the EcoLogo, and approximately 2,000 household, commercial and industrial products certified by the ECP (TerraChoice 1997).

Use of eco-labelling programmes, such as the ECP, is an effective means of identifying greener procurement options. However, these programmes alone are not sufficient to inform government decision-makers because only a small portion of products and services required by the federal government have obtained certification. This is due to many factors. First, these programmes typically focus on commonly purchased goods such as office products and household items, and not the unique or highly specific products often required by the federal government. Second, rapid technological change results in the introduction of new products or goods that have not gone through the certification process. Third, low Canadian demand for greener goods results in the fact that the EcoLogo is not broadly promoted or communicated by Canadian companies in their major marketing efforts (NRTEE 1997). Fourth, certification and licensing costs may limit participation by those firms, particularly small and medium-sized enterprises, that do not anticipate sufficient economic benefits through these programmes. Industry reluctance to market environmental attributes and the low market demand are mutually reinforcing, with the end result being a limited number of greener goods and services that are advertised and available in the Canadian marketplace.

In an effort to make incremental improvements to procurement practices, federal departments, such as Environment Canada, are broadening their definition of what constitutes a greener good and are starting to include notions such as greener production processes. This provides a larger range of greener goods to choose from and also reinforces industry efforts to apply more comprehensive approaches such as environmental design, environmental management systems and life-cycle analysis.

A national electronic greener procurement database called the *Environmental Information Service* is currently being designed by Public Works and Government Services Canada (PWGSC), another federal department, which will be based on a more comprehensive definition of greener goods and services. The evaluation and selection criteria are expected to include concepts related to the overall environmental management of a firm, including its use of natural resources, new or modified production processes, as well as the environmental performance of suppliers. Environment Canada is also seeking to improve its procurement practices by buying greener goods and services where certified 'green' options are not available. To this end, it exchanges greener procurement tools and criteria, such as greener product lists, with other federal departments, provincial governments and other countries. While these tools may not represent perfect solutions, they enable Environment Canada to benefit from the work of others and, in turn, make incremental improvements to purchasing practices.

While some progress is being made to better identify greener goods and services, more work is required nationally and internationally so that consumers have the necessary information to evaluate confidently and select greener goods across different product attributes and categories.

▌ *Environment Canada's Approach to Greener Procurement*

Environment Canada tabled its first sustainable development strategy in Parliament in April 1997 in support of the Government of Canada's commitment to the environment and sustainable development. The department's strategy is an important step in comprehensively assessing the economic, environmental and social impacts of its policies, programmes and operations. Environment Canada's current work to design and implement an EMS represents the operational component of its sustainable development strategy. An EMS will enable Environment Canada to manage strategically its environmental risks and opportunities, including greener procurement.

Prior to the implementation of its EMS, Environment Canada employed a pragmatic, results-oriented approach to increase the quantity of greener goods and services it purchased. Ministerial approval of Environment Canada's *Green Procurement Policy* in 1994 was an important first step. The policy provides direction in guiding employee purchasing decisions, while at the same time leaving room for flexibility in decision-making. This policy directs employees to:

▶ Consider the 'cradle-to-grave' impact of goods and services.

▶ Use EcoLogo-certified products wherever feasible.

▶ Adopt greener criteria in purchasing decisions (i.e. select recycled or energy-efficient products).

▶ Include environmental terms and conditions within the selection criteria of Environment Canada contracts.

Effective training programmes and information tools are essential in increasing employee awareness so that this policy becomes a daily reality for departmental personnel. Environment Canada has developed several useful greener procurement tools to assist employees in making better purchasing decisions. Environment Canada's recently developed catalogue, *51 Green Products Guide*, identifies greener product options for those items—such as computers, office furniture, paper products—that are most commonly purchased by the department. Electronic greener procurement databases have also been developed by regional Environment Canada offices to meet their local purchasing needs.

To promote awareness and use of these tools, Environment Canada developed a 'green suite' of computer-based training courses which is available to employees through its departmental computer system. The department also designed and piloted a half-day *Greener Procurement Workshop* which is to be offered to those personnel that have a direct procurement role. This workshop focuses on concrete ways of encouraging greener procurement by making small changes to employee purchasing practices and applying practical procurement tools. It also introduces social marketing concepts by eliciting employee commitments to greener procurement.

These efforts have emphasised a pragmatic, small-steps approach which encourages employees to take responsibility for their procurement decisions. However, as the department implements its EMS, it is beginning to take a more strategic approach to the management of its internal operations and greener procurement efforts. The department's *Operational Environment Policy*, approved in 1997, identifies greener procurement as a key component of Environment Canada's internal environmental strategy. This view was reinforced in the findings of a department-wide initial environmental review (IER) which identified greener procurement as a priority environmental aspect for the department. As a result, Environment Canada's National EMS Team established a departmental procurement working group in 1997. This group will be responsible for conducting a 'mini-EMS' for greener procurement issues by systematically applying the following EMS principles:

▶ Securing departmental commitment

▶ Developing concrete action plans

▶ Implementing action plans and ensuring departmental capacity to do so

▶ Measuring and evaluating progress

▶ Continuously reviewing and improving Environment Canada's performance

At the present time, the working group is developing a database which will be used for Environment Canada contracts. An important next step will be to develop better means of tracking greener purchasing within Environment Canada and to create progressive greener procurement targets that can be effectively measured and monitored. The establishment of a working group represents a positive step forward toward a more strategic and co-ordinated approach in managing Environment Canada's greener procurement efforts.

▍▍ *Targeted Greener Procurement Strategies*

In order to achieve the greatest results in the most efficient manner, federal government departments, including Environment Canada, are working in partnership with non-governmental organisations and industry to develop practical options. This work has typically focused on those products and services that have significant environmental and economic impacts, and on those transactions that are carried out by a relatively small number of employees.

▍▍▍ Vehicles

Procurement and management of the federal fleet represents an important opportunity area for greener procurement. The passage of the *Alternative Fuels Act* by

Parliament in 1995 demonstrates the Government of Canada's commitment to environmental leadership by reducing a broad range of air pollutants through the increased use of alternatively fuelled vehicles. This act requires that 50% of Government of Canada eligible new vehicle purchases in fiscal year 1997/98 operate using alternative fuels where cost-effective and feasible. This requirement rises to 60% in 1998/99 and 75% in 1999/2000.

In addition to the environmental benefits, it is thought by some that this act may support an increase in the demand for alternatively fuelled vehicles in Canada. However, it is important to recognise that the Government of Canada's total fleet of 25,000 vehicles represents less than 1% of the on-road vehicles in use in Canada. Federal departments, even as a collective, may not have sufficient power to impact on the alternative fuel supply infrastructure given the geographic dispersion of federal operations. The *Alternative Fuels Act* does, however, underline the federal government's commitment to environmental leadership through the implementation of a greener procurement strategy for its fleet to reduce its environmental impact.

All federal departments are working towards compliance with this act as part of their overall environmental management programmes, and are looking toward automobile and alternative fuel suppliers to design creative technologies that will facilitate compliance. As part of its broader fleet strategy, Environment Canada's Minister, in 1995, committed the department to reduce its fleet size by 30% over three years, to increase its use of alternative fuels (such as propane and natural gas), to increase its use of car pooling and leasing, and to use recycled motor oils and coolants. A departmental fleet policy was approved by senior management and a comprehensive training programme was implemented to educate drivers on the benefits of environmentally sound driving, maintenance and procurement practices. To share best practices and implement regional action plans, a departmental ground transportation working group, composed of fleet managers, was formed in 1997.

Environment Canada has reduced its fleet from 711 to 570 vehicles to date. Furthermore, approximately 60 vehicles have been converted to use alternative fuels. However, these conversions have not yet led to the environmental and economic benefits originally forecast. Major financial, technical and emission issues have been identified: conversions have resulted in some unanticipated operating problems, have proven to be costly, and have occasionally resulted in increased air emissions. This experience is an important reminder that leading-edge greener technologies may not always live up to supplier claims. Given this reality, it is felt that the long-term success of Environment Canada's efforts to comply with the act will depend, in part, on a reduced reliance on conversion technologies and the development of greener options by original equipment manufacturers.

||| Building Management

Building management represents an important greener procurement opportunity where a co-ordinated federal programme can result in significant environmental and economic savings. The *Federal Buildings Initiative* (FBI), designed by the federal department of Natural Resources Canada (NRCan) in 1991, helps managers to take advantage of long-term cost savings of greener building operations. The FBI involves an innovative partnership between the public and private sector to improve the energy efficiency in federal-owned facilities without financial investment or risk on the part of the Government of Canada. The FBI programme uses private capital, resulting from longer-term cost savings, to finance building energy, water and air system retrofits.

Environment Canada issued the first energy performance contract awarded under the FBI in 1993 to retrofit the Canada Centre for Inland Waters in Burlington. The FBI retrofit programme included upgrades to the building's electrical and mechanical systems, targeted reductions in water consumption, and the installation of a new electricity and heating production system. These initiatives will result in an annual reduction of carbon dioxide emissions by 12,700 metric tonnes and yearly savings of $850,000 after a 7.2-year payback period. Following the expiry of the contract, these savings will be retained by the department. Opportunities to implement the FBI programme for other Environment Canada sites across the country have also been undertaken. The FBI is considered to be one of the most successful environmental programmes for federal operations as it has resulted in significant environmental and financial savings, and supports Canada's environmental industry.

Work is also under way to promote environmental stewardship and greener procurement in the management of office accommodations. In 1995, Environment Canada and Public Works and Government Services Canada (PWGSC) created *The Environmentally Responsible Construction and Renovation Handbook*. The *Handbook* is a compilation of practical information to help federal property and facility managers address two common environmental concerns: solid waste reduction and the selection of greener building materials and products.

To build on this work, Environment Canada and PWGSC are now developing a more comprehensive set of environmentally sensitive accommodation standards called *The Green Office Plan*. Its objective is to ensure that building selection and design, construction and demolition, electrical and mechanical systems, furnishing materials and facility management strategies incorporate measures to maximise energy and water conservation, improve indoor environmental quality (i.e. indoor air, lighting) and implement sound waste management principles. Because *The Green Office Plan* is intended to be integrated into existing procurement processes on a federal public-service-wide basis, it is expected to have many positive environmental impacts and should also help to increase the demand for greener accommodation goods, services and processes.

To pilot *The Green Office Plan*, Environment Canada initiated the *New Officing Strategies Project* for an Environment Canada office floor. This project incorporates new planning and design concepts such as improved functionality, team work settings and non-territorial meeting rooms. As an important part of this demonstration project, environmental criteria were specified in all facets of the endeavour, ranging from product selection to construction and demolition waste diversion plans. To this end, the project employed life-cycle (cradle-to-grave) concepts which included considerations on how to minimise the amount of waste entering landfills. For example, existing components were salvaged, carpet was recycled and drywall was installed between wall panels to increase sound insulation.

As part of this project, Environment Canada worked in partnership with PWGSC and industry leaders to establish and apply a remanufactured standard for systems furniture which is the first of its kind within the federal public service. Through remanufacturing, previously used panels and furniture components are refurbished to 'as-new' quality. The standard specified a minimum 60% remanufacturing requirement for panels and systems furniture used in the project. In addition, non-refurbished products featured environmental attributes, such as recycled content in carpet, steel, sound insulating material and particle board.

In September 1997, this Environment Canada office floor was the first in Canada to be ECP-certified because of the environmental considerations accounted for in its design, construction and day-to-day operations. Environment Canada will continue to work with PWGSC and industry partners to develop more precise environmental specifications for future projects. For example, minimum quantities of recycled material, such as steel, will be identified for use in furniture components.

||| Energy

Concrete steps are also being taken to create markets for greener energy through first-purchase strategies. As part of its sustainable development strategy, Environment Canada committed to purchase 15%–20% of its building energy from renewable sources by 2010, and to commence greener power pilot projects in fiscal year 1998/99 (Environment Canada 1997: 16). To realise this commitment, Environment Canada, along with Natural Resources Canada (NRCan), signed a greener energy purchasing agreement with an Alberta energy company. In it, the two federal departments agreed to purchase up to a total of 13,000 megawatt hours of greener power per year for their Alberta facilities over the next ten years. This agreement demonstrates true environmental leadership, as both Environment Canada and NRCan will be paying a premium for the wind power generated by this energy company. It is thought that this agreement could, in turn, stimulate interest by energy companies of other provinces to develop greener power alternatives.

||| Hotels

Environment Canada is also working in co-operation with the Hotel Association of Canada, TerraChoice Environmental Services and other government departments to develop an independent *Hotel Eco-efficiency Rating Program*, which will be the first of its kind in the world. This work reinforces and supplements voluntary efforts already undertaken by the lodging industry to adopt best practices in environmental management. In this programme, hotels are independently evaluated on their corporate environmental management practices in areas such as guest and food services, meeting facilities and grounds maintenance. An evaluation has already been conducted for nine Canadian hotels as part of the programme's initial introduction and it will soon be promoted to all hotel chains in Canada.

To encourage federal use of the forthcoming one-to-five 'green leaf' rating system, the hotel ratings are expected to be incorporated into the 1999 *Federal Government Directory for Government Employees*. Environment Canada will direct its employees to use this rating system when selecting hotels for accommodation and conference purposes. Work is also under way to complete a pilot with three other countries to extend these efforts internationally.

||| Telephones

In a direct effort to foster life-cycle management and demonstrate that eco-efficiency can improve competitiveness over the complete product life-cycle, Environment Canada has entered into a partnership with Nortel, a Canadian telecommunications company. In 1997, Nortel and Environment Canada announced a CDN$1.2 million research project to explore environmentally preferable design technologies. The project aims to explore sustainable telephone design and production practices that decrease environmental impacts and provide a competitive edge in the global economy. Environment Canada will be contributing $250,000 to sponsor a life-cycle assessment to identify and verify potential environmental improvements. In this project, Nortel will use environmental design standards and practices to explore 'concept' telephones with leading environmental features such as lead-free interconnection technology, fewer parts and a reduction in the number of materials for ease of recycling. This initiative represents the first time that the Government of Canada and private industry have worked together to examine an entire product life-cycle.

||| Photocopiers and Paper Products

Environment Canada initiated the creation of an inter-departmental working group composed of departments operating within a federal building complex (of 6,000 employees) to leverage the building's total spending power in photocopier purchases. A contract was issued for the approximately 200 photocopiers required in the complex. This co-ordinated approach significantly improved the price and service levels received. In addition, it enabled departments to insist on certain environmental criteria, such as default double-sided copying, machine components that are recycled and recyclable, and packaging, such as toner bottles, that is taken back by the supplier.

To increase the use of greener paper procurement, this same inter-departmental working group issued a second contract to ensure these photocopiers would be supplied with EcoLogo-certified paper (50% recycled, 10% post-consumer fibres) and not virgin copy paper. Environment Canada is also working with a stationery supplier located in the complex to increase the number and visibility of the greener products it offers. These efforts should help to increase the amount of greener stationery products federal employees purchase within the complex.

||| Government Partnerships

As part of its broader policy agenda, Environment Canada is also developing effective partnerships with different orders of government to advance greener procurement thinking and practices both nationally and internationally. Within Canada, Environment Canada has worked through different venues to encourage an effective dialogue. In November 1996, Environment Canada and PWGSC sponsored a two-day *National Procurement Workshop*. Federal, provincial and municipal representatives, as well as participants from private-sector organisations and suppliers, came together to better understand different perspectives in accelerating progress in greener government purchasing.

In addition, a Federal Green Procurement Task Force was created by the National Round Table for the Environment and the Economy (NRTEE) in 1994 to assist federal departments and agencies in greening their procurement practices. This group of industry, not-for-profit and governmental participants, including Environment Canada, has been actively working to advance its mandate. In 1996, the Task Force commissioned a report, entitled *Development of Criteria for Green Procurement: Summary Report* (Delphi Group 1996), which outlined the state of green procurement for private and public sectors in Canada and identified possible criteria that could be used to increase greener procurement. One of the study's key findings was that gains in green procurement can only be made when an organisation has a clear, public commitment from senior managers supported by adequate resources and implementation strategies.

A second study, *Going For Green: Meeting Foreign Demand for Environmentally Preferable Products and Services through Federal Procurement* (NRTEE 1997), was completed in 1997 and was followed by an expert stakeholder workshop to discuss its findings. The study identified trends for greener products in some of Canada's major trading markets, and the role of the Government of Canada as a public purchaser. Most recently, the NRTEE published a *Statement on Federal Green Procurement* in January 1998 which included a series of conclusions and recommendations to inform and guide the procurement efforts of federal government decision-makers.

Environment Canada is also building closer working relationships with member countries of the Organisation for Economic Co-operation and Development (OECD) and the Asia-Pacific Economic Co-operation (APEC) forum. Environment Canada chaired the working group which led to the February 1996 passage by OECD ministers of a Council Recommendation on *Improving the Environmental Performance of Government*. This recommendation is intended to encourage member-country governments to reduce the environmental impacts of their own operations and decision-making processes. As a follow-up to this resolution, several OECD meetings have been held to encourage member-country governments to share practical information and best practices. To facilitate the exchange of information, Environment Canada also initiated the creation of a *Greening Government* website for the OECD. The department has also been an active participant in the OECD's *Green Goods* conferences on greener public purchasing and its associated working group (OECD 1997).

Work is also under way to collaborate with Asia-Pacific countries on greening government and greener procurement practices through workshops and meetings. Examples include a Canada–Japan Workshop on *Greening Government* in 1996 (Environment Canada and the Environment Agency of Japan 1996) and an Environment Canada workshop on *Asia-Pacific Sustainable Cities* in 1997. These partnerships and meetings are beneficial because different orders of government learn from the experiences of others. By exchanging valuable tools and best practices, governments can save time and money by minimising the duplication of effort. Moreover, such exchanges can also help to gradually raise the overall bar of performance across governments.

||| Lessons Learned: Key Components of an Effective Greener Procurement Strategy

Over the years, Environment Canada has learned many important lessons through partnerships with other governments and through its experience in implementing its own greener procurement strategy. In order to advance greener procurement effectively within government organisations, it is useful to apply the following change management principles:

▶ **Secure a champion from senior levels** to establish organisational commitment, drive the change process and achieve real success. Leadership from senior managers is essential to send the necessary signal that greener procurement is a real priority.

▶ **Encourage a culture of environmental awareness** by emphasising incremental, pragmatic changes to the day-to-day decision-making and responsibilities of all managers and employees.

▶ **Involve key employees** in the design and implementation of the greener procurement strategy. Employee participation will increase 'buy-in' and help to ensure the strategy is designed to meet the organisation's unique characteristics and needs.

▶ **Simplify the environmental decision-making process** by integrating tools that are easy to understand and use into the organisation's procurement processes. Employees are less likely to use complicated tools when dealing with time pressures, competing purchasing priorities and the intimidation factor of selecting greener goods and services.

▶ **Define clear environmental accountabilities** throughout all managerial and employee levels to strengthen commitment, stimulate action and facilitate the examination of past greener procurement efforts.

▶ **Limit the scope** of initial efforts by reaching for 'low-hanging fruit': those areas that have the greatest opportunity for positive environmental change in the short term. For example, organisations could develop specific strategies for high-volume goods or could focus training efforts on those employees that make the largest proportion of procurement decisions.

▶ **Establish realistic, but challenging environmental targets** to focus efforts, maintain momentum and encourage a culture of continuous improvement.

▶ **Recognise innovative initiatives and reward successes** to foster creativity and risk-taking within the organisation.

▶ **Foster partnerships** with other governments, non-governmental organisations and industry leaders to increase practical knowledge, share best practices, minimise duplication of effort and initiate joint greener purchasing initiatives.

▋▋▋ *Additional Opportunities for Advancing Greener Government Purchasing*

Although some positive steps have been taken, there is a great deal of additional work that is required to leverage the Government of Canada's purchasing power and increase the quantity of greener goods and services that departments buy. Some important steps that could be taken over the next years include:

▶ Creating a *Greener Purchasing Forum* of Canadian governments (Government of Canada 1996) with appropriate private-sector involvement that could share information, leverage collective purchasing power and, ultimately, develop common procurement standards based on best practices. These standards could then be used by all orders of government to provide suppliers with greater certainty and consistency in developing greener products and services.

▶ Instituting, as part of federal government procurement processes, the requirement that potential suppliers fully describe the positive environmental attributes of their products, processes, services and environmental management systems (NRTEE 1998).

▶ Fostering greater collaboration and exchange of greener procurement tools across governments, both nationally and internationally. In Canada, this could be encouraged through the creation of a national website.

▶ Fostering greater collaboration with other federal departments to better leverage federal government purchasing power and to develop shared performance indicators in assessing the efficacy of governmental procurement strategies.

▶ Developing additional partnerships with industry and non-governmental organisations to design and develop greener goods and services.

▶ Capitalising on future technological advances in electronic commerce over the longer term. Greener criteria could then be seamlessly embedded into electronic procurement systems to make greener purchasing a default option and to facilitate the tracking of greener purchases for government departments.

▐▐ *Conclusion*

Government of Canada departments and agencies are striving to better incorporate the environment into the management of their policies, programmes and operations. As part of this larger effort, progress has been achieved in promoting and implementing greener government purchasing strategies. Environment Canada has been able to realise many important successes by fostering effective partnerships and emphasising a pragmatic, small-steps approach to achieve concrete results. However, more work can and should be done. As a result, Environment Canada remains committed to continue working both internally and with external partners to advance greener procurement as part of its overall environmental mandate.

3
Environmentally Preferable Purchasing
The US Experience

William Sanders

▮▮ *Introduction*

Consumers can play an integral role in improving the environment through their purchasing patterns. By demanding certain products, consumers can send a clear signal to the manufacturers about their preferences for those products and services that pose fewer burdens on the environment. By leveraging their purchasing power, consumers are voting with their wallets, directly affecting manufacturers' bottom lines. Some manufacturers are attuned to this market signal and have recognised that differentiating their products on the basis of environmental attributes can serve as a competitive advantage.

'Consumers' include anyone in the private or public sector that buys goods and services, including individuals, institutions (e.g. universities, hospitals, all levels of government) and companies. 'Products and services' also cover a wide spectrum: anything from soaps to satellites and from cleaning services to healthcare services.

As the single largest consumer of goods and services, expending over $200 billion annually on a wide variety and large quantity of products and services, the US Federal government leaves a large environmental footprint. By the same token, it can wield its purchasing power to propel companies to manufacture products and services that place fewer burdens on the environment and thereby leverage and jump-start the market for 'green' products both in the public as well as in the private sector.

Certainly, the concept of leveraging Federal dollars to move the marketplace is nothing new. Federal procurement has been used as a tool in accomplishing socio-economic goals for decades, with procurement preference programmes for small business concerns, labour-surplus area concerns and US-made products (Conrad 1993: 2). In the environmental arena, the fact that paper with recovered materials content has become the norm is an example of how purchases of such goods by the Federal government made it more widely acceptable and available (see Fig. 1).

However, despite this potential, the US Federal government has not relied heavily on demand-driven policies to achieve environmental improvement and the market for 'green' products remains a niche market. Why? In part, this is because there is currently no existing infrastructure that can easily facilitate the identification of 'green'

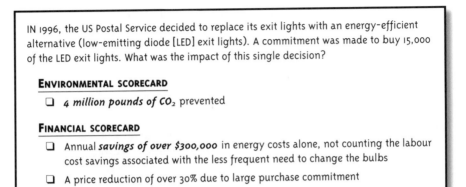

IN 1996, the US Postal Service decided to replace its exit lights with an energy-efficient alternative (low-emitting diode [LED] exit lights). A commitment was made to buy 15,000 of the LED exit lights. What was the impact of this single decision?

ENVIRONMENTAL SCORECARD

❑ *4 million pounds of* CO_2 prevented

FINANCIAL SCORECARD

❑ Annual *savings of over $300,000* in energy costs alone, not counting the labour cost savings associated with the less frequent need to change the bulbs

❑ A price reduction of over 30% due to large purchase commitment

Figure 1: Buying Green Makes Environmental and Financial Sense for the US Postal Service

products and services for consumers. Although there are a number of private-sector environmental labelling or certification organisations in the United States that are attempting to fill this gap, these programmes have not yet made deep inroads into consumer buying patterns.[1] This lack of infrastructure has served as an obstacle for widespread purchase of 'green' products.

The absence of an infrastructure is even more pronounced in the public sector. Whereas consumers in the private sector have begun to take advantage of existing information about the environmental performance of products and services, and are factoring this in their purchasing decisions, environmental considerations traditionally have not been a factor within the Federal government purchasing process. Instead, the Federal acquisition community has relied primarily on cost and performance, and, to a certain extent, health and safety issues as deciding factors.

This chapter will discuss the evolving debate about green procurement in the United States within a broad context of current environmental management practices and the changing acquisition landscape. The chapter will examine the role of the Federal government and particularly the role that the US Environmental Protection Agency (EPA) has had to play in advancing, shaping and putting into practice the concept of green procurement.

▌▌ *Background*

The commitment for government to be an environmentally responsible consumer is ensconced in a number of national statutes, including the following.

▶ **The Resource Conservation and Recovery Act (RCRA) of 1976**, the solid and hazardous waste statute, includes a provision—Section 6002—which directed government agencies to promote recycling by increasing the purchases of products made with recovered materials and thereby develop markets for products made from materials recovered from the solid waste stream.

---

1. Two notable examples are Green Seal and Scientific Certification Systems.

‣ **The Pollution Prevention Act of** 1990 establishes an environmental management hierarchy and places pollution prevention[2] as the approach of first choice. This Act directed EPA to identify opportunities for Federal procurement to encourage source reduction.

‣ **The Energy Policy Act of** 1992 emphasises energy efficiency and renewable energy and promotes, for example, the use of alternative fuels and encourages the purchase of alternative-fuelled vehicles.

Yet, although these laws have been on the books for a number of years, the potential for the use of purchasing power to achieve environmental objectives has not been fully utilised and the progress made was limited until recently.[3] These statutory mandates were given a major boost in 1993 with a series of Presidential Executive Orders signed by President Clinton, which, in sum, require the Federal government to improve environmental performance in its daily operations and practices—i.e. to 'green' its decision-making process (see Fig. 2).

An integral component of these Executive Orders and US 'greening of government' efforts is the use of its purchasing power to achieve environmental improvement (see Fig. 3). The Executive Orders require Federal agencies to purchase products ranging from energy-efficient computers, recycled-content products, to 'environmentally preferable' products. The Executive Orders also require changes in the standards, specifications and regulations guiding purchasing in the Federal government to be modified to allow for 'green' purchasing.

These Executive Orders served as important catalysts for rejuvenating existing or, in other cases, creating new 'green' procurement programmes in the United States. These include the following.

‣ **'Buy Recycled' programme.** Originating in Section 6002 of RCRA (see above), the 'Buy Recycled' programme is the oldest and the most well-established environmental procurement programme in the US. RCRA requires EPA to 'designate' products that can be made with recovered materials and to recommend practices for buying these products, including the recovered materials content levels and specifications. These recommendations are made based on a market survey to ensure sufficient availability, reasonable price and competing vendors. Once a product is designated, purchasing agencies

---

2. Pollution prevention means 'source reduction', as defined under the Pollution Prevention Act, and other practices that reduce or eliminate the creation of pollutants through: increased efficiency in the use of raw materials, energy, water or other resources; or protection of natural resources by conservation. The Pollution Prevention Act defines 'source reduction' to mean any practice that: reduces the amount of any hazardous substance, pollutant or contaminant entering any waste stream or otherwise released into the environment (including fugitive emissions) prior to recycling, treatment or disposal; and reduces the hazards to public health and the environment associated with the releases of such substances, pollutants or contaminant.

3. For example, between 1976 and 1992, only five products made with recovered materials—paper, cement and concrete containing fly ash, building insulation, re-refined oil and retreated tyres—had been designated by EPA under Section 6002 for purchase by government agencies.

★ 12843 **Procurement Requirements and Policies for Federal Agencies for Ozone-Depleting Substances** (21 April 1993) directs Federal agencies to change their procurement policies to reduce the use of ozone-depleting substances earlier than the 1995 phase-out deadline called for in the Montreal Protocol.

★ 12844 **Federal Use of Alternative-Fuelled Vehicles** (21 April 1993) places the Federal government in a leadership role in the demand and use of alternative-fuelled vehicles, calling on each agency to adopt aggressive plans to exceed the purchase requirements of such vehicles established by the Energy Policy Act of 1992.

★ 12845 **Requiring Agencies to Purchase Energy-Efficient Computer Equipment** (21 April 1993) encourages market transformation through increased purchase of energy-efficient computer products that save money and reduce pollution.

★ 12856 **Federal Comspliance with Right-to-Know Laws and Pollution Prevention Requirements** (3 August 1993) includes Federal agencies in mandatory Toxic Release Inventory (TRI) reporting, which was originally restricted to manufacturers in the private sector. A key initiative to include pollution prevention practices in the Federal agencies, this Executive Order demonstrates that pollution prevention and reduction of hazardous chemicals is as important in the public sector as it is in the private sector.

★ 12873 **Federal Acquisition, Recycling and Waste Prevention** (20 October 1993) directs Executive agencies to increase the purchase of products containing recovered materials and environmentally preferable products. The Order also encourages agencies to increase their recycling and waste prevention activities.

★ 12902 **Energy Efficiency and Water Conservation at Federal Facilities** (8 March 1994) encourages increased use of energy- and water-saving products in Federal facilities. By purchasing products that are in the top 25% of the market for energy and water efficiency, the Federal government reduces energy consumption in its facilities and demonstrates how simple changes in procurement decisions can lead to large savings on annual utility bills.

★ 12969 **Federal Acquisition and Community Right-to-Know** (8 August 1995) extends the reporting requirements under the Toxic Release Inventory to contractors who provide goods and services to Federal agencies. Information concerning chemical release and transfer can assist the government in purchasing efficiently produced, lower-cost and higher-quality supplies and services that also have a minimum adverse impact on community health and the environment.

Figure 2: Presidential Executive Orders Related to the Environment

Source: Excerpt from US EPA 1996

❝ Federal facilities will set the example for the rest of the country and become the leader in applying pollution prevention to daily operations, purchasing decisions and policies. In the process, Federal facilities will reduce toxic emissions, which helps avoid cleanup costs and promotes clean technologies. ❞

President Clinton
Executive Order 1285

Figure 3: Top-Level Commitment for the 'Greening of Government'

are required to buy the product with the highest recovered material content level practicable (US EPA Office of Solid Waste and Emergency Response 1997).

The Executive Order on Federal Acquisition, Recycling and Waste Prevention (Executive Order 12873) helped streamline the process by which EPA could designate the items and thereby helped spur the addition of a large number of new items to the designated list. As of March 1998, 36 items have been designated by EPA, and additional items are about to be added (see Fig. 4).

▶ **'Energy Star' programme.** Originally begun for private-sector purchases, this tremendously popular programme—and probably the most well known internationally of the US green procurement programmes—establishes energy-efficiency levels for computers and other energy-consuming products. Executive Order 12902 requires Federal government only to buy computers, monitors and printers that meet the Energy Star requirements for energy efficiency. Though the programme began with its emphasis on computers and computer-

---

▶ **Paper and paper products**

▶ **Vehicle products**
- ❑ Engine coolants
- ❑ Re-refined lubricating oils
- ❑ Retread tyres

▶ **Construction products**
- ❑ Building insulation products
- ❑ Carpet
- ❑ Cement and concrete containing coal fly ash and ground granulated blast furnace slag
- ❑ Consolidated and reprocessed latex paint
- ❑ Floor tiles
- ❑ Patio block
- ❑ Shower and bathroom dividers and partitions
- ❑ Structural fibreboard
- ❑ Laminated paperboard

▶ **Transportation products**
- ❑ Channelisers
- ❑ Delineators
- ❑ Flexible delineators
- ❑ Parking stops
- ❑ Traffic barricades
- ❑ Traffic cones

▶ **Park and recreation products**
- ❑ Plastic fencing
- ❑ Playground surfaces
- ❑ Running tracks

▶ **Landscaping products**
- ❑ Garden and soaker hoses
- ❑ Hydraulic mulch
- ❑ Lawn and garden edging
- ❑ Yard trimmings compost

▶ **Non-paper office products**
- ❑ Binders
- ❑ Office recycling containers
- ❑ Office waste receptacles
- ❑ Plastic desktop accessories
- ❑ Plastic envelopes
- ❑ Plastic rubbish bags
- ❑ Printer ribbons
- ❑ Toner cartridges

▶ **Miscellaneous products**
- ❑ Pallets

Figure 4: List of EPA-Designated Items with Recovered Materials

related products, it has in recent years expanded to include products such as furnaces, air conditioners, etc.

▶ **'Energy Efficiency Challenge' programme.** Under the Energy Policy Act, Federal agencies are required to purchase energy- and water-efficient products. To spur the trend towards such purchases, the US Department of Energy (US DOE) in 1995 challenged other Federal agencies to purchase products from among those tested and found to be most energy- and water-efficient (rated in the upper 25%) or at least 10% more efficient than the minimum levels set by Federal standards. Twenty-two Federal agencies pledged to meet this challenge. The US DOE has tested and recommended products ranging from energy-efficient chillers and refrigerators to fluorescent lamps.

These programmes have a number of common elements. First, they are **important pioneers** in the area of green purchasing. They have helped to establish the US Federal government's presence in demand-driven policies for environmental improvement. They have been instrumental in getting the environment on the radar screens of many of the Federal purchasers. Additionally, each of these programmes is focused on a very clear mission that is based on a **single attribute** of the product: for example, recycled content or energy efficiency.

This single-attribute focus is not surprising, given that environmental management in the first twenty or so years of EPA's history has centred around controlling and cleaning up industrial pollution in disparate pieces—often shifting the pollutant from one medium to another. This is not to criticise or underplay the tremendous success of this approach in cleaning up the most egregious and noticeable environmental problems.

Thus, not unlike the Agency's past policies in the industrial sector, the few policies and programmes directed at influencing consumer behaviour and consumer products have been driven by concerns related to single-medium issues (e.g. solid waste ['Buy Recycled'], air quality ['Energy Star', 'Green Lights'], water quality, etc.). However, as the Agency moves away from addressing environmental problems on a single-medium-by-single-medium basis to a multi-media, systems-based approach that focuses on preventing pollution by targeting the initial source of pollution, through process redesign, material substitution, etc., the Agency's programmes targeted at the consumer sector will also have to evolve to reflect this paradigm shift. Thus, we need to build on the successes of the single-attribute green procurement programmes to introduce the Federal purchasers to a more comprehensive approach to buying green.

This broader perspective is reflected in EPA's Environmentally Preferable Purchasing (EPP) programme, which aims to minimise environmental impacts across all environmental media.

▍▍ *Environmentally Preferable Products and Services*

The Environmentally Preferable Purchasing programme is an outgrowth of President Clinton's mandate in Executive Order 12873 to have the US Federal government identify and give preferences to those products and services that are environmentally preferable, i.e. those that place fewer burdens on the environment in comparison to other products or services that perform the same function.[4] This definition goes on further to say that this comparison could consider environmental impacts across the various life-cycle stages of the product.

The Executive Order called on the EPA to issue guidance that Federal agencies should use to identify and give preference to environmentally preferable products and services.[5] Arising out of this mandate, three inter-related roles can be identified for EPA. First is one of a national policy-maker. Second, EPA needs to provide practical guidance to Federal agencies that must interpret the national policy and apply it to their own acquisition and procurement situations. Third, as a consumer of goods and services itself, though it may be small in comparison to many of the other agencies, EPA must put into practice what it expects other agencies to do. Each of these roles are examined more closely below. Through each of these roles, EPA must help build an infrastructure that can support environmentally preferable purchasing within the Federal government.

▌▌▌ Framing the Debate

Although Executive Order 12873's specific mandate is to target and influence Federal government buying patterns, given both the intended and real effects of the Federal government market pull, establishing a national policy on environmental preferability needed to involve all stakeholders—both in the public and the private sector. To begin, EPA held extensive discussions with key stakeholders, including: major Federal purchasing agencies (such as the Department of Defense, the General Services Administration, Department of Energy, etc.); manufacturers and trade associations; environmental organisations; as well as academics and other interested organisations and individuals. To help frame these discussions and to solicit general comment from the public, EPA published a discussion paper in which it laid out the issues associated with determining environmental preferability and possible approaches for incorporating such a concept into the Federal procurement process (US EPA Office of Pollution Prevention and Toxics 1994).

This public process helped identify a number of key factors that influenced policy development. First, during the early 1990s, there was tremendous changes in the US Federal acquisition landscape—from streamlining to reforming the way Federal agencies should purchase commercial products, all with the goal of expediting government purchases and saving taxpayers' dollars.[6] Within this context, many in the Federal procurement community raised concerns that adding environmental considerations into the purchasing equation would add more complexity rather than simplicity to the acquisition process.

---

4. Environmentally preferable products and services are defined in the Executive Order on Federal Acquisition, Recycling and Waste Prevention (EO 12873), October 1993.
5. Executive Order 12873, Section 503.
6. These changes resulted in the passage of the Federal Acquisition Streamlining Act of 1993, a legislation that seeks to simplify contract solicitation and administration. In addition to the legislative changes, there was also a major effort by the Clinton–Gore Administration to 'reinvent' the government to be more efficient and quality-conscious. Reform of acquisition practices was a major priority in the series of 'reinventing' initiatives.

Second, with the diversity interests came a wide variety of interpretations of what 'environmental preferability' meant (see Fig. 5). And, by extension, there was very little consensus on the approach that EPA should adopt to advance environmentally preferable purchasing. Instead, there emerged a spectrum of suggested approaches. At one end of the spectrum, some recommended that EPA come up with a list of environmentally preferable products. Proponents of this approach argued that this would ensure ease of implementation by the buying agencies.

Figure 5: Key Stakeholders in Environmentally Preferable Products and Services Policy Discussions

However, others raised concerns about this approach because they felt that a list would freeze technology and stifle continuous environmental improvement. Many private-sector stakeholders felt that a government-generated list could not keep up with the rapid changes in technology—for example, in the electronics sector. Instead, a number of companies suggested that they should be allowed simply to provide environmental information as they would any other information about their products. Rounding off this end of the spectrum, some recommended that the government not get involved in such preferential programmes.

There was also a great deal of discussion about the appropriate role that third-party environmental labelling or environmental certification programmes could play in helping Federal purchasers identify environmentally preferable products. Unlike many other countries, the US does not have a government-run or -sanctioned multi-attribute, life-cycle-based eco-labelling organisation. Thus, this debate—which continues even now—is hindering the free flow of information between these organisations and the Federal buyers.

What could be taken away from these discussions? The concept of environmental preferability is multi-faceted and there is no single, 'right' approach to incorporate this concept into the Federal procurement process.

Taking these many views into account, in September 1995, EPA published a proposed *Guidance on the Acquisition of Environmentally Preferable Products and Services* (US EPA 1995). This represented the first articulation of the US's policy on green products and services and serves as a broad framework within which Federal agencies can initiate efforts to make more environmentally preferable purchasing decisions. The proposed *Guidance* errs on the side of those who wanted a less prescriptive and more flexible approach. This is reflected in the seven principles included therein (see Fig. 6). However, EPA recognised that this broad policy articulation fell far short of Federal agencies' expectations for a more specific set of 'how to' directions from EPA.

I. Consideration of environmental preferability should begin early in the acquisition process and be rooted in the ethic of pollution prevention, which strives to eliminate or reduce, up-front, potential risks to human health and the environment.

2. A product or service's environmental preferability is a function of multiple attributes.

3. Environmental preferability should reflect life-cycle considerations of products and services to the extent feasible.

4. Environmental preferability should consider the scale (global versus local) and temporal reversibility aspects of the impact.

5. Environmental preferability should be tailored to local conditions where appropriate.

6. Environmental performance of products and services should be a factor in competition among vendors.

7. Agencies need to examine product attribute claims carefully.

Figure 6: EPA's Seven Guiding Principles

‖ Putting Policy into Practice

Recognition of this shortcoming led EPA to initiate a number of pilot projects in co-operation with key purchasing agencies to apply the broad principles to specific acquisitions. The primary intent behind the pilots is, first, to demonstrate and test the workability of the concepts and principles in the *Guidance*. Second, while the *Guidance* is aimed at public- and private-sector policy-makers, the results of these pilot projects are intended to provide more detailed, practical and 'user-friendly' tools for use by procurement and contracting officers.

Four pilots have been under way. Two pilots (hard surface cleaning products; interior latex paints) were initiated by the US General Services Administration (GSA), which is the largest provider of products and services to the rest of the Federal government as well as the owner and manager of a large portion of civilian buildings and properties. Two others have been initiated by the Department of Defense (DOD) and have involved the interior and exterior building renovations at the Pentagon and a number of other buildings in the metropolitan DC area.

For the cleaning products pilot, GSA and EPA co-operatively identified seven attributes that can serve as indicators of a cleaning product's environmental performance. The seven attributes include:

▶ Skin irritation

▶ Food chain exposure

▶ Air pollution potential

▶ Presence/absence of fragrances

▶ Presence/absence of dyes

▶ Reduced packaging/recovered-content packaging

▶ Features to minimise exposure to concentrates

Vendors were asked to provide information, on a voluntary basis, on these attributes for inclusion in GSA's 1996 *Commercial Cleaning Supplies* catalogue. Federal purchasers can use this information, presented in a matrix form, to compare cleaning products based on the environmental attributes most critical for their geographic region and intended use. After the initial environmental performance matrix was published, sixty additional vendors expressed interest in the GSA's product catalogue. Adding more vendors to the schedule will bring more competition and a wider array of products available to the Federal purchasers.[7]

An approach similar to the cleaning products pilot is being adopted for interior latex paints in a partnership between GSA and EPA. In addition to the environmental attributes, however, the matrix will also include functional performance (e.g. durability) information as well.

In the DOD–EPA exterior renovation pilot, a slightly different approach was adopted, where environmental preferability is incorporated into DOD's contracting process. In June 1997, DOD awarded a five-year, $1-million-per-year contract to maintain and repair the parking lots and access roads at four Washington, DC-area facilities, including the Pentagon's 67 acres of parking. This contract includes several unique features to ensure that the work not only meets all price and quality concerns, but also incorporates the use of products with multiple environmental attributes whenever feasible.

The most innovative aspect of the exterior renovation contract provides the contractor with a financial incentive to use products with the greatest number of environmentally beneficial attributes. Contractors can earn a 2% price differential for each environmental attribute. The attributes eligible for the price differential are identified in the contract, although the contractor can suggest additional attributes for any product required under the contract. The contractor can also suggest changes in construction practices that improve environmental performance. If DOD approves the changes, the contractor can receive a price differential for using them. In the few months after beginning work, the winning contractor has already identified several products and a new process—all of which appear to significantly improve environmental quality while continuing to meet or exceed DOD's mandatory performance

---

7. For further information about this project, please refer to US GSA/US EPA 1997, or visit the Environmentally Preferable Purchasing programme's website at *www.epa.gov/opptintr/epp*.

criteria. With this unique approach, the task of incorporating environmental prefer-ability into the purchasing process is shared between DOD and the contractor.[8]

Although the financial incentive aspect of the exterior renovation project could not be applied to the much larger interior renovation pilot project, DOD and EPA also worked to incorporate environmental preferability considerations into the con-tract process, including ensuring that the overall performance of the contract would be based in part on how well the contractor performed on environmental prefer-ability factors.

However, another approach was adopted for a pilot project on computers. EPA and GSA began work on this project intending to build on the success of EPA's 'Energy Star' programme by expanding the number of attributes considered in purchases of environmentally preferable computers. This pilot sought direct involvement of industry stakeholders in identifying the key factors for determining environmental preferability. Despite extensive information about environmental characteristics of computers, agreement on ways to capture this information for use within the Fed-eral purchasing context was difficult to reach. The electronics industry also expressed its interest in maintaining its focus on other EPA initiatives and work on the com-puter pilot was suspended. Of note on this pilot was the absence of a strong demand push by GSA. This uncertainty of demand for computers with environmentally prefer-able characteristics added to the electronic industry's concerns about investing its time and resources in this pilot project.

In all of these pilots, the role of EPA has been to serve as the environmental consultant and advocate for environmental preferability issues, while the procure-ment decisions and strategies have been left to the purchasing agencies. The intent behind using different approaches in these pilots is to match more closely the needs of the individual agencies, the type of product or service being purchased and the acquisition method being used. Rather than attempting to find a single approach that can address all circumstances, particularly in this early stages of implementa-tion, EPA's EPP programme's focus has been on understanding the process by which decisions are made and asking the questions: What are the best ways to put envi-ronmental considerations into the purchasing equation in the first place? And how can it be institutionalised?

▌▌▌ 'Walk the Talk'

In the first three years of implementation, EPA's focus has been external—develop-ing a national policy and assisting other agencies in implementing this policy within these partnering agencies' acquisition processes. It has been just this past year that resources and attention have been directed towards making EPA's own procurement practices reflect EPA's guidance to the other agencies. This effort has recently been integrated into a larger 'greening EPA' initiative, which is looking comprehensively at improving the environmental performance of all aspects of EPA's operations—from management of EPA's facilities to how laboratories operate. Although EPA is very small compared to many other US government departments and agencies,

---

8. For further information about this project, please refer to US EPA 1997a, or the EPP programme's website (see footnote 7).

EPA should lead by example. Also, invaluable lessons can be learned through working directly with EPA's own procurement staff. To this end, EPA is currently examining more closely the process by which the results of the GSA–EPA cleaners pilot can be instituted within EPA through changes in the contract language in EPA's lease (most of EPA's buildings are leased from GSA or private owners). Other efforts include drafting of contract language to identify and purchase environmentally preferable paper (going beyond recycled content) and greening of EPA buildings (both new construction and renovations).[9] To identify other opportunities, a procurement audit will be conducted in the autumn of 1998. Over the next few years, EPA will need to ensure that it balances the internal and the external focus of its EPP activities.

▌ Lessons Learned

An important part of EPA's EPP programme is to evaluate and learn from the pilot projects and to share this learning with others in the Federal government. A number of observations can be made.

1. Results from our early pilots indicate that the issue of environmental preferability is, in fact, complex. However, viewed within the context of rapid changes occurring within the US Federal acquisition landscape and the variety of products and services that the Federal government buys, this is not surprising. Rather than moving forward with an expectation that there will be a short-term solution for incorporating environmental preferability into the acquisition process, the EPP programme will build on small successes while looking for opportunities to make a quantum leap towards institutionalising this concept into everyday practice for Federal purchasers.

2. 'Greener' public purchasing requires the expertise of both the environmental and the acquisition/procurement experts. This is because EPP in the Federal government context presents at least two challenges. First is the challenge of how to define what is environmentally preferable. As EPA has defined it, environmental preferability depends on numerous and specific product or service factors, including the local conditions within which the product will be used, available alternatives, life-cycle impacts, etc. The second part of the challenge is how to ensure that those products or services that do place fewer burdens on the environment are indeed purchased. The Federal acquisition process involves complex and sometimes arcane sets of rules and regulations (even with the recent reforms to the acquisition process) which may make it difficult for new environmental products and services to compete on an equal footing with traditional products and services.

Traditionally, however, the two—environmental and procurement—communities have not come together. Our early pilots have shown that it takes flexibility and innovative thinking by both environmental and procurement experts to overcome these dual challenges. Unfortunately, however, the two communities—often with seemingly competing interests, goals and priorities—traditionally have not come together on this issue. Thus, much work needs to be done to bridge this gap.

9. For examples of EPA's 'green building' initiatives, please refer to US EPA 1997b, or the EPP programme's website (see footnote 7).

3. Purchasers in Federal government are constrained by the complex set of laws and regulations that they must follow when making purchases. Often the existing specifications and regulations dictate the use of certain products that place greater burden on the environment than available alternatives. Recent changes to the US Federal Acquisition Regulation (FAR), which provides the basic contracting guidance and implementing regulations used by Federal agencies for buying products and services from the private sector, will go a long way to rectifying this situation.[10] Specifically, the FAR was formally revised in August 1997 to incorporate policies for the acquisition of environmentally preferable and energy-efficient products and services. These changes require consideration of environmental factors in all aspects of Federal acquisition, including acquisition planning, describing an agency's needs, conducting market surveys, and evaluating and selecting a vendor, etc. However, despite these changes to the policies, again, translating these acquisition policies into practice will require time and resources as well as innovative approaches in order to ensure that practices and processes that take environment into account are favoured above those more familiar and traditional practices that do not.

4. The changing acquisition landscape will dictate special considerations for environmentally preferable purchasing. For example, recent streamlining reforms allow for more direct purchasing decisions to be made by non-procurement personnel through the use of credit cards. This decentralisation of purchasing means that there will be an ever-increasing number of purchasers—purchasers that will go outside of the traditional government supply systems to buy their products. This decentralisation can be best demonstrated by the meteoric increase of credit card use by Federal buyers. For example, in 1989, the number of credit card holders in the Federal government was only 10,000; in 1996, this number had jumped to 250,000. Likewise, the dollar volume has also increased significantly: from $460,000 in 1989 to $2.96 billion in 1996 (Laurent 1997).

This trend highlights the importance of reaching out to those beyond the acquisition community with the environmentally preferable purchasing message. For the large purchasing agencies, such as GSA and DOD, who serve as suppliers of goods and services to the rest of the Federal government, they are concerned about losing their business to non-government supply sources. They view inclusion of environmentally preferable products in their product catalogues as an opportunity to provide an added service to their Federal customers, and thereby remain competitive in an increasingly decentralised supply system.

5. Our early pilots indicate that different approaches are needed for different types of procurement and product category for how we can best incorporate environmental preferability into the purchasing equation. Using common sense, we need to tailor our approach and level of analysis to fit the complexity of the product categories.

6. Environmental information on life-cycle impacts is scarce and, where available, is often difficult to translate into useful formats to allow for decision-making. Given this, we need either to look for existing sources of information or devise a creative way of overcoming insufficient or difficult-to-understand information. In

---

10. For additional information, consult the Federal Register, vol. 62 no. 163 (22 August 1997), pp. 44809-13.

our DOD–EPA pilot project on exterior and interior renovation, the primary responsibility for finding and using environmental information on environmental preferability is placed on the contractor who will be conducting the renovations. To encourage and, in some sense, reimburse for the administrative costs associated with this new approach, the DOD contract allows for a price differential incentive.

In this regard, we also need to look to see whether there are private-sector sources—information sources, approaches, institutions (e.g. standard-setting organisations, etc.)—that can be relied upon. Short of this, another approach EPA has adopted is to fund development of tools that can be used to facilitate purchasing decisions based on life-cycle considerations. One such tool is decision-support software developed by the Department of Commerce's National Institute of Standards and Technology (NIST), which incorporates a life-cycle approach that considers the economic and environmental impacts of numerous building materials. The *Building for Environmental and Economic Sustainability* (*BEES*) software presents users with overall performance scores for the products being compared based on the weights set by users for each product's economic and environmental performance data. Individuals using the *BEES* software can also select the relative importance for each of the six environmental impact categories: global warming, acidification, nutrification, natural resource depletion, indoor air quality, and solid waste. Though originally designed for use in comparing building materials, the software and information base will be expanded to include other categories of product.

7. Anticipated spill-over effects are already occurring. Many local and state governments are looking to the Federal government lead or are taking the lead. Looking at the spill-over effect in the private sector, interestingly, with the results of the GSA–EPA cleaning products pilot project, there has been tremendous interest from large corporations who are interested in incorporating environmental preferability within their own organisations

▍ Looking to the Future: Challenges and Opportunities

Greener public purchasing is an evolving issue. And, because of this, the debates about approaches and goals will certainly continue. This is desirable, given the complex and dynamic nature of this issue. Answers for the best way to make a strong environmental improvement through the use of public purchasing power may be, at times, elusive. Having said this, however, that is not to say that we cannot move forward. We can certainly make incremental progress and 'learn by doing'.

Given the environmental management trend in recent years—one that is based on pollution prevention—and the key role that the Federal government can, and should, play as a large consumer of goods and services, the use of public purchasing power will remain an important policy vehicle for environmental improvement.

4
The Greening of Public Procurement in the Netherlands

Nicolien van der Grijp

II Introduction

Changing production and consumption patterns is a focal point of current environmental policies at both national and international level. On the consumption side, three different groups of consumers can roughly be distinguished: individuals, companies and governments. This chapter deals with the greening of purchasing practices performed by the last category, i.e. government, which includes a wide variety of procurement officers belonging to local and central governments and other state-funded or state-managed organisations.

The term 'public procurement' is used to indicate the process of purchasing and tendering by public authorities undertaken primarily to fulfil public responsibilities. It concerns not only day-to-day purchases but also major investments. Significantly, up to three-quarters of expenses are incurred in purchasing consumable goods and services, while the remainder goes on the acquisition of capital goods (OECD 1997). In accordance with the present regulatory approaches, four different areas of public procurement can be distinguished:

▶ Product supply contracts

▶ Public work contracts

▶ Service contracts

▶ Contracts in the utility sector

The bulk of product supply contracts as far as public administrations are concerned relate to office equipment. Common examples of office supplies are stationery, computers, photocopiers, lighting and office furniture. Service contracts in relation to the public sector generally apply to cleaning, maintenance, catering and waste removal activities. Public work contracts apply to the construction of housing, public facilities, roads and hydraulics; and utilities contracts apply to water, energy, transport and telecommunications companies. The financial value of public procurement is considerable: among OECD countries, for example, government consumption of products and services equates to 5%–15% of total Gross Domestic Product (GDP) (OECD 1997).

The outline of this chapter is as follows. First, attention is paid to the relevance of public procurement as an instrument of environmental policy; the process of purchasing and tendering is then examined, followed by the present regulatory scope for the greening of public procurement. The final part of the chapter describes the development and application of environment-oriented public procurement in the Netherlands. This section is largely based on a case study conducted by the Institute for Environmental Studies (IVM), a Dutch university research centre, in the framework of the EU project 'Product Policy in Support of Environmental Policy', which inventoried product policy in the EU and its member states, and sketched future possibilities for environment-oriented product policy.

ⅠⅠ *The Relevance of Public Procurement as an Instrument of Environmental Policy*

Gradually, public procurement has gained importance as an instrument of public policy. Given its side-effects on economy and environment, it has been recognised that public procurement may be used to realise policy objectives in these fields. After all, as public authorities are among the largest consumers, the way they use their purchasing and contracting power can influence the markets for environmentally sound products and services. By expressing their environmental preferences, public purchasers can contribute to a better environment in several ways (Oosterhuis, Rubik and Scholl 1996):

▶ Directly, by demanding products and services with a lower overall environmental impact

▶ Indirectly, by putting pressure on producers to develop products and services with a lower environmental impact

▶ Indirectly, by improving the market position of environmentally preferable products and services

▶ Indirectly, by setting an example for other consumers

In its role as an environmental policy instrument, public procurement can be defined in a narrow and a broader sense. In a narrow sense, greener public procurement only includes purchasing and tendering of environmentally less harmful products and services. In a broader sense, it also includes other environmentally relevant behaviour by public authorities and institutions, such as a reduction in consumption or the environmentally responsible disposal of products. In this connection, the OECD (1997) makes a comparison between 'hardware' tools, including measures that enable the selection, identification and purchase of environmentally preferable goods, and 'software' tools, including measures that modify the environmental behaviour of organisations using and consuming goods.

Recently, the potential of public procurement as an instrument for environmental policy has been recognised by public authorities from several countries and international organisations. The European Commission, for example, stated that 'the role of public procurement policies as they affect the environment needs to be considered by all levels of administration' (CEC 1996a). The OECD has also given a high priority to 'green' public procurement. In February 1996, the OECD Council adopted a Recommendation on Improving the Environmental Performance of Government, which advocates that member countries should 'establish and implement policies for the procurement of environmentally sound products' (C[96]39/FINAL). In February 1997, the OECD organised an International Conference on Greener Public Purchasing to stimulate the development of the instrument.

Ill *The Process of Public Procurement*

The process of public procurement is influenced by several factors, including the structure of the public administration, the availability of information, and the regulatory framework. Countries have different purchasing structures which are largely connected to their constitutional and administrative organisation. Therefore, some countries have a more centralised approach than others. Generally, each level of the public administration has its own procurement competence which is in most cases further delegated to several functions. As a result, the network of procurement officers is very complex in most countries.

Identifying greener products and services is a crucial aspect of greener public procurement. In addition to more conventional information on products and services, procurement officers aiming to lower the environmental impacts of consumption will need extra information on:

▶ Environmental criteria and assessment methods

▶ Range of products offered, including their environmental characteristics, preferably from cradle to grave

▶ Practical experiences with environmentally less harmful products, as their technical qualities may differ from conventional products

The General Agreement on Tariffs and Trade (GATT)/World Trade Organisation (WTO), as well as the EU, have issued procedural rules applying to procurement contracts that exceed certain financial thresholds. These rules are aimed at requiring minimum levels of transparency and establishing obligations to follow open procedures for the awarding of contracts. For this reason, tendering practices are undergoing a continuous process of formalisation aimed at reducing the scope for subjective decision-making. In the last few years, the regulatory framework has increased. This is due on the one hand to an extension of the scope of the relevant regulations and, on the other hand, to a stricter supervision of compliance with procurement rules. Recently, procurement regulations have become so complicated that consultancies now offer to take over the entire procedure from public authorities; they claim that specialised legal, technical and business-economic knowledge is essential and that mistakes are easily made.

The EU began its legislative efforts in the 1970s. The first EU directive on public procurement was issued in 1971 and concerned public work contracts. In 1978, a second directive, on the supply of products, came into force. Both directives were amended several times and finally replaced in 1993 (product supply: 93/36/EEC; public works: 93/37/EEC). In the 1990s, a directive on contracts in the utility sector

(93/38/EEC) and a directive on service contracts (92/50/EEC) were issued by the EU. The latter completed the system by including all the remaining public orders.

The GATT/WTO issued the first Agreement of Government Procurement (GPA) in 1979. This agreement was twice amended; the latest version dates from 15 April 1994. It consists of the actual agreement containing basic principles, procedural rules and challenge procedures, and a number of appendices. The GPA applies to procurement of products as well as services, but its coverage is not as broad as that of the EU directives. It does, for example, not apply to telecommunications, railways, hydraulics, energy provisions and local transportation. The GPA has been part of official EU legislation since 1 January 1996.

The present rules require that procurement officers in member states of the EU comply with the official EU procedures if their intended purchases or tenders exceed certain financial thresholds. Below the thresholds, procurement officers are free to make their own choices within the general provisions of the Treaty on European Union and, possibly, national regulations. The present thresholds are shown in Figure 1.

TYPE OF CONTRACT	EU THRESHOLDS (ECU)	GATT/WTO THRESHOLDS (ECU)
Product supply	200,000	128,771
Services	200,000	128,771
Public works	5,000,000	—
Utilities	various	—

Figure 1: Financial Thresholds for Procurement Officers

Public authorities who intend to place an order that exceeds the financial limits have to make an announcement in the *Official Journal of the EU*. In their call for tenders, the public authorities are obliged to publish the tendering specifications and selection criteria to be applied. These specifications have to be based on financial-economic qualities and/or technical specifications. The prohibition on including technical specifications with a discriminatory effect has been concretised by means of obliging contracting authorities to make, as far as possible, reference to European standards. By European standards are meant the standards approved by the European Committee for Standardisation (CEN), by the European Committee for Electronic Standardisation (CENELEC) or by the European Institute for Telecommunication Standards (ETS).

After the submitting of tenders, the public authorities may award the contract to one of the interested parties. The two alternative criteria for the award of contracts are:

- ▶ The lowest tender, or
- ▶ The economically most favourable tender

The first option, the 'lowest price', leaves little flexibility to include additional aspects in the selection process. The second option, however, permits the selection of those tenders that are most favourable from a business or economic point of view. This criterion leaves room to take into account aspects such as service and quality. After the award of the contract, the public authorities have to inform the Commission about the results of the procedure. Subsequently, the name of the contractor and the price are published in the *Official Journal*. An unlawful procedure may lead to a ruling by the European Court, resulting in suspension of the tendering procedure, or, when the contract has already been carried out, to a sentence for compensation.

In 1996, the European Commission adopted a Green Paper on 'Public Procurement in the European Union: Exploring the Way Forward' (COM[96] 583 final) (CEC 1996b). This discussion paper aims to launch a wide debate on how the Commission can make the most of the opening of public procurement markets. The Commission pointed out that the regulatory framework for public procurement has been established, but that some problems remain: first, implementation and application of the public procurement directives by the member states are inadequate, and, second, the policy applied to date has had little economic impact. In addition, the Green Paper calls for discussion on certain points, including the link between public procurement policy and environmental policy. The Commission received several, quite contradictory, reactions on the linkage issue and is now preparing a communication. However, it has not come to any conclusive decisions yet about the course to pursue.

III The Regulatory Scope for the Greening of Public Procurement

Since the regulatory framework prohibits discriminatory tendering practices, procurement officers may need clarification about the possibilities available to pursue environmental objectives. It has even been claimed that, in order to avoid difficulties, there is a tendency among procurement officers to leave environmental demands out of calls for tenders.

In its Green Paper (CEC 1996b), the Commission states that 'the application of the public procurement directives does indeed leave scope for public authorities to promote environmental protection' and it recognises that 'it would undoubtedly be desirable . . . to clarify the possibilities offered . . . for taking environmental concerns into account'. In the same paper, the Commission is establishing a first step in the clarification process by summing up several possibilities:

▶ Environmental protection considerations can be incorporated into the technical specifications.

▶ Environmental protection objectives can be included among the criteria for selecting candidates.

▶ Environmental factors can play a part in identifying the most economically advantageous tender during the award phase.

▶ Purchasing entities can pursue environmental protection objectives through performance conditions imposed contractually.

These possibilities are only roughly defined; they are all subject to certain conditions that will need a further elaboration in the near future. In practice, some further steps have already been taken. As yet, there is consensus that procurement officers may ask for a product that satisfies eco-labelling criteria or its equivalent, but that they are not allowed to refer to a particular kind of eco-labelling scheme. Also, public authorities may demand that the latest technology is applied in the product. It is, for example, allowed to specify that cars should meet the highest emission standards.

Public purchasers may also give preference to companies with environmental management systems. Such systems might be preferable to eco-labelling schemes because they are able to capture the overall behaviour and performance of a company. This trend is being reinforced by the introduction of ISO 14001 certification. Furthermore, tenders may demand that a certain number of delivery conditions have to be met: for instance, they can require that goods be shipped by bulk rather than individually, that empty packaging and the discarded product be taken back by the supplier, that products be delivered in re-usable containers, etc. They can also require that suppliers give precise information regarding—or warranties for—a product's expected life-span. As yet, it is doubtful whether it is permissible to specify criteria concerning manufacturing processes and distance between purchaser and supplier. It remains unclear as no such cases have yet come before the courts.

Instead of asking for clarification, there is, in principle, another way to handle the present 'lacunae' in the procurement regulations, namely to exploit the legislative gap. Some parties involved actually prefer the option of legal uncertainty, because it presents an opportunity to experiment with environmental requirements. The afterthought is that it is sometimes not sensible to ask for clarification when you cannot predict the answer. However, in a democratic system it seems a better idea to force a political debate in such a case.

As things stand now, it may be concluded that the regulatory framework cannot be considered a real obstacle to the greening of public procurement. However, neither is the present framework a stimulating factor, and it certainly does not provide an invitation for a revolutionary approach.

▌ *The Greening of Public Procurement in the Netherlands*

▐ *The Policy Framework*

Until 1989, public procurement was not explicitly used as an instrument for environmental policy in the Netherlands. This changed with the publication of the first National Environmental Policy Plan (NEPP) in 1990 which was a milestone in the development of an integrated approach to environmental problems. In the NEPP 1990 it is stated for the first time that public authorities should fulfil an exemplary function regarding environmentally sound behaviour. In this context, the NEPP puts forward two action points:

▶ All ministries should establish an environmental management system in their own organisation.

▶ Environmental aspects should play an important role in public procurement.

In the Netherlands, an environmental management system (EMS) is considered to be a good starting-point for the greening of public procurement. Public administrations are not obliged to implement such a system, but the government has provided some strong incentives to do so. The Dutch EMS roughly corresponds to the approach pursued in the EU Council Regulation (1836/93/EEC) on the voluntary introduction of Eco-Management and Audit Schemes (EMAS) which was adopted in 1993. However, the scope of this EMAS regulation is only restricted to companies performing 'industrial activities', thus excluding public administrations.

In the IVM study on public procurement (van der Grijp 1995), it appeared that in 1994 all ministries had meanwhile developed their own environmental management activities, and that nearly all had implemented three elements that are essential for environment-oriented public procurement, namely: an environmental programme; the integration of environmental management in the organisation; and the appointment of an environmental co-ordinator. The majority of the ministries had started the implementation process in 1990 or 1991. The 1994 study showed that the provinces had not made much progress in implementing environmental management systems and greening of public procurement, but this situation seems to have changed only shortly after (van Scheppingen 1995). Furthermore, the study demonstrated that the municipalities, after a slow start, had been quite active in implementing EMSs; most of them began the implementation process in 1992 or later.

The Memorandum on Products and Environment, issued in 1996 by the Ministries of Environment and Economic Affairs, recommended the addition of environmental clauses to tendering specifications and proposed making it compulsory for suppliers to give environmental information on their products to public purchasers. In a later stage, the idea of a legal obligation to provide product information has been abandoned. The Ministry of the Interior was the first to publish environmental clauses to be included in all invitations to tender and terms of delivery. According to the Ministry (1997), tenders should specify at least:

▶ The raw materials that have been used in the product, and the environmental impacts that are caused during its production, use and waste stages

▶ The parts of, or raw materials in, the product that cannot be recycled

▶ The identification of any possible alternatives that are less harmful from an environmental point of view

Terms of delivery should include the following conditions (Ministry of the Interior 1997):

▶ The supplier must guarantee that the composition, means of production, packaging and use of the product, and the waste associated with it, do not cause a larger environmental burden than is specified in the tender.

▶ The supplier is obliged to take back end-of-life products that are fully or partially recyclable and to ensure that they are processed, unless explicitly agreed otherwise.

▶ The supplier must guarantee that the use of the product will not exceed the MAC (maximum accepted concentration) standards (on working conditions) applicable at the time of delivery.

▓ Sample Products: Paper and Concrete

The IVM study (van der Grijp 1995) focused specifically on two sample products. Paper was chosen as the product from the office environment, mainly because of the long and eventful history associated with the issue of recycled paper. Paper is also the subject of the only action the EU has taken so far to stimulate environmentally sound public procurement. When recycled paper was introduced in the 1970s, the Netherlands' public authorities reacted enthusiastically at first. However, negative experiences in the early years, when paper quality was low, have had long-lasting implications. It even seems that there is still a serious aversion to large-scale use: the study confirmed that the use of recycled paper in the Netherlands is limited because of a perceived short life-span and lack of user convenience (van der Grijp 1995). In addition, the Dutch still have a preference for a high level of whiteness associated with virgin paper. However, separate collection of waste paper and paper reduction measures have been adopted by most public administrations.

The second product that has been examined in more detail is concrete. It was found that, in spite of their positive attitude towards sustainable building, the municipal authorities in the Netherlands hardly ever insisted on concrete with a specified granulated rubble content (van der Grijp 1995). This could be attributed to factors related to the relatively recent introduction of the product, such as ignorance of its existence and doubts about quality. These doubts may be removed when the product is officially certified in the future.

▓ Barriers to the Greening of Public Procurement

In the IVM study (van der Grijp 1995), hypothetical barriers were formulated to create a structure for evaluation. They were classified into six categories: awareness and motivation; economic; legal; information; organisational; and technical barriers. It should be emphasised that these barriers are largely sequential: they are related to different stages of the purchasing or tendering process. For example, lack of awareness and motivation may make other barriers further along the sequence—such as economic, legal and technical—irrelevant. Some of the present experiences have indeed revealed that, once a barrier had been overcome, others appeared.

Awareness and motivation barriers refer to consciousness of environmental problems connected to public consumption patterns and the willingness to do something about it. In the Netherlands the awareness about the possibilities for greener public procurement is developing steadily. There is a general consensus about the role model that the Dutch public authorities should present with regards to environmentally sound behaviour. In addition, most procurement officers claim to use environmental criteria in their procurement decisions, but the extent and the type of criteria appeared to be largely subjective. One ministry has taken a particular measure that may have a stimulating effect: the fact that public purchasers should take environmental aspects into account when making purchasing decisions was added to job specifications.

Until now, the emphasis in the Dutch situation has been on the substitution of products and services with environmentally preferable ones. According to pioneers in the field, the discussion should take a new turn: the crucial choice should be made to reduce the *amount* of products used. Furthermore, the study shows that greening of public procurement is usually initiated by a few active people, among whom are the environmental co-ordinators of EMSs. The passivity of the majority might be an obstacle for the further development of the instrument.

Economic barriers refer to the costs of alternative products in comparison with conventional products, and to (dominant) market positions of suppliers. With respect to costs, it is relevant which methods are used for cost–benefit analysis. The outcome of such an analysis may be different when environmental costs are internalised to a larger extent. The Dutch authorities were not able to make a general statement about relative prices of alternative and conventional products and services, because some alternatives are more expensive and others are cheaper. They expect prices eventually to level out and the alternatives to become cheaper in an expanding market. Finally, it should be emphasised that all measures leading to a reduction in consumption will clearly reduce costs.

Dominant suppliers may abuse their market power to prevent the breakthrough of environmentally sound products. The present experiences with environment-oriented public procurement in the Netherlands, however, do not suggest that the attitude of suppliers is an obstacle to the development of the instrument. However, there are some examples of unco-operative or even negative attitudes among interested parties.

Information barriers refer to problems in collecting product information—for example, about product content or alternative products—and assessment of environmental characteristics of products. An significant bottleneck in the Netherlands is the inadequate supply of information on products and services, which is complicated by the never-ending flow of new issues and new products. Public purchasers generally cannot operate with abstract concepts such as sustainability; they need concrete and specific information, preferably on a brand-name level. Furthermore, the discussion of products is often confused due to a lack of clear information and a lack of consensus about the overall environmental impacts of a product. Well-known examples in the Netherlands are the discussions on which type of paper (recycled or new) or milk packaging (bottle or carton) is to be preferred from an environmental point of view.

Eco-labelling schemes may offer help in selecting greener products because the products are easily identified. However, the range of products covered by the present schemes is still rather limited. In the Netherlands, the independent environmental consultancy agency PMA is in fact the only provider of environmental information. The Ministry of Environment has repeatedly taken initiatives to establish some sort of product information centre, but these attempts have failed because of its vulnerable position as a public institution. PMA has gradually filled the information gap by publishing loose-leaf manuals about environmentally sound products and services. Subsequently, manuals have been published on office stationery, office machinery, cleaning, catering, building maintenance services and office furniture. These provide general guidance on choosing environmentally preferable products, and, moreover, contain 'positive' lists of brand-name products, divided into best and second-best options. The manuals have been a big success among procurement officers, who are grateful to have access to information that needs no further interpretation. At present, the manuals provide *the* standard in the Netherlands; they are used by approximately one-third of national and local authorities and a growing number of companies. Recently, PMA extended its activities with the development of computer software to determine the eco-profile of offices.

Legal barriers refer to the procedural framework of international and national regulations. In a study of procurement of office furniture (van Scheppingen 1995), it was found that Dutch procurement officers were ill-informed about the EU public procurement procedures, and that they were often not aware of the sanctions that are connected to non-compliance. In addition, procurement officers seem to perceive the EU directives as a barrier to the greening of public procurement. However, as yet, it is not possible to draw firm conclusions about the extent to which Dutch procurement officers are reticent in taking environmental concerns into account in 'European' tendering procedures in order to avoid judicial procedures.

Organisational barriers refer to the division of procurement competences and the availability of structures that enable communication and exchange of information within and between public administrations. In the Netherlands, the competences for public procurement are largely split up and the functions involved are quite independent. It is therefore necessary to motivate a lot of people to effect a change in public procurement. However, this does not appear to be an insurmountable obstacle, but rather, at most, a delaying factor. To support and facilitate the 'greening' process, there are platforms and consultative bodies at various levels of the administration.

Technical barriers refer to problems associated with different characteristics of alternative products and the market availability of environmentally sound products. Dutch procurement officers are largely of the opinion that the quality of alternative products is lower than that of conventional ones. One reason for a negative perception may be the fact that several alternative products that have recently been introduced into the market lack official recognition by way of certification or established norms. Another reason for a negative perception may be the different appearance and characteristics of alternative products. Both these obstacles have occurred in relation to paper: namely, colour and user convenience. In relation to concrete with a granulated rubble content, there are some indications that the parties involved have doubts about the appropriate methods of calculating the supporting power of structures that use this material.

||| Perspective for the Future

From the above, it may be concluded that environmental aspects are increasingly taken into account in procurement decisions in the Netherlands. However, it is not possible to give an assessment of the environmental and economic impacts of the current policy, because there are no specific targets, and monitoring only takes place on an incidental basis. A new impetus for greener public procurement may be given by the Memorandum on Environment and Economy published in 1997. The memorandum is the result of a collaborative effort by four ministries: the Ministry of Environment, the Ministry of Economic Affairs, the Ministry of Agriculture, Nature and Fisheries, and the Ministry of Transport and Water Management (1997).

The memorandum sketches a perspective for a sustainable economic development. One of its starting-points is that the transformation process towards a sustainable, environment-efficient economy is a joint responsibility of companies, consumers and public authorities. The greening of public procurement should be one of the means of integrating environmental and economic objectives. Moreover, environment-oriented public procurement should counteract the deadlock that has been reached in the market penetration of less environmentally harmful products and services. The present state of affairs in the Netherlands is summarised as follows: **producers argue that consumers do not show the willingness to pay for environmentally sound alternatives, and that there is a lack of demand; consumers argue that the alternatives are too expensive and that there is a lack of supply.**

A few activities to spur the breakthrough of greener public procurement have already been started. The Ministry of Economic Affairs, for example, is examining the possibilities of procurement officers becoming 'launching customers' (first buyers) of environmentally friendly technologies, and is exploring the possibilities of introducing 'technology procurement' in the Netherlands. What is meant by 'technology procurement' is a push strategy involving the setting of requirements by large buyers, or combinations thereof, to force innovative product development. Moreover, in the period from 1998 to 2003 the government will make available a budget of 10 million guilders to facilitate, *inter alia*, the establishment and implementation of a monitoring system to identify failures and successes of current governmental procurement, and to develop resources for procurement officers in order to provide them with clear and unambiguous criteria for assessing the environmental impacts of product groups.

5 Issues for Environmental Purchasing in Australian Local Government

Wayne Wescott

▌▌ Introduction

As communities explore more ways to become sustainable, local government is starting to examine its own purchasing practices. Councils buy a range of goods and services, which creates, on a national scale in Australia, a $15 billion industry. How can we leverage the impact that this may have towards promoting sustainability?

Environs Australia, a non-profit, non-government organisation working with local governments to improve environmental management, has designed a project to address this question. Working in close conjunction with the City of Manningham, Environs Australia is setting out to discover practical policy initiatives, joint purchasing practices, accounting packages and successful experiences in orienting purchasing towards sustainability. In Australia's rapidly changing local government context, it is looking at: the impact of the Internet and electronic commerce on purchasing; increased competition, deregulation and the green market; integration with competitive tendering principles; and various international approaches.

This is all within the context of examining the increasingly potent powers that local governments have in determining the country's future sustainability. The environmental debates of the last few decades have become a part of mainstream debate within many councils. Councils are realising that they contribute directly in their own operations to major environmental issues, such as greenhouse gas emissions, the reduction of biodiversity and the endless creation of further waste, and are also major local determinants of their communities' responses through the policies that they enact on matters such as land use and transportation. This has fuelled the growth of many different environmental initiatives, from the sectoral approaches of waste management or Local Conservation Strategies through to overall integrative approaches such as Local Agenda 21.

Within that general context, the purchasing practices of councils can be an important tool as part of a wider effort to re-orient councils and their communities towards a more sustainable future.

▌ What Environs Australia is Doing

The project seeks to:

▶ Produce an issues paper that outlines the generic issues relating to green purchasing in Victoria, Australia, and internationally, and overviews the current state of play and resources

▶ Audit the key resource expenditure areas of the City of Manningham

▶ Develop a set of criteria for green purchasing, based on the key resource areas of local government (extrapolated from Manningham and others)

▶ Workshop these criteria with other purchasing agents, such as MAPS (Municipal Association Purchasing Service) and Purchasing Victoria

▶ Present an alternative green purchasing approach for councils, with measurable results

▶ Produce and launch a generic model for other councils to introduce green purchasing approaches

▌ The Aim of this Chapter

In order to set the scope of environmental purchasing, this chapter will address a variety of issues and identify some key opportunities. It will also provide some practical steps relating to the work being done at Manningham Council. This chapter also examines the role of purchasing, both in the context of Victoria and the country as a whole. The importance of purchasing is seen as vital, given the increasing globalisation of markets and the potential impact of electronic commerce.

▌ Local Government and Purchasing

Local government purchases a range of goods and services from a wide variety of suppliers. Below is an examination of: the scope of the purchasing; the main methods used by councils; and the main sectors of goods that are being purchased.

▌ Scope of Purchasing

Total outlays by Victorian local government in 1995/96 were $1,474,000,000. The total aggregate outlays for Australian local government were $15,495,000,000. Although this includes interest payments and other financing and transfer strategies (including different state approaches to assets and so on), clearly we are talking about a potentially enormous amount of collective purchasing power in local government, both in Victoria and nationally.

Individually, there are enormous variations in the ways councils nominate, categorise and spend their resources. Indeed, a long-standing complaint against the types of benchmarking that became popular some years ago has been that they have failed to compare like with like. Some councils include a variety of services under one banner, while others break them down and across other categories. Some gather staffing into one category; others break it up into units. Some councils gather their car fleet into one management unit; others spread it (and the related expenditure) across the different units. The advent in Victoria of Compulsory Competitive Tendering (CCT) has led to slightly greater uniformity, as there are requirements to segment expenditure in a more effective manner to assist the tender process.

Major areas of environment-related expenditure are the traditional operations where there is an easily defined direct impact on natural resources, such as waste creation and energy management. These are the areas in which conservation officers have had the greatest success in arguing for adding environmental criteria to purchasing policies. Rough calculation of these is possible through extrapolation from individual councils.

Figures 1–3 describe the rate allocation for three councils' budgets in 1996/97 and indicate which environmental considerations apply to each category. From these, we can see that nearly half of councils' direct expenditure from rates falls into traditional environmental areas of expenditure. Strategically, these should be the areas where there are the greatest opportunities for early success.

ITEM	**POTENTIAL ENVIRONMENTAL CRITERIA**	**% OF RATES**
Street trees	Indigenous trees	0.6
Parks, open space	Grey water recycling; low water-use planting	5.5
Civic buildings	Low-energy lighting; insulation; energy-efficient appliances	11.12
Waste and recycling	Recycling content in materials; waste reduction in contracts	6.97
Street lighting	Green power (from renewable energy)	2.0
Economic development	Sustainable technologies support	1.53
Roads, footpaths	Recycling of materials: asphalt, concrete	18.9
Street and toilet cleaning	Environmental cleaning products; recycling of street leaves	2.18

Figure 1: The City of Darebin, Victoria: Budget Allocation 1996/97

▐▐▐ Joint and Individual Purchasing

Councils in Victoria have changed their purchasing practices over the years. There has been a steady growth in joint purchasing and, recently, the advent of CCT. There are two main organisations providing joint purchasing in Victoria: Purchasing Victoria and MAPS. Although accurate figures are difficult to come by, one organisation considers that Purchasing Victoria covers about 10% of the existing Victorian Local Government market and MAPS about 35%. (The total size of that Victorian market, according to a MAPS estimate, is $400 million per annum.) The rest of

ITEM	POTENTIAL ENVIRONMENTAL CRITERIA	% OF RATES
Parks, open space	Grey water recycling; low water-use planting	7.0
Waste services	Recycling content in materials; waste reduction in contracts	10.0
Street lighting	Green power (from renewable energy)	3.0
Economic development	Sustainable technologies support	2.0
Roads, footpaths	Recycling of materials: asphalt, concrete	9.0

Figure 2: The City of Greater Dandenong, Victoria: Budget Allocation 1996/97

ITEM	POTENTIAL ENVIRONMENTAL CRITERIA	% OF RATES
Street trees	Indigenous trees	3.5
Parks, open space	Grey water recycling; low water-use planting	11.92
Civic buildings	Low-energy lighting; insulation; energy-efficient appliances	4.45
Waste and recycling	Recycling content in materials; waste reduction in contracts	12.3
Street lighting	Green power (from renewable energy)	3.14
Economic development	Sustainable technologies support	2.4
Roads, footpaths	Recycling of materials: asphalt, concrete	12.0
Street and toilet cleaning	Environmental cleaning products; recycling of street leaves	0.6

Figure 3: The City of Boroondara, Victoria: Budget Allocation 1996/99

the purchases (or over half of all council purchases) in these categories made by Victorian councils are made individually.

An interesting trend is that Victoria-based purchasing schemes are being adopted by other states—primarily New South Wales—as the potential efficiencies are recognised across state borders.

||| MAPS

The MAPS Group was formed in 1985 when fourteen of the inner municipalities in Victoria agreed to organise common-use item contracts through MAPS in order to obtain a higher-quality product at a better price. The scheme was made available to other councils in 1987/88 and, more recently, to other statutory bodies who now total over 170 separate offices. Until 1992, MAPS was administered by the City of Melbourne on behalf of its members. In October 1992, the Minister for Local Government approved the establishment of MAPS Group Ltd as a public company limited by shares. In April 1993, a prospectus was floated offering all 'eligible persons' the opportunity to take up shares in MAPS. At the close of the prospectus, over 90% of members had taken up shares. The Group is controlled by a board of directors elected by the shareholders.

MAPS has a very large membership base in the metropolitan area of Melbourne, supplemented by a substantial base in the major provincial centres, and the organisation claims about 75% of the total Victorian local government joint purchasing market share. Examples, as cited by MAPS, of the types of product it purchases are: aluminium foil containers, batteries, bitumen, boots, shoes, protective clothing, brushware and brooms, chemicals, computers, pipes (plastic and concrete), fax machines, telephones, fuels, oils, vehicles, trucks, mowers, chainsaws, office machinery, paints, paper, photocopiers, plumbing products, quarry products, steel, and many others. MAPS uses a set of general selection criteria to evaluate suppliers.

▶ **Service and distribution.** The ability and/or willingness of tenderers to provide goods/services to all members and the degree of distribution points to allow 'local' supply is taken into account.

▶ **Quality.** Product quality as regards content, design features and other benefits, including in-service support from the supplier, is taken into consideration.

▶ **Quality assurance.** Certification to AS 3900/ISO 9000 series is considered when evaluating submissions.

▶ **Testing.** Laboratory and/or in situ tests of samples are carried out where appropriate.

▶ **Standards.** Compliance with relevant standards (Australian, British or American) is confirmed as detailed in each specification where applicable.

▶ **Product selection.** Product comparison on the basis of other public authorities' experience—as well as the impact of staff recommendations—and preferences is taken into account. The suitability of equipment, conformity with contract specifications and compatibility with existing equipment is taken into account.

▶ **Member input.** Recommendations by members following evaluation and review of products are considered. The review of tenders by scheme member representatives includes, where appropriate, occupational health and safety advisors and outside industry specialists.

▶ **Australian preference.** The purchasing scheme gives full consideration to the commercial advantages and economic benefits of purchasing goods and services of Australian or New Zealand origin. Tenderers must indicate where applicable the percentage of imported content in their offers.

▶ **Supplier history.** The scheme takes into account supplier history such as: demonstrated track record, financial capacity, occupational health and safety, capability and qualifications of personnel, equal employment practices, etc.

▶ **Price.** Price in the context of cost-effectiveness and value for money is considered.

▶ **Special requirements.** Where appropriate, additional 'contract-specific' criteria are used in conjunction with the 'general selection criteria'.

The above general selection criteria are utilised to evaluate all tender submissions and are allocated weightings in accordance with their significance to the contract requirement.

⦀ Purchasing Victoria

Purchasing Victoria was begun as a co-operative under the auspices of the Municipal Association of Victoria (MAV) in 1987. At the beginning of 1996, it was formally spun off from the MAV and became an entity that offers purchasing services for a whole range of councils, community groups and other organisations, such as water boards. Its turnover in 1996/97 was $60 million. Purchasing Victoria works with all councils in Victoria (except the City of Melbourne, which has a strong connection with MAPS) and provides suppliers across the full spectrum of council activities. Its method of operation is through an annual tender process—each year, half of its tenders are let for a two-year period.

As with MAPS, Purchasing Victoria very much reflects the policies and approaches of its member councils and clients. It tends not to take a proactive approach to user demand, though it is open to persuasion on such issues.

⦀ Purchasing Australia

Purchasing Australia, based with the Department of Administrative Services, covers federal departments' procurements on a nationwide basis. Its mission is: 'To work in partnership with government buyers, suppliers and industry to optimise outcomes through purchasing consistent with government objectives'. Purchasing Australia administers the broad policies and guidelines within which all Commonwealth departments and agencies make their purchasing decisions. Some of these requirements are overtly environmental, as set out in the *Commonwealth Procurement Guidelines*. The *Guidelines* require buyers to:

▶ Seek to buy goods and services with the least adverse environmental impact

▶ Work with industry to encourage continuous improvement in the environmental impact of the goods and services they buy

▶ Assess the environmental impacts of goods and services against informed and common standards and methods

The *Guidelines* can also require that goods and services:

▶ Comply with occupational health and safety requirements

▶ Meet environmental best practice in energy efficiency and/or energy consumption

▶ Are environmentally sound in manufacture, use and disposal

▶ Are re-usable or recyclable, are designed for ease of recycling, or otherwise minimise waste

It is also to be noted that, in order to meet the Commonwealth's obligations arising from the *Revised Strategy for Ozone Protection*, buyers should:

▶ Not buy products or equipment manufactured with or containing the ozone-depleting substances halons, chlorofluorocarbons (CFCs), carbon tetrachloride or methyl chloroform

▶ Decommission and replace fire protection equipment containing halons

▶ Not buy products or equipment manufactured with or containing the ozone-depleting substances hydrochlorofluorocarbons (HCFCs), where products using environmentally friendly refrigerants are available and fit for the intended purpose

Agencies are also advised to minimise waste by:

▶ Reducing overall fleet fuel consumption

▶ Improving the energy efficiency in Commonwealth-occupied buildings, new buildings (including residential buildings) and major refurbishments

▶ Considering strategies to maximise the recycling of paper, plastics and packaging materials

It is unclear as to how the implementation of any of these guidelines are assessed, or if there are requirements to ensure compliance by means of an auditing body.

▋▋ Compulsory Competitive Tendering (CCT)

CCT is a method of enforcing market-testing of services. Legislation by the State government effectively requires most councils to market-test all but a very few of their council activities. The advent of CCT in Victoria has led to the diminution of the role of environmental policy in some areas and, paradoxically, the strengthening of environmental policy in other areas. This paradox has occurred because the most fundamental result of the introduction of CCT in Victoria has been in clearly defining the expectations of the purchaser. Some councils had been doing this all along, but for most this was a difficult process that required a re-examination of current practices.

In councils, such as Manningham and Frankston, where the existing officer(s) were quickly able to put into place environmental frameworks, there has been a very positive impact in terms of the consideration of environmental issues in key tender areas. Where this did not occur, the overwhelming weighting in the evaluation of tenders has been regarding price.

▋▋ The Role of Purchasing in Sustainability

Increasingly, councils in Australia have begun to re-orient themselves around the concept of sustainability. In practice, this means:

▶ Thinking and planning for the long term

▶ Involving a wider group of stakeholders

▶ Integrating council policy and operations across the entire organisation

What is the role of purchasing in this? Can councils assist in creating new sustainable technology markets?

Such considerations take us beyond the more traditional approach to green purchasing which essentially attempts to provide purchasing checklists for 'greener' products. Although this has value in the short term, there is a problem in applying such strategies to dynamic markets (i.e. where there is constant change in products and standards) and in building coherent policy-based purchasing strategies (because they too readily become limited by the scope of the original checklist). There has also been considerable difficulty in keeping material up to date with changes in both purchasers and providers.

▌▌▌ Creating New Sustainability Industries

The first role that purchasing can play is in creating and developing new 'sustainability industries', especially locally. These industries generate products and services that encourage greater sustainability locally, and are also 'future-oriented' in that they are in the early stages of their industry development. Examples of such products and services are:

▶ Energy efficiency industries (solar hot water services, photovoltaics, insulation, high-efficiency windows) that encourage reduced greenhouse gas emissions

▶ Waste and recycling services (such as products created from green waste materials recycling, waste exchanges, tyre recycling plants) that minimise the impact of waste creation on cities

▶ Information services (such as community information systems, Internet-based global networks, skills training and development of expertise) that spread important information about new products, services and approaches

By actively working towards developing local expertise in these areas, a purchasing policy can assist in developing the local infrastructure that will enable a more sustainable community. This includes taking into account the life-cycle costs of products (including, for example, the energy costs of transporting these same products and services from other regions), as well as the important social benefits of maximising local employment.

▌▌▌ Creating New Markets

The second key role is in creating and developing new 'sustainability markets'. To some extent, this has already become part of many councils' policies through a determination to 'buy recycled: many councils request that recycled products be part of the mix of purchases if there is rough equivalence on price.

There have also been attempts actively to create markets through the purchasing of recycled plastic street furniture and litter bins. Some tenders, as part of the CCT regime, have also specified that the successful tenderers must either use recycled products (such as the City of Stonnington's Waste Transfer Station), or dispose of their materials, such as concrete and asphalt, to the appropriate recycling industries. Most of these criteria will be limited by the industry's potential at any one time. Products with percentages of recycled materials always have to compete with raw materials in price, and it has proved hard to leverage the gains from one product—say, recycled street furniture—into other products beyond that particular niche market.

Other approaches could be to look at policies that can be more easily adapted to new conditions. The Greenlight Consortium has developed with the Sustainable Energy Development Authority (SEDA) in New South Wales the 'Energy Smart Homes Policy', which encourages councils to set minimum performance standards for new homes and extensions. This has the advantage that, over time, there will be 'knock-on' effects of the expansion of energy efficiency markets through price reductions, greater supply, better deliverability, and so on.

▌ *Key Barriers to Environmental Purchasing*

The most significant issue for Victorian councils as regards environmental purchasing is the undertaking to increase the amount of products with recycled content. This was driven by the State government and community organisations.

The first problem was the essential conservatism of the purchasing process. As there are often significant time-lags between the cycles of purchasing—driven by the length of the contract to the supplier—it was often impossible to implement a policy decision straight away. And that led to councils either losing interest or impetus, as well as being unable to capitalise on the community involvement or councillor direction that had been generated by the debate.

Purchasing officers, and clearer purchasing policies, became more prevalent in the early 1990s in Victoria, but this often merely exacerbated things by tying up suppliers over long periods to maximise economic gains, but thus minimising the capacity to move quickly or react to new community demands. Additionally, many suppliers had secured their contracts through close and long-term personal relationships with the council officers making the purchasing decisions. This is not meant to suggest any impropriety, merely that the council officers preferred to deal, in a very direct and personal way, with suppliers that they felt were able to meet their needs.

The second problem was the difficulty in matching purchasing policy requirements to new markets. Recycled plastic products in street furniture, for example, faced a whole range of perceptions about their quality: Were they reliable? Would they stand up to extreme weather conditions? Would the community object? Would they be easier to vandalise? Were they out of keeping with heritage areas? and so on. The reality was that, as with any new product or practice, continual public explanation and education of the long-term benefits of using these products was required. Indeed, in many cases, it could be argued that reduced costs will accrue over the long term through price reductions driven by growing markets, reduced maintenance on certain products, and so on. This is only possible when there is enough time given in the contract to amortise costs of increased up-front investment over the appropriate time-frame. Short-term contracts will rarely allow for this sort of innovation, as many waste management industry representatives point out.

Notwithstanding all of this, there is the essential issue that many virgin materials are still under-costed in our economy, as they fail to take into account life-cycle costs, such as waste creation, which are passed on and externalised or are subsidised in other ways. Until this is equalised, some recycled products will suffer a continuing cost impost.

▌▐ *Environmental Purchasing: The Opportunities*

From this consideration of the issues and experiences so far, we can begin to identify some clear next steps that can harness the influence of purchasing to assist in re-orienting local government towards sustainability.

▌▐ Joint Purchasing Schemes

Given that half of all purchases in certain categories are done via joint purchasing schemes in Victoria, there is great potential to add sustainability criteria to existing criteria. This could leverage the policy formulation in councils so that any price differentials that may already exist (say for recycled materials, or greater energy efficiency) can be reduced.

There is also the potential for one or other of the major competing joint purchasing organisations to use the new sustainability criteria as part of their marketing. The advantage of this is that the organisation will have a competitive advantage with councils that have existing policies or that develop new policies supporting sustainability purchasing. The organisation will thereby not only have a marketing edge, but can also become a powerful advocate for the success of such criteria. Suggested strategies to take advantage of this opportunity are:

▶ Encourage councils to develop, adopt or enforce existing environmental purchasing policies

▶ Use these policies to pressure the joint purchasing organisations to offer environmental criteria as part of their tender process

▶ At the same time, convince the joint purchasing organisations that they can be market leaders by adding environmental criteria right now to their tender process

▶ Assist the current council purchasing officers through the development of a support network for environmental purchasing that links to similar existing networks overseas

▌▐ The Internet and Electronic Commerce

There has been great interest for many years at different levels of government in the potential of micro-economic reform in councils that specifically focuses on development, especially concerning building and planning applications. But the new forms of purchasing that electronic commerce may allow are also opportunities for re-orienting existing practices. Interest in electronic systems has two key drivers:

▶ The desire to reduce developer costs by speeding the process as quickly as possible

▶ The need to provide better-quality information to all community sectors concerned with any particular development

In general, there has been great interest around the world in the potential for electronic transactions—often called 'e-cash' (by analogy with e-mail) or 'digital cash'. It should be noted that many councils already perform many cashless transactions, such as their use of existing ATM systems for electronic payment of salaries. The reason for the appeal of electronic transactions is the incredible ease for the customer with which they can be completed—often a simple clicking of a button or, at most, filling in a form. The cost of these transactions, given the steadily decreasing costs of the Internet and the software and hardware associated with it, is also very attractive.

An issue for councils is the potential to buy goods and services across national boundaries. This is greatly enhanced by the ease of purchasing through electronic means, as opposed to bank orders and other processes. This opens up the potential to tap into overseas suppliers that can—through the expansion of their markets globally—begin to offer sustainable technologies and other environmentally friendly products at costs that reflect new economies of scale.

There is a dilemma here, however. As with the other areas of life that are facing increased globalisation, the issue of 'buy Australian', a concept that is cherished at least in theory in many councils around the country, could become a major stumbling block. Reconciliation probably lies in the long-term building-up of the local capacity for new sustainable technology industries, and therefore local jobs.

Overseas organisations already provide some similar services related to environmental purchasing: the International Council for Local Environmental Initiatives (ICLEI) runs a programme in Europe called 'PROCURA'. This initiative entails research, an environmental procurement campaign, the production of a guide for local authorities, and a series of conferences and exhibitions leading to the creation of a municipal purchase officers' network throughout Europe.

Network of Municipal Procurement Officers. The training seminars and workshops, as well as the congress and exhibition projects, are intended to serve the development of a network of municipal procurement officers, a 'Municipal Green Purchasers Club', which would be facilitated by ICLEI. This network will be linked to the European procurement officers' network that the European Partners for the Environment (EPE) network plans to establish, and will cover the local government sector.

Guide for Purchasing Officers. ICLEI plans to publish a guide to environmentally conscious procurement in its series of *Policy and Practice Manuals*. This activity will be co-ordinated with the 'public procurement' module projected by the EPE's network, of which ICLEI is an active member. ICLEI's guidelines for local authorities will be designed so that they fit into the guideline framework defined by EPE and will cover the municipal sector.

Training Seminars. Training seminars, as well as workshops, are needed in order to provide opportunities for purchasing officers to learn of the necessity to influence the market through environmental demand, and to meet and exchange information and experiences. ICLEI's International Training Centre (ITC) will be liaising with the association of professional eco-counsellors, 'Eco-Counselling Europe', to design and offer these seminars and will be organising such workshops for municipal purchasing officers.

PROCURA **Congresses and Exhibitions.** A series of biennial congresses and exhibitions under the name PROCURA are being planned in order to: raise awareness of the strategic importance of the local and regional authorities purchasing sector in 'greening the market'; make the European Eco-Label scheme better known to municipal purchasing officers; and provide for contacts between the purchasing officers on the demand side and the suppliers. ICLEI has been negotiating with congress venues as well as fair and exhibition companies in a number of European cities.

Municipal Pilot Project and Case Studies. Under consideration is the launch of a pilot project on 'green purchasing' with some ten European local authorities involved. Experiences from these cities would be evaluated and laid down in case studies that would be provided through the 'Local Sustainability' European Environmental Good Practice Information Service managed by the EURONET/ICLEI consortium. It is predicted that these types of initiative will only increase as other cities and communities become active in this area.

The suggested strategies to take advantage of this opportunity are:

▶ Seek links with overseas organisations implementing environmental purchasing and assist them to market their existing suppliers electronically direct to councils and/or to the joint purchasing groups

▶ Publicise Internet commerce potential and reality to councils

⫿⫿ Creating New Markets through Competition

As the waves of deregulation and increased competition become more frequent after the Hilmer Report,[1] there are new opportunities for a purchasing policy that explicitly tackles sustainability as part of the new competitive markets. In some areas, this is already happening. The deregulation of energy markets is assisting the growth of 'green energy' (that is, energy from renewable sources) as it has become a marketing tool. Integral Energy (New South Wales) and Citipower (Victoria) are both involved in this. This can be combined with explicit policy to become a powerful driver for change.

The key is to develop realistic sustainability product targets that slowly build markets, and to avoid the ill-matching of supply and demand that has caused problems in the recycling industry by slowly increasing the amount of sustainability products. This allows the targets to be fed into the tender situation in a way that allows equal access to all potential tenderers. But it also allows innovative tenderers to reap the benefits of their initiative.

There is also the potential for this to provide a 'quality' future, in that it allows tenderers and suppliers to see the vision of the local community more clearly. This may be simply in understanding the large-scale impact of green waste recycling, or it may be part of a community-wide initiative to reduce greenhouse gas emissions in programmes such as 'Cities for Climate Protection'.

---

1. The Hilmer Report, a report to the Federal government, created a new national competition framework which has encouraged reform in both the private and public sectors.

Suggested strategies to take advantage of this opportunity are:

▶ To be prepared to offer realistic and competitive targets for adoption by councils

▶ To broker deals from the councils to the new deregulated industries through knowledge of the targets and the capacity to group together significant amounts of resources

▌▌▌ Local Economic Development, 'Buy Local' Schemes and Sustainability

Criteria that assist new sustainability industries would seek to encourage all existing council services to use these new sustainability services where possible. For example, maintenance on existing buildings could be focused on ensuring local suppliers of sustainability products (insulation, low-wattage lights and so on) are used.

The potential breadth of this is apparent if we simply look at the resources that flow across almost all council operations (such as energy, paper, information technology, waste creation and disposal). By ensuring that some of this is re-oriented to local sustainability suppliers, an immediate impact can be gained.

It is possible to link some of these policy initiatives to existing schemes, such as 'buy local' programmes. These tend to take the view that, if there is rough equivalence in price and other factors (though some councils such as Tweed Heads in New South Wales will go as far as 10% variation on price), then local suppliers should be used where possible. This is seen as legitimate local economic development, and the linking to developing local sustainability industries could therefore also avail itself of some of the investment strategies that are commonplace for this type of infrastructure development. This may include a greater tolerance of variation on price and other criteria, 'co-partnerships' with key local suppliers to develop expertise or purchase required equipment and the development of long-term contracts that are geared to become more competitive as the up-front investment costs are absorbed.

This type of arrangement also has the potential to reduce the incipient antagonism between existing local businesses and sustainable industries. By providing a 'even playing field', all local industries have the potential to take part in new growth industries. As an active job creator, it also crosses much of the political boundaries that can otherwise exist for green initiatives.

Suggested strategies to take advantage of this opportunity are:

▶ Linkage of existing 'buy local' and 'buy Australian' schemes to the development of local sustainable technology policies

▶ The development of partnerships with national associations and industry organisations, as well as significant industry leaders, that represent sustainable technologies

▶ The marketing of government funding and resourcing opportunities, especially prevalent in export-oriented industries, that can be used to fund sustainable technology development

III Conclusion

This chapter has suggested some actions that could be undertaken by Australian local government organisations to further environmental purchasing. To recap, these are:

▶ Encourage councils to develop, adopt or enforce existing environmental purchasing policies

▶ Use these policies to pressure the joint purchasing organisations to offer environmental criteria as part of their tender process

▶ At the same time, convince the joint purchasing organisations that they can be market leaders by adding environmental criteria right now to their tender process

▶ Assist current council purchasing officers through the development of a support network for environmental purchasing that links to similar existing networks overseas

▶ Seek links with overseas organisations implementing environmental purchasing and assist them in marketing their existing suppliers electronically direct to councils and/or to the joint purchasing groups

▶ Publicise Internet commerce potential and reality to councils

▶ Be prepared to offer realistic and competitive sustainability targets for adoption by councils

▶ Broker deals from the councils to the new deregulated industries through knowledge of the sustainability targets and the capacity to group together significant amounts of local government resources

▶ Link existing 'buy local' and 'buy Australian' schemes to the development of local sustainable technology policies

▶ Develop partnerships with national associations and industry organisations, as well as significant industry leaders, that represent sustainable technologies

▶ Market government funding and resourcing opportunities, especially prevalent in export-oriented industries, that can be used to fund sustainable technology development

Environs Australia will be assisting local governments and their representative bodies to undertake these tasks over the next few years.

6 Nordic Countries' Green Public Procurement of Paper

Tito Gronow, Tapio Pento and Alain Rajotte

▌▌ Introduction

In 1991, ministers of OECD countries recommended that member governments develop ways of greening their operations and practices. This call for action may be explained in part by the fact that the combined purchasing power of government expenditures can exert a considerable influence on the development of environmentally sound production and consumption patterns, thereby promoting the convergence of economic and environmental objectives.

Although comprehensive programmes have yet to be defined, initiatives have already been launched by national governments in order to take environmental considerations into account in their operations. Moreover, it is expected that these experiences will provide empirical evidence on the main factors governing efficient programmes. In this regard, the OECD's Pollution Prevention and Control Group (PPCG) has mandated the authors to review current procurement policies and programmes in Nordic countries with a view to suggesting recommendations for promoting efficient initiatives. Empirical practices of programmes in Finland, Norway and Sweden that incorporate environmental aspects into the public procurement of paper were examined. This chapter builds from this earlier work, studying the following questions in more detail:

▶ What volume of paper is consumed by public bodies?

▶ How is public procurement organised?

▶ How are products' environmental and other performances defined?

▶ What types of green procurement programme are in place and what has been their effect?

▶ What have been the effects of these programmes on industry?

The report was prepared by Tapio Pento, with the exception of the section on Sweden, which was researched and written by Tito Gronow. In addition, Alain Rajotte reviewed current practices and guidelines in other OECD member countries in order to allow comparison with the Nordic approaches.

II‖ Public Procurement of Paper in Three Nordic Countries

Finland, Norway and Sweden are major producers of paper but consume only a small part of their own domestic production (see Fig. 1). With regard to uncoated wood-free paper, which is used mainly as copier and office paper, Finland consumes 11% of its own production. Most domestically produced tissue paper is consumed domestically.

Country	UNCOATED WOOD-FREE		OTHER PRINTING PAPER		TISSUE PAPER		PACKAGING PAPER AND BOARD	
	Consumption	Percentage of production	Consumption	Percentage of production	Consumption	Percentage of production	Consumption	Percentage of production
Finland	126	11	600	9	?	?	522	22
Norway	70	130	278	16	61	235	253	49
Sweden	227	26	585	17	161	55	638	15

Figure 1: Consumption of Paper in Three Nordic Countries (1,000 tons)
and the Percentage of Consumption of Domestic Production, 1995
Source: Pulp and Paper International 1996

The amount of unprinted paper purchased for consumption by governmental organisations is not known. Estimates by manufacturers and distributors range from 25% of domestic consumption of tissue paper to as high as 45% of uncoated wood-free paper, and practically zero in other grades. This implies that the total public consumption of unprinted paper in the three countries is approximately 250,000–300,000 tons, or 5%–7% of total consumption.

The amount of paper that Nordic governments purchase in printed form or which they consume in the form of packages, advertising material and the like are also not known. Some rough estimates for the countries under review are given in the following sections.

Most local governments in the three countries have begun Local Agenda 21 programmes, which include, among others, green procurement practices for paper. Central governments have no formal national programmes, but the Norwegian government has initiated a three-year (1994–96) project: 'Green Government Procurement Policy'. Many less formal programmes in different areas of government are in place.

Green products are commonly defined by the 'Nordic Swan' eco-label, which is generally considered a public institution, regardless of its semi-independent status.[1] Products that are accepted in such procurement programmes are either 'Swan'-

---

1. The Nordic Swan is administered by the Standards Authorities of Finland and Sweden, The Ministry of Environment of Iceland, and a government-backed foundation in Norway. Its co-ordinating body represents consumers, environmental authorities, NGOs, industry and research institutions.

certified or satisfy most of its life-cycle environmental criteria. Some programmes accept the EU Eco-label or labels awarded by environmental organisations such as the Swedish *Bra miljöval*, and Type II declarations by manufacturers. This is particularly the case for tissue, where not enough suppliers have applied for the Swan label. The Nordic Swan is used even in larger procurement programmes, because their administrators consider that they do not have the resources to make exhaustive lists of green products themselves.

Sixty-six manufacturers of uncoated wood-free paper with hundreds of brand names have received the Nordic Swan label (Nordisk Miljømerking 1996). These products form a very large majority of the copier paper market of the three countries. Products that do not bear the Swan are usually confined to small market shares. Supplies of eco-labelled grades appear to be sufficient and the market remains competitive. To date, only one manufacturer of hygiene papers has secured the Nordic Swan. Some tissue brands on the Nordic markets have Type I eco-labels awarded by other bodies, or use their own Type II labels, some of which have the backing of environmental NGOs.

III Green Public Procurement of Paper in Finland

The purchase of uncoated wood-free paper by public organisations is estimated by trade experts at somewhere around 3.5 million reams per year, or around 42% of the country's total consumption, of which some 1.5 million reams are acquired by local government.[2] The percentage is explained by the fact that, due to high unemployment, almost every other employed person in Finland works either in the public sector or in publicly owned corporations. The proportion of public consumption is lower in tissue paper, where governmental purchases are estimated at around a quarter of the total annual consumption, or approximately 25,000 tons. Estimates from different sources of the total consumption of all paper products by the public sector centre around 50,000 tonnes per year.

No statistics are available for governmental purchases of printed products, such as contract printed materials, newspapers, magazines, books, booklets and other printed material. A rough estimate is that the central government uses some 2,500–3,000 tons of different grades of paper in its contract printings.[3]

Finland used to have a centralised government supply house, VHK, which provided most of the unprinted paper used by the central and many local governments. Since 1st January 1995, it operates under the name Hansel as a government-owned distributor which competes for the custom of public buyers on the open market, offering frame agreements, stocking and direct deliveries, and drop-shipments from manufacturers. Its market share is considered to be less than 25% of the governmental market in both copier and tissue paper. Hansel is conscious of environmental

---

2. Estimates by manufacturers and trade. The consumption estimate of local communities is calculated as the same amount per capita as in the City of Helsinki, which consumes 210,000 reams annually, and Espoo, Vantaa and Kauniainen, which purchased 85,000 reams in 1995 (communication with P. Kettumäki).

3. Communication with S. Tvorek.

aspects in procurement, and has made it a point to offer environmentally sound products whenever available.

Previously, Finland's government printing house, VPK, had been privatised in 1989 under the name Edita, and this organisation still commands a majority share of contract printings to central government. From the start, Edita has had strong in-house environmental programmes and was the second printing house to meet the more stringent criteria of the Nordic Swan for printed products in March 1996.

Within central government, local organisations, such as offices, hospitals or (departments of) universities, are typically entitled to select their own preferred brands of paper. Local governments operate either a central purchasing system, as when a city's procurement department takes delivery of products and supplies different administrative units, or, less commonly, allow the departments to acquire their own products, assisting them only with frame agreements and technical expertise.

The central government of Finland does not have a comprehensive green procurement programme that covers all its organisational units. A study and a plan for green procurement was devised (Väisänen and Nissinen 1994), but was not put into effect. The Ministry of Environment and several other departments have their own green office programmes, which include the purchase of environmentally preferable products (Vesi- ja ympäristöhallitus 1994). The existence of informal green procurement is evident in many central government institutions through initiatives taken by the purchasers themselves, to the extent that trade experts state that the Nordic Swan has become a *sine qua non* for all tenders and smaller purchases of copier paper.[4]

All cities, most large towns and many smaller municipalities in Finland have instituted Local Agenda 21 sustainable development programmes since 1992. Practically all of these programmes incorporate green office practices and many set green paper purchasing and recycling goals (Huovila 1996; Helsingin kaupunki 1993, 1995, 1996; Silver 1993; Lankiniemi and Annala 1996).

Success in instituting environmental considerations into local community paper procurement has been varied. Some cities have achieved and even exceeded their stated goals, while most have made some progress and have switched to environmentally better products. A small number have produced only few explicit changes in their purchasing patterns. Several success factors have been mentioned in discussions. Good project management and the continuous support of high-level decision-makers are important. Many programmes were started with a decision by the city council, which is the highest level of authority, and were then channelled to the environmental department. However, the lack of further support and control from the council has made it difficult to implement programmes fully across departments. Some programmes were planned by the environmental people with little participation from buyers, users or suppliers, which lessened their impact. Programme management by environmental departments alone, especially when undertaken by environmental experts with little management experience, and without the participation of other categories of personnel, has apparently slowed down the change toward greener purchasing. Thus, a closer participation of buyers in the design and implementation of procurement programmes appears to be a key factor, especially

---

4. Communications with H. Husso, B. Nygård, M. Uotinen and J. Uotinen.

if the co-operation of environmental and procurement management produces both cost savings and environmental improvements.

A significant proportion of all paper bought by public authorities in Finland has become environmentally more preferable over the last few years. Practically all copier paper purchased today bears the Nordic Swan eco-label. Tissue paper with a recycled content has become the norm. The majority of printed material acquired either as contract jobs or books and paper are produced by firms that have been awarded with eco-labels or that have implemented environmental programmes. These improvements have been accomplished in most cases via informal methods rather than via formal programmes, with the active participation of manufacturers, printers and supply houses.

▌ *Green Public Procurement of Paper in Norway*

Norway's central and local government organisations purchase unprinted paper on the open market. Buyers have the option of using frame agreements which are awarded by the Government Procurements Division, a central procurement advisory body within the Ministry of Planning and Co-operation. The division co-ordinates public procurement and concludes frame agreements and group purchases between government entities. For instance, the 1996 frame agreement contains fourteen brands of copier paper offered by three supply houses (Statskjøp 1996). All brands offered bear the Nordic Swan eco-label, some being made of totally chlorine-free pulp. The frame agreements are in common use, but some government units use them only as a starting point for direct negotiations with suppliers.

Local governments make their purchases independently, without central guidance. Some operate centralised purchasing, while others have delegated the purchasing authority to lower-level cost centres. The City of Oslo did have a central purchasing organisation until the end of the 1980s, but has replaced it with an advisory body, acting within the department of finance and planning. This body also acts as an advisor to buyers and provides frame purchase agreements for paper and many other goods. Due to delegated procurement from the open market, no data exist about the quantity of paper purchased by public bodies.

Furthermore, the Ministry of Environment launched a study of the criteria for a green office in 1992, in which paper procurement was one of the main areas (Toft and Dall 1992a, 1992b). The use of the Nordic Swan eco-label was employed in this programme for the product groups for which it was available, and criteria were developed for products that the label did not cover (Miljøverndepartementet 1993, 1994).

The central advisory bodies of the Ministry of Planning and Co-operation play a pivotal role in the greening of procurement practices. Experts on both unprinted and printed paper procurement are highly informed on environmental issues and, in effect, strongly promote the use of eco-labels and other environmental criteria in central government procurement.

The Ministry of Environment, together with the Lillehammer Olympic Organising Committee, established a 'Green Office' programme in 1991. Seven municipalities and two counties in the region took part in the project (MiljøKompetans

1992). The goals of this programme were to avoid waste, to reduce environmental damage arising from products' manufacture, and to prevent toxic emissions by the selection of appropriate goods and packages. The results of the programme underlined the importance of green procurement criteria. In fact, two-thirds of the participating communities did switch to Nordic Swan copier paper (MiljøKompetans 1994). Later, the 'Green Office' expanded and, by the end of 1993, 120 out of a total 450 municipalities had adopted it.

As a follow-up, a central government programme on green procurement was initiated in 1994 to reduce environmental impacts and set a good example for the rest of society, and to encourage Norwegian enterprises to build up environmental expertise, notably to increase their competitive edge in the future. The programme encompassed a number of projects concerned with professional purchasing, and directed at trade and industry. Within this programme, the Ministry of Environment was responsible for the project entitled 'A Green Government Procurement Policy'. The project has outlined a proposal for criteria and guidelines for a green governmental procurement policy. The proposal included environmental criteria for selecting products and suggests how they could be incorporated into procurement policies. This work has been compiled in a guidebook for procurement officers. There is an ongoing revision of the regulations for governmental procurement (Statens förvaltningstjeneste 1996a), which was expected to be completed in 1997. The incorporation of environmental aspects into purchasing will be considered in connection with this work.

Many procurement programmes in local government have been launched in Norway during the 1990s. A nationwide 'Green Working Life in Practice' (GRIP) programme contains green procurement as one part of its activities, and paper products are among the first items on the agenda. The programme uses the Nordic Swan as the criterion for copier paper, and requires non-bleached recycled content for hygiene papers. The programme also contains objectives for reducing paper consumption through efficient use and electronic mail, as well as enhancement of paper recovery (Grønt Arbeidsliv 1994). The GRIP programme also embodies nationwide informational and educational tasks (GRIP 1996).

Practically all copier paper purchased by public bodies in Norway today bears the Nordic Swan eco-label, and most hygiene papers have recycled content. Again, it is difficult to attribute this environmentally commendable record entirely to the greening of procurement programmes, since the switch by manufacturers and markets toward eco-labelled and recycled paper had already taken place.

▌▌ Green Public Procurement of Paper in Sweden

The Swedish government began to adopt certain laws and statutes regarding public procurement policy in 1992 because of the impending EES agreement. The new public procurement legislation came into force on 1st January 1994 as Swedish Civil Law 1992: 1528. Further harmonisation with existing European laws followed. The 1992: 1528 Law was then renewed and republished under SFS 1993: 1468. Some further changes were also enacted during 1994, SFS 1994: 614, and 1995, SFS 1995: 704.

The basic principle of the Swedish legislation is that public procurement must be conducted on commercial principles, and in accordance with EC directives, objectively, without discriminating any party. The purpose of environmental considerations in public purchasing is to promote and increase environmental awareness among suppliers, to support environmentally sound technical innovations and best production practices, and to facilitate structural changes that enhance the growth of a sustainable economy. At the same time, environmentally motivated public procurement programmes serve as models for private organisations, and will inevitably improve the competitiveness of Swedish products (SOU 1996: 23).

However, the programmes have been criticised by Swedish industry on the grounds that the ongoing discussion on public procurement policies and even the current application of procurement legislation concentrate too much on environmental issues and do not pay enough attention to free trade and competition, which are the main items in European public procurement legislation (Industriförbundet 1996). As such, the EC has criticised Sweden, among several other countries, for its implementation of the EC directives on public procurement.

A Public Procurement Board has been created to oversee public purchasing in Sweden. Its main tasks are to ensure that:

▶ Swedish legislation as well as the EC directives and WTO rules are followed.

▶ The latest developments in the EU and the WTO are acknowledged.

▶ Information and relevant statistical data on public procurement are collected and disseminated in order to improve the programme's efficiency.

The body covers procurement at the three administrative levels in Sweden: state, county (*landsting*) and commune, as well as in publicly owned companies, foundations, associations and the state-controlled Swedish Lutheran Church.

Public procurement at state level is decentralised to fourteen procurement units, each one covering one or several functional areas, such as postal service, lower or higher educational units, road and water administration, higher civil administration, medical care, etc. The main task of these units is to negotiate frame agreements with suppliers at advantageous prices. They also act as wholesalers, stocking and delivering products to governmental customers. Counties and municipalities have their own procurement units. In practice, the county and the municipalities within a nearby geographical area often have a common public procurement unit. Public institutions are, in principle, allowed to run their own procurement programmes, but the specialised larger procurement units handle a large majority of purchases because of their better economic performance and expertise.

Environmental aspects have already been taken into account in supplier selection since the development of the first green procurement programmes at the end of the 1980s. The programmes commonly include a training section, in which the importance of environmental criteria for different products is explained.

The Swedish Environmental Protection Agency (EPA), which acts under the Swedish Ministry of Environment, has recently published recommendations, jointly with the Public Procurement Board and the Chemical Inspection Office, regarding the formulation of public procurement policy (Naturvårdsverket 1995, 1996). The role of price has been recognised, but it is proposed to leave the procurement unit with some freedom regarding environmental criteria. In the case of paper products, the main recommendations include eco-labels and recycled fibres (Naturvårdsverket 1996: 38). Eco-labels are not recommended as a mandatory requirement, but it is recommended that paper products should at least fulfil the criteria of eco-labels such as the Nordic Swan. This latter recommendation is commonly followed in public procurement practice. It is not known how much of this practice is derived from procurement programmes, because copier paper on the Swedish market is already Nordic Swan-certified.

In addition, a recommendation promotes recycled fibre content as an important criterion for procurement guidelines. In this regard, the Swedish EPA claims that the use of recycled paper saves global forest resources and results in reduced environmental impacts because of reduced transport and energy savings. However, the impact of the Swedish EPA proposals has not yet been assessed.

In the case of tissue, purchasing practices are more heterogeneous because there are not enough Nordic Swan products on the market. Some municipalities require that the pulp used for manufacturing tissue paper is not chlorine-bleached. Others accept the *Bra miljöval* ('good environmental choice') eco-label issued by the Swedish EPA, or the EU's Eco-label. It is also common for public buyers to request details of suppliers' environmental policies in order to rank firms on environmental grounds.

It is impossible to calculate the exact quantity or value of publicly purchased paper, as no complete statistics are available. A government report (SOU 1996) estimates that the total value of public procurement in 1993 was 280 billion Kroner, of which some 27% was spent on products. Services were the largest procurement item, but state investments and municipalities' subcontracts had also an important influence. Indeed, paper and paper products was the fourth largest group in procurement contracts of municipalities and counties in 1994 (SOU 1996: 21-30).

In 1993, the Swedish National Board for Industrial and Technical Development initiated a project, also called the 'Green Office'. The project aims are to develop procurement recommendations, product lists and handbooks (Naturvårdsverket 1995: 111). Swedish counties are also developing an on-line database to facilitate electronic procurement. Environmental criteria of products will be included in the selection database. This is expected to help public procurement units and single buyers to select environmentally preferable products.

||| Impacts of Green Procurement Programmes in the Nordic Countries

As indicated above, Nordic countries do not produce precise statistics that would enable comparisons of paper procurement patterns before and after the implementation of green procurement practices. Therefore, the following analysis of the changes in consumption, impacts on industries and nations, and other effects are extrapolated from the review of experiences of involved parties.

||| Experiences with Product Use and Performance

Many users of copier paper cite inferior performance of early recycled-content papers. Dust and equipment malfunctions were cited as problems in Norway. Väisänen and

Nissinen (1994) state that 'recycled papers have produced some fluff in printing machines' and frequently tend to jam copying machines. The early problems were apparently caused by inadvertent introduction of mechanical pulp into fine papers via recycling. The interviewees state that the quality of environmentally preferable copier paper has improved rapidly and that technical problems have mostly been solved. National archives may still have reservations about the advisability of using recycled-content paper for documents that are to be preserved indefinitely, because it is possible that some of the recycled fibres are from mechanical pulp or have not been manufactured in an alkaline process.[5] This means that the recycled paper may disintegrate over time and would subsequently be very costly to preserve. At present, there are plenty of types of uncoated fine paper available with the Nordic Swan eco-label and which also satisfy the archive standards (Johannesen 1996: 2).

Few responses regarding the performance of hygiene papers were received and only one was negative. A Finnish user considered the performance of some green brands of hygiene papers considerably worse in quality when compared with regular brands. A trade expert on hygiene papers commented that there are few complaints today, because buyers and the users are already familiar with the products they order, and know what they are getting.[6]

It appears that a substantial proportion of users and buyers are not aware of the environmental aspects of the products they are using, and are not capable of making comparisons between green products and others. Some do not even know the meaning of the Nordic Swan eco-label. Some Finnish users confuse the Nordic Swan eco-label with another and somewhat similar 'swan' label, which has been used for a long time in Finland to indicate a domestically manufactured product.

‖‖ Environmental Improvements over the Life-Cycle

Nordic Swan-certified copier paper has become the norm for public authorities. For hygiene papers, there is a trend toward the use of recycled-content products, but the rate of change is not as clear as it is for copier paper.

The switch to environmentally preferable paper has been accompanied by a considerable reduction in environmental impacts. If the approximately 100,000 tonnes of copier paper purchased by Nordic governments now implies a generation of nearly 0.3 kg of AOX in waste-water per tonne of pulp produced, instead of 1 kg or more, the amount of AOX will have been reduced by some 70,000 kg. Such effects are substantial across the products' life-cycles.

However, it is not possible to state unequivocally that the governments' green purchasing practices are the sole cause of these environmental improvements. Green purchasing of paper was begun mostly during this decade. At the same time, Nordic manufacturers of copier paper were making voluntary investments in chlorine-free bleaching of pulp, and the number of paper brands awarded the Nordic Swan increased rapidly. This meant that public organisations could remain loyal to certain brands, the environmental credentials of which were being improved by the

---

5. Nordic countries have standards that define the criteria for paper that is fit for archives, e.g. the SFS 5453 of Finland.
6. Communication with R. Immonen.

manufacturers, and improve their own environmental performance without any additional effort.

The purchasing patterns for hygiene papers in public organisations may also have changed during recent years when environmentally preferable purchasing programmes have been in place, mostly in favour of paper with recycled content. Purchased paper may now contain up to 100% recycled fibres and Type III environmental brands—with names such as 'Nature Saver'—have become established in many public organisations. Again, the extent to which this switch may be related to the implementation of procurement programmes is difficult to assess, because a similar development has also taken place in private markets, in part due to the active efforts of manufacturers to offer greener products.

Substantial reduction of paper consumption has not been reported by governmental buyers, nor by representatives of distributors or manufacturers. Only some organisations in Finland have reduced their purchase volumes, most likely as a result of streamlining during the tight governmental budgeting that has taken place since 1991. But significant increases have been achieved in the recovery of used paper in public organisations. The sustainable development programme of the City of Pori in Finland reports a doubling of paper recovery from 71 tonnes in 1993 to 141 tonnes in 1995 (Lankiniemi and Annala 1996). National paper recovery rates have increased rapidly and two-thirds of recoverable paper was collected for re-use in 1996. Informal estimates by paper collection firms confirm that source separation and recycling programmes in governmental locations in Finland have become significant sources of recovered paper, but have not succeeded in providing sufficiently effective fine paper segregation.[7] Most office paper waste still comes in mixed batches to the collectors, who then have to provide a sorting process.

||| Economic and Other Effects of Purchasing Bodies

The prices of environmentally preferable paper, such as recycled-content hygiene papers and non-chlorine-bleached printing paper, were originally higher, in part because some paper was not made by domestic manufacturers and prices reflected the costs of import as well as the relatively small volume of the trade. The lack of availability of environmental printing paper has been overcome, and plenty of Nordic Swan-certified brands are now offered by domestic and foreign manufacturers. Deliveries and terms for the environmentally preferable paper are no different than for normal paper, with the possible exception of totally chlorine-free copier paper, which still may command a slight price premium in some instances.[8]

The procurement practices of governmental organisations have changed in many departments. The participation in procurement of environmental staff and experts has become more common. Buyers at all levels of government have become more aware

---

7. Communication with J. Juutilainen.
8. The Statskjøp frame agreement (Statskjøp 1996) shows totally chlorine-free (TCF) copier paper to be slightly higher in price in Norway than other brands that satisfy the Nordic Swan criteria. Hansel price lists (Hansel 1996) do not indicate any difference in Finland. All interviewed manufacturers' experts state that no premiums are paid today to manufacturers for the use of TCF pulp.

of environmental considerations. Indeed, responsible negotiation bodies, which often include environmental experts routinely consider environmental aspects in decision-making.

Effects on National Economies and Industries

If all public procurement were to move into recycled-content copier paper, the paper manufacturing industry would move closer to sources of waste paper. This would cause substantial negative economic effects in Finland and Sweden, who exported 1.1 and 0.7 million tons of copier paper in 1995 respectively (Pulp and Paper International 1996). Approximately 1.5 million annual tons of newsprint capacity has already moved out of the Nordic countries to central and southern Europe since 1985 as a result of the increasing recycled content of newsprint. This corresponds roughly to an investment of five large newsprint machines, 38 million ECU of lost annual revenue to the forest owners,[9] and some 680 million ECU of lost annual exports to the three Nordic countries.[10]

Increased preference for recycled tissue paper has not caused an influx of imports in Finland and Norway. The import of tissue paper in Sweden has increased from 6,000 to 79,000 tons between 1985 and 1995 (Pulp and Paper International 1996), but largely from foreign mills owned by Swedish firms.

The rapid transfer to elementally chlorine-free (ECF) and totally chlorine-free (TCF) pulp bleaching has required heavy investments by the pulp and paper industry. Nordic manufacturers have already switched all of their operations to ECF and TCF processes. No data are available on the size of the investments that were required in this change.

The stance of Nordic paper producers toward environmental matters has traditionally been relatively open. Manufacturers have worked to achieve the criteria required for Nordic Swan certification. Effluent and emission statistics of mills are published routinely,[11] and environmental management systems are being implemented at mills. Most importantly, the strategy of Nordic manufacturers in the last decades has been to gain competitive advantage by always using the newest, largest and most efficient production machinery. The strategy has benefited the environment, because the new equipment has, as a rule, almost always produced lower effluents and emissions, as well as using less wood fibre and energy. Not all firms or individuals accept green governmental procurement programmes, and all complain about the need for high-volume orders for green goods and the necessity of charging a higher price when costs of manufacturing are higher. A typical example of this is a comment by the Swedish Industrial Federation on the governmental study on environmental procurement, which considers it a prerequisite for such programmes that industry receives enough turnover for the green products (Industriförbundet 1996).

Manufacturers complain that public procurement programmes are increasing their costs even when they satisfy all of the criteria that are embedded in the programmes.

---

9. Calculated at a volume of 1.5 million m³ of spruce pulpwood at 25 ECU/m³ (Aarne 1994: 164).
10. At a price of 450 ECU per ton.
11. E.g. *Finnish Forest Industries Federation Environmental Yearbook.*

Most countries have their own programmes, which have their own widely different criteria (cf. Milieukeur 1994; Nordisk Miljømerkning 1996), and require special handling even for each bid made. Transaction costs are expected to increase in systems such as these, as more bureaucracy is needed to deal with the continuously revamped criteria, even when no compliance measures are needed. Some managers expressed the hope that public procurement could make use of the information produced by environmental management systems, or that nations would work out a common standard to avoid constant duplication of work.

Effects of the public green procurement programmes of Nordic countries on the strategies of pulp and paper manufacturers are also difficult to estimate. Nordic companies export most of their production and their own governments are relatively small customers. The Nordic paper industry manufactures over 16 million tons of the paper grades shown in Figure 1, of which Nordic governmental organisations consume approximately 1.5%. Nordic manufacturers of copier paper express rising resentment toward eco-labels, and many are planning to discontinue the current eco-labelling of their products because of the competitive cost disadvantage. The complaint concerns the imbalance of revenues and costs associated with eco-labels. All interviewed corporate managers state that their firm has found no competitive advantage from an eco-label. The large majority of consumers bypass eco-labels and give them little or no consideration in their purchasing decisions. In addition, even when all important competitors have secured their eco-labels, there has been no change in market shares. The companies consider that they have annual costs of millions of ECU in eco-label fees which their less environmentally conscious competitors do not have to pay. If a sufficient proportion of buyers does not react to eco-labels, these costs are seen as a punishment on the environmentally better firms. As a result, the number of eco-labelled brands of copier paper that are available on the Nordic markets is expected to fall rapidly in the next few years.

Distributors have expressed few negative effects arising from green public procurement programmes. Some cite an increase in their workload caused initially by having to learn about the environmental effects and the selection criteria of the multitude of products that they handle. The development of revised purchasing processes and negotiation practices and, finally, informing customers represent additional tasks. Education of retailers and sales staff has not advanced very far, judging from a quick survey in Finland and Norway, where staff were selling eco-labelled paper without even knowing the implications of the label.

||| Legal and Trade Issues

Current legal considerations lead to severe constraints on environmentally preferable purchasing. Public procurement is controlled by complex sets of laws and ordinances adopted by international bodies and central and local governments.[12] Legislation and the multitude of rules and regulations do not always recognise existing environmental

---

12. Central government laws and ordinances on public procurement in Finland add up to some 600 pages (Julkiset hankinnat 1994). The German administrative system governs procurement practices with laws and ordinances at four administrative levels: *Bund, Land, Kreis* and *Kommun,* and also recognises EU regulations (Umweltbundesamt 1992).

attributes. Domestic laws and EC directives have hindered the implementation of environmentally sound procurement programmes. For example, the Finnish government-owned distributor Hansel states that actions taken by the EC have made it hesitant about actively promoting eco-labelled products.[13] The firm promotes green products, but not aggressively, and no longer stocks only Nordic Swan products (Hansel Kampanjat 1996).

In Norway, legal considerations have not significantly affected procurement programmes. A representative of the Government Procurements Division did not consider that legislation hindered the green procurement programme, and added, in a discussion about the ambiguities of EU and EEA contract directives: 'We proceed with our EPPP [environmentally preferable purchasing] programme, anyway.'[14]

The environmentally conscious public procurement programmes for paper have not had noticeable effects on either competition or on market shares. All major suppliers of copier paper have acquired the Nordic Swan eco-label, and market shares have not changed. For hygiene papers, domestic manufacturers have opted to increase the recycled content of their products and existing market shares have been retained.

Finally, Nordic pulp and paper manufacturers do not seem to be overly worried about the potential market-distorting effects of eco-labels or environmental public procurement programmes. Several managers state that they consider their mills to be the most environmentally friendly in the world, and consider it unlikely that the use of life-cycle criteria by buyers would put them at a disadvantage.

▮ Conclusions

Public procurement programmes of paper that take environmental effects of the products into consideration are expected to yield a meaningful impact on the environment with very small costs to the purchasing parties. Such programmes are promoted as a 'soft' policy tool in comparison to the usual command-and-control schemes. Commercial interests of suppliers are expected to make them accept the actions prescribed by their governmental customers.

None of the three Nordic countries has an official green procurement policy for paper, but there are many formal and informal programmes and projects that aim to purchase only the environmentally best-performing paper. Practically all copier paper purchased in these countries has been awarded an eco-label, and a substantial portion of tissue paper brands have recycled content. Developments on the market as a whole have been similar, where paper manufacturers have applied for and have received eco-labels, and have increased their use of recycled fibres.

Practical difficulties abound in running environmental procurement programmes. Public procurement organisations are not particularly well equipped to determine which criteria should be employed to define the set of environmentally best products; neither do they have the expertise, facilities, organisation and funding to continually revise their green lists. The use of third-party Type I eco-labels has been seen

---

13. Communications with T. Hailikari and S. Terho.
14. Communication with R. Johannesen.

as a solution in the Nordic countries, but this route may be closed if paper manufacturers cease to apply for eco-labels in order to avoid the associated costs.

An unspecified number of environmentally conscious procurement programmes are in operation in the national and local governmental units of the Nordic countries. More and more experiences are being gathered on the related management issues in different types of organisational structures. The days of centralised government purchasing organisations are over in most countries, and the running-in of new practices requires expertise in organisational motivation and environmental marketing. The important notion of instituting green purchasing programmes in tandem with advantageous operating practices, such as efficient collection and source separation programmes and the use of the right paper for the right application cannot be overemphasised.

Collaboration between the managers of green procurement programmes and the manufacturers and distributors enhances the potential of least-cost results. Many major manufacturers are, in principle, willing to participate in such programmes and are not averse to making the required environmental improvements, given that they are offered adequate inducement in the form of sufficient order volumes.

The status of green public procurement in international legislation and trade agreements is most unclear. The PPM (production and process method) rules of the World Trade Organisation expressly prohibit the use of production emissions as a purchase criterion, yet many governments are already adopting such criteria as an almost standard practice in programmes toward sustainability.

7 Greener Purchasing and Trade Rules
Can they be Reconciled?

Stig Yding Sørensen and Trevor Russel

THE POTENTIAL for conflict between the environmental and trade agendas has been a matter for growing concern to both business and environmentalists, if for different reasons: and some rulings by the World Trade Organisation (WTO)—such as the recent interim ruling that found US legislation designed to protect endangered sea turtles was in violation of multilateral trading rules—have heightened the unease on both sides. One of the areas of concern is the relationship between international trade rules and greener public procurement initiatives and programmes—whether, on the one hand, WTO agreements will be a barrier to sustainable development as set out in Agenda 21, and, on the other hand, whether greener purchasing schemes can become a barrier to international free trade.

The question is whether greener purchasing and trade rules can be reconciled. In this chapter, we identify the international rules and principles that regulate public procurement and examine how they can limit or further the potential of greener public purchasing as an instrument for sustainable development. The chapter considers the international agreements under the World Trade Organisation's auspices, and the trade principles behind the agreements. After discussing the WTO agreements, it considers the key issue of including demands relating to the manufacturing process in tendering procedures. The chapter concludes with some suggestions on how environmental issues could be incorporated into international procurement agreements—without harming the principles of free trade.

‖ The WTO Agreements and Government Procurement

International trade agreements have covered government procurement—up to a point. The 1979 Tokyo round of the General Agreement on Tariffs and Trade (GATT) included an agreement on government procurement (the Code), but it was limited in scope and was also a plurilateral agreement—meaning that the parties to the original 1947 GATT were not required to become signatories. In fact, only 19 GATT contracting parties, mainly the most developed countries, acceded to the Code, thereby accepting limited GATT discipline for certain procurement decisions. The Code allowed parties greater access to a relatively small number of foreign procurement opportunities in signatory countries on a national treatment basis, but because it did not contain a most-favoured-nation (MFN) provision, it excluded non-signatories from its benefits. Environmental specifications fell within the Code but, since it did not apply at sub-national level, there was a substantial gap in its coverage.

The trend towards integrating procurement rules into the international trade regime continued in the Uruguay round negotiations. In January 1996, a new plurilateral Agreement on Government Procurement (AGP) came into force. While the membership is broader than that of the former Code, it still consists primarily of the developed countries. Unlike its predecessor, the AGP applies to both national and sub-national procurement activity, although it does not cover all industrial sectors—while the sectors that are covered are often subject to reciprocity provisions, and certain financial thresholds must be met before the AGP applies. A national treatment provision only exists among signatories, and the market access and transparency rules of the AGP are not applied on an MFN basis to all WTO members.

Article VI of the AGP covers technical specifications, mandatory or voluntary, which are an essential element of all procurement schemes. The relevant parts say:

> Technical specifications laying down the characteristics of the products or ser-vices to be procured, such as quality, performance, safety and dimensions, symbols, terminology, packaging, marking and labelling, or the processes and methods for their production and requirements relating to conformity assessment pro-cedures prescribed by procuring entities, shall not be prepared, adopted or applied with a view to, or with the effect of, creating unnecessary obstacles to international trade.
>
> Technical specifications prescribed by procuring entities shall, where appropriate,
>
> a) be in terms of performance rather than design or descriptive characteristics,
>
> and
>
> b) be based on international standards, where such exist, otherwise on national technical regulations, recognised national standards or building codes.

Nothing in Article VI prevents a 'procuring entity' from using environment-related technical specifications; indeed, certain technical specifications relating to processes and production methods would appear to be permissible.

Environmental and business interests agree that green procurement schemes must be fair and not further trade discrimination. The objective of green procurement is not to create trade discrimination but to further a competitive market which includes environmental issues *on equal terms* with price, quality, delivery terms and so forth.

Transparency throughout the procurement process is needed to ensure these goals, and this depends on a formalised procurement system providing for timely notice of procurement opportunities as well as reasonable and uniform conditions for the participation of potential suppliers, and the administration of the tendering process. Articles VII–XIV and XVIII–XX of the AGP establish international rules for pro-curement, which are designed to increase transparency and fairness in the procurement process.

Another issue is the question of participation by both business and environmen-talists in a procurement programme. This would allow them to work with government bodies on developing procurement specifications. Article VI of the AGP prohibits procurement authorities from soliciting or taking advice that would preclude competition from a firm with a commercial interest in the procurement process. This excludes neither business nor environmentalists from the process.

Business is often invited on a general level (i.e. specialists or branch organisations) in the early stages of the procurement process as advisors on technical matters. To represent wider interests such as the environment, public health and consumer needs in the procurement process, NGOs can be invited—but this is still a rare practice.

Harmonisation is obviously a key issue. In the area of procurement, harmonisation can refer either to the development of standardised procurement procedures (procedural harmonisation) or to the development of uniform procurement specifications (substantive harmonisation). Procedural harmonisation, in the form of the AGP, is beginning to occur among those countries who have signed the agreement. Substantive harmonisation suggests the international harmonisation of technical standards—the pros and cons of which are now discussed.

International Standards and Technical Specifications

Article VI establishes a preference for existing international standards, or national technical regulations or recognised standards. Standards adopted by the International Standardisation Organisation (ISO) tend to be regarded as international ones; what is much less clear is when, or if, the provisions of multilateral environmental agreements, or those of an international non-governmental certification organisation such as the Forest Stewardship Council, could form the basis for international AGP standards.

There are pros and cons to relying on international environmental standards in drafting technical specifications. For business, international standardisation means certainty: when companies know what is expected, they can find it easier to compete internationally. However, if the standards are set too low, this can put businesses capable of winning contracts requiring technically superior environmental performance at a disadvantage—setting the standards too high will disadvantage companies with less technical expertise and resources.

Similar concerns arise from an environmental perspective. The protracted effort to negotiate the ISO 14000 series of environmental standards shows that the convoy moves at the pace of the slowest ship where international environmental negotiations are concerned. International standardisation of environmental norms at the lowest common denominator is a cause for worry, because it can mean that industry loses the incentive to invest in environmentally superior technologies—and can also mean that governments find it difficult to implement procurement programmes that address local environmental conditions. Also, industries in countries with fewer resources and less sophisticated environmental technologies could be disadvantaged by higher foreign environmental standards.

The work in international standardisation organisations is hugely decentralised and, in the EU alone, over 100,000 national standards are going to be replaced with 9,000–12,000 European standards over the coming five to ten years. The work in the groups is characterised by changing participants with different experience in the standardisation work. It is difficult to participate in the groups, which generate huge amounts of paper in very technical language. Furthermore, the meetings are held at different locations in Europe and in the rest of the world. The ISO is also an acronym for 'International Sightseeing Organisation'. This makes it very expensive to participate in the work, especially for environmental NGOs and consumer groups; very often, only businesses with specific interests in the standard can afford to participate, and wider interests enjoy only sporadic representation (Goldschmidt 1995).

Since most standards are important in public procurement and already have considerable environmental impact, this is an unfortunate situation from an environmental point of view. A study by CASA (Bauer and Hermind 1995) has illustrated this and points out that, although the *raison d'être* of the standardisation organisation is to further the common interests of society as a whole, at ISO level society is largely represented by business interests.

A central issue is the adequacy of technical specifications used in government procurement programmes. When international or national specifications cannot be relied on, technical specifications can be designed to procure environmentally suitable products; at the same time, however, they can be used to protect domestic industries. Article VI of the AGP tries to address this problem by requiring that technical specifications 'not be prepared, adopted or applied with a view to, or with the effect of, creating *unnecessary* obstacles to international trade (emphasis added). However, it does not specify what type of technical specification constitutes an 'unnecessary' obstacle to international trade.

Article V does imply that a technical specification is more likely to be accepted as necessary if it is written in terms of performance, rather than design or descriptive characteristics, and if it is based on international standards (where they exist). Business argues that, since it permits standards to be drafted in a way that quantifies a product's environmental characteristics (such as emissions), the Article's preference for performance over design or descriptive characteristics should pose no problems from an environmental, as well as business, perspective. But, as shown above, there is little incentive to include environmental characteristics into international standards.

The preference for international standards over national technical regulations could be a different matter entirely. This is likely to mean that bodies such as the ISO will continue to assume more importance—which, however, could lead to governments postponing the implementation of national standards because of ongoing international negotiations, and also could make it more difficult for governments to tailor technical specifications to address national environmental concerns when faced with the fact that international standards should take precedence. At the same time, no government can afford to participate in the huge number of standardisation groups.

III *Environmental Impacts from Cradle to Grave*

One of the strongest potentials of greener purchasing is the possibility to pull the development and innovation of cleaner products and technologies through the supply and demand mechanism of the market. The environmental effect of a product or technology differs on its way from cradle to grave. Sometimes, the most serious effects arise from use of the product; in other cases, problems do not materialise until disposal stage. Also, environmental impact is connected to raw material acquisition or the production process. To exploit the full potential of greener purchasing, public purchasers must be able to stipulate environmental requirements in the production process.

The issue of process and production methods is where the environmental and trade communities are most divided. Business is claiming that environmentalists encourage governments to develop domestic technical regulations that govern how a particular product—and, worse still, even an imported product—is produced. The issue becomes a cause of tension when governments attempt to influence foreign non-product-related processes and production methods unilaterally, rather than resolve them multilaterally. According to business, procurement specifications could be designed to influence how foreign products are manufactured—or designed to exclude foreign products because of the techniques used to produce them. Business wants the AGP provisions amended to remove this risk.

The Danish Ministry of Business and Industry has highlighted the equation between trade and environmental requirements as they apply to greener public purchasing by examining the European Union's rules on public tendering. Its conclusions can to some degree be applied to the AGP since the EU follows the AGP (Danish Environmental Protection Agency 1995). The general advice is that, in a tendering procedure, the purchaser can choose either the lowest price or the economically most favourable offer in awarding a contract—and, in the ministry's judgement, if purchasers opt to apply the principle of the economically most favourable offer as the award criterion, they are free to set out environmental requirements or preferences for the product(s).

However, the ministry has pointed out the conflict between greener public purchasing and trade by stating that purchasers are restricted as to how they can apply environmental requirements to the manufacturing process, if the process is not significant to the properties of the finished product and does not affect the environment in the country where it is used. While the reasoning behind this is that such requirements could lead to the suspicion (indeed, the practice) of favouring national suppliers—in particular, if that means that suppliers from other member states are prevented, in practice, from participating in the tendering process—it does suggest that EU tendering rules are hampering the effectiveness of greener public purchasing initiatives.

That said, the ministry has identified some openings for environmental requirements. For instance, it is still possible to require compliance with national environmental legislation concerning the manufacturing process with regard to public works contracts performed within the national boundary. The ministry also considers it is in accord with EU legislation to give preference to companies participating in the EU's environmental management and audit scheme (EMAS) or its equivalents; and also believes it is possible to give preference with regard to the manufacturing process if that preference is based on reasoned environmental considerations crucial to environmental impact.

It is a fact that the EU rules do set limits on the requirements that can be applied to the manufacturing process: what is not clear is exactly where the limits are, for there is no clear definition of when an environmental impact can be considered transboundary. The consequence is that the legal status for such requirements remains in a grey area—leaving purchasers to word their tender documents carefully, and hope they do not violate international trade rules. In Denmark and elsewhere in the EU, there is pressure for public authorities to adopt greener purchasing policies, yet they have to implement greener purchasing decisions within an unclear, uncertain legal framework. The threat to greener public purchasing in these circumstances is that public authorities will be unwilling to 'take a chance', and instead opt for the status quo (Sørensen 1998).

Denmark has proposed a revision of the EU directives, which would allow environmental considerations to be integrated into tendering procedures, while preventing unfair discrimination against companies (Danish Environmental Protection Agency 1996). Its proposed rule changes include:

▶ When instituting tender procedures, purchasers can require documentation relating to ISO 14031 (performance) and ISO 14040 (life-cycle assessment) or similar CEN standards relating to the environmental aspects of a product, and give preference to products which, according to the information received, have the lowest impact on the environment.

▶ Purchasers can require that a product carries an EU Eco-label.

▶ Purchasers can give preference to products satisfying the criteria for the award of the European Eco-label, when the label has been published in the official journal.

▶ Purchasers can require that the producer of the product be certified under the EU's EMAS scheme or a similarly certified environmental management system (such as ISO 14001).

▍ Reconciling Free Trade and Greener Public Purchasing

There does not have to be a conflict between free trade and sustainable development. Both business and environmental interests have to search for strategies to make sustainable development both a competitive and a natural part of free trade. As has been pointed out by the Danish government, the present situation is unsatisfactory and a clarification of the rules is badly needed. Several actions could be taken.

The simplest, and probably most effective, solution to further free and non-discriminatory markets would be to expand the membership of the AGP—or, failing this, to develop some system or mechanism to bring more procurement activity into a multilateral, as opposed to plurilateral, framework. This approach—essentially a first step towards procedural harmonisation of procurement schemes—ought to prevent green procurement programmes run by non-signatories to the AGP from becoming barriers to international trade. There also needs to be a focus on ensuring even greater transparency in the public procurement process—and this could be linked to the disposition of international development assistance.

At the same time, the AGP and trade blocs such as the EU or NAFTA must incorporate clear agreements on how greener public purchasing can be undertaken. Consideration should be given to including several points in the rules:

▶ Environmental labels focusing on a specific environmental issue or taking the whole cradle-to-grave cycle into consideration. Preference for products with, for example, the EU's flower, Nordic Swan, US Energy Star and so forth should be explicitly allowed and encouraged.

▶ Public purchasers must be able to support environmental management systems such as EMAS and the ISO 14000 series.

▶ Public purchasers must be able to support industries that give priority to eco-design, eco-efficient products or are working to implement cleaner technologies.

▶ Public purchasers must be able to gain access to all environmental information they may find relevant.

▶ Public purchasers must not be forced to trade with what they consider environmentally 'criminal' industries, i.e. industries exporting hazardous waste to the third world in conflict with international agreements or industries using ozone-depleting substances.

▶ Environmental requirements should constitute a mandatory and standardised part of any public tender procedure—just as price is a part of any consideration.

Finally, it is paramount to keep an eye on the work of standardisation groups. Governments must insist that environmental considerations are taken into account when standards are agreed upon. Governments could consider giving active economic support to the participation of NGOs and environmental interests in the standardisation process. And, if governments signing international agreements bind themselves to follow the standards in the procurement process, international government institutions such as the WTO or the EU must be able to veto or reject standards that do not include environmental considerations in a dynamic way (Sørensen 1998).

The lack or inadequacy of legislation and international agreements is an obstacle to the inclusion of environmental considerations as a natural part of the market. This is a constant frustration to producers, purchasers and users alike. It is not satisfactory—there are ways to make trade and environment reconcile.

Section 2
Private Purchasing

8
Encouraging Green Procurement Practices in Business
A Canadian Case Study in Programme Development

Michael J. Birett

III *Introduction: The Need to Establish a Market*

The procurement of goods and services is a daily occurrence for most businesses. Yet the choices made can have a critical impact on the long-term well-being of both the environment and local economy. Environmental initiatives such as waste reduction are particularly dependent on the procurement activities of private-sector and government operations.

Municipal 'Blue Box'[1] collection programmes, for example, rely heavily on revenues generated by the sale of processed, recyclable materials into what are essentially commodity markets. Between 1995 and 1996, open-market prices for recycled #11 corrugated cardboard ranged from a high of $340 to a low of $50 in North America. Combined with fluctuations in the value of other Blue Box materials, operating revenues in the Region of Waterloo, Ontario, alone dropped by $1.9 million or almost 50% as a result. Justification of waste-diversion programmes in private-sector businesses is equally dependent on market values for recyclable materials. Revenues from the sale of office fine paper and Blue Box materials were sufficient in 1995 for most local haulers to offer free collection services and even pay generators where sufficient volumes were involved. Two years later, most were charging fees equivalent to $275/tonne to provide the same service. With local landfill disposal fees at $50/tonne, the justification for waste-diversion programmes was seriously jeopardised.

The underlying problem in both of the examples above was ultimately the lack of market demand for the materials collected. As with all commodities, low demand translates into low prices. In the case of recycling programmes, low prices result in insufficient revenues being generated to offset collection and handling costs relative to the alternative of disposal. Establishment of strong, stable markets for recyclable materials is therefore critical. And it is here that government and private-sector purchasers can play a key role. The government of Canada alone procures more than

---

1. A municipally based kerbside collection programme for selected household recyclable materials, such as newsprint, fine paper, steel, aluminium or plastic food and beverage containers.

$8 billion in goods and services annually. Consider the ramifications that a policy by this one government preferentially to procure products with recycled content could have on the market demand and value of recycled materials.

The influence of employees involved in purchasing decisions goes well beyond the impact on municipal and private-sector recycling efforts, however. Regular disposal of large quantities of waste packaging materials, disposable products and partially used or stale-dated inventory are all indicative of poor decision-making within a business. As a result, profitability is impacted by high material and disposal costs, and valuable landfill space is unnecessarily wasted. Ultimately, these decisions directly affect the financial strength of the businesses involved and the local communities they support.

▌ Awareness-Raising

It was for these reasons that staff at the Regional Municipality of Waterloo, Ontario, Canada, developed a series of initiatives to encourage environmentally responsible or 'green' procurement among local businesses. The first of these initiatives was to organise and host a one-day conference entitled 'Closing the Loop' in late 1994. The primary objective of the conference was to raise awareness of the underlying issues among local purchasers. It also served as a first step toward raising the profile of successful procurement professionals as potential 'champions' of the environment. Notable presentations included an overview of relevant legislation, environmental standards and important trends. Displays highlighting over thirty new products, technologies and private-sector initiatives were also featured. Over 100 participants from across the province attended the successful event.

▌ Strategies for Behavioural Change

It is important, however, to recognise that awareness-raising initiatives such as the one mentioned above are, in isolation, largely ineffective in causing changes in behaviour to occur. Studies in behavioural change have repeatedly demonstrated that awareness does not necessarily translate into action. An informal study conducted by Regional staff six months after the 1994 conference eloquently demonstrated this point. Of the attendees contacted, over 87% indicated a greater appreciation and concern for the need to support green procurement within government and business. Yet less than 9% could cite specific actions they had taken to change their own procurement practices or those of their company.

Increasingly it is recognised that a number of key elements must be present in voluntary initiatives for sustainable change to take place. First, a solid understanding of the target audience, their attitudes and receptivity to the proposed change is required. Second, an appropriate strategy to cause change must be selected and carefully developed. Finally, the role of 'change agents' and 'catalysts' or 'champions' must be thoroughly understood and their involvement approached correctly.

Fundamental to behavioural change efforts is a clear insight into the target audience. An accurate assessment of existing attitudes and receptivity toward the proposed message is necessary. Problems such as racial intolerance, for example, can be extremely pervasive because they often stem from attitudes and beliefs shared within families for generations. Increasing competition with immigrants for jobs or negative experiences with affirmative action programmes can strengthen such beliefs, despite public support for racial equality. Understanding the underlying source of exhibited behaviour in combination with an appreciation of the competing pressures or barriers to change is required to formulate an effective change strategy.

Behavioural change strategies fall into three basic categories or variations thereof. Normative strategies, those that motivate change by drawing on the strength of intrinsic beliefs and values of the target audience (e.g. honesty, kindness to children, protection of the environment) are generally found to be the most sustainable. Coercive strategies, those that rely on force (e.g. legislative requirements, disciplinary action) and utilitarian strategies, which rely on direct rewards, tend only to be effective so long as they are enforced. A law without enforcement, for example, is unlikely to be followed if the general public does not believe in its inherent value.

||| Credibility of Information

Equally important to the success of behavioural change initiatives is the need to recognise that individuals evaluate information in part on the basis of the credibility of the information source. Voluntary government programmes are particularly suspect for this reason. Therefore, individuals and organisations seeking to initiate change must objectively evaluate their credibility as proposed agents of change and take action to address potential image problems. One effective way to bridge the credibility gap, for example, is the identification and use of the leaders from within a target audience to deliver the change message. Related professional associations serve a similar purpose in communicating outside messages to the target audience on a broader basis. Respected peers of the target audience can serve as powerful 'catalysts' or champions of change, motivating others by example. They lend important credibility to the efforts of outside advocates of change.

||| *The Role of Purchasers*

||| Constraints

In examining the opportunities to encourage green procurement among local purchasers, it was therefore important to understand the context within which purchasers work. Routine job responsibilities for most purchasers focus on daily efforts to secure various commodities at the lowest available price through an efficient, standardised process. The majority do not have the latitude or authority preferentially to procure goods at a higher price on the basis of qualitative benefits such as environmental strengths. Nor do they have to time to explore the relative benefits of various products unless specifically requested to do so. Decisions to include specifications such as recycled content are generally made either by the department requiring the commodity in question or by the senior management of the company in the form of corporate policy. Therefore, while potentially receptive to the concept of green procurement, corporate buyers are not in a position to act on the issue.

To further complicate matters, it is important to recognise that many companies have been aggressively downsizing their central administrative services over the past decade. Due in part to advances in technology and the proliferation of contract services, these changes were dramatically accelerated during the last economic recession in Canada. Many companies have effectively gutted their procurement departments and decentralised these functions. As a result, most procurement professionals are struggling to retain employment in the face of dwindling resources and responsibility. New challenges such as procurement of green products are not likely to be a priority under these conditions unless support is provided from external sources.

Decentralisation of procurement activities has also created several additional barriers to green procurement. Monitoring procurement of green products by staff in different organisational units is both a time-consuming and potentially complex process. Co-ordination and communication of new procurement directives in this environment requires substantially greater efforts. These challenges represent a significant barrier to purchasers in light of their limited resources.

⫾ Drivers for Change

However, several factors continue to drive change forward in this area. Many larger corporations have faced substantial public pressure to accept greater responsibility for the environmental impacts of products they produce. As a result, companies such as Xerox and Nortel have made significant advances in the procurement of goods and services to address these concerns. Issues such as employee health and safety and indoor air quality have also driven change in the procurement of raw materials for building products, cleaning chemicals and coatings.

In addition, most organisations representing procurement professionals recognise the downsizing pressures their members face and have been working to enhance their skill-sets and profile. These groups are generally supportive of green procurement initiatives because of the opportunities created for their members to increase their profile and value within their individual companies.

⫾ Developing a Strategy to Promote Greener Purchasing

Development of a strategy to address these factors was therefore necessary: the Region would be required to do more than merely raise awareness of green procurement issues. The approach taken recognised that most purchasers are effectively choice-makers rather than decision-makers, in that they have limited authority to make policy decisions. A combination of normative and coercive techniques was therefore considered most appropriate. Specifically, the emphasis in subsequent initiatives was on both motivating individuals to take action and also providing them with an understanding of how to secure support within their companies for change. The underlying message emphasised the benefits to purchasers' professional careers, their companies and the local environment.

As part of the strategy, both direct and indirect communication links were established with local procurement professionals. Leaders or 'champions' in the field with whom local purchasers could relate were recruited as spokespersons for the Region; supportive associations were contacted to assist with promotional efforts; success stories were collected and cultivated locally for later use; distinct efforts were made to develop the credibility of the Regional government as an advocate of green procurement;

specific tools to facilitate the procurement of green products and services, and mechanisms to provide ongoing support, were developed as part of the plan.

Ongoing communications with local purchasers were established through a variety of approaches. A database was initially developed based on the list of local purchasers to whom the conference was advertised. This list was consolidated with a pre-existing database of contacts responsible for environmental issues within local manufacturers (approximately 1,200 contacts). Those individuals who were unable to attend the conference were sent a summary overview highlighting its success and the list of local companies who did attend (essentially a 'Who's Who' of local manufacturers and institutions).

Topical information was then distributed to the entire group on a regular basis over the next two years. This information consisted primarily of one-page fax bulletins. Topics included legislative and voluntary trends in environmental management and, in particular, green procurement. Success stories featuring prominent companies' green procurement efforts and overviews of non-profit associations active in the subject area were highlighted. Useful tools, including a directory of local waste management services and guide on waste reduction, were also distributed, along with information about other green procurement information sources: the intent being to develop credibility with this group as an informational source and to reinforce the fact that other businesses were actively pursuing green procurement.

Concerted efforts were also made to cultivate relationships within key non-profit organisations involved with professional purchasers (including GIPPER, PMAC, OPBA and GPI). Financial and 'in-kind' support was provided to several related organisations. Regional staff participated actively on committees and at a board level in order to gain first-hand experience in working with purchasers. This background work was particularly helpful in identifying influential members of the purchasing community and subsequently in soliciting their support for the Region's initiatives.

At the same time, Regional staff began work to improve their own corporate performance or credibility with respect to green procurement. A specific bylaw supporting green procurement was developed and passed by Regional council, the focus of which was to review existing tenders and specifications to identify opportunities where recycled content could be specified.

In addition to the efforts of Regional purchasing staff to implement the bylaw, a separate pilot study was conducted of procurement opportunities within the corporation. The objectives of the pilot included development of an efficient mechanism for reviewing and evaluating alternative products and identification of immediate opportunities for change within the division. Materials with a dollar value of over $10,000 or of substantial volume were selected for review. The Region's Transportation and Design & Construction (D&C) divisions were selected as the focus of the pilot because of the large volumes of construction materials procured annually. Staff from the Waste Management, Purchasing, Transportation and D&C divisions were actively involved in the process. Materials reviewed were organised into eight general categories, including aggregate, asphalt, concrete, lumber, paint, signage (notice boards and roadside signs) and erosion control materials. In total, purchases of over $375,000-worth of inventoried and $674,257-worth of non-inventoried materials were reviewed. Thirteen tenders from 1994 worth approximately $11,300,000 were also reviewed from a process perspective. Over eighteen economically viable alternatives were identified for consideration by the division as a result of the pilot.

||| Resistance to Change

Development of internal procurement practices within the Regional corporation proved to be invaluable in understanding the barriers that green procurement initiatives face. Despite the presence of a specific bylaw and awareness of its importance among staff, significant resistance to change existed throughout the organisation. Regional purchasers faced many of the same problems as their private-sector counterparts in trying to adopt green procurement practices. Problems such as having difficulty securing support from senior management and fellow staff were common to both groups. Informal discussions with local purchasers at the time also revealed a continuing desire for additional information. Others reported having difficulty assessing the validity of and comparing the performance claims of green products. Time requirements to perform cost comparisons were also identified as a concern.

||| A Green Procurement Pilot Programme: 'Striking the Balance'

In response, a new pilot programme was developed in the latter part of 1996 and launched in the autumn of 1997. The underlying objective was to work with participants over the course of a three-month period to implement the core elements of a successful green procurement programme within their own companies. The intent was to provide participants with current information, better tools and contacts to accomplish this task within an atmosphere of ongoing support. Secondary objectives included evaluation of this format as a means of achieving sustainable change, and developing working relationships between participants and local suppliers of green products and services.

Strategic partners were sought out early in the development of the pilot. The Green Procurement Institute (GPI; previously the Canadian Buy Recycled Alliance) was approached to act as lead organisation. The GPI was selected because of its established credibility as a non-profit organisation focused on promoting green procurement issues. The Ontario Ministry of Environment's Green Industry Office was secured as a funding partner because of its knowledge of and support for local suppliers of green products. The Purchasing Managers Association of Canada (PMAC), Ontario Public Buyers' Association (OPBA), Waterloo Regional Co-operative Purchasing Group and the Chambers of Commerce of Cambridge and Kitchener, Waterloo, were also secured as supporting community partners. These organisations played a key role in promoting the pilot and lending it credibility. It is also important to recognise that the willingness of these groups to support this initiative was a direct result of having cultivated meaningful relationships with them from the outset. The University of Waterloo volunteered to host the event and also participated directly in the pilot.

The pilot, entitled 'Striking the Balance', took the form of a series of six half-day workshops spread out over a three-month period. The intent of this approach was threefold. The primary reason was to minimise the impact of the time commitment on participant's workload; second, it also provided participants with the opportunity to apply the course materials at work and review their results with the instructors at a subsequent session; finally, it facilitated development of relationships among participants and other attendees in the pilot, such as suppliers.

Course layout included in-class exercises, take-home assignments, speakers and open discussion. Participants were provided with a balance of information on new products and trends, practical tools to facilitate decision-making, and ideas on promoting their efforts and gain support from their management and fellow employees. Success stories were used extensively to motivate participants and encourage those with doubts to be more open-minded. Motivational speakers from prominent companies spoke about the difficulties and successes their organisations encountered in implementing green procurement initiatives. Suppliers were invited to speak about their experiences in trying to develop and gain acceptance for new products and services: the intent being to encourage discussion around the need for greater co-operation between suppliers and buyers in developing new solutions. New and innovative products and services were also displayed by local suppliers at each of the six sessions, based on themes reflective of the day's discussions.

The course material was organised to take participants through a step-by-step process, from background information to specific action necessary to implement change within their organisations. A template of the process was provided to assist participants in visualising the interdependency of the concepts being discussed. The initial session provided an overview of the current trends in green procurement. Emphasis was placed on redefining green procurement, the idea being to move participants beyond basic concepts such as recycled content in fine paper to the broader issues such as energy efficiency and indoor air quality. Issues with which purchasers have traditionally not been involved were highlighted to demonstrate the opportunities that exist for them to get more involved in key areas of decision-making. Success stories highlighting the actions of other procurement professionals were used to drive home the point that others have been successful in raising their profile within their companies by taking an environmental stance.

The importance of senior management support as a coercive technique in programme development was reviewed with participants. The role of policy, mission and vision statements as enabling tools and sources of visual reinforcement during programme implementation was also discussed. Participants were also asked to review their own organisations for the presence of these and other fundamental components of a successful programme, so that they might better understand the potential barriers they would face in the absence of visible senior management 'buy-in'.

The second session reviewed current standards, definitions, labelling systems and criteria for defining green products and services. Participants were provided with an overview of available reference sources for obtaining additional guidance, including new websites, directories, documents and applicable organisations. As an assignment, participants were asked to review their major purchases and select several to examine for green alternatives during the remainder of the pilot. The role of suppliers and means of developing effective communications with suppliers was emphasised during this module. The need for purchasers to learn how to communicate their needs and preferences effectively was emphasised in this module as a tool for effecting change.

Session three was designed to provide participants with insight into the human-istic aspects of implementing changes in a company's procurement practices. This included effective strategies for dealing with the resulting dynamics both within their own organisations and with suppliers. Particular emphasis was placed on practical tips for anticipating and dealing with employees' reactions to changes in purchas-ing procedures and for building commitment to new initiatives.

Session four focused on aspects of evaluating and justifying the purchase of green products and services. Developments in the practical application of product life-cycle analysis were reviewed with the participants. The financial impact of indirect costs such as hazardous materials management, indoor air quality problems and employee absenteeism were also discussed. Approaches to quantifying these costs and the benefits of products offering improvements in durability and energy, fuel and water efficiency were reviewed and applied through in-class exercises.

Participants were also provided with a number of tools for facilitating the decision-making process. These included checklists, for example highlighting often-neglected aspects of typical commodities such as associated packaging waste, re-usability and recyclability. The use of pre-tender meetings, expressions of interest and performance-testing as a means of securing additional product information was also discussed. The benefits of incorporating qualitative factors such as recycled content or employee health into the tender process through mechanisms such as weighed, price, and balanced budget preferential purchasing policies was debated at length.[2] Partici-pants were then asked to apply these tools to an evaluation of several purchases made by their own companies as part of the take-home assignment.

In the fifth session, participants were challenged to explore the broader aspects of green procurement by reviewing opportunities in the areas of energy efficiency, resource conservation and pollution prevention. New trends, such as contract man-agement of chemical applications in facilities, and new technologies, such as waste treatment through solar aquatics, were highlighted. An overview of existing federal and provincial funding and technical assistance programmes for facilities retrofits was also provided to participants. The potential application of consulting services such as ESCOs (Energy Service Companies) in providing alternative financing options for retrofit commercial projects was discussed at length.

Discussion during the final session focused primarily on measuring and com-municating success. The objective of this session was to ensure that participants understood the need to reinforce the justification of decisions after they have been made and to build on initial successes. The application of benchmarks and per-formance indicators in isolation and as part of a broader programme such as an environmental management system was reviewed. The importance of securing employee and supplier feedback as a means of proactively identifying problems with selected products or practices and alternatively to build support for their use was

2. 'Weighed' purchasing preferentially adjusts the price of a desired product by a set amount based on its qualitative attributes. 'Price'-based purchasing permits selection of a pre-ferred product within a predetermined range where its price exceeds that of its com-petition. A 'balanced budget' approach permits allocation of budgetary savings from one or more initiatives to cover the higher cost of a related preferred product or service.

also discussed. Participants were provided with a variety of suggestions for supporting their initiatives, including examples of successful reward and incentive programmes. A communications template was also provided to participants to facilitate identification and regular contact with both internal and external target audiences.

▌ Evaluation of the Pilot

Participation in the pilot was limited to twenty companies for budgetary purposes. In selecting companies to be invited, emphasis was placed on obtaining representation from each of the major business sectors in the Region. This included companies from the automotive, manufacturing, food-processing, electronics, commercial retail and financial sectors. In addition, local institutions such as the hospitals, universities, school boards and municipalities were represented. A discount was also provided to companies interested in sending more than one employee. This was done in order to encourage companies to send individuals responsible for both environmental and purchasing functions within the same organisation. As a result, a total of 37 individuals representing twenty local major corporations attended. The individuals in question represented three groups of employee—procurement professionals, operations and environmental staff—in relatively even proportions.

Advance promotional efforts included general advertisement of the pilot by fax bulletin to the Region's database of local companies, fax-out notices by the partner associations and articles in their newsletters, and through an article in the local newspaper's business section. Targeted promotion included invitational letters to the environmental and purchasing staff and senior management of approximately eighty selected companies followed up by personal calls where appropriate. As a result of these efforts, the pilot was sold out within weeks. This positive response is notable in light of the fact that several green procurement seminars offered in Ontario at the same time were cancelled due to poor advance registration. In the end, over 43 suppliers, 10 speakers, 7 facilitators and 37 participants were involved in making the pilot a success.

Feedback from the participants was, in general, excellent and word-of-mouth support for the programme has generated interest in several other municipalities. Plans are in place to run the programme in both Toronto, Ontario and Ottawa (Ontario in the spring of 1998). A net profit exceeding $5,000 was generated from the pilot to serve as seed money for the GPI to deliver the programme nationally. More importantly, in a follow-up survey of participants, over 73% indicated that they had made at least one change in the procurement practices of their company as a result of their participation in the pilot. Of those that hadn't, the majority indicated plans to do so in the future. This represents a significant improvement in terms of tangible results when compared with the survey of attendees at the Region's 1994 conference on green procurement. In addition, a number of the suppliers who participated in the pilot were successful in securing additional business and/or good leads from the participants. In several cases, suppliers were made aware of opportunities to bid on sizeable contracts.

As with all pilots, a number of areas of improvement were identified. The majority of participants felt that the twelve-week duration of the course, while conducive to relationship development, was too long. For many, it spanned the beginning or end of a new business cycle making consistent attendance difficult. A maximum of four half-days or several full days spanning a two-week period was therefore recommended for future venues. The majority of participants also had difficulty completing the assignments on their own time. Additional time in class for this work as part of break-out groups was preferred by the majority of participants.

Perhaps most troubling was the noticeable variability among suppliers regarding knowledge of the environmental aspects of their products. Surprisingly few could discuss the benefits of their products on more than a superficial level. This basic lack of understanding of the very issues their products are reportedly addressing represents a serious barrier to the successful marketing of green products and services. It also leaves one to wonder whether this lack of product knowledge is the source of many of the concerns raised about the credibility of performance claims related to green products. Participating consulting firms, in contrast, were well versed and consequently had good success identifying and capitalising on new business leads.

Despite the relative success of the pilot, it is also worth noting that, of the various participants, the purchasers were, as a group, by far the most resistant to the ideas and suggestions put forth in the pilot. Participants with operational and environmental responsibilities were the most willing to explore new concepts. The purchasers present often felt that many of the issues raised were not within their areas of responsibility. In addition, several were uncomfortable with taking a leadership role on such matters. The other groups present often expressed frustration with their perception of 'purchasing' as a barrier to implementing changes within a company. This frank discussion of each group's concerns among the attendees proved to be very enlightening.

▌ Conclusions

In conclusion, it is clear that, if the concept of green procurement is to progress significantly, several changes must take place among the main stakeholders. The majority of supplier representatives clearly need basic training in the marketing of the environmental benefits of their products and services. In addition, procurement professionals need to recognise the role they play in improving the environmental performance of their companies. They must also endeavour to become more comfortable with leading the drive to change procurement practices in business.

9

Do-It-Yourself
or Do-It-Together?

The Implementation of Sustainable Timber
Purchasing Policies by DIY Retailers in the UK[1]

David F. Murphy and Jem Bendell

Ill Introduction

> Acting independently we don't stand a hope in hell's chance of influencing any-
> thing. We might just stand a chance if we all work together on it . . . I think
> that we all share the same view that it is an extremely important issue and is
> not one that will go away if we simply turn our back on it and say we are going
> to ignore this.
>
> *Mike Inchley, Do It All* [2]

What happens when leading UK do-it-yourself (DIY) retailers collaborate with a
major wildlife organisation on a complex environmental purchasing initiative? This
chapter describes how B&Q, Texas Homecare, Do It All, Homebase, Great Mills
and Wickes agreed and implemented a joint policy with the World Wide Fund for
Nature (WWF) to source all their wood products sold from well-managed forests.
The fact that these companies, operating in a competitive market sector, found cause
to work together on a greener purchasing initiative makes it a particularly important case to describe. That they worked in close collaboration with a high-profile
member of the environmental movement makes it even more compelling. The subsequent spiralling of the initiative from a handful of companies in the early 1990s
to a group of 86 companies, including Tesco, Habitat and Tarmac, by 1998 indicates its importance to managers and policy-makers concerned with greener purchasing in a variety of trade sectors.

In this chapter we outline some of the common themes in the implementation
of this policy. In doing this, we aim to portray the benefits of collaboration on greener
purchasing initiatives: between buyers and suppliers; between competing companies;
and between companies and environmental groups.

---

1. This chapter is based on a case study (Murphy 1996a) prepared for a research project
    undertaken by the School for Policy Studies and New Consumer with funding from the
    Economic and Social Research Council (ESRC), entitled 'The Implementation of Social
    Responsibility Policies in UK Companies'.
2. Interview with D.F. Murphy, 2 December 1994.

||| *In a Competitive World*

The UK's DIY home improvement retail sector has experienced a boom over the past three decades, with total sales reaching more than £9 billion by the mid-1990s. The rise of the DIY sector can be attributed to three inter-related factors. First, home ownership has increased dramatically—from 43% in 1960, to 59% in 1980, to almost 70% by 1990. The introduction of the 'right to buy' by the first Thatcher government in 1980 gave many public-sector tenants the opportunity to purchase the freehold on their homes. The second major factor contributing to the growth of the DIY sector has been the increased costs of employing professional carpenters, plumbers, electricians and other home-construction specialists. Third, market research indicates that many home-owners have had more leisure time available to undertake home improvements.

In parallel with this increase in consumer demand, the supply side of DIY also changed radically. The traditional high-street DIY stores of the 1960s were superseded by aircraft-hangar-sized, out-of-town superstores in the late 1970s. In some cases, prior secondary sites such as factories, cinemas, garages and bus depots were acquired for the emerging DIY superstores. In other cases, new stores were built at relatively low costs. The larger shed-like, one-stop shops were able to beat their high-street competitors on quantity and variety of goods, advertising expenditure and, most importantly, price.

However, during the 1990s, the sector had to adjust to the impacts of recession and the related slump in the housing market. With brutal price wars, volatile market shares and a series of take-overs characterising the sector in the UK during the 1990s, DIY retailers were having to survive in a competitive world.

||| *In a Critical World*

> The Big Six DIY superstores are major outlets of tropical timber products. As it is very difficult to distinguish between rainforest timber and wood from other areas, shoppers should boycott all timber products from these stores.
>
> *Friends of the Earth Press Release, 8 November 1991*

In contrast to many other industrial sectors, purchasing was one of the earliest and most visible of environmental issues for DIY retailers. This was due to the work of environmental pressure groups during the late 1980s and early 1990s. Campaigners from Friends of the Earth (FoE) and Rainforest Action Groups (RAGs) conducted a series of protests against DIY retailers because they sold tropical timber. 'Chainstore Massacre' demonstrations in DIY car parks graphically linked violence against forest peoples to logging with chainsaws and, in turn, to market demand from DIY chainstores (see Chapter 24). With the media focusing on tropical deforestation, the DIY stores faced an increasingly critical world.

Initial responses to this criticism were, for the most part, ill-judged and cosmetic. In 1990, Payless (merged with Do It All later that year) claimed that it purchased hardwood doors 'from *reputable* suppliers dealing through *proper* forestry plantations' (quoted in Murphy 1996a: 7; emphasis added). Around the same time, Texas Homecare argued that, for the 'countries that supply Texas, their Governments [must] have an active policy on reforestation, thus ensuring that Texas Homecare only uses products from a sustainable source' (Texas Homecare 1990). This was at a time when many companies did not know the origin of their timber products, as illustrated by research from B&Q's new environmental manager, Alan Knight. He found that, although 50% of its suppliers said their products came from well-managed forests, only 10% were willing or able to identify the forest of origin. Knight also contacted forest campaigners with WWF, FoE and RAGs, as well as key people involved with the timber trade, including suppliers. This open approach to the problem of B&Q's role in tropical deforestation was to lead to a process of mutual learning and the development of a comprehensive wood-sourcing programme for the company (see Chapter 24).

||| In a Brave New World

At the Rio Conference in June 1992, delegates agreed *A Non-Legally Binding Authoritative Statement of Principles for a Global Consensus on the Management, Conservation and Sustainable Development of all Types of Forests*. For the environmental movement, this was not enough. WWF's Forest Conservation Officer Francis Sullivan believed that 'you can't just sit back and wait for governments to agree, because this could take forever'[3] and so WWF turned its attention to industry. WWF set a target of 1995 for the world's timber trade to be based on sustainable utilisation of resources and invited industry to work with it towards this target.

> WWF . . . believes that partnership is always preferable to confrontation. Many other NGOs do not agree . . . Now is the time to prove that conservationists and industry can work together constructively . . . We stand at a crossroads in our relationship between NGOs, the public and business, and this is the time for us to attempt to move forward in a spirit of cooperation (WWF 1991: 11-12).

Retailers found themselves in a brave new world: activists were saying that deforestation was no longer merely the domain of governments but was actually a company's responsibility. Some of these activists were even asking companies to work with them. The response of managers in most of the DIY trade and the subsequent collaboration is, we believe, a testament to the importance of imaginative and progressive management.

Following the WWF seminar 'Forests Are Your Business' in 1991, ten companies committed themselves to reaching the 1995 target and agreed to work with WWF. Initially, the companies and WWF had agreed to a target without knowing how it would be achieved. Later, WWF felt it was necessary to formalise arrangements and the WWF 1995 Group was formed, with five requirements (see Fig. 1). As part of the monitoring process, WWF also agreed to respond individually to each company commenting on progress. Results from progress reports were published in the WWF's six-monthly *Forests Newsletter*.

B&Q was the first company to join the WWF 1995 Group, its board formally adopting the policy in September 1991. For B&Q, 'the prime motivator . . . was the fact that [the timber issue] was a real problem which needed solving'.[4] The company

---

3. Interview with D.F. Murphy, 11 November 1994.
4. Interview with D.F. Murphy, November 1994.

I. Obtain board approval to adopt the target date as company policy.

2. Designate a 'senior executive' with responsibility for policy implementation and reporting to WWF.

3. Provide WWF with a written action programme detailing how the company would reach the 1995 target.

4. Submit regular six-monthly progress reports by to WWF.

5. Agree to the immediate phase-out from all wood products sold by the company, all labels and certificates claiming sustainability or environmental friendliness, until such a time as a credible independent certification and labelling system was established.

Figure 1: Original Requirements for Membership of the WWF 1995 Group

recognised that the marketplace was changing and saw a need to make radical changes in its relationships with its suppliers. Two projects featured prominently in this shift. B&Q started by focusing on timber suppliers, requiring its 100 suppliers to provide precise information by May 1992 on where their wood supplies originated. In reality this proved overly ambitious and the target was revised to the end of 1993.

In December 1991, B&Q then launched a general environmental audit programme based on a lengthy questionnaire to over 500 suppliers (including timber and non-timber products). The quality of supplier responses was variable and B&Q was unable to respond as promptly or as thoroughly as the company had intended. The supplier audit strategy was reworked and, by 1993, the timber and general environmental audits had been merged. The 1993 questionnaire was shortened and more emphasis was placed on face-to-face contact with suppliers. Although the company was clearly breaking new ground, many of B&Q's strategies were later adopted by other DIY members of the 1995 Group.

▌▌ *Policy Development and Implementation*

Analytic decision-making on environmental policy is often assumed to be characterised by structure, consistency, explicit definitions and bounded choices (Moss *et al.* 1994). The actual experience of formulating and implementing environmental purchasing policy involves complexity, uncertainty, ambiguity and shifting boundaries. Given that so few of the implications of the sustainable timber purchasing policies were known at the outset, most of the detailed aspects of the policy only evolved during the course of implementation. In retrospect, however, we can identify some common themes. To provide a structure for the practitioner, we translate these themes into ten 'steps' in the implementation process. Each step is best considered as part of an evolutionary process where policy is regularly updated or refined in response to changing circumstances (Murphy 1997).

▌▌ *Step 1: Find Language*
At the outset it is important to agree on the language and terms to be used in the development and implementation of the greener purchasing initiative.

For participants in—and critics of—the timber trade, the word 'sustainable' was problematic. In the late 1980s and early 1990s, many countries were claiming that their forests were 'sustainably managed'. Such claims became a major point of contention which led to breakdowns in communication: between NGOs; between NGOs and industry; and between NGOs, industry and governments. WWF and its partner companies decided it would not be good idea to use the word 'sustainable' for the WWF 1995 Group.

Another problem was that a lot of product information was using the word 'sustainable' indiscriminately. Alternatives considered were 'environmentally appropriate forestry' and 'low-impact logging'. For the companies and WWF, the term 'well-managed' offered a clearer business context. It was therefore adopted to describe what was desired from timber producers.

||| Step 2: Agree Standards

Once a common language is found, real negotiations on environmental and social standards can commence.

Soon after its inception, Group members realised they needed to be working towards the same goals. Consumer confusion and, worse, scepticism was rife. Well-managed forestry needed to be defined. Negotiations towards an international standard for well-managed forests culminated in the formation of the Forest Stewardship Council (FSC) in 1993. The 'Founding Group' consisted of environmental groups, forest industry representatives, community forestry groups and forest product certification organisations. Financial and logistical support was provided by both WWF and B&Q, among others. The original FSC Mission Statement committed members to 'promote management of the world's forests that is environmentally appropriate, socially beneficial and economically viable'—language consistent with the principles of sustainable development. The council's ten principles therefore represented a widely agreed standard for well-managed forests (see Fig. 2).

||| Step 3: Define Targets

Translating a commitment, in principle, into a programme of action requires a target or set of targets.

While most companies, and indeed WWF, felt that the 1995 target was probably an extremely ambitious one, from the point of view of getting people motivated to take action it proved to be the best option. In reflecting on the early stages of the process, Francis Sullivan of WWF noted that 'although we had committed ourselves to a target date, we still didn't know how it was going to be done'.[5] WWF wanted to get the ball rolling by getting 'members of the wood product trade [to] commit to the principle of taking responsibility for their supply chains and to purchase only products from well-managed forests' (WWF 1996: 4). Despite the fact that no one knew the financial or logistical implications of the policy at the outset, WWF and the companies agreed that specific details could be worked out during the course of implementation. This is consistent with the idea of an evolutionary policy process.

---

5. Interview with D.F. Murphy, 11 November 1994.

1. **Compliance with laws and FSC principles.** Forest management shall respect all applicable laws of the country in which they occur and international treaties and agreements to which the country is a signatory, and comply with all FSC principles and criteria.

2. **Tenure and use rights and responsibilities.** Long-term tenure and use rights to the land and forest resources shall be clearly defined, documented and legally established.

3. **Indigenous peoples' rights.** The legal and customary rights of indigenous peoples to own, use and manage their lands, territories and resources shall be recognised and respected.

4. **Community relations and workers' rights.** Forest management operations shall maintain or enhance the long-term social and economic well-being of forest workers and local communities.

5. **Benefits from the forest.** Forest management operations shall encourage the efficient use of the forest's multiple products and services to ensure economic viability and a wide range of environmental and social benefits.

6. **Environmental impacts.** Forest management shall conserve biological diversity and its associated values, water resources, soils and unique and fragile ecosystems and landscapes, and, by so doing, maintain the ecological functions and integrity of the forest.

7. **Management plan.** A management plan—appropriate to the scale and intensity of forest management—shall be written, implemented and kept up to date. The long-term objectives of management, and the means of achieving them, shall be clearly stated.

8. **Monitoring and assessment.** Monitoring shall be conducted—appropriate to the scale and intensity of forest management—to assess the condition of the forest, yields of forest products, chain of custody, management activities and their social and environmental impacts.

9. **Maintenance of natural forests.** Primary forests, well-developed secondary forests and sites of major environmental, social or cultural significance shall be conserved. Such areas shall not be replaced by tree plantations or other land uses.

10. **Plantations.** Plantations shall be planned and managed in accordance with principles and criteria 1–9, and principle 10 and its criteria. While plantations can provide an array of social and economic benefits, and can contribute to satisfying the world's needs for forest products, they should complement the management of, reduce pressures on and promote the restoration and conservation of natural forests.

Figure 2: FSC Principles of Forest Management
Source: FSC 1994

▍ Step 4: Assign Tasks

The implementation of a greener purchasing initiative must be assigned to a particular department. Preferred options have included quality assurance, technical services, environment or buying.

Once the DIY retailers had formally adopted the 1995 target and associated requirements as policy, the first major step for each company was to develop a written action programme for submission to WWF. As part of this process, each company had to decide where the timber sourcing policy would be most effectively situated. Below are examples of five companies' responses.

▶ **Example 1.** The policy was seen as a quality assurance issue with major commercial implications. Within this company, the policy was originally handled by the buying department. As the workload increased, it was shifted to quality assurance. The QA manager of timber products attended external seminars and meetings related to the timber policy. He was expected to provide buyers with a sense of direction. The QA manager met regularly with the buyers to negotiate the nuts and bolts of replacing product x with product y. This was a complex process of negotiation which also involves discussions with suppliers.

▶ **Example 2.** From the start, the policy was situated within a new environmental department. The environmental manager had a timber buyer seconded to his department full-time, for one year, to lend a buyer's perspective to the 1995 target. This arrangement facilitated mutual learning about the links between environmental and commercial aspects of timber sourcing. The company also hired a timber technologist as a full-time consultant. Buyers were expected to start grading all their suppliers on their environmental performance, including the timber policy. A league table was published each month with each buyer's name and all supplier grades listed. Top buyers were identified. Although no bonuses were given, buyers could see how their colleagues were performing. League tables were also distributed to all directors. This introduced an element of accountability.

▶ **Example 3.** This company situated the policy within timber buying from the start. The company did not have a specific scientific or environmental services department. While there were some discussions with the holding company's environmental people, implementation was left to the DIY company. The timber buyer, as one of fifteen DIY product buyers, co-ordinated the process. Each buying area was required to identify sources of timber in their products. The timber buyer provided briefing notes and standardised supplier questionnaires to the other buyers, and maintained a company-wide database to which all buyers had access. After some initial misgivings, but with pressure from senior management, the buyers slowly came on board over a period of about a year.

▶ **Example 4.** This company initially assigned day-to-day responsibility for the policy to the environmental manager. Early in the process, this manager identified staff awareness workshops as a priority, particularly for buyers. He became frustrated by what he saw as a lack of enthusiasm on the part of the buyers. The environmental manager felt that they were not spending enough time communicating with suppliers, discussing the policy with them and raising the issue when new products were being introduced.

▶ **Example 5.** The policy was situated within the quality assurance area. The quality assurance manager hired a specialist timber technologist who was instrumental in moving the policy forward. The introduction of the timber-sourcing policy coincided with a restructuring of all of the company's major processes (supply performance reviews; supply business reviews; promotions management; promotions pricing; etc.). This enabled the company to develop procedures for the timber policy that were compatible with procedures for other company processes.

As can be seen from the above, very few timber buyers in the DIY companies were actually responsible for policy development, or directly answerable for the degree of policy implementation. In most cases, both contact with WWF and contact with suppliers on environmental issues came from environmental or quality assurance managers, often backed up by specialist timber technologists.

Ultimately, however, the key people on whom action depended were the buyers and product managers responsible for wood and wood products. Communication within the companies, between buyers and quality or environment managers became more complex. Product managers and buyers, for whom timber sourcing and environmental matters were not previously important, now had to juggle a number of priorities in making their purchasing decisions.

||| *Step 5: Inform Stakeholders*

Collaborative initiatives to achieve greener purchasing can lead to disbelief, scepticism or even confrontation from those with an interest at stake; therefore clear communication with stakeholders is essential.

In January 1994, WWF and the four DIY retailers in the Group at the time released a joint accord signed by company managing directors 'to send a clear and consistent message' to over 500 wood product suppliers in the UK and overseas. In addition to restating the 1995 target, the accord specified that 'independent certification is the key' to meeting the target. It further stated that 'independent certification bodies should be accredited by the Forest Stewardship Council' (WWF 1995 Group 1994). The Joint Accord got very little publicity in terms of the printed media, but the timber press did take notice.

Signing the Joint Accord was a natural progression, given that all companies were working toward the same goals. It was released at a point when suppliers felt they were getting mixed messages from the DIY retailers; in some cases, suppliers were using these inconsistent messages to play one retailer off against another to avoid taking action. The Joint Accord was meant to overcome such situations by making suppliers aware that the DIYs were a united force. Each company circulated the same press release and information to its suppliers, which meant that most suppliers received three or four copies. One of the DIY interviewees illustrates how the first Joint Accord had a major impact on one of his company's suppliers:

> I had a supplier come to see me just after the Joint Accord was published and he said: 'That was the last straw, I was trying to resist it, I didn't believe you were serious and suddenly I saw this Joint Accord. I don't even supply the others but when I saw that I suddenly realised this is a major change in business culture.' [6]

---

6. Interview with D.F. Murphy, November 1994.

Meanwhile, scepticism began to rise within the NGO community about the route that WWF was taking. Groups that were not inclined to partner industry at the time, such as Friends of the Earth and the German group Rettet den Regenwald, raised difficult questions concerning WWF's role. WWF's Forest Conservation Officer, Francis Sullivan, attended meetings with NGOs in order to alleviate their concerns. However, WWF was beginning to receive commercially sensitive information from companies in the Group, relating to both environmental performance and supply chain structure. This meant WWF could not be entirely open with others in the environmental movement. When FoE asked member companies about their timber supplies, a number replied that they would only give such information to WWF. Relations with stakeholders were smoothed somewhat because of the Group's commitment to the FSC process, which aimed to be fully inclusive.

When overt confrontation did occur, it was not with the environmental groups but with sections of the trade that felt threatened by the rapidly expanding collaboration. The UK's Timber Trade Federation (TTF) constantly criticised the group's allegiance to the Forest Stewardship Council system of timber certification as anti-competitive and threatened to take WWF to court over what the TTF saw as an emerging buyers' cartel. In response, WWF revised the Group's structure and commitments to what they are today (see below).

||| Step 6: Provide Resources

Greener purchasing initiatives have resource implications. Although many companies can get by without additional resources, performance is increased with targeted funds.

Over time, membership of the WWF 1995 Group began to generate a significant amount of work for the companies. Quite simply, additional time to open and maintain dialogue with key players was required. Internally, dialogue with buyers, marketing and PR managers was required, often through training workshops. Externally, dialogue with suppliers about environmental issues, and with WWF on the details of policy implementation, was essential. These often involved the co-ordination of, or attendance at, special seminars. External advice, in the form of consultancy, was also required by a number of companies: advice on timber re-sourcing from timber technologists, and on the management of supplier assessment data from information technology (IT) specialists was widely sought.

It was therefore surprising that over half of the member companies questioned in 1996 had not yet allocated additional resources towards achievement of WWF 1995 Group objectives (Bendell and Warner 1996). For example, the environmental manager of one company had his budget request for awareness-raising activities, specifically for the buyers, rejected. The fact that some of the companies could implement the new policy without additional funds points to the benefits of collaboration. Many companies had little or no internal expertise in the areas of timber sourcing and sustainable forest management, but in WWF they had a partner that knew a lot about these issues. As one of the DIY interviewees noted, 'we needed guidance and one way of getting that guidance is to join up with people who know what they're talking about' (quoted in Bendell and Warner 1996).

There were also major resource implications for WWF. As the Group expanded and the task of implementation became clearer, the Forest Unit supplied additional finance for a group manager, Justin Stead. His task was to increase the size of the Group, help companies and assess their progress. As the Group expanded and the 1995 deadline loomed, a consultant, Jem Bendell, was employed to develop a reporting system and database to monitor company performance (see below). Other consultants were brought in to help with external communications and promotion of the WWF 1995 Group and the FSC. In total, it was estimated that WWF had spent around £1 million on the WWF 1995 Group and the FSC by the end of 1995.

||| Step 7: Monitor Progress

Monitoring the progress of a collaborative greener purchasing initiative is crucial—for all partners—and requires the development of common indicators.

This greener purchasing initiative was primarily an exercise in data collection. Most companies began to gather data in the following sequence:

1. Identify products with wood content.

2. Identify the forest(s) of origin of the wood content.

3. Assess management practices at forest level.

4. Assess suppliers' attitudes to certification.

5. Assess forest managers' attitudes to certification.

To gather this data, questionnaires were sent to all suppliers of products containing wood. Because many questionnaires were either returned with assurances about the environment but with no evidence, or apparently discarded by their recipients, retailers realised they would need to monitor suppliers' responses to the timber policy.

Therefore companies placed more emphasis on using indicators of suppliers' commitment and progress, such as the prompt return of questionnaires, the adoption of environmental policies, the ability to estimate the volumes of timber involved, and the identification of forests of origin. Different companies used different indicators. Some companies asked questions relating to management techniques used at forest level, such as the volume of timber harvested each year per hectare of forest. Other companies placed greater emphasis on the attitudes of forest managers to being certified under the FSC scheme and on developing programmes of action towards certification.

Initially, WWF gave little guidance on which questions were the most important to ask. However, complaints from suppliers, who were receiving four or five different sets of questionnaires, prompted WWF to make its requirements clearer. In 1995, it prepared a detailed proforma for companies to complete every six months. To complete this proforma, companies needed to obtain information from their suppliers on the value (£ sterling) and the timber volume (wood raw material equivalent) of wood products by species type and country of origin. This was further subdivided into performance categories:

▌ **A:** certified

▌ **B:** known 'well-managed'

▌ **C:** unknown origin

Some companies had difficulty classifying products in category B rather than C, due to the subjective nature of determining 'well-managed' in the absence of certification. In addition, where information was not available, it did not always indicate bad forest management. For example, B&Q identified two types of failure in sourcing: critical and non-critical:

> Critical are far more serious [than non-critical]. These are sources where our judgement says the sources are badly managed or the information is so poor that we cannot make any judgement. Non-critical failures are sources where the company policies and/or the quality of the information is not sufficient but it is our judgement based on other information that the source is probably well managed (Knight 1996: 37).

Eventually, WWF recommended that companies should grade supplies as 'B' if they were able to obtain details of the forest of origin and of the forest manager's willingness to undergo a certification assessment.

In turn, WWF needed a clear system for monitoring members and assessing their progress. The indicators they chose included:

- Number of 'supplier action plans' agreed (this entails a written agreement between buyer and supplier that the supplier will achieve certain goals relating to timber sourcing or certification within a specified time-frame)
- Number of suppliers de-listed due, in part, to a failure in responding to the new environmental sourcing policy for timber products
- General participation in seminars and supplier visits
- Punctual submission of six-monthly reports
- Percentage of trade in certified material (category A)
- Percentage of trade in material of unknown origin (category C)
- Progress in these categories over the last six months

Step 8: Verify Results
For companies to achieve all the benefits of a greener purchasing policy, they need credibility with all stakeholders: independent verification is the solution.

Although WWF was monitoring companies, the system was based on self-assessment. With a Group of 47 members by 1995, WWF's limited staffing levels and other resources precluded any formal, on-site verification of policy implementation. Besides, WWF was keen not to be seen as actually endorsing the companies: WWF–company relationships were founded on trust. There were three major reasons for this approach:

- WWF believed companies would have run a higher risk scenario by maintaining membership of the Group under false pretences rather than leaving the Group.
- By not taking any subscriptions from member companies, WWF maintained [its] financial independence from members of the Group . . .
- Member companies were committed to a separate product monitoring and standard verification system through their commitment to the FSC (Bendell and Sullivan 1996: 15).

The last of these points is key. The FSC system was important to this purchasing initiative not only because of the setting of standards for well-managed forests but also because of the procedure it administered to verify whether those standards are being implemented. The FSC operated an accreditation programme. This meant certification companies such as SGS Qualifor or Scientific Certification Systems were accredited by the FSC as being competent to certify when forest managers are implementing the FSC's principles and criteria. The accredited certification organisations could also check the chain of custody of timber products so that the end-products could be guaranteed to come from an FSC-endorsed forest. After a chain-of-custody certificate was obtained, manufacturers and retailers could display the FSC logo and consumers could then buy certified products with confidence.

‖ Step 9: Manage Information

Greener purchasing initiatives require major information technology resources, particularly the ability to revise and rework company systems of information management.

The supplier environmental questionnaires generated a lot of data. Information on products, companies, forests, species, countries, volumes, tonnes, labels, people, and even attitudes, needed to be stored in a useful format. With different suppliers using different measures for volume and different taxonomies (including local trade names), the ability to collate and manipulate the information gathered from the questionnaires was difficult. For all partners, no matter what approach they took to supplier assessment, database development went hand in hand.

Some companies decided to use existing company database systems so that information could be stored under, for example, a particular product's barcode. Inputting data from suppliers into a database designed for storing information on individual products proved a major technical challenge. Companies such as Do It All and Great Mills went down this route, seeing that it would be better in the longer term to have environmental information in the nerve centre of the company. Other companies decided to set up specific databases for their supplier environmental assessments, and only cross-reference data with other company systems when necessary. B&Q's database was designed in such a way, as was 'TimberTracker', the Sainsbury system that was used to assess Homebase's suppliers. George White of Sainsbury's TimberTracker programme recalls:

> In April 1995, Timber Tracker was established. Between May and November 1995 information on all Group suppliers and their products was analysed for a timber content. Over 200 Homebase suppliers were sent questionnaires, covering approximately 8000 products.[7]

The variety of database systems being developed by member companies posed problems for WWF's Forest Unit, which had to identify common denominators of information in the company questionnaires and databases so that they could report to WWF on the same proforma.

---

7. Personal communication with D.F. Murphy, 30 May 1996.

Ⅲ Step 10: Evaluate and Report Achievements

As collaborative greener purchasing initiatives introduce unfamiliar roles for organisations and their managers, it is important to evaluate performance, report openly and refine procedures.

The fact that the WWF 1995 Group happened at all was a huge success. By the end of 1995, it was time to assess how close the initiative had come to the original targets. By the year-end, four of the DIY companies had less than 5% of their product sources unaccounted for. In the wider 1995 Group, 24 of the 47 1995 Group companies had identified all of their product sources. All DIY members of the 1995 Group had purchased some independently certified products. In the wider 1995 Group, 18 of the 47 member companies had achieved this result. The others had yet to purchase any, either due to the non-availability of products (e.g. no certified paper or pulp products available) or due to logistical delays associated with certification and reluctant suppliers.

WWF published results in a special newsletter, *WWF 1995 Group: The Full Story* (WWF 1996). In addition, most of the member companies publicised how far they had come with timber sourcing and certification. Do It All's timber technologist summed up his company's achievements at the time, reflecting the real sense of collaboration and commitment the initiative had instilled in all partners:

> We have visited the Far East and educated our suppliers on the Group requirements and commitments . . . We have encouraged a number of our suppliers to join the 1995 Plus Group . . . Our Information Technology team has devoted considerable time in adapting the existing database to read the volumes and label each product . . . according to WWF guidelines . . . We are developing a new database in line with our new Information Technology and the revised 1995 Group requirements . . . Since 1993 all of our new suppliers have been issued with a Quality and Environment Questionnaire and this has recently been upgraded . . . Today the role of the WWF 1995 Group is much more readily recognised and accepted. Consequently our suppliers are more likely to accept and conform to the action plans we have agreed . . . Our PR department will participate in the combined launch of the FSC logo to both our customers and our staff . . . Our employees, our customers and our company has gained many benefits from being members of the WWF 1995 Group. Our continued association with and the success of the 1995 Plus Group will enable us to meet some of our moral obligations to the environment (Magill 1995).

Although the partners were able to report their achievements and failures, very little evaluation of the costs and benefits of the initiative took place. For example, WWF made no attempt to assess the area of forest saved per pound spent on the initiative. Most companies did not thoroughly assess the commercial benefits versus the financial costs of their membership of the WWF 1995 Group. On both sides there was a feeling that this had to be done, and mutual recognition that partnership made both environmental and commercial sense.

Ⅲ New Relationships

In addition to these steps in the implementation of sustainable timber purchasing policies, there are a number of issues that emerged concerning inter-organisational relationships: between buyers and suppliers; between competitors; and between companies and non-governmental organisations (NGOs).

▌▌ *Between Buyers and Suppliers*

Initially, the policy was perceived by suppliers as an idea that was being imposed on them either by WWF or by the DIY retailers. Gradually, this view changed as suppliers began to realise that the policy had the potential to provide suppliers with secured orders. For example:

> B&Q has stated that products which have been independently certified and carry the FSC logo will not be de-listed in favour of equivalent but non-certified products (unless there are serious quality or supply problems, and only then can the decision be made by the B&Q Board) (Knight 1996: 44).

Consequently, there was the feeling that, after some initial disturbance and selective de-listing (by 1996, 99 suppliers had been de-listed due, in part, for failing to respond to the new environmental purchasing policies), supplier–buyer relations gradually became more collaborative. Now, while there is evidence that the policy did in many cases facilitate collaboration between the DIY retailers and their suppliers, head-to-head, hard financial negotiating was not eliminated. Despite the introduction of the new policy, most DIY product managers and buyers continued to have much more frequent contact with suppliers than environmental and/or quality managers. Buyers also continued to use the commercial clout of their relatively large companies to carry out tough negotiations with their much smaller suppliers. From the DIY retailer point of view, an essential part of a buyer's role is to negotiate the best deal possible and this did not change. From the suppliers' point of view, they wanted assurances that new investments in timber sourcing and certification would result in commercial benefits.

In reviewing progress, some of the companies noted the insufficient 'buy-in' to the process by product managers and timber buyers. Given their traditional focus on low prices and high quality, some of the buyers found it difficult to integrate environmental issues into their negotiations with suppliers. Timber buyers co-operated more fully where clear direction was given from the top of the organisation and where environment and/or quality assurance managers were empowered by senior management to obtain results via training programmes, secondments and other non-financial incentives. Most of the DIYs acknowledged that effective company action will ultimately depend on the presence of motivated and environmentally aware product managers and buyers. In the words of one of the company interviewees, the buyers need to become more accountable for the policy and will only do so by 'eating, sleeping and drinking this issue in their particular areas and putting much more pressure on their suppliers to be doing something'.[8]

The way forward for all the DIY retailers has been to integrate environmental issues into the core functions of buying. The experience of Great Mills is illustrative:

> The Company now has in place a self-certification system which requires suppliers to provide source details of all new timber products before they are accepted

---

8. Interview with D.F. Murphy, 2 December 1994.

for sale. This information is stored in an electronic database which is integrated into the Company's Management Information System. Up to date information concerning the source of any 'timber' product currently on sale is thereby readily available to buyers and can be provided to customers on demand (Crewe 1996).

||| Between Competitors

Given that all the DIYs had signed up to the same set of rules, it was inevitable that there would be opportunities to work together. Although each company insists that no commercially sensitive information was exchanged, the nature of the business is that most either share or are aware of the other's suppliers. For example, when Company A visits a Finnish supplier to discuss certification issues, it may also represent the interests of Company B if they share the same supplier. Company B would then reciprocate on a similar fact-finding visit to Malaysia. Co-operation was also facilitated by the strong and mutually supportive inter-personal relationships that developed within the Group.

The bottom line for co-operation between the DIY retailers was the need to send consistent messages to all suppliers. The DIYs agreed that they should be asking the same questions to get comparable information on product sources and to facilitate progress towards certification. To this end, the process of receiving and interpreting supplier information also became more similar during the collaboration.

||| Between Business and NGOs

The WWF 1995 Group was a major departure both for an environmental charity and for retailers. Never before had a major environmental group acted in such close partnership with industry on internal company matters. This publication is not the place to describe the full implications of business–NGO partnerships (for this, see Murphy and Bendell 1997), but we can summarise some of the benefits of the partnership approach for WWF and the DIYs.

For WWF, partnership was a useful way of promoting its conservation goals. For business, there were certainly benefits from being a partner of a high-profile environmental group. Much of the DIY co-operation described above was facilitated by WWF through its regular seminars for the DIYs and other WWF 1995 Group members. The DIYs also saw WWF as the 'honest broker' between retailers and suppliers. WWF advised all the 1995 Group companies on key aspects of policy development and implementation, including complex sourcing and certification issues associated with products such as plywood and chipboard. The environmental group also helped with promoting the greener purchasing initiative and giving it credibility with the media and potential critics in the environmental movement.

||| Beyond the 1995 Group

After 1995, the Group has continued—with a new target to trade in only FSC-endorsed wood products by 2000. The agreement no longer states this target explicitly because of concerns about anti-competitive trading, but individually companies have stated their commitment to the '100% FSC by 2000' goal—an ambitious target which, like the 1995 target, will not be met by the majority of retailers. However, it is a target that is helping galvanise everyone into action. By the end of 1997, there were over 80 companies in the WWF 1995+ Group. The annual turnover in wood products was £3 billion, including 67,400 product lines, of which 3% were certified.[9]

In 1998, the wider impact of this collaboration, on the timber trade worldwide and even in other industrial sectors, is being felt. Growing numbers of companies in the Netherlands, Sweden, Austria, Belgium, Switzerland, Australia and North America have bought into the idea of independent timber certification. WWF and other NGOs such as Milieudefensie (Friends of the Earth Netherlands) have taken leadership roles in facilitating so-called buyer groups and/or FSC working groups. At the 1995 UN Commission for Sustainable Development (CSD) meetings in New York, a straw poll found that two-thirds of member-state respondents supported the idea of independent voluntary certification. What started as a fairly limited policy initiative between WWF and a small group of UK companies has now become a significant policy issue for the UN and its member states.

In his assessment of the WWF 1995 Group, George White of J. Sainsbury's Timber-Tracker Programme rather prophetically concluded that:

> The 1995 Group has been a major success; it is a public demonstration of our commitment to addressing this issue responsibly. We may yet see the 1995 Group/FSC model applied to problems with responsible sourcing [of] other natural resources.[10]

Indeed, since 1995 there has been a growing momentum for collaboration on greener purchasing and/or ethical sourcing initiatives. In 1996, Unilever, one of the world's largest buyers of frozen fish, formed a partnership with WWF International to develop global standards for sustainable fisheries management under the auspices of a Marine Stewardship Council (Maitland 1996). Key players in the WWF 1995 Group were consulted by WWF International and Unilever in the early stages, including B&Q's Alan Knight and WWF Forest Unit's Jem Bendell. J. Sainsbury plc and other retailers have also become involved in the development of the Council, which now has a set of principles and criteria for sustainable fishing and several pilot certification schemes under way.

The processes involved in the new collaborative efforts to raise labour standards in less industrialised countries, and to promote ethical sourcing generally, share similarities with the WWF 1995 Group and FSC initiatives. The Social Accountability standard, SA 8000, draws on the verification model of the FSC, while the Ethical Trading Initiative (ETI) is bringing together retailers, NGOs, trade unions and consumer groups—a development of the partnership model pioneered by the WWF 1995 Group.

▐▐ Conclusion: Do-It-Together

Improving a company's environmental performance through greener purchasing can be much more complex than other environmental management initiatives. By

---

9. V. Sequeira, WWF UK, personal communication with J. Bendell, 11 December 1997.
10. Personal communication with D.F. Murphy, 30 May 1996.

its very nature, greener purchasing involves people, companies and organisations external to the company taking the initiative. Therefore dialogue and collaboration is imperative. This chapter has demonstrated that much can be achieved when organisations and companies work together.

The chapter also revealed that an independent body can be very useful in facilitating dialogue on environmental matters between buyers and suppliers and between competitors. WWF and other NGOs are beginning to see the role they can play in facilitating progress in this area. Jean-Paul Jeanrenaud, one of original organisers of the 1995 Group, offered the following:

> Real progress will only be made, both in terms of solving environmental problems and enabling business to be put on a firm social and environmental footing, by forging partnerships between industry and environmental groups to collaborate in promoting solutions that are positive for both business and the environment (WWF 1995: 4).

If partnerships can be forged in such a highly competitive (and previously 'irresponsible') retail sector, then there should be scope for similar initiatives in a variety of other trade sectors. Despite this, some managers may shy away from the daunting complexity of this kind of environmental purchasing initiative—and this chapter has not described a simple straightforward process. However, by working together to develop multi-stakeholder agreed and independently certified standards of environmental quality, individual company workloads can be reduced. B&Q's Alan Knight explains:

> What we need to do is to create an environment where we don't really have to do any work. [We need] people to realise that if you want to do trade with the DIY sector in the UK, you have to be independently certified and you have to know where your timber comes from, and there is no point in even approaching us unless you have that information.[11]

This is the ultimate solution to the business problem of implementing greener purchasing, eventually eliminating the need for reams of questionnaires. One company would nevertheless be incapable of promoting such profound change alone. In a competitive world, the business response is often to seek commercial advantage by going it alone. This chapter has shown that there is much to be gained by business competitors and environmentalists doing it together for the mutual benefit of business and society.

---

11. Interview with D.F. Murphy, November 1994.

IO Small and Medium-Sized Enterprises
The Implications of Greener Purchasing[1]

Robert Baylis, Lianne Connell and Andrew Flynn

▌ Introduction

Small and medium-sized enterprises (SMEs)[2] have been recognised increasingly by policy-makers as playing a vital role in preserving a stable and diverse economic base in many countries. In the case of the United Kingdom, they account for 99.9% of all businesses and provide two-thirds of all private-sector employment (CBI 1993). Our work focuses on SMEs in manufacturing and processing sectors, since SMEs, and companies in these sectors in particular, are responsible for a large proportion of environmental degradation (de Boer 1997; CEC 1993a: 28) and are therefore more likely to come under pressure from their customers to improve their environmental performance than service or merchant sectors.

We have limited our work to manufacturing and processing sectors since, as Hill (1997) points out, these sectors invite a life-cycle perspective due to the wide range of environmental implications that may apply to them. Therefore, since greener purchasing represents a move towards addressing the life-cycle of products, manufacturing and processing industries are where the impact of greener purchasing is likely to be felt most.

This chapter explores the implications of greener purchasing for SMEs and shows that their responses are far from uniform. We therefore conclude that the pressures from customers to improve environmental performance should be tailored to individual SME circumstances. This contrasts with a discourse among some practitioners and academics that advocates the implementation of environmental management

1. We acknowledge gratefully the assistance of Joek Roex in completing the statistical analysis on which this paper has been based. We are also indebted to the European Regional Development Fund which part-financed the empirical work without which this paper could not have been written.

2. SMEs are defined by the European Union as companies with fewer than 250 employees worldwide, an annual turnover of less that ECU 40 million (around £25 million), an annual balance sheet total not exceeding ECU 27 million (around £17 million) and an upper level of 25% external ownership by companies that do not fit the other criteria (CEC 1996). In this chapter, all companies that fall outside this definition have been referred to as being 'large' companies.

systems (EMSs) or, at least, the formulation of written environmental policy documents as being appropriate for all SMEs irrespective of size or circumstances.

We base our arguments on a questionnaire survey undertaken in South Wales in the UK during the winter of 1996–97. The questionnaire was sent to 914 manufacturing and processing companies; 420 replied, representing a 46% response rate. Of these, 216 replies were from SMEs and 204 were from large companies (see Baylis, Connell and Flynn 1997 for a detailed analysis of the ways in which SMEs and large companies responded). The questionnaire contained 42 questions covering a range of environmental management and regulatory topics. In addition to the survey, this chapter draws on data obtained during detailed site tours and interviews with managers having environmental responsibilities at 25 of the SMEs that responded to the survey.

∥ SMEs as Customers and Suppliers

Hill (1997: 1258) reminds us that companies are usually both customers and suppliers. This is equally true for large companies and for SMEs. For example, SMEs may be the customers of large companies supplying raw materials such as metals, plastics or chemicals used in manufacturing processes. Other SMEs may supply their goods direct to the public as in the case of bakeries, ice cream manufacturers or furniture manufacturers. Of course, many SMEs will be suppliers to large companies but, as demonstrated below, this does not necessarily result in their being the subject of greener purchasing initiatives.

Our survey has illustrated the complexities of supply chains by revealing that both large companies and SMEs are more likely to receive helpful environmental advice and/or guidance from their suppliers than from their customers. Greener purchasing therefore entails obtaining environmental support as well as the more obvious matter of assuring good environmental performance in suppliers. Nevertheless, the balance of power between suppliers and customers is such that the former, and SMEs in particular, are less persuasive in greener purchasing (Hill 1997). It may be possible for SMEs to make internal changes to practices and performance but, we suggest, few large companies will entertain making changes to accommodate requirements of SME customers or suppliers. For instance, a small plastics injection moulder we visited had found that it was impossible to persuade either its large customers or its large suppliers of raw materials to make changes that would make its process more efficient.

Notwithstanding the complexities of purchasing and supply relationships, our research shows that large companies, as a whole, are more aware of environmental pressures on them than SMEs. Indeed, it is a fact that many SMEs have fewer environmental pressures on them due to their lower public profile and lower individual environmental impacts. By exploring the numbers of sources of motivation for environmental improvement that companies declared, we were able to establish that large companies are motivated by 48% more pressures than SMEs (see Baylis, Connell and Flynn 1997 for the detailed data). This confirms similar conclusions reached by Williams, Medhurst and Drew (1993) and results in large companies being more likely to be implementing environmental improvement programmes that will, as a minimum, demand more environmental information from their suppliers. As we will demonstrate below, this is by no means universal for all large companies and we therefore disagree with common perceptions that SMEs are always in a supply chain with a large company at the top, which will exert pressures to make environmental improvements (see, for example, Holland and Gibbon 1996).

Before considering the implications of greener purchasing for SMEs, we must remind ourselves of the wider context in which this occurs. This is, according to our respondents, that customers represent a relatively low-level source of environmental motivation, being only the sixth driver for SMEs and the seventh for large companies (see Fig. 1). Furthermore, while these placings appear to provide some evidence to corroborate popular perceptions of supply-chain pressure being focused on SMEs, the absolute proportion of large companies being driven by supply-chain pressure is 67% higher than for SMEs.

	SMEs %	LARGE COMPANIES %
Compliance with environmental regulation	65	86
Potential to increase profits by reducing costs	51	64
Good neighbourliness/public concern	48	63
Personal concern for the environment	51	56
Employee concerns	38	48
Customer pressure (supply chain)	26	43
Company environmental policy	14	50

Note: Percentages are based on the number of questionnaires returned in each category.

Figure 1: Most Common Stimuli Encouraging Environmental Improvements

Even though customers may not be the main source of motivation for industry to improve its environmental performance, there are a number of factors that have contributed to their having an environmental agenda that they may wish to fulfil through greener purchasing. These can be summarised as:

- Implementation of corporate environmental policies either as part of, or independent of, an EMS
- Compliance with legislation: for example, with respect to hazardous substances or packaging
- Participation in supply-chain initiatives led by business support organisations such as the Welsh Development Agency's Supplier Association programme
- As participants in alternatives to regulation[3]

3. It has become clear from numerous discussions with regulators and business-support bodies that supply chains will be used to provide a practical and cost-effective means of encouraging SMEs to tackle environmental issues without the need for direct regulatory intervention.

▶ Pressure from their own financiers and other stakeholders (see, for example, NPI 1997)

▶ 'Green consumerism' on the part of individuals

We now turn to consider the implications for SMEs of customers pursuing their environmental agenda through greener purchasing.

II Implications of Greener Purchasing for SMEs

As Hill (1997) points out, there are two strategies that customers adopt in pursuing their environmental agenda:

1. Seeking 'information about the environmental aspects of policies, processes and systems from their suppliers' (Hill 1997: 1262)

2. Imposing specific requirements on their suppliers

We add a third possible strategy:

3. Ceasing to purchase from suppliers with unsatisfactory performance or that fail to co-operate with the customer in meeting its environmental objectives

We now consider the implications of these three strategies in more detail.

1. Customers Seeking Information

Environmental questionnaires, environmental questions in quality questionnaires and supplier audits are examples of supplier-focused information-gathering activities of customers. Such activities will often be the first indication an SME will have regarding a customer's environmental agenda. However, our survey showed that it is large companies that are the most likely target for supply-chain initiatives, with 61% of large companies compared to only 35% of SMEs having received environmental enquiries. Despite this comparatively low level of impact on SMEs at present, we join with other commentators (see, for example, Christie, Rolfe and Legard 1995; Hillary 1995) in anticipating that growth in industrial implementation of certified EMSs will lead to increasing numbers of environmental enquiries being received by SMEs from their customers. We now support this forecast using data from our survey.

The international standard for environmental management systems, ISO 14001, contains no specific requirement for companies to address the environmental aspects of their suppliers, but that the associated general guidelines indicate that purchasing and contracting are among the activities that should be considered. The European Union's Eco-Management and Auditing Scheme (EMAS) is more specific when it calls for the 'environmental performance and practices of contractors, subcontractors and suppliers' to be addressed (CEC 1993b: 10). Thus, both of the major routes to implementing an EMS are expected to lead to increased attention being paid to the environmental impacts of suppliers.[4]

---

4. See also Clayton and Rotheroe 1997, who concluded that BS 7750, the British Standard for environmental management systems which was superseded by ISO 14001, was a powerful source of motivation for companies to carry out assessments of their suppliers' environmental performance.

Figure 2 illustrates the level of implementation of EMSs at the time of our survey and how this is likely to change, assuming that those companies that said they were considering implementing a system will do so.

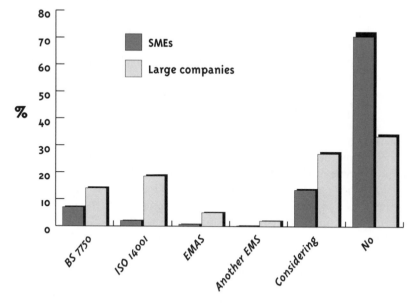

Note: BS 7750 is now superseded by ISO 14001.

Figure 2: Implementation of Environmental Management Systems in Industrial South Wales

Further analysis of the data included in Figure 2 shows that only 22% of companies (irrespective of size) were implementing any form of EMS and 21% were considering it. This suggests that EMS activity, and therefore greener purchasing, is likely to increase by around 95% in the short term. This may even be an under-estimate as more companies are persuaded of the efficacy of implementing an EMS or are forced to do so by their customers. The impacts of this will be felt most by large companies in the short term, but it is inevitable that it will affect many SMEs in the long run. Only the extent of the effect on SMEs is open to conjecture.

Implementation of certified EMSs is not the only reason why customers might wish to evaluate environmental performance when deciding which companies to buy from or what requirements to impose in purchasing contracts. Indeed, one of the leaders in this field is the British DIY chain, B&Q, and this company does not have an EMS that is certified to a particular standard. However, in view of the high level of interest being shown by large companies in EMS implementation, we suggest that it is likely to be the predominant environmental activity being carried out by large companies for the foreseeable future. In turn, EMS implementation will lead to an increasing focus by customers on the environmental performance and practices of their suppliers.

Questionnaires are likely to remain the most common form of information-seeking carried out by all but the most environmentally active customers. This is because of the human and financial resource implications of carrying out more detailed work. Thus, where customers do perform detailed evaluations of their suppliers' environmental performance, prioritisation of scarce resources means that the main pressure will be focused on key suppliers. For example, one large telecommunications equipment manufacturer in South Wales has an EMS certified to ISO 14001 and has instigated a programme of auditing the environmental performance of suppliers. The nature of the company's work necessitates a diverse supply-base of over 250 companies and so it has only been possible to carry out audits in the largest suppliers. The task of auditing smaller companies is, at the present, considered by the customer to be too onerous to entertain.

Chapters 9, 20, 23 and 24 have reported on supplier environmental rating initiatives carried out by customers. In B&Q's case, the impact has been enormous since its programme commenced in 1991. By 1995, the company had obtained 1,290 individual supplier reports and 850 completed questionnaires. It had also carried out 195 site visits, 140 clinics and 18 seminars and conferences (Knight *et al.* 1995). Through our work in South Wales, we are also aware that B&Q's supplier programme is now having an impact on second-tier suppliers, i.e. those that are suppliers to B&Q's suppliers. Clearly, the availability of resources that can be committed to such programmes is a crucial factor in their impact on SMEs. This is illustrated in the case of the South Wales telecommunications equipment manufacturer discussed above. The medium through which data is collected may be another limiting factor.

2. Imposing Specific Requirements

Customers seeking environmental information are unlikely to impose specific requirements on their suppliers in the first instance. However, this might follow from responses perceived by the enquirer as being unsatisfactory or when a supplier audit has revealed unsatisfactory environmental performance or practices. Where customers are sincere about greener purchasing, we forecast that the impact on SMEs has the potential to be large since our site visits have not revealed any SMEs that are free from a need to make environmental improvements. Furthermore, many are failing to understand or comply with environmental legislation.

In the case of customers that have limited resources or inclination to work with their suppliers to improve performance, we anticipate a growth in demands that suppliers should have written environmental policies. In the longer run, and as EMSs become more commonplace, some commentators believe that SMEs will be forced to implement them if they are to continue receiving the business of their customers.[5] Christie, Rolfe and Legard (1995) found evidence that this would happen, while other commentators view it as a certainty based on industrial adoption of ISO 9000 series quality management systems (see, for example, Euro Info Centres 1995; Sunderland

---

5. Peter Wilson of the European Commission's Environment Directorate is reported as stating that the main driver for EMAS registration in the European Union will be supply-chain pressure and cites the example of Volvo which called its 850 suppliers to Sweden to encourage adoption of certified EMSs (ENDS 1996).

and Thomas 1997). Clarke and Fineman are more cautious when they suggest that the greenness of a company would be an 'order qualifier not an order winner' (Clarke and Fineman 1995: 45).

Figure 2 has already illustrated the future trajectory of EMS implementation but does not support those who believe in universal implementation. Furthermore, many of the companies that we have visited have reported that, despite initial fears that they would have to implement a certified quality management system in order to supply the majority of their customers, those fears were unfounded. Indeed, 40% of manufacturing and processing SMEs responding to our survey reported that they had no quality management system. On this basis, we dispute that quality management systems are a universal condition of trade or that EMSs will become so in the future. As with quality management, questionnaires and supplier audits may obviate the need for certified systems as far as a significant number of customers are concerned.

The position in August 1997 is that relatively few companies, approximately 310 in the UK (ENDS 1997b), have a certified EMS. As a result, customers insisting that their suppliers implement an EMS are similarly rare. Nevertheless, some larger customers are encouraging it. For example, we understand that some large companies are now beginning to make their suppliers aware of a British Government scheme to provide subsidised environmental consultancy work to help SMEs implement an EMS.[6]

Documents and management practices may have their place in improving environmental performance, but some customers may be more precise in the material changes that they wish SMEs to make. In the case of B&Q, the company considers that implementation of EMSs can, in many cases, stand in the way of suppliers making tangible environmental improvements (ENDS 1995). This is because implementation of a system takes up resources that might be spent more productively in tackling the environmental aspects of a company directly. The SME suppliers of customers that take a more active role in improving environmental performance through their supply chain are therefore expected to demand practical environmental improvements in technologies employed, management practices and in the formulation of products supplied. Evidence that this is already occurring is discussed below with respect to responses made by SMEs.

3. Ceasing to Purchase from Suppliers with Unsatisfactory Performance

The ultimate sanction for any customer evaluating the environmental performance of its suppliers is to find an alternative source of supply. During the first three years of its supplier environmental audit programme, B&Q ceased purchasing from ten

---

6. Reported by Howard Metcalfe at 'Environmental Management: The Inside Track', a workshop held at the All Nations Centre, Cardiff, on 12 September 1996. Mr Metcalfe is the Managing Director of the NIFES environmental consultancy which manages the Small Company Environmental and Energy Management Assistance Scheme (SCEEMAS), which is funded by the UK Department of the Environment, Transport and the Regions to provide for grants of up to 50% of consultancy costs incurred by SMEs implementing EMSs. The scheme is designed to promote EMAS registration.

of its 661 suppliers due to their failure to improve despite being given an extension to B&Q's original deadline (Knight *et al.* 1995). Clayton and Rotheroe (1997) found that 26% of a sample of companies assessing the environmental performance of their suppliers had ceased to use suppliers on environmental grounds. However, further discussions with those customer companies revealed that the reasons for such actions were rarely related solely to environmental matters. Rather, environmental performance was just one of several factors. Given the paucity of data in this area, it is instructive to reflect on Robinson's (1991) findings in relation to the implementation of quality management systems, since these have a longer history than EMSs and are more widely implemented.[7]

Robinson carried out a survey examining the changing relationship between large companies and their small suppliers as a result of the introduction of quality management systems. He found that close customer–supplier relationships had led to a trend towards fewer suppliers in the supply chain. The reasons he gave for this were: perceived benefits of single sourcing; inability of some suppliers to meet vendor certification requirements; and increased management time invested in suppliers. These factors constrain the number of suppliers it is possible to work with and are equally applicable in the case of greener purchasing, as is Robinson's conclusion that:

> Large companies are moving towards close supplier relationships and rationalising their supply bases will invariably lead to winners and losers among the suppliers, as some suppliers win business at the expense of others, and the losers may disappear from these companies' supply chains altogether if they remain oblivious to the changing environment around them (Robinson 1991: 6)

Robinson added that the more enlightened large companies would not simply leave their smaller suppliers to fend for themselves. Rather, they would work with them to meet the stringent standards that they required. Again, as in the example of the British Government's subsidy for EMS implementation, this also holds true with respect to greener purchasing.

III Implications of Greener Purchasing for Industry Sectors

Greener purchasing initiatives are most likely to affect industrial sectors that are perceived to have a poor environmental image, a high risk of causing significant environmental problems or are closer to end-consumers. Figure 3 illustrates this convincingly in its representation of our data. The chemicals sector receives the highest proportion of environmental enquiries because it is widely perceived as having the greatest potential to cause pollution. This is followed by the electrical and electronics sector. The reasons for this probably lie in the variety of components that are used in the sector's products. The sector is also close to end-consumer markets and is often a first-tier supplier to wholesalers and retailers. This may have resulted in a culture in which customer requirements are acknowledged more readily. The metals

---

7. Of the SME respondents to our survey, 57% had a formal quality management system, compared to 10% with an EMS.

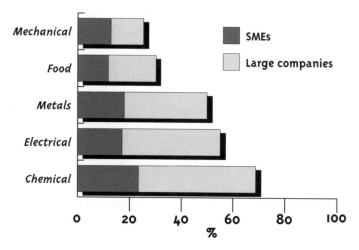

Figure 3: Environmental Enquiries or Questionnaires Received by Key Sectors

and metal-processing sector also receives a relatively high level of customer environmental enquiries since it is a 'dirty' industry processing raw materials often for use by cleaner industries.

Figure 3 appears to reflect the size structure of each sector since it is the food and mechanical engineering sectors that have higher proportions of SMEs than the others.[8] Thus, both of these sectors show little difference between large companies and SMEs with respect to the numbers receiving environmental enquiries from their customers. Given that we have shown that supply-chain pressure affects large companies more than SMEs, the greater proportion of SMEs in the food sector could also explain why it experiences a relatively low level of customer environmental enquiries despite often being a supplier to retailers and close to end-consumer markets. However, we suggest that its lower level of activity is more likely to be a manifestation of the laggardly performance that the sector is noted for, since food manufacturers tend to be unaware of the harmful impacts of their activities on the environment and, consequently, have a bad record for pollution incidents (ENDS 1994).

The proportions of SMEs receiving customer environmental enquiries is remarkably even across sectors but, in the case of large companies, the sectoral differences are much more marked. Thus, the sector in which an SME is placed appears to have little bearing on the amount of supply-chain pressure it is likely to experience, whereas the opposite applies for large companies.

▌▌ SME Perceptions of Greener Purchasing by their Customers

Before looking at how SMEs may respond to greener purchasing initiatives, it is instructive to consider their perceptions about their customers. Welford (1994) reports

---

8. Proportions of SMEs by sector: chemicals (41%); metals (50%); electrical and electronic (42%); food (63%); and mechanical (76%).

on two consecutive surveys carried out during 1992 and 1993 which purported to focus on SMEs.[9] The surveys revealed more companies reporting that environmental issues would become increasingly important or to some extent important to their customers in 1993 than in 1992 (Welford 1994: 155). Furthermore, by 1993, only 10% of Welford's respondents answered that environmental issues would have no importance to their customers. He considers that this increase in awareness was due to a heightened level of actual customer pressure which often took the form of environmental enquiries.

Our survey explored SME awareness of customer environmental agendas by asking whether respondents considered that an EMS could or does help them meet the needs of their customers. The response we received was that only 22% of SMEs believed that this would be the case. In contrast, 57% of large companies responded positively. Of course, there may be other ways of meeting customer needs, but we were able to discount these to a large extent by asking for reasons from those who had been undecided or responded negatively to the question. These reasons are identified in Figure 4.

Figure 4 shows that customer-specific reasons were relatively few. This either suggests that relatively few customers have environmental agendas or confirms that SMEs have a low level of awareness thereof. Only 7% of SMEs and, coincidentally, 7% of large companies had anything to say about their customers. 'Customer ambivalence' describes the answers from companies that reported that their customers were not interested in environmental performance or were only interested in cost or quality. It is suspected that 'customer ambivalence' could also describe many more companies that gave other responses: for example, those that responded that their existing practices were satisfactory or that their wastes were insignificant in quantity or environmental impact.

▌ *SME Responses*

The answers to our survey show us that there is a low level of supply-chain activity affecting SMEs with respect to environmental matters in comparison to large companies. We also disagree with Welford's optimistic results showing a high level of awareness of customer environmental agenda among SMEs. This leads us to conclude that most SMEs are unlikely to take steps to anticipate greener purchasing initiatives. Indeed, it provides one explanation as to why SMEs tend to adopt the reactive strategies that, according to Welford (1994), are stereotypical. This pattern is not limited to environmental issues, since the managerial style of most (but not all) SMEs is one of reaction to crises of any nature or origin. However, like all of our findings, there are exceptions. For example, a high-technology SME that we visited was at an advanced stage of implementing an EMS as a response to anticipated customer demands with respect to environmental performance.

Irrespective of whether anticipatory or reactive, greener purchasing initiatives can certainly encourage suppliers to take action. For example, Dr Alan Knight of B&Q is reported as believing that the company's purchasing policy led to a supplier of

---

9. The author omitted to explain how he had defined an SME.

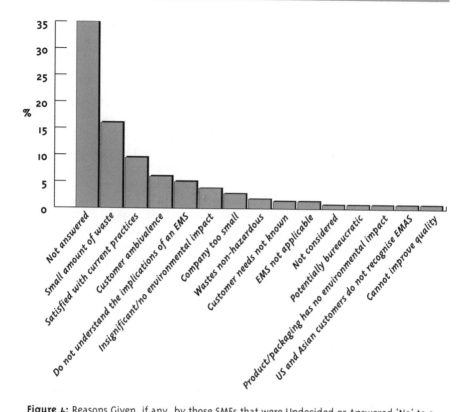

Figure 4: Reasons Given, if any, by those SMEs that were Undecided or Answered 'No' to a Question Asking if an EMS would Help them Meet the Needs of their Customers

light-shades formulating its own environmental action plan and sending out questionnaires to 200 of its suppliers (ENDS 1993). Similarly, Hillary (1995) reports on an SME that was encouraged to commission an environmental review following an initiative involving Hoover's suppliers. Greener purchasing initiatives have contributed to a growing number of SMEs which have availed themselves of free or subsidised environmental reviews carried out by business-support organisations. Moreover, a small number of SMEs are going further by implementing EMSs, usually with outside financial assistance. We suggest that these steps may be driven partly by supply-chain pressures.[10] In contrast, Gouldson argued that greener purchasing policies are unlikely to result in significant environmental improvements in SMEs (Gouldson 1995). We therefore turn to an evaluation of our survey data to establish the extent to which SMEs are, or are not, responding to greener purchasing initiatives.

We found that 35% of SMEs had received enquiries from their customers but that only 26% reported being driven (or anticipated being driven) by customers to make

10. According to the consultancy administering the scheme, as at 2 July 1997, a United Kingdom total of 170 SMEs have applied for grant assistance under SCEEMAS (see footnote 6).

environmental improvements. Although this difference suggests that 9% of *all* SMEs received environmental enquiries that made no impact on their practices, further analysis of how companies answered both questions reveals that 56% of those SMEs that had received customer enquiries reported that they were not being driven to make environmental improvements.[11] This suggests that many of the enquiries received might have been rather undemanding and tends to confirm Gouldson's fears.

This low level of reported motivation attributed to customers does not mean that all greener purchasing initiatives are a failure. On the contrary, Figure 5 shows clearly that the pressures felt by some SMEs are being translated into practice across a range of possible environmental improvements. The figure shows the responses of SMEs and large companies to a question exploring what environmental improvements had been made by them. Companies were asked to select the improvements made from a list that we provided. The figure presents an analysis of their answers according to whether or not the respondents had received environmental enquiries from their customers. A similar pattern to that of SMEs, albeit more marked, can be observed in the responses of large companies. This puts the SME responses in perspective by showing that large companies, even those without supply-chain pressure, are carrying out more environmental improvements than SMEs.

Environmental improvements can also result from the implementation of environmental management tools such as policies, audits and systems. We have explored the influence of greener purchasing on the implementation of these tools and have found a similar pattern to that revealed in Figure 5. This is shown in Figure 6.

The results should be viewed in perspective, in that they do show a higher level of activity among SMEs (and large companies) that have received environmental enquiries, but this activity is of a lower order of magnitude in comparison with the numbers of enquiries being made by customers. For example, among those SMEs that had received customer enquiries, only 35% reported that their operations had been the subject of an environmental review or audit.[12] Given that undertaking an environmental review represents a modest step toward environmental improvement, this is more evidence that many greener purchasing initiatives are failing to encourage SMEs to take action. Indeed, we are unable to identify whether those reviews or audits that had been carried out had been prompted or carried out by customers, but we do know from our site visits that some SMEs had said that an environmental review or audit had been carried out when, in fact, they were referring to something else, such as a health and safety assessment. Our survey results are therefore likely to provide an optimistic impression of this aspect of SME action in response to customer pressure.

Our site visits have revealed that only one or two customers have been involved when SMEs have received enquiries and this may explain the limited success of greener purchasing activities that has been revealed by our analysis. Furthermore, these enquiries have often been limited to asking if the SME has a written environmental

---

11. Forty-two not driven by customers out of 75 receiving environmental enquiries from their customers.

12. Twenty-six had been the subject of a review or audit out of 75 receiving environmental enquiries from their customers.

	SME[a]	SME[b]	Large Company[a]	Large Company[b]
	%	**%**	**%**	**%**
Input improvements				
Reduced energy use	32	25	58	43
Changed fuels/feedstocks/raw materials	26	9	36	22
Output improvements				
Reduced/re-used packaging	48	31	59	48
Provided equipment to control/reduce/prevent waste-water discharges to sewers or water courses	25	19	63	34
Provided equipment to control/reduce/prevent gaseous/particulate emissions to atmosphere	22	16	65	32
Found alternative off-site uses for materials otherwise considered to be wastes	19	13	40	32
Managerial improvements				
Improved housekeeping	68	50	80	72
Provided employees with environmental training	12	2	48	23
Invited employee suggestions to assist in compliance or identification of potential environmental improvements	8	3	34	16
Erected environmental awareness-raising signs around the premises	4	5	21	13
Processing improvements				
Changed materials-handling practices	32	14	48	30
Changed process/manufacturing equipment	22	14	52	28
No improvements				
No improvements have been made	7	26	2	8
Other improvements				
Other	4	4	2	5

[a] *Companies answering that they had received customer enquiries*
[b] *Others*

Figure 5: Environmental Improvements Made according to whether or not the Respondents had Received Environmental Enquiries from their Customers

policy. SME responses to such enquiries tend to be that the company does not have a policy or may entail procuring one without giving much thought or subsequent commitment to it. Although this picture is a generalisation, only three of the companies we have visited that claimed to have an environmental policy have been able to produce a copy. In one of those, a company representative said that the policy had not been implemented. Furthermore, none of the SMEs that we interviewed reported that its customers had taken any action when told that a policy

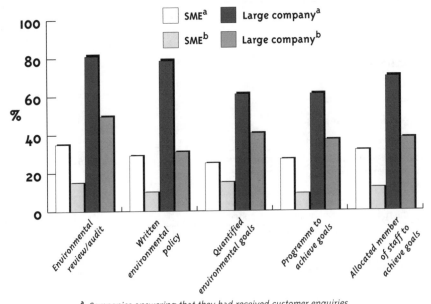

Legend:
- SME[a]   Large company[a]
- SME[b]   Large company[b]

[a] Companies answering that they had received customer enquiries
[b] Others

Figure 6: Implementation of Environmental Management Tools according to whether or not the Respondents had Received Environmental Enquiries from their Customers

was not in place. Not even a company with a reputation for being among the most advanced with respect to environmental protection declined to purchase from an SME that stated in a supplier questionnaire that it had no environmental policy.

This low level of commitment to environmental policies which was apparent on-site is also apparent in our survey results. The survey revealed that only 29% of SMEs that had received environmental enquiries from their customers had written environmental polices.[13] This is a surprisingly low proportion, given that environmental policies are often the main focus of greener purchasing strategies. What is more remarkable is that only 41% of those with policies *and* receiving customer enquiries stated that they would be motivated by their policies to make environmental improvements (see Baylis, Connell and Flynn 1997 for a detailed discussion of the failure of environmental policies to motivate). This is consistent with the findings reported in Figure 5 and indicates clearly that supply-chain pressure that requires written environmental policies is unlikely to deliver real environmental improvement in the majority of SMEs. If, as is forecast above, customers require their SME suppliers to implement certified EMSs, the level of meaningful response is likely to be even less than we have found with environmental policies.

Figure 6 repeats the behaviour pattern we have observed above with respect to companies adopting quantified environmental goals, having programmes to implement them and designating staff with environmental responsibilities. Explanations

13. Twenty-two with policies out of 75 receiving environmental enquiries.

as to why different environmental management tools are more or less popular are linked to factors other than related to customers and so we have not explored these here (Baylis, Connell and Flynn 1997).

Of course, it is in the nature of SMEs that some will not co-operate with their customers' greener purchasing initiatives. As we have seen above, this may result in a customer ceasing to purchase from a supplier that behaves in this way. However, the extent of this will vary from sector to sector and according to individual circumstances. Thus, non co-operation may not necessarily lead to the demise of the SME, especially given the pragmatic way in which some customers implement their greener purchasing strategies. Furthermore, it has become clear through our interviews that some SMEs with wide customer bases are prepared to withdraw from supplying any customer that attempted to force them to make environmental improvements.

So far, we have focused on the direct actions that SMEs may or may not take in response to greener purchasing initiatives. However, it is possible that some might be prepared to do the bidding of their customers and then increase their prices to cover any associated costs such as might be incurred in implementing an EMS. Others might consider developing or reformulating products with a view to exploiting a 'green' premium. Welford explored these possibilities in his surveys carried out in 1992 and 1993 but only three companies (3%) in 1992 and six (6%) in 1993 thought that their customers would be prepared to pay higher prices (Welford 1994). He concluded that:

> The perception seems to be that customers are price-sensitive and that, in general, they are not willing to pay more for a product with green credentials. Whether this view is true or not is less important than the fact that there is a perception that customers are not willing to pay more for green products, since that is what firms will base their actions on (Welford 1994: 156).

▌ *Conclusions*

Our research in South Wales suggests that the impact of greener purchasing initiatives is limited for SMEs and, for them, varies little between industrial sectors. Nevertheless, we have shown that greener purchasing activities are moving a significant minority of SMEs towards making real improvements to their environmental management practices and performance. Greener purchasing has not, however, achieved the status of being the main or even a powerful source of motivation to make environmental improvements among manufacturing and processing SMEs.

SMEs tend to react to, rather than anticipate, the requirements placed on them by customers, although there are exceptions to this pattern. This reactivity is partly due to the generally poor level of environmental awareness and understanding of the environmental agenda of their customers. The availability of human and financial resources also dictates the level of anticipatory action and the extent to which the SME responses to supply-chain pressure are substantive. The result of this is that SME responses to greener purchasing initiatives may be, in many cases, little more than hollow gestures.

In order to overcome gesture responses, customers themselves will have to adopt active strategies. The alternative is passive strategies, which are characterised by supplier questionnaires and failure to provide feedback to suppliers (Clayton and Rotheroe 1997). Customers will have to appreciate that greener purchasing strategies that focus on SMEs having to implement environmental management tools such as policies or EMSs will only have a limited influence on SME activity. As both our survey and B&Q have found, focusing on environmental management tools may be ineffectual and may be a distraction from carrying out real environmental improvements. Indeed, even in larger companies, EMSs do not guarantee good environmental performance, as has been shown in the case of two companies with an EMS which were prosecuted for environmental offences (ENDS 1997a).

For the many customers for whom resources are limited, it may be difficult for them to work with all of their SME suppliers to make real environmental improvements. However, rather than focus on environmental management tools and passive data-gathering exercises, their efforts may be more usefully directed towards forming close working partnerships with key suppliers to meet their environmental agenda in the first instance. They may also reflect on the fact that SMEs are not necessarily large companies in waiting and therefore solutions appropriate for the customer may not be appropriate for the supplier or their organisational structure (Palmer and van der Vorst 1996). Thus, they may wish to consider employing organisations with expertise in environmental management in SMEs to ensure that their SME suppliers meet environmental performance criteria in the most cost-effective and appropriate manner, both for the SME and the customer. In the case of Wales, there is a number of organisations able to fulfil this role. For example, the Welsh Development Agency has a Supplier Association programme which can work with suppliers to help them meet the environmental needs of their customers.

11 An Exploratory Examination of Environmentally Responsible Straight Rebuy Purchases in Large Australian Organisations[1]

Michael Jay Polonsky, Harry Brooks,
Philip Henry and Craig Schweizer

||| Introduction

There is growing evidence that firms are becoming more concerned about how their activities affect the natural environment (Cairncross 1990; Langrehr, Langrehr and Tatreau 1992; McDaniel and Rylander 1993; Nichols 1993; Walley and Whitehead 1994). The growing number of firms that are modifying their products or implementing environmental management systems is one indication of this increasing environmental concern. These systems are often based on standards developed by third-party organisations such as the International Standards Organisation (ISO 14001) or the British Standards Organisation (now-defunct BS 7750) (Hamner 1996; Zeffane, Polonsky and Medley 1994). However, many firms are not modifying their behaviour simply because of governmental pressure, as research suggests that there are organisations who believe improving environmental performance is also a business opportunity (Jay 1990; Langrehr, Langrehr and Tatreau 1992; Menon and Menon 1997; Porter and van der Linde 1995; Zeffane, Polonsky and Medley 1994).

Much of the research examining firms' environmental behaviour has focused on various aspects related to the firm's production activities. For example, many organisations are becoming more concerned with their waste-generating activities and have designed various programmes to reduce these by-products. Such a corporate focus has the advantage that it often generates substantial cost savings, reduces the firm's negative environmental impact (Walley and Whitehead 1994), enhances the firm's 'green appeal' and provides consumers with less environmentally harmful alternatives. In their role as consumers, organisations can also stimulate suppliers of environmentally responsible products to produce more such goods (Glover 1994). For example, McDonald's was actively involved with recyclers of polystyrene, both as a supplier of waste materials and a purchaser of the recycled product, stimulating

---

1. We would like to thank Philip Rosenberger III, Gary Mankelow and the anonymous reviewers at the *Journal of Business and Industrial Marketing* for their useful comments. This chapter was originally published in the *Journal of Business and Industrial Marketing* 13.1 (1998): 54-69.

both supply and demand (Polonsky 1995). Thus, firms marketing goods with environmental attributes have to understand the way in which purchasing decisions regarding these goods are made, if they are to satisfy organisational consumers.

To date, there has been a limited amount of research examining organisational purchasing behaviour of products with environmental attributes (Drumwright 1992, 1994). From an environmental marketing perspective, it may be more important to understand environmental organisational consumption, given that organisational buying represents a majority of all marketing activities, far overshadowing purchases by final consumers.

The purpose of this exploratory study is to examine the organisational purchase of one environmental straight rebuy product and provide some insights that may assist marketers of products with environmental attributes in being more effective. The examination of purchasing agents' (PAs') attitudes and perceptions towards the purchase of recycled paper products has several advantages: (a) these products tend to be straight rebuy purchases; (b) they tend to have a similar buying centre structure; (c) they can be used across industries in a similar fashion; and (d) PAs have a majority of the influence in the purchase of supplies (Jackson, Keith and Burdick 1984), such as recycled paper.

To examine this issue, this study undertook in-depth interviews with PAs of eleven large (i.e. having more than 100 employees) organisations in one of Australia's largest cities. While the study examines one of the least complicated environmental purchase activities, that of the straight rebuy of recycled paper products (i.e. a supply), it should be noted that other non-supply straight rebuy decisions involving products with environmental attributes may be more complex. Thus, these results may not be generally applicable to all types of 'environmental' straight rebuy situations or to other purchasing situations.

▍▍ *Environmental Organisational Purchasing*

It has been suggested that company efforts to 'buy green' can have the makings of a purchasing manager's nightmare. For example, recycled paper products offer limited colours, are of poorer quality than virgin paper (which can lead to jams in printers), and may cost more (Nichols 1993). However, in other areas buyers have found that recycled paper products are in fact a better buy than virgin paper. More recently, laser printer manufacturers and paper manufacturers have been keen to point out that recycled paper is in fact superior to non-recycled paper, as it holds toner longer (Xerox 1994).

While around the world some firms have been proactive in becoming more environmentally responsible (i.e. less environmentally harmful), there are still many firms who have been motivated to act solely because of external governmental pressure. Firms have often been pushed to make their offices 'greener'. For example, in Singapore, the government has undertaken to persuade businesses to exchange data electronically, in order to cut back on the amount of paperwork generated (Mackenzie 1993); and, in the US, all federally purchased paper must contain 20% post-consumer recycled content (Peattie and Ring 1993). These and other governmental actions

(Commonwealth Environmental Protection Agency 1994) indicate that policy-makers have an understanding of the green revolution's importance.

While many companies are voluntarily pushing ahead, the average office has a long way to go. The purchase of recycled products moves the firm one step closer to the green 'ideal', i.e. minimising their negative environmental impact. Compared with ten years ago, or even five years ago, managers' attitudes and understanding of the importance of the natural environment has improved considerably (Mackenzie 1993).

While managers are becoming more environmentally aware, there has been limited research examining organisational environmental purchasing behaviour (Apaiwongse 1991, 1994; Drumwright 1992, 1994; Langrehr, Langrehr and Tatreau 1992). The most comprehensive research to date to examine environmental organisational purchasing behaviour was a US study that undertook 63 in-depth interviews in ten organisations to determine 'how and why socially responsible buying comes about in organisations' (Drumwright 1992, 1994) It was found that organisations and buying centres were comprised of three different types of individual: 'policy entrepreneurs', 'converts' and 'resisters'.

'Policy entrepreneurs' were identified as individuals who are prepared to go to personal expense to put important issues forward within a company, i.e. champion the environmental issue. They use their knowledge of an issue as a power base, to 'prick the corporate social conscience' (Drumwright 1992). 'Converts', on the other hand, are people within the organisation who embrace the policies put forward by policy entrepreneurs, often after initial resistance. It was suggested that once an individual converted, they often fervently believe and preach social responsibility themselves. The last group, 'resisters', is self-explanatory: they are individuals within the organisation who do not see the need to modify existing behaviour.

Based on this previous work, organisations can be classified into four categories, which are described in Figure 1 (Drumwright 1992, 1994). There are two major groups that can then be further subdivided. The first of these two groups has a deliberate strategy to undertake socially responsible buying activities and can be subdivided into the groups of 'founder's ideals' and 'symbolism'. The second group does not have a deliberate strategy for undertaking socially responsible buying and can be subdivided into the groups of 'opportune' and 'restraint'. If they (the 'opportune' and 'restraint' groups) are making environmental purchases, they may be doing so for 'other' reasons, such as they face external pressure. For example, governmental regulations requiring the phasing-out of CFC-based products forced all firms in the aerosol industry to purchasing non-CFC propellants. Firms that modified their behaviour prior to the introduction of the regulations might be classified as firms based on 'founder's ideals' or 'symbolism', whereas those firms that only modified their behaviour due to governmental action might be classified as 'opportune' or 'restraint'.

▌▌ *The Buying Centre*

As this work broadly examines organisational purchasing, it is useful to examine briefly the buying centre and some issues relevant to this study. There have been

SRB: DELIBERATE ORGANISATIONAL STRATEGY

Founder's ideals

The founder viewed the organisation as a bully pulpit for social change and a social laboratory. The company had a formal stated social mission, a social responsibility officer and social responsibility audits for itself and its vendors.

Symbolism

SRB was used to symbolise the company's efforts at socially responsible behaviour in other realms in which such efforts were complex and not easily communicated. Top management recognised that social responsibility was linked to success because the business was subject to heavy public and/or regulatory scrutiny.

SRB: NO DELIBERATE STRATEGY

Opportune

The company engaged in SRB when cost savings or competitive advantage resulted. The company was responding to what it perceived to be as a hot topic among customers or competitors at the moment.

Restraint

Rather than buying something that would be more advantageous, the company voluntarily exercised restraint and engaged in SRB at a non-negligible cost. At times, the company began to resemble other types.

Figure 1: Drumwright's Classifications of Socially Responsible
Buying (SRB) by Organisations

Source: definitions are taken from Drumwright 1994: 15.

numerous attempts to model the purchasing process (Johnson and Lewin 1996) and it would be impossible to examine all these models in this chapter. It is, however, important to identify some basic similarities in the models, especially those related to purchase of straight rebuy products.

Most earlier work suggests that the nature of the purchase will influence who is involved in the decision-making process. The structure of the buying centre is usually comprised of a number of individuals including users, buyers, influencers, deciders and gatekeepers. In some cases, an individual may occupy several buying centre roles, i.e. they may be buyer, decider and influencer. In addition, each individual involved in a buying centre is motivated by different forces, which will depend on their role in the buying centre and their role in the organisation (Johnson and Lewin 1996; Webster 1993). Given the number of individuals involved in the buying centre decision-making process, research examining this area has tended to be more complex. To be comprehensive, a buying centre study needs to identify and interview all buying centre members (Drumwright 1994).

Another important buying centre issue is that the type of purchase influences the buying process and the buying centre structure. Industrial purchases have been classified into three different buying categories: 'new task', 'modified rebuy' and 'straight rebuy'. There have been many differences found between the types of purchase, with 'new task' purchases being the most complex and 'straight rebuys' being the most straightforward. For example, it has been found that straight rebuy purchases take less time, involve fewer decision-makers, and usually deal with less complex products, compared to the other decision types (Doyle, Woodside and Michell 1979).

In terms of influence of individuals within the buying centre, it has been suggested that PAs were more influential in selecting suppliers and making purchase decisions in straight rebuy situations (Jackson, Keith and Burdick 1984). PAs were also found to be responsible for the majority of the purchases of supplies, which are goods that do not become involved in the final product, but are essential to everyday operations (Jackson, Keith and Burdick 1984). Thus, examining the attitudes of PAs towards recycled paper should give an indication as to buying centre members' attitudes, although this may vary based on the specific rebuy situation.

III *Methodology*

Data were collected from eleven organisations in one large Australian city. All organisations examined were of sufficient size to support a specialised purchasing department. An examination of two separate mailing lists identified sixteen organisations within the targeted region as employing more than 100 employees. These organisations were contacted by telephone to explain the research project and determine whether the PA would be prepared to participate in the study. Eleven of the sixteen PAs agreed to participate in the study (a 69% response rate), representing the following industries: manufacturing (4); utilities (3); governmental/statutory bodies (3); and communications (1). Interviews were conducted under the condition of confidentiality and thus no data on individual firms or PAs are reported.

PAs responsible for the purchase of paper products were considered the best people to interview, due to the assumption that a supply type of straight rebuy was being examined and they (the PAs) would have the most influence (Doyle, Woodside and Michell 1979; Jackson, Keith and Burdick 1984; Mattson 1988). A preliminary question was asked to gauge the extent of the PA's role in the process and whether any other individual was involved. It was found that PAs believed that they had the most purchasing influence (i.e. they were the key informant) for this product and thus no additional organisational informants were sought. While it is recognised that self-reported nature of the response may introduce some bias, no attempt was made to verify respondents' views.

The interview protocol was semi-structured in nature and was designed to allow flexibility while still maintaining a standard set of questions. Semi-structured interviews were considered the most appropriate, as they were used in the earlier literature (Drumwright 1992, 1994) and, in addition, they are often used in exploratory research. The questions used were designed based on information obtained from an industry expert and the previous literature (Drumwright 1992, 1994; Langrehr, Langrehr and Tatreau 1992). However, given the narrow area examined in this study (supply type of straight rebuy) and differing data collection processes (one key informant versus multiple informants), this work is not directly comparable to earlier quantitative results.

The final interview protocol contained fifteen questions that could be divided into five issues: (1) organisational demographics; (2) the environment as an organisational issue; (3) buying centre function issues; (4) suppliers' influence; and (5) recycled paper usage and evaluation criterion issues (see Fig. 2 for the interview protocol).

QUESTION	ISSUE COVERED
Demographic questions (e.g. size, industry). What is the main function of your firm?	The environment in the organisation
Do you consider the environment to be an issue for your organisation? Will it continue to be an issue in future years?	The environment in the organisation
How do you rate the performance of your industry generally in its response to environmental issues?	The environment in the organisation
What areas of your business are currently using recycled products? What areas could use recycled products in the future?	Recycled paper issues
What sort of incentives would encourage you to use recycled and recyclable products now?	Supplier issues
What sort of written/unwritten policies are in place regarding the firm's environmental stance? How does this affect everyday purchasing decisions?	Buying centre issues
Which department within your firm has the most influence over the purchase of paper for office and administration work? Why?	Buying centre issues
Are you aware of recycled paper and packaging products available that could be used within your company? Are you aware of potential suppliers?	Recycled paper issues/supplier issues
How do you perceive suppliers of recycled products? Can they adequately satisfy the needs of your company? Do the suppliers of recycled products communicate their product offerings effectively?	Supplier issues
What criteria do you consider most important for evaluating paper-based products?	Recycled paper issues
What information sources would be considered important when purchasing recycled paper products?	Supplier issues
What are your perceptions about recycled paper products?	Recycled paper issues
Have you had any experience with recycled paper products in the past? Why/Why not? What happened?	Recycled paper issues
Do you see any problems or benefits in being seen by stakeholders and the public as being an environmentally aware company?	The environment in the organisation

Figure 2: Semi-structured Interview Protocol and Issue Covered

The objective of the study is to highlight trends and examine the views of a key informant in the buying centre (i.e. PA) for a straight rebuy purchase with environmental attributes. However, as has previously been mentioned, it is not clear whether these findings can be generalised to all environmentally oriented straight rebuy situations.

Each semi-structured interview lasted approximately thirty minutes. Notes were taken, the data were then reduced as suggested by the literature (Drumwright 1992, 1994; Miles and Hubberman 1984). Given the qualitative nature of the data and small sample size, only descriptive analysis and the examination of broad trends of respondents' attitudes are provided. This type of exploratory study has inherent limitations, most notable being the potential for respondent and interviewer bias. As suggested by earlier research, respondents interviewed may, at times, reflect their own attitudes and not necessarily the organisation's attitudes. For example, PAs with a strong personal conviction towards the environment may inadvertently bias their response. In addition, key informants may have an inflated view of their importance to any decision process and thus further introduce bias into the data.

‖ Results and Discussions

As was discussed earlier, four broad issues relating to recycled paper were examined in this study. In this section, each of these issues is individually examined, based on the information obtained in the eleven PA interviews.

‖ The Environment as an Organisational Issue

Not surprisingly, all the PAs felt that the environment was an important issue for their firm and they believed it would continue to be an important issue in the future. This result is confirmed by other studies, which found most managers believed the environment was an important issue today and would be in the future (Peattie and Ratnayaka 1992; Peattie and Ring 1993; Vandermere and Oliff 1991). All the organisations examined had some type of paper recycling programme in place to reduce waste.

In probing the PAs in more depth, it was found that a small number of organisations (three) had policy entrepreneurs or, as they stated, ‘greenies on staff to push the company to act’. Other PAs said that their organisations were facing environmental pressures from various external groups, including regulators and the local community, from which could be implied that many organisations are taking a more ‘opportunistic’ approach towards purchasing environmental products. They appear to be ‘responding to what it perceived to be as a “hot topic” among customers or competitors at the moment’ (Drumwright 1994). This perspective was supported by two PAs who felt that their organisations could achieve a ‘competitive’ advantage by going green.

The more ‘committed’ organisations, or those that might possibly be based on ‘founder's ideals’, went further and established environmental departments to ensure that all individuals in the organisation behaved responsibly. There were two organisations that had integrated environmental training into all levels of the organisation in order to ensure that their employees understood the environmental imperative.

PAs in these firms believed that their firms were leading the way in terms of integrating recycled paper into the organisation.

Firms undertaking the above activities might be classified in the 'founder's ideals' or 'symbolism' category but, without an indication of organisational involvement with environmental issues, it is difficult to distinguish between these two categories. As none of the PAs suggested that they were individually responsible for the establishment of broad-based environmental purchasing criteria, it is therefore unclear if PAs were acting as 'policy entrepreneurs'. If they were, it would be inconsistent with the findings of other researchers (Drumwright 1992, 1994).

When examining the organisation and its relationship to the environment, six PAs indicated that they felt they were constrained by the supplier inability to provide innovative solutions, i.e. the recycled paper was not satisfactory for all organisational uses. In these cases, the organisations may ultimately be able to assist suppliers in developing new products to meet organisational needs appropriately.

⦀ Buying Centre Issues

In the sample, six of the eleven organisations had policies dealing with the purchase of recycled paper, though not all of these were formal written policies. In one case, a PA took it upon itself to develop appropriate purchasing criteria for recycled paper. At least two organisations had formal buying lists that restricted their purchases to approved companies. Thus, if a supplier of recycled paper was not on the list, then their products could not be purchased.

As suggested by the buying centre literature (Doyle, Woodside and Michell 1979), PAs felt that they had the primary responsibility for the purchase of recycled paper. They considered its purchase to be a routine activity. Two PAs felt that, on occasions, there was a minor influence from the firm's computer department, which consumed large amounts of the paper purchased. Another respondent said that, on occasions, individual departments made specific requests for certain types of paper, though even in these cases it was up to the specific PA to find an appropriate supplier.

⦀ Supplier-Related Issues

All PAs said they could easily identify suppliers of recycled paper, with nine PAs naming specific brands. While awareness was high, PAs were less than satisfied with the service and information provided by recycled paper suppliers. It was felt that suppliers did not 'push' recycled paper over virgin paper. This comment was also made when PAs were asked about suppliers' ability to satisfy the company's general needs. There was 'scepticism' by PAs relating to the quality of products produced, which may have been due to poor past experiences. It was felt that sometimes the product characteristics were exaggerated by marketers, leaving PAs 'dissatisfied' with the recycled paper products purchased.

Overall, PAs identified that newer recycled paper products were of higher quality than were earlier products. This may imply that the resources spent on communicating environmental characteristics of recycled paper, by large organisations such as Xerox (Xerox 1994), might be changing PAs' attitudes toward recycled paper. At least two PAs favoured additional supplier-based promotion of their recycled paper products. However, it may also reflect real improvements in the quality of recycled paper. PAs indicated that, to be effective, any supplier information on recycled paper products had to differentiate itself from the regular flow of junk mail coming across their desk.

PAs suggested that suppliers could provide incentives such as lower costs, which would increase organisational use of recycled paper. Such supplier incentives were favoured over governmental or tax incentives. It was felt that the quality and value of recycled paper had to be communicated more clearly to encourage purchase. Finally, six of the PAs believed there was a promotional bias by suppliers towards virgin paper, which may have been attributable to the higher margins associated with that product or the fact that the higher price 'dissuaded' organisational purchases.

⫴ Recycled Paper Issues

It was found that eight of the organisations sampled were presently using recycled paper somewhere in their organisation though, as mentioned above, all PAs were aware of recycled paper suppliers. PAs identified a variety of different recycled paper items available including: computer paper, envelopes, letterheads, note pads, photocopying paper, printing paper and toilet rolls. Not all firms that used recycled paper used all available recycled products. Interestingly, some firms would only use recycled paper internally, while others only used it on letterhead and external materials. This difference in usage might indicate a difference in organisational categorisation, with those only concerned with outward appearances being less environmentally 'concerned' or involved.

Six of the PAs indicated that previously they had had negative experiences with recycled paper and that it not been 'up to scratch'. These PAs suggested that, in the past, using recycled paper had resulted in damage to office equipment. These negative experiences might, therefore, increase the perceived individual risk to PAs in regards to purchasing recycled paper and thus more communication from suppliers regarding product quality improvements would be required to stimulate purchase.

PAs were asked to identify the most important criteria when evaluating paper products. The two most identified criteria were quality (four) and price (three), with factors such as delivery, service, recycled content and country of origin each being identified as the 'most important' by at least one PA. Thus, it appears that PAs are very concerned about paper performance, although respondents were not asked to rank evaluation criteria in terms of importance.

There were some contradictory findings in this area of the study: for example, two PAs said that recycled paper was not white enough to use for letterhead, while another PA suggested that product quality had improved to such an extent that, without the 'recycled' logo, consumers would not be able to identify the paper as recycled. Another contradictory result was that two of the PAs said that they were willing to pay more for recycled paper products that performed well yet, as mentioned earlier, three PAs indicated price was their primary evaluation criteria. These differences might be explained by the environmental orientation of the firm and the PA. An alternative explanation might be that perceptions are heavily influenced by the diverse previous experiences of the respondents. There is strong evidence to support this alternative view as 54% (six) of the PAs indicated they had had negative previous experiences and only 18% (two) had positive past experiences. While most PAs had previously had negative experiences, on the whole they believed that quality was improving, but that product quality was still inferior to virgin paper.

There was also a question asked regarding perceptions, as distinct from past experience. Seven of the respondents had had negative perceptions towards recycled paper's effectiveness. The reasons given for these negative perceptions relate directly to their negative previous experiences mentioned above. Of those who had had positive perceptions towards recycled paper, two PAs felt that it was important for their organisation to use recycled paper for a 'solid' public image. Thus, PAs may not necessarily be commenting on their past organisational use, but rather on broader business benefits. If this is the case, then these firms would be classified as 'opportunists'.

‖ *Managerial Implications and Recommendations*

This study highlights the fact that industrial buyers seem to require products to have attributes additional to those that have been traditionally offered. Not only do organisations want a quality product at a reasonable price, but they also appear to want that product to be less environmentally harmful. It does not appear that organisational buyers are placing environmental purchasing criteria above all others, i.e. price, quality, etc. As such, marketers must provide a balanced marketing mix and not necessarily focus solely on environmental attributes (Ottman 1995). Marketers should, however, not ignore environmental attributes when marketing and promoting their products either—although the importance of the environmental attributes to the industrial buyer may be dependent on where the buyer's organisation fits within the four-firm classification: 'founder's ideals', 'symbolism', 'opportune' and 'restraint'.

It is possible that the specific marketing strategies used might be modified depending on the environmental orientation of both the firm and the individual purchasing agent. This may result in marketers segmenting organisations and developing specific strategies to target each segment. For example, in Australia, Kyocera has run several different print advertisements for their Ecosys laser printer, in which environmental information has been included with varying degrees of emphasis (Kyocera Electronics Australia 1994, 1995, 1995–96). Thus, some marketers may already be trying to use an organisation's environmental involvement to segment industrial consumers.

To assist marketers, it may be useful to identify a process by which organisations can be segmented. Figure 3 puts forward a segmentation model that relies on three main criteria. These criteria were suggested in the previous research and are supported by this study. First, marketers need to identify if firms have an environmental purchasing policy (Drumwright 1992, 1994). Second, marketers must identify the specific criteria used to evaluate the product purchase. In firms with environmental purchasing policies, these criteria should be more easily identifiable, as they will be established in the policy. For firms that do not have environmental purchasing policies, it will be important for marketers to identify individual PAs' purchasing criteria, which will often be more difficult given their often subjective nature.

The third step is to identify the PAs' involvement with environment issues and their involvement in the purchase of products with environmental attributes. Identification of PAs' involvement level will be important, even in firms where there are

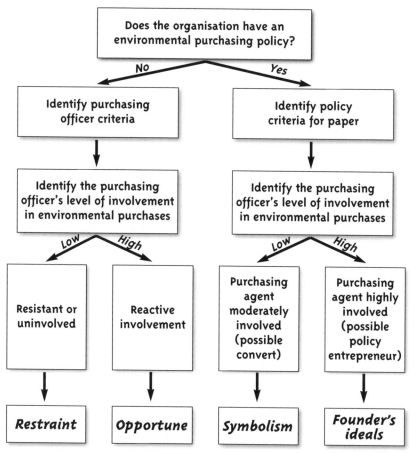

Figure 3: Model of Recycled Paper Purchasing Behaviour

environmental purchasing policies, as the PA will be responsible for the implementation of environmental purchasing policies. The higher the PA's involvement with environmental issues, the more marketers may need to emphasise the product's environmental attributes. If the PA is not actively involved with environmental issues, it is most likely more important to highlight other product attributes. However, the product's environmental attributes should also at least be mentioned, even if they are not emphasised.

Thus, strategies for marketing products with environmental attributes can be developed by understanding how involved both the organisation and individual PA are with the environment. While the proposed process is based on an examination of a supply type of straight rebuy products, it is suggested that it may also apply to other types of purchase: non-supply straight rebuy, modified rebuys and new products. However, the identification of the overall importance of environmental product characteristics and environmental involvement of all buying centre individuals will be more difficult to identify and evaluate for these other types of purchase.

Managerial recommendations can also be based on the fact that products, especially those with environmental attributes, are evolving at a rapid rate. As with all types of product, marketers need to communicate continually with buyers to identify problem areas to assist in improving their existing offerings. More importantly, marketers need to communicate how their products have been improved. It appears that negative past experiences may have a long-term influence on perceptions and future purchase behaviour. Marketers must develop effective methods of communication to ensure that attitudes and perceptions change as the products and quality levels change.

Strategies to overcome past product deficiencies may also attempt to minimise the risk to the purchasing organisation. Minimising risk through various types of guarantee or warranty may be one method of encouraging trial or retrial. In other cases, firms may attempt to obtain third-party endorsement or certification for products with environmental attributes as a way of reducing consumer uncertainty (Mendleson and Polonsky 1995; Stafford and Hartman 1996). For example, the Kyocera laser printers are endorsed by the Australian Conservation Foundation (Kyocera Electronics Australia 1994), which is a highly credible environmental organisation in Australia. This endorsement may encourage some organisations to purchase a product that utilises new environmentally less harmful technology, which they might have not otherwise considered.

▮ *Conclusions and Future Research*

In terms of this exploratory research, it appears that PAs are buying recycled paper products for many different reasons. 'Going green' may be an important organisational issue, but it seems that, when evaluating purchases, environmental product attributes are only one component of the overall evaluation process. It does appear that products must have a minimal set of acceptable characteristics to be purchased. From this research, it is still unclear, however, how PAs trade off environmental characteristics with other product characteristics. Clearly, quality and value (as distinctive from price) are two important characteristics that need to be present for purchase to occur.

Organisational purchasing behaviour is shaped by many different forces. If recycled product producers, straight rebuy and others are to become in-suppliers, they must understand the organisation's product use and buying centre behaviour. Simply appealing to organisations' desire to 'be green' is most likely not enough to sell to all organisations.

It appears that the marketers of environmentally responsible products may have to overcome other problems as well. For example, potential consumer may have inaccurate perceptions of product quality due to poor past product performance. Marketers must ensure that they communicate environmental product attributes and changes in those attributes effectively to key decision-makers in the buying centre. However, the communication of environmental product attributes is not an easy task. There is a growing stream of literature discussing the problems faced by consumer goods manufacturers in communicating environmental information (Carlson, Grove and Kangun 1993; Davis 1993). Given the buying centre's diversity, marketers may need to provide extensive information to address all members' needs.

The research examining environmentally responsible buying behaviour is, at present, very limited and requires additional academic investigation. This is not to imply that the existing buying centre literature needs to be ignored or re-invented. Applying existing buying centre theory to other types of purchasing criterion may yield other useful insights and findings. An area of theory that may need to be further developed is the linkage between organisational activities and non-financial motivations. If environmental criteria are becoming more important to organisations, the marketers need to have a method of developing strategies that will achieve desired organisational outcomes.

There are a number of other areas that could also be examined. For example, research could examine a wider range of product types, other straight rebuy, new purchases and modified rebuy purchases, to determine if the type of purchase decision has an influence on the purchasing of products with environmental attributes. It could be hypothesised that new product purchases are already risky decisions and thus firms would be less willing to purchase products with environmental attributes, especially if the products themselves are new to the market. If there are quality concerns by industrial consumers, it may be difficult for products with environmental attributes, of any type, to be adopted.

There is also an opportunity to examine this phenomenon cross-culturally. While this study examined supply types of straight rebuy products in large Australian organisations, it was not directly comparable to the previous US work in this area, given the different focus of the two studies. Another area that could be examined is the difference between small and large organisations. Small organisations often are considered to have a more family/community focus and are often more flexible than larger organisations. They may, thus, be more likely to purchase products with environmental attributes. In general, there appears to be extensive room for research into the purchasing of products with environmental attributes.

I2

Integrating Environmental Criteria into Purchasing Decisions
Value Added?

Jim Hutchison

||| Introduction

The emerging concept of life-cycle thinking suggests that environmental concerns extend beyond an organisation's own boundaries, and that improvements in environmental performance can be gained through supply chain relationships. Current thinking also suggests that environmental performance improvement must also create value for the business. Using findings developed from a period of research on organisations in 1997,[1] this chapter explores the factors motivating organisations to integrate environmental criteria into purchasing and supply decisions. In addition, it examines the value perceptions from applying or receiving supply chain pressure.

Improving environmental performance has become an established goal in business. Many companies are facing new challenges brought about by growing ecological problems, societal concerns and changes in the attitudes of consumers. The speed of change in these areas places pressure on organisations to adapt strategies and operating procedures that reflect developing good practice. Organisations are confronted by two major challenges: (1) to improve the quality of the environment; and (2) to improve their competitive position in the marketplace.

Environmental issues challenge the evaluation criteria of traditional competitive advantage. In the past, aspects such as costs, quality and delivery were considered to be the critical success factors. The traditional criteria remain fundamental indicators of competitiveness while the introduction of environmental management further increases the scope to create competitive advantage.

The influence of these characteristics on integrating environmental criteria into the supply chain is more obvious for some than others. Larger organisations are beginning to take a proactive approach and are developing environmental purchasing policies that will enable them to add or create value for the organisation. There is likely to be far greater incentive for these organisations to take opportunities, both internally and externally, that provide some form of competitive advantage. It is also likely that

---

1. This work was carried out as an MBA thesis by the author (Hutchison 1997), and focuses on organisations in the Milton Keynes area.

organisations in business sectors experiencing the greatest environmental pressure are those who will be exposed to more opportunities to add value.

In contrast, there is little evidence to suggest that small or medium-sized enterprises (SMEs) are addressing their environmental performance in this manner, and are more likely to develop environmental initiatives as the result of external pressure. SMEs are invariably the suppliers to larger companies with more advanced environmental policies and it is often the case that it is the smaller firm that has to adapt to the purchasing policy of the larger company.

Organisations buy goods and services to satisfy a variety of goals, such as making profits and reducing costs. In order to support these goals, purchasing behaviour must be carried out under the guidance of formal purchasing policies, constraints and requirements established by the organisation. It is important to understand that environmental criteria must co-exist within the organisation's overall purchasing objectives.

❙❙❙ Purchasing Objectives

The importance of procurement as a key function in the management of business can be emphasised by considering the total cost of materials in relative terms. The chemical or car manufacturing industries can find that their purchases amount to approximately 70% of turnover (Baily and Farmer 1990). Up to 75% of IBM UK's annual input costs relate to products and services bought in from other companies or other parts of the IBM corporation. In 1992, more than £1.6 billion was spent in the UK alone with 2,000 suppliers, many of whom have long supply chains of their own across a wide spread of countries (Gillett 1993). All this suggests that the effects of good purchasing management on the profitability of a typical manufacturing or service organisation can be considerable.

While the cost of bought-in goods and services is one of the principle measures of purchasing effectiveness, it is by no means the only one. There are many and varied objectives for those involved in the purchasing function. This list includes:

▶ Ensuring security and continuity of supply

▶ Obtaining 'best' value while maintaining a balance with desired quality

▶ Maintaining working relationships with other departments within the organisation

▶ Ensuring selection of the best suppliers

▶ Negotiating with suppliers and building mutually beneficial relationships

▶ Development of policies and procedures to support the achievement of objectives

▶ Monitoring market trends

▶ Providing information and advice, including input into the development of new products

However, while this provides a list of generic objectives that can be applied to most organisations, how the objective is reached (or even set in the first place) will often depend on the characteristics of the supply chain within which it operates. Bytheway (1995) notes that the characteristics of a supply chain include such elements as:

> ❫ The length and breadth of the business activity involved
> ❫ How and where power is deployed within the chain
> ❫ The maturity of the supply chain
> ❫ The adversarial or co-operative attitudes of those involved
> ❫ The nature of demand—it might be constant or not
> ❫ The type of product—perishable, life-threatening, etc.
> ❫ Volume of goods involved—are they slow-moving?
> ❫ The level of consistency—is there a variety in levels of performance?

The influence of these characteristics on integrating environmental criteria into the supply chain are more obvious for some industrial sectors than others.

The extent to which companies in different sectors of industry and commerce have adopted environmental management principles varies. Some sectors are heavily involved, others moderately, and for many it is not even considered an issue. There are distinct groupings that have been identified as being more susceptible than others to the need for environmental management. These include energy providers, heavy engineering, waste disposal, chemicals and plastics, road transport, and pulp and paper products.

Scott Ltd is the largest producer of disposable tissue products in the UK and in 1992 committed the organisation to taking a life-cycle approach to understanding its environmental impacts. The initial assessment of suppliers' performance across a range of performance criteria resulted in the worst 10% of suppliers being dropped. In addition, those suppliers with the best performance were given added preference in purchasing decisions (Kybert 1993).

Within this supply chain, the nature of the product plays an influential role. Scott recognise that they have 'bought in' a significant proportion of their major environmental impacts through suppliers' commercial forestry and pulp-manufacturing operations. In addition, the consistency of Scott's suppliers, in environmental performance terms, was very erratic. For example, emissions of carbon dioxide per tonne of pulp were found to vary by a factor of seventeen between suppliers of kraft pulp (pulp supplied for a strong type of paper). The range reflected not only different energy efficiencies, but also the balance in terms of renewable and non-renewable energy resources. These results provided the basis for the dropping of some suppliers.

It can be seen that a variety of supply chain characteristics, such as the high level of purchasing power (wielded by Scott), the type of product (produced by an environmentally sensitive process), and the extremes in levels of supplier environmental performance all play a role in shaping Scott's environmental purchasing objectives.

Environmental pressures have provided an unexpected catalyst for organisations reviewing customer–supplier relationships. The traditional relationship is often viewed as an adversarial one, with both having different objectives. However, many organisations are now coming to realise that having a good supplier base is one of the key factors in achieving corporate improvement and profit goals. Suppliers should also realise that, if their customers are doing well, then they will benefit—the purchaser and supplier have a common goal. Despite this change in attitude, pressures on suppliers are, in fact, becoming more acute with the trend for large firms to cut down on the number of suppliers with the aim of improving productivity and saving money (Gillies 1995).

For many companies, partnership sourcing—when customer and supplier develop a close and long-term relationship—can provide advantages, reducing stock levels, helping to improve the company's response to customer needs and so on. There are also benefits for the supplier who, on surviving a rigorous vetting procedure, can expect the relationship to be viewed as a long-term one.

Large firms use a wide variety of means to monitor suppliers: financial ownership, quality (e.g. commitment to ISO 9000), benchmarking performance, consistency in pricing, timely delivery and flexibility in adapting to change. Suppliers are required to be open about their working practices when dealing with larger organisations, and increasingly this includes their attitude to environmental concerns. This is partly because companies worry that a supplier that has poor standards in these areas will reflect badly on them, but it is also a fact that there is a distinct advantage to be gained through proactive involvement in environmental issues.

While there is little evidence to suggest that companies address environmental issues purely on profit-motivated grounds, it is an inescapable fact that, for the majority of businesses, the process of environmental performance improvement must carry with it some form of business gain. A clear example of this is the Unipart Group of Companies (UGC)'s 'Ten(d)-To-Zero' programme for supply chain management. This was launched in 1989 to build relationships between UGC and their suppliers and provide the basis for continuous improvement in performance. One of the key UGC buyer values is to work towards 'zero environmental harm' with the objective being 'to continually highlight, refine and minimise the adverse environmental aspects of the DCM [Demand Chain Management] product range' (UGC 1997).

The objectives and methods for this programme are clear in addressing areas within the chain that are likely to have an adverse environmental impact. Guidance notes for Unipart buyers clarify these aims further. These notes cover the reasons for addressing specific issues and focus heavily on risk reduction. For example, in the section dealing with suppliers who have not demonstrated compliance with relevant legislation, the guidance states that 'this point is aimed at minimising the risk to the supply chain. If a company is prosecuted, or worse, if operations are stopped by the regulators, it could lead to a disruption in supply and/or extra costs'(UGC 1997). There is clearly a risk to the environment from companies operating outside of legislation as well as to the supplier. This risk extends to UGC and can be readily translated into the generic objectives previously discussed. Reducing environmental impact is an important goal, although from a business point of view UGC is also concerned over continuity and security of supply.

Now consider the following statement from Michael Hepher, Group Managing Director of British Telecommunications (BT):

> . . . as environmental standards tighten, disposal costs rise. For items bought for use with BT, disposal costs have a direct impact on BT's bottom line. Such costs can be minimised—and in some cases totally eliminated—by consideration at the procurement stage . . . BT's reputation depends on supplying a quality product to customers . . . BT sees a strong correlation between environmental issues and quality. The view that environmental performance is a quality issue,

with waste and poor performance being linked to quality failure, has been accepted by the organisation (Hepher 1994).

This statement picks up on many of the generic purchasing objectives and shows how BT is using the environment to expand on key elements of its business strategy. By focusing on environmental issues, the purchasing function can deliver on objectives related to cost reduction, quality enhancement and product development.

In a similar approach, the following points were raised by John Gillett, Regional Procurement Manager of IBM:

> . . . by helping its suppliers in a disciplined and structured approach to compliance, IBM anticipates benefits not only in terms of its environmental credentials, but also in reduced costs and quality improvements . . . but more work is needed, in particular on preparation for Eco labelling where the failure of suppliers to comply in certain areas could mean that IBM would lose the right to use the label and forfeit the competitive edge to be gained from early compliance with the new European environmental labelling requirements (Gillett 1993).

Again, this statement considers environmental criteria in terms of cost, quality and also considers the effectiveness of IBM's operations in maintaining a competitive edge. The provision of an environmentally conscious product, however, must also meet the traditional criteria of delivery, price and quality in order for it to meet IBM's requirements fully.

Although this approach may be regarded as cynical, in that it appears that any environmental improvement must equate to competitive advantage, current literature on business management does not focus on ecological problems for their own sake, but on their implications for their effect on the value of the organisation affected. The Chartered Institute of Purchasing and Supply (1994) has developed guidelines on environmental purchasing which recommend that the costs and benefits of environmental purchasing are considered. This includes the identification of:

▶ The legislative pressures and understanding of the operational implications

▶ Suppliers where environmental risks are important enough to represent a threat to security of supply

▶ Main market opportunities and pressures where environmental policy in purchasing has a role to play

▶ Resource needs and evaluation of the costs and benefits of building the environment into purchasing and supply

▶ Suppliers who contribute to the organisation's performance and therefore image in the local community

It is clear that, for any organisation intent on the development of an environmental purchasing programme, there needs to be some form of tangible evidence that it will improve the bottom line. It is in the understanding of where an organisation sits in the supply chain, the nature of the chain and in what area organisations can gain maximum value that allows us to evaluate what motivates them to introduce an environmental purchasing programme.

⏐ *Motivation and the Creation of Value*

Porter's (1985) value chain analysis suggests that an understanding of a firm's internal value chain, as well as its role as part of an overall sectoral value chain, provides insights that can lead to the generation of competitive advantage. Every organisation can be seen as a collection of activities that are carried out to design, produce, market, deliver and support its product or services. Each of these activities can be a source of competitive advantage through its ability to add value. Many value chain activities occur outside an organisation in relationships with suppliers and distributors. Suppliers will, in turn, experience their own set of value activities and competitive advantage is likely to be sustained by linkages made between these and those of their customers. A key issue worth considering is whether these key linkages can be sustained when there are differing perceptions between customer and supplier of the value to be gained. Should a supplier view a customer's environmental requirements as an additional cost (rather than an opportunity), then what level of commitment is it likely to apply to the issue?

Studies show that, where suppliers are coming under pressure to improve their environmental performance, they view this as 'neither desirable nor helpful' (Winter and Ledgerwood 1994; Hillary 1995; Hutchison 1997; Elliott, Patton and Lenaghan 1996). One explanation for this may lie in the concept that value should be assessed from the viewpoint of the final consumer or user of the product or service. This may not happen among suppliers for a variety of reasons. For example, they may be distanced from the final users by several intermediaries, i.e. other manufacturers and distributors. The understanding of creating value by addressing environmental issues does not come directly from the consumer or user but from other parties that may separate the supplier from the realities of their markets. Also, those suppliers reacting to pressure, particularly from larger customers, are then forced to address those issues seen by the customer to be important. This raises the question of how much value is added to the supplier through management of an environmental issue of relevance to the larger organisation.

It is obvious that customers' and suppliers' value interests will overlap very broadly in the overall sectoral value chain. It is also the case that both parties' perception of value may also differ within a common linkage in the chain. Before we can begin to discuss why this is so, there needs to be careful consideration of what motivates organisations to develop environmental purchasing criteria in the first place.

If it is assumed that organisations are pursuing a coherent business strategy, the role of environmental purchasing should be looked at in the context of how environmental performance helps to deliver competitive advantage. Environmental performance can then be seen to be driven by three key factors (CBI 1994):

▶ Market expectations

▶ Risk management and regulatory compliance

▶ Business efficiency

Environmental purchasing and supply has a key role to play in ensuring that all of these factors are fully addressed.

III *Market Expectations*

An organisation's marketplace is the logical starting point in any assessment of its competitive ability, although where the environment is concerned it is still a new and evolving concept. Awareness of an environmental issue does not always translate into a purchasing decision. Competitive companies are increasingly focusing on customers' needs and the development of value-added products and services. Creative and far-thinking organisations are increasingly willing to utilise environmental performance as a tool to enhance market response.

B&Q, the leading DIY retailer, is perhaps the most well-known example of large-scale integration of environmental criteria into purchasing decisions. Since accusations of irresponsible timber sourcing against the store in the early 1990s, B&Q has focused attention on its environmental performance (see also Chapters 9 and 24). Alan Knight, Environmental Policy Controller, is quoted: 'As the DIY market leader, B&Q has a responsibility to learn and an opportunity to profit by being ahead of its competitors on a course that they will inevitably be required to follow' (Hill, Marshall and Priddey 1994).

The launch of its Supplier Environmental Audit (SEA) in late 1991 led to a forty-page questionnaire being sent to all suppliers. This provided a picture of its supply base's environmental performance, showing that 8% had an environmental policy, 29% were found not to have taken any environmental action at all, while 25% did not even complete the questionnaire. A shorter follow-up questionnaire in 1993 discovered that many suppliers were actually unaware of what their environmental impacts were. Following a communications programme to raise awareness, B&Q began to give suppliers a rating dependent on their environmental commitment. In spite of some progress by December 1993, only 35% of suppliers were at an environmentally acceptable level. The company concluded that, until the environment was made a truly commercial issue for suppliers, the impact would be limited. The company introduced an environmental policy stating: 'B&Q will de-list suppliers who show no commitment to improving their environmental performance' (B&Q 1994). The total of suppliers with an environmental policy had risen from the initial 8% to 97% of the total by May 1995!

In practice, suppliers recognise the value of B&Q as a large buyer, and it is claimed that the practice of de-listing tends to occur where a combination of poor quality, service and environmental performance occurs. This supports the view that the use of environmental purchasing criteria will be carried out within certain economic boundaries. The real value to B&Q is undoubtedly in the fact that it is in its interests as a business to be an environmental leader in the retail sector. However, how do suppliers regard the pressure to improve their environmental performance?

The evidence shows quite clearly that suppliers did not become fully committed until it became a commercial issue. The real value to them will be in retention of business with B&Q. However, it is also stated that 'B&Q's suppliers "of all shapes and sizes" have discovered new opportunities for waste reduction and increased efficiency, as well as reporting positive benefits in employee morale' (Barry 1996). While this, presumably, is a welcome side-effect of the initial pressure, B&Q lists *its* four major achievements of the Supplier Audit as:

- Compliance with the company's environmental corporate policy
- Written commitment to improvement by all suppliers
- Development of a body of information on the environmental impacts of B&Q's products
- A major increase in understanding by suppliers

It is difficult to ascertain whether the last benefit alludes to suppliers' understanding of B&Q's demands or the real economic and environmental value of assessing their own impacts.

It is also interesting to note the pressure does not stop at B&Q's immediate suppliers. These suppliers are also expected to audit *their* suppliers as part of the environmental programme. Barrett and Murphy (1995) quote one B&Q employee on the difficulties faced with tracing a paint brush back to the forest of origin:

> . . . he bought his paint brushes from a company in Germany who bought the timber from a company in Italy, who bought it from a company in America, who bought it from a range of sawmills in America, who bought it from an even wider range of forests. So it essentially was a bit of a nightmare.

This represents an extremely complex chain which necessitates tracing all the connections involved, from the production and sourcing of each component back to the origin of raw materials and methods by which they have been obtained. The value to B&Q of this complexity comes from fulfilling policy requirements towards life-cycle management of products. This in turn was inspired by pressure from consumers and environmental pressure groups. The difficulty for these suppliers will be in determining the value to be placed in changing or amending processes to meet the demands of an organisation they are unlikely to have contact with. They will be dependent on intermediaries in the supply chain to translate this for them. As many of these suppliers are so far divorced from the viewpoint of the final consumer (who represents the ultimate value assessor), they are likely to view this pressure as 'unwanted' and a cost of doing business, rather than an opportunity to add or create value.

The marketplace represents a complex web of buying and selling and it is important that organisations look beyond their immediate links in the supply chain both to anticipate and to utilise environmental pressure to their best advantage.

▌ *Risk Management and Regulatory Compliance*

Realisation that any environmental impropriety can be easily traced upstream and downstream in the supply chain can influence a company's purchasing and selling criteria. Some organisations are more exposed than others, but many realise that the environmental impacts of products and services can be traced back to the raw materials bought in by the producer or assembler. Legislation plays a key role in defining supplier risk: for example, through the treatment and disposal of hazardous wastes. The waste management chain places a responsibility on the producer to ensure that waste is dealt with in a responsible manner.

The risk-based approach to managing supply chain issues is a common one. IBM, with more than 2,000 suppliers spread across many countries, recognises that it is exposed to risk on many fronts. IBM's first move was to categorise the types of risk presented by different groups of suppliers, and the extent to which IBM could be judged responsible in the event of an environmental impact. Six key risk factors were identified:

- Geographical proximity to supplier
- Extent to which product design has been specified
- Use of contract workforce
- Hazardous materials and processes
- Waste disposal
- Level of dependency of supplier on IBM business

The view was taken that liability will increase in proportion to IBM's involvement in specifying the design and production processes for a product, and to the percentage of a supplier's output that the IBM work occupied.

Underpinning IBM UK's approach to supplier performance is a range of management guidelines which set out the levels of control required for different types of supplier. Five categories were established, according to the level of commercial involvement and to the extent to which products and services are provided to IBM's own specification. Category 1, where IBM buys products, processes or services such as airline tickets off the shelf, is at the low-risk end of the scale, and no environmental evaluation is required. At the highest end of the scale is category 5, where IBM furnishes some or all of the chemicals used by a supplier, where IBM has chemical containment equipment cleaned or decontaminated, or where an IBM location is the sole or primary customer for a given supplier location. Between these two extremes, every level of involvement is defined, and documented procedures have been drawn up specifying the level of environmental control required for each, carefully matched to the potential environmental risk.

Gillett states that IBM's aim was 'to raise the capability of the supplier base gradually to a position where it could match IBM's overall environmental objectives' (Gillett 1993). Clearly, any added value to a supplier's programme will be dictated by IBM's objectives for adding value. These may not always coincide; for example, IBM is concerned to retain its image as a world leader. For most suppliers in the SME category, there are few resources to exploit this new image. The possibility of adding value through promoting this image in the marketplace will be substantially less than the opportunities open to IBM.

However, there are instances where value-added objectives will be broadly similar. This is particularly the case with category-5 suppliers, where an IBM location is the sole or primary customer for a given supplier location. The level of integration in this relationship is such that it could realistically be expected that an understanding of the need for environmental improvement will be more readily communicated. The motivation to act may be different, i.e. IBM is concerned over the risk to its image while the supplier is concerned about the risk of not fully meeting customer requirements. However, the situation essentially revolves around an issue of quality, which can be more readily integrated into existing business practices. The perception by suppliers of environmental purchasing pressure will determine their response.

If it is 'sold' on the basis of reducing risk and liability for IBM (looking internally), suppliers may become confused over how these changes add value for them.

Incentives such as cost reduction and quality improvements may provide value of a more tangible nature and lead to a more positive response. Where customers can translate the value of their actions into something tangible for the supplier, then there is a greater chance of this linkage being sustained. The supplier is, therefore, more likely to view the environmental pressure as an opportunity rather than a cost.

ABB Power Generation is a leading contractor for the design, supply, installation and commissioning of power stations and has committed itself to adhering to a number of protocols and initiatives, such as the Montreal Protocol on Substances that Deplete the Ozone Layer. The company realises that, to keep its commitments, it is heavily reliant on subcontractors and suppliers.

With this in mind, ABB has developed an environmental policy and also specific environmental requirements for suppliers. For suppliers working with paint, ABB specifies low-solvent or aqueous paint systems. In its tender specification, ABB states that these types of paint are widely available, although generally more expensive owing to a higher solids content. However, the document also states that, due to this, fewer coats are required, which should result in an overall financial saving. The value to ABB in this linkage is in meeting policy commitments while the supplier can readily see the economic value of helping ABB to meet its commitments.

It is difficult to equate risk with competitive gain, as, for many organisations, management of risk is an essential requirement for operating. However, it is an established fact that poor risk management can have disastrous results, both environmentally and financially. The purchasing department provides an important screening process to ensure that unnecessary risks are not introduced into an organisation.

▌▌ *Business Efficiency*

Organisations are also becoming increasingly aware of efficiency gains to be made through addressing environmental issues. This is often translated into minimising costs through efficient raw material utilisation or a decrease in wastes generated. It is often the case that the ability to achieve improvement is dependent on other parts of the supply chain—especially in the case of those companies who buy in the vast majority of their goods and services. More efficient and effective uses of packaging has been a common issue for customers and suppliers working in partnership in the past. The introduction of legislation on packaging waste has helped to focus efforts even further in this area.

British Telecommunications plc (BT) is the UK's largest company and principal supplier of telecommunications services. It is also a major supplier, but not manufacturer, of associated products. With a procurement budget of £4.5 billion (1994/95), BT is also the UK's largest civilian purchaser (BT 1995).

BT is actually perceived by the general public as having little impact on the environment. However, the organisation recognised that, in addition to threats posed by consumer attitudes and changing legislation, opportunities were also appearing for a proactive approach to environmental issues. As a major purchaser of goods and services, BT feels it can have a significant influence on environmental performance by pushing environmental issues along the supply chain. BT has developed an environmental purchasing standard to ensure that environmental considerations are taken into account during the tendering process. This is used for all tenders exceeding a certain limit on the value of supplies or for purchases that represent a potentially high environmental impact (or risk).

The standard requires suppliers to respond in a number of areas—sourcing of raw materials, manufacturing processes, subcontractors' activities, environmental aspects of use, recycling, disposal and improvement programme. For a particular purchase, each potential supplier is asked to respond to each area of the standard for their particular product or service. BT then assesses each supplier's response against a template, and assigns a numerical score so that the potential environmental impact of similar products from different suppliers can be compared. This feeds into the overall contract adjudication decision and is weighed alongside other more traditional factors—whole-life costs, product reliability, quality, delivery and technical performance. In this way, companies can gain competitive advantage by demonstrating commitment to environmental improvement. The weighting given to environmental aspects varies according to the type of product being purchased, and its associated whole-life environmental impact. For certain products—e.g. batteries, paper and print—environmental considerations may have a significant effect on who wins the contract.

A benefit of this approach has been to create a better understanding and recognition of life-cycle management issues and the avoidance of unplanned costs. BT is now able to address disposal issues at the acquisition stage, either to discriminate against items with known environmental hazards in disposal or to make arrangements for the supplier to be responsible for the eventual disposal of the product. This, in turn, has encouraged suppliers to manufacture less environmentally damaging products. As long as these products continue to meet performance specifications, then it is easy to see how an increase in business efficiency and environmental improvement go hand in hand.

Although there are a number of similarities between BT and B&Q, such as the reliance on suppliers as the basis for environmental programmes, there is one distinct difference in their motivation to develop such programmes. This will influence the value judgements suppliers will make in responding to pressure.

B&Q initiated its environmental programme largely as a response to external pressure from consumers and environmental groups. The reluctance of suppliers initially to develop environmental policies is likely to have been aggravated by the fact that they were distanced from the value judgements that ultimately mattered: those of the consumers. In BT's case, the organisation is not perceived as a major source of adverse environmental impact. In fact, it could be argued that their global telecommunications technology is environmentally positive, in that it can substitute for more energy-intensive forms of physical travel. BT's environmental programme was initiated internally and is regarded as a quality issue. The value judgements on BT's products and services largely emanate from within the organisation itself, and are thus likely to be more easily translated to, and understood by, suppliers dealing directly with the value source. It is possible that, by integrating environmental issues into its existing quality programme, BT has found a way of effectively communicating the value of addressing environmental performance.

▮▮ *Linking the Environment with Quality Management*

Many commentators have stressed what they see as natural linkages between quality management and the improvement of environmental performance (Welford and Gouldson 1993). The argument is based on the similarities in the two approaches. The control of both can be achieved by essentially the same management principles such as policy and planning, communication, evaluation, personnel and organisation and assurance.

Oakland (1993) states that throughout and beyond all organisations there is a series of quality *chains* of customer and suppliers that may be broken at any point by one person or one piece of equipment not meeting the requirements of the customer, internal *or external*. In terms of quality, Oakland suggests that this failure usually finds its way to the interface between the organisation and its outside customers. As in quality, an organisation's environmental performance is only as strong as its weakest link, and where quality management plays a role in supplier evaluation and rating there should be an opportunity to combine this with an environmental programme.

The objective of a purchasing system is fairly simple: to ensure that the purchased products or services conform to the requirements of the buyer. The implication, then, for suppliers, in environmental terms, is that they will have a set of performance requirements to meet. In quality terms, business can use quality system standards as tools to establish appropriate practices and procedures to assure the delivery of these requirements. The quality management standard ISO 9000 acts as a benchmark.

ISO 9000 is a voluntary standard, though many view this with some scepticism owing to the increasing regularity in which it is quoted as a contractual necessity for carrying out business. The pressures for implementation come not only from those organisations searching for reliability and security of supply, but also from within the standard itself. Organisations operating under ISO 9000 have an obligation to ensure that their suppliers are selected on the basis of their ability to meet defined requirements and objective documentary evidence will be required to show that the supplier:

▸ Has the capability to do so; and

▸ Will do so reliably and consistently.

Often, the evidence required is for the supplier to show that its quality system has been independently certified to ISO 9000. In effect, the pressure for achieving performance requirements is passed down the supply chain. The point to be made here is that, if we view quality and environment as being interlinked and the management approaches similar, then it would be logical to expect the knock-on effects to suppliers to be similar.

In environmental terms, there have recently been developments of principles and techniques for improving environmental performance by a number of groups. The most prominent of these tools is ISO 14001, the international standard on environmental management systems, which takes a quality systems approach to environmental management. While the requirements of the standard are open to interpretation, there are clear hints that the environmental probity of suppliers should also be considered with regard to their products and services. Current literature, overwhelmingly, expects that the introduction of standardised management systems will create supply chain pressure (Hutchison 1997). The use of the standards themselves are likely to be promulgated through the supply chain.

One unlikely source of dissent about this theory has come from B&Q, one of the pioneers of corporate supply chain greening, who has decided not to force suppliers to comply with BS 7750 (now superseded by ISO 14001). Only a few of their suppliers were planning to obtain certification and the company claimed that implementing the standard was proving a distraction from real environmental improvements (ENDS 1995). A review of suppliers noted that many companies with limited resources were unable to spend time and money on the management systems and the issues they were designed to address.

What can we read into this decision? The issues that an organisation's environmental management system are supposed to address are those that are significant to the organisation itself. If it is the case that suppliers are being pressurised into addressing the issues that are of importance to the customer, there is the distinct possibility that they may be forced into activities that are not necessarily adding optimal value, both in an economic and environmental sense.

Looking at the situation from a quality point of view, it is obvious that customers are essentially trying to achieve the environmental performance levels required of them. This may necessitate working with suppliers whose activities will almost certainly be taken into account should a life-cycle management approach be taken. This may well be in the form of a partnership, but it is customers' environmental or financial objectives that will drive this activity.

The problem with trying to equate quality with environmental management is in trying to reconcile the differences in objectives and scope of the two systems. The implementation of management systems is pushed forward by the need to improve performance in quality and environmental management. Each of these is driven by a set of external or internal factors, the drivers, which in turn have to be put into the context of an organisation's own ambitions, culture and policies. For quality, the scope of the issues to be considered will tend to be narrow and will focus directly on the organisation and its products and services in the context of customer requirements. With respect to the environment, the scope is much broader and impacts on a wider range of issues, which may even be global in nature.

A supplier can focus on a partnership with a customer far more easily when dealing with quality issues, because meeting customers' needs is a fundamental requirement for staying in business. In environmental terms, however, the performance levels are dictated by a much broader range of pressures than the customer. Suppliers who are forced to meet their customers' requirements in environmental terms can find themselves addressing the wrong issues. To what extent does the environment and quality interlink, then, for the supplier? Could a supplier become certified to an environmental management system standard by concentrating on its customers' expectations? In theory, the answer is 'no', as, for example, ISO 14001 requires the organisation to address its own significant environmental impacts.

How an organisation determines the significance of an environmental impact will depend on many issues. The concerns of customers is one issue, but others such as legislation, local community concerns, investors and health of employees can be just as important. All these have to be considered, as well as the not unimportant issue of the actual or potential impact on the environment of an activity, product or service! In practice, current evidence does suggest that suppliers guided by customers towards environmental management are taking the decision on a commercial basis. The environmental scope then becomes as narrow and focused as that of quality.

Consider the case of an electronics components distributor (sixty employees) based in Buckinghamshire, UK (Hutchison 1997). It has become certified to ISO 14001, largely in response to customer pressure. Customer demand for recycled materials is the main motivating factor in considering environmental performance, with these customers also certified to ISO 14001. The organisation lists, as its three key environmental issues to address: waste, packaging and transport. It is interesting to note that these are issues that are all under the company's direct management control and therefore present an opportunity to address key internal value-added activities, such as cost savings and efficiency gains. However, on being questioned on what it regards as the main benefits to be gained from responding to customer pressure, the comments were as follows:

> An opportunity to cement our relationship with the customer.
>
> To keep the business . . . like we would address any other customer concern.

When questioned on the likely benefits to the customer, the organisation was unsure but felt it was likely to be reduced costs or liability.

As discussed above, the perception of value in addressing environmental issues can differ between customer and supplier. How effective will an environmental management system be that is run to satisfy customer demands as opposed to one that is motivated by internal considerations? It is often the case that quality management systems fail to deliver quality improvements because they are seen as an imposed bureaucratic cost rather than a tool to help drive the business. There is a real danger that, without an in-depth evaluation of the long-term costs and benefits of an environmental programme, ISO 14001 may follow a similar route.

The organisation did state that its actions were not symptomatic of the industry as a whole, although such actions are 'beginning to take root'. It could be that, as experience grows within the industry sector, then knowledge of the benefits of addressing environmental issues will accumulate and be put to a profitable use. At the moment, the organisation appears not to regard supply chain pressure as providing internal value other than the retention of the customer's business. Concentrating on ways of meeting the customers' environmental performance may obscure the real benefits to be gained from focusing on their own internal issues.

In many respects, it makes sense for organisations to utilise existing quality management systems in building environmental programmes. It also a fact of business life that suppliers will be expected to comply with many and various requirements from customers in order to maintain their custom. However, should customers look to suppliers as an integral part of environmental improvement, there needs to be an understanding on both sides of the value to be gained from these links. The quality management approach is known and understood, but if it is to result in real environmental improvement then the relationship must be on the basis that both customer and supplier are aware of why they are involved and what the benefits will be.

▌▌ *Conclusion*

For many organisations, the use of environmental purchasing criteria is a value-driven activity and the implication is that gains in environmental performance must be both economically feasible and in tune with overall business objectives. However, as purchasing pressure is driven by the customer's objectives, it is debatable whether this value is both understood or transferred to suppliers. As a consequence, suppliers will be driven by their customers' environmental objectives, which may take them away from areas of environmental performance most likely to add value for them.

Supply chain pressure will increase as the use of environmental management system standards spread, both horizontally across business sectors and vertically through product chains. Pressure is likely to spread upstream, affecting several layers of suppliers in the product chain.

The introduction of environmental purchasing is not essentially a new concept for many organisations, and it does not necessarily stand in isolation. For many organisations, environmental activities will be considered as an extension of quality management and be judged as such. It is unlikely that environmental issues will be the sole criteria for a purchase decision, but they will increasingly be used to define key purchasing objectives.

13 Global Environmental Management
An Opportunity for Partnerships[1]

Julie M. Haines

||| *The Environment and Sustainable Development*

With the globalisation of the world economy and pockets of exploding industrial growth, it is difficult to discuss the world marketplace without touching on the notion of sustainable development. Sustainable development not only means viable economic growth, but all aspects of sustainability, including the environment. With this phenomenon, global corporate leaders have carved an important niche—in promoting global environmental management practices, not only for their own facilities, but often for the industrial sectors in which they operate, including their horizontal and vertical partners, vendors and suppliers.

Promotion of sound environmental practices by corporate leaders should not be simply dismissed as self-interested protectionism or improving their own environmental competitiveness, it can also be seen as an altruistic move to promote a more harmonious balance between the industrial market and the world in which they operate. Whether the motive is self-interested or altruistic is not centrally important: what is most important is the result or benefit to the companies, the communities and the global environment.

The new emphasis on the environment is becoming increasingly evident in the multiple ways in which corporations are now promoting environmental management programmes. Many corporations have environmental mission statements; they have dedicated environmental, health and safety (EH&S) staff; they publish environmental reports; and they promote, fund and participate in community-based environmental initiatives. In GM's 1997 *Environmental Report*, such lofty ideals are not only articulated, but put into practice through their 'WE CARE' programme. In the global context, these global environmental programmes translate into practices that can potentially have a multiplier effect. In the developing world, large multinational corporations (MNCs) are increasingly committed to complying with

---

1. A wider discussion of the issues raised in this paper can be found in the report, *The Global Environmental Management Report: Candid Views of of Fortune 500 Companies*, prepared by Riva Krut and Carol Drummond for the US–Asia Environmental Partnership, October 1997.

❏ Apple Computer	❏ General Motors Corporation	❏ Motorola
❏ ARCO Chemical Company	❏ Georgia-Pacific Corporation	❏ NEC Corporation
❏ BankAmerica	❏ Hewlett Packard	❏ Nissan
❏ Bristol Myers Squibb	❏ ITT	❏ Occidental Petroleum Corporation
❏ Canon	❏ John Deere	❏ PPE
❏ Compaq Computer Corporation	❏ Kimberly Clark	❏ Premier Group
❏ Digital Equipment Corporation	❏ Korea Special Chemical Machinery Company	❏ Rockwell International
❏ Du Pont	❏ Lockheed Martin	❏ Tenneco Packaging
❏ Eastman Kodak	❏ Microsoft Corporation	❏ Texas Instruments
	❏ Monsanto	❏ Union Camp
		❏ Weyerhaeuser

Figure 1: The Thirty Companies Interviewed for the
Global Environmental Management Report

home-country standards when entering new markets, often introducing a new level of voluntary environmental performance based outside the traditional regulatory regime.

Based on an increasing number of private, market-based initiatives, the United States–Asia Environmental Partnership (US–AEP) developed the 'Clean Technology and Environmental Management' (CTEM) programme. The US–AEP is a US government interagency programme administered by the US Agency for International Development (USAID). The ten-year programme seeks to foster partnerships between the US and Asia as a means of promoting sustainable development. The CTEM programme of the US–AEP compliments a Public Policy Programme which concentrates on promoting sustainable development through enhancing partnerships between US and Asian government policy-makers, the general public and communities.

In a recent study initiated and sponsored by the CTEM programme, environmental managers and directors at thirty MNCs, all *Fortune 500* companies (see Fig. 1), were interviewed to identify their corporate environmental strategies and how these strategies effect corporate practice and performance. The study focused on voluntary environmental practices of companies: i.e. the activities that these corporations believe take them beyond compliance into a new level of commitment and consciousness about their own environmental performance. Also of interest was how, and if, their own internal environmental standards are transferable to others in their industries including their own supply chain. Voluntary environmental business standards appear to achieve great results, but can these voluntary programmes of large, resource-rich companies be translated effectively into supply chain environmental management programmes? The resulting publication, *The Global Environmental Management Report: Candid Views of Fortune 500 Companies* reveals many thoughts on this subject. The responses from the thirty MNCs proved that their views are as unique as their companies, but helps to identify trends and potential areas for increased partnership as the world looks for collaborative solutions to global environmental issues.

The US–AEP undertook the study in order to establish what a sample of global firms are doing in both corporate environmental management and supply chain management, and what relationship these programmes have to ISO 14001. The study was organised so that respondent firms answered four key questions that directly address those issues. Of particular interest to US–AEP was the reach of these global firms into the Asian marketplace, where development of an industrial base is growing faster—and is projected to grow faster in the next decades—than in any other geographic area in the world. Even with the financial crisis in Asia, these high, albeit slightly slowed, growth scenarios indicate that the industrial base will no doubt contribute significantly to the total pollution load of each country, the region, and globe. However, with the adoption of strong, market-based voluntary standards and global environmental management programmes to compliment regulatory regimes, the potential to reduce total pollution loads can also be significant. With this in mind, the *Global Environmental Management* report posed some basic questions of these global leaders:

> Do global US and Asian firms have environmental management systems? What is their reaction to ISO 14001?

> Do firms set supplier environmental conditions?

> Do firms set standards for supplier environmental management systems?

> Is ISO 14001 a supplier condition for business with global firms?

The study resulted in a variety of answers and situations; although each was unique, there are some notable trends in environmental management strategies. Most global firms do have formal EMSs in place and are well aware of ISO 14001 and its potential ramifications for the global marketplace. Firms are formulating strategic positions on ISO 14001 implementation, should it become a market condition, and often these leaders have extracted certain aspects of ISO 14001 to compliment and add value to their own customised EMSs. The issue of supply chain environmental management is not nearly as far along in its evolution as the use of corporate EMS. Whereas there are small pockets of industrial leaders in specific sectors (automobiles, computers and electronics, textiles, and chemicals) that are leading the trends in outreach and standard-setting for their supply base, most supplier criteria are linked specifically to product specifications rather than environmental performance. No firm interviewed absolutely requires ISO 14001 certification as a criterion for continued business relationships; however, a small minority of firms are exploring the possibility of requesting ISO 14001 being utilised by suppliers, more for compliance and performance assurances rather than for certification. These results are certainly worth a closer look.

▌ Do Global US and Asian Firms Have Environmental Management Systems? What is their Reaction to ISO 14001?

The study shows clearly that most of the firms do indeed have elaborate EMSs that have been developed and customised over time, and that these firms do not consider

EMSs to be synonymous with ISO 14001. Dwane Marshall, Union Camp's Director, Corporate Office of Environmental Affairs, states:

> There is a tendency, an inappropriate one in my belief, to consider environmental management systems and a certifiable ISO 14001 programme as being synonymous . . . Union Camp's environmental management 'culture' has evolved over two decades and led to a collection of practices which we would characterise as our environmental management system. In many respects, that system parallels some features of the ISO 14001 standard.

Union Camp, after commissioning a consultant to undertake a gap analysis, found that no significant gaps exist between their internal system and ISO 14001 requirements, and indeed the Union Camp EMS posed no barriers to meeting the intent of an ISO 14001 system. Mr Marshall goes on to say that, although it is conceivable that ISO will become a competitive feature in the marketplace, Union Camp has not yet experienced any significant customer pull for ISO 14001 certification.

Other firms espouse beliefs that ISO 14001, although not the only way to implement an environmental management system, is an appropriate EMS solution with global application to their company. These firms, such as Rockwell International, are using ISO 14001 as a management tool that not only puts in place proactive environmental programmes, but offers a competitive advantage. In the interview with Rockwell International's Vice President for EH&S, Dr Reisenweber, he states that Rockwell's customers, particularly in Europe are beginning to demand ISO 14001 certification, but it is unclear whether those same demands are heard in the US and Asia. However, Dr Reisenweber makes it clear that Rockwell's decision to become ISO 14001 certified was not based on real or perceived customer demand—rather, Rockwell International's corporate decision to be proactive and a leader on major environmental initiatives, such as ISO. At the time of the interview, Rockwell did not have plans to require ISO 14001 certification of its supply base.

Not all the respondent firms agree that ISO 14001 certification is becoming a customer demand or even a competitive advantage. For example, Motorola currently perceives no customer demand for ISO 14001 certification. Du Pont, which has based its corporate EMS on the chemical industry's Responsible Care Programme rather than on ISO 14001, does see a potential competitive advantage in Asia and therefore is certifying facilities only in that region. Lockheed Martin Corporation officials believe that ISO 14001 is a competitive advantage within the electronics sector, and assert that there exists a growing sense that it will evolve into a customer requirement. To this end, Lockheed has announced that it expects to complete certification to ISO 14001 by mid-1998, but only for its electronics facilities.

Clearly, the debate continues to rage as to market pressures that exist for the voluntary ISO 14001 certification: consensus can not even be reached within a single industry sector. Although Lockheed's prediction that ISO 14001 certification will be important in the electronics sectors is impetus enough for them to act, interviews with Microsoft, Motorola, Apple and Digital show that these firms in the same sector have not experienced any indication that their customers will require ISO

❑ *Does your company have an environmental programme?*

❑ *Does your company have written environmental procedures?*

❑ *Has a summary of legal requirements applicable to your operation been compiled?*

❑ *Do you have environmental goals?*

❑ *Do you have a pollution prevention programme?*

❑ *Do you have an emergency response plan?*

❑ *Has an environmental audit been conducted in the last three years?*

❑ *Has an environmental assessment been conducted in the last three years?*

❑ *Has the company made a determination of whether any environmental approvals or permits may be required by law or regulations?*

Figure 2: Questions Eastman-Kodak is Developing for Key Suppliers

certification. The complexities in the marketplace and the difficulty of making strategic decisions in such a context continue to plague environmental managers. Another interesting question for these same managers is the relevance environmental standards should play among suppliers.

❙❙❙ Do Firms Set Supplier Environmental Conditions?

Answers to this question were quite varied. Clearly, firms are concerned that suppliers meet 'environmental requirements' that are driven by regulations. These requirements tend to be centred around packaging, recycled paper content and ozone-depleting chemical specifications. Firms will also uphold standards for product content that tend to minimise environmental impact, such as prohibiting the use of cadmium or lead-based materials; however, these specifications are frequently tied to a regulatory requirement which may be a prerequisite for the sale of goods by the MNC in a particular market or geographic region.

Although the majority of firms tend not to monitor, audit or specify environmental *standards* or *conduct* in any way for suppliers, these same firms do tend to ask environment-related *questions* of their suppliers. Eastman Kodak Corporation seems to be one firm on the leading edge of understanding supplier environmental programmes, although it does not impose standards or specify environmental conduct. Eastman Kodak is currently developing a series of questions that they will put to key suppliers, which not only includes permitting and compliance issues, but goes beyond the compliance arena (see Fig. 2).

Whereas it appears that most MNCs do not specify environmental criteria or standards specifically for the environment, many firms ask their suppliers about environmental performance. Almost regardless of the answer, however, firms tend to purchase from suppliers based mostly on price and quality drivers, except in some emerging arenas. Apart from the electronics and computer industry, as well as some ground-breaking supply chain programmes in clothing and textiles, most firms are adopting a 'wait-and-see' attitude. If indeed customers demand that MNCs accept accountability for suppliers' environmental performance, these firms will be ready to act. Who will pay for it? Ultimately, the customers who demand it.

▍ Do Firms Set Standards for Supplier Environmental Management Systems? Is ISO 14001 a Supplier Condition for Business with Global Firms?

The strong majority of firms are not currently requiring ISO 14001 certification or specifying voluntary environmental standards for their supply chain; however, it is clearly an emerging issue. Some companies, such as Nissan Corporation, have announced that they intend to become fully ISO 14001 certified, and will expect it of their suppliers. But, at this point in time, Nissan is in the minority of companies towing a hard line. Others have taken a somewhat softer tact. General Motors Corporation, for example, is merely encouraging suppliers to evaluate the benefits of implementing structured EMSs, using ISO 14001 as one potential model. Although GM is not requiring ISO 14001 certification, it does have numerous supplier programmes that focus on performance improvement. To this end, GM has recently completed a multi-industry benchmarking study to learn about additional methods for improving overall supplier environmental performance. It is likely that the benchmarking study could result in newly structured supplier outreach programmes for GM and others who participated.

There are also many experimental supplier programmes that exist today. In addition to voluntary internal programmes, such as Responsible Care and the CERES (Coalition of Environmentally Responsible Economies and Societies) principles, there are pockets of MNCs that are coming together to standardise supplier reporting information, often specifying environmental standards that must be met. The Computer Industry Quality Council (CIQC) is one of these groups. Comprised of fifteen to twenty of the largest computer companies in the world (Apple, Compaq, Hewlett Packard, IBM, Sun Microsystems and others), the CIQC, in collaboration with the Pacific Industry Business Association (PIBA), has developed a supply chain management standard for environmental performance, which, coincidentally, is called CIQC 0014 and, like ISO 14001, focuses entirely on environmental management. Suppliers, frustrated by the barrage of environmental questionnaires from their customers, appear to welcome this standard which provides a common tool for gathering and reporting environmental information. Through these standard CIQC 0014 reporting mechanisms, the MNC buyers are assured that suppliers are meeting compliance standards, which ISO 14001 will not guarantee.

▍ The Bottom Line

While it is true that the 'bottom line' is still by far the most significant driver for all action in the corporate industrial world, more than ever corporate bottom lines are being affected by the environmental performance of their own facilities and that of their affiliates. After undertaking this study, what do we know?

▶ Large, resource-rich corporations use environmental management systems not only as a way of meeting regulatory requirements, but to manage production better, reduce risk and liability, and improve their bottom lines.

▶ MNCs have a tremendous amount of leverage when it comes to promoting certain behaviours within the marketplace. Smaller corporations will often look toward MNCs, who can typically set performance standards for the rest of the industry and provide guidance and incentives.

▶ Supply chain management is a fairly new initiative, but seems to be gaining momentum. Large firms are concerned with key supplier environmental performance and are starting to experiment with supplier outreach programmes and standards for their supply chain.

▶ ISO 14001 offers some solutions for EMSs, but is not the only effective tool. Most MNCs utilise the 'smart' parts of ISO 14001 to customise their own systems, and only a small minority of firms are requesting ISO 14001 certification of their supply base.

▌▌ *Opportunities for Partnerships*

The industrial world has changed significantly in the last two decades, and newly emerging environmental awareness around the globe offers additional momentum for increased change in the years to come. In regions of the world with strong regulatory regimes, voluntary programmes appear to offer the 'icing on the cake' for industrial leaders looking for competitive advantage and beyond-compliance status. In the developing world, voluntary environmental programmes also have a important role. In the absence of a developed or strong regulatory environment, market-based programmes and market pressures can lead to industrial behaviour change. In Asia, ISO 14001 has attracted more attention than in many other areas of the world because it is viewed as a potential barrier to trade. Asian industrialists, eager to reach the world market, keep a vigilant watch over real or perceived market trends that could potentially impact their export markets. Over the last few years, environmental performance is increasingly becoming a real issue for industry as many MNCs set expected behavioural standards and the public watches closely.

Governments have a key role in this evolution of environmental performance through partnership programmes or regulatory relief programmes. Particularly relevant in the developing world, a strong market push for environmental standards and performance made by industrial buyers and the public may decrease the pressure on the already overburdened government policy-makers and environmental enforcers. It is also through these outreach programmes and voluntary systems that information is efficiently shared through vertical and horizontal business relationships, where ideas *can* 'change the world'.

Section 3
Innovations

14
The Green Purchasing Network, Japan

Hiroyuki Sato

‖ *Outline*

The Green Purchasing Network (GPN) was established in February 1996 to promote green purchasing in Japan. As of April 1998, it has over 1,300 member organisations, including corporations, local autonomous bodies, consumer groups, environmental NGOs and co-operative associations. The GPN promotes and disseminates green purchasing practices, draws up purchasing guidelines for each type of product, publishes *Environmental Data Books* on various products, holds seminars and study meetings, and awards commendations to organisations that have shown outstanding performance in implementing green purchasing.

‖ *Background of the GPN's Establishment and its History*

Developing a sustainable society has emerged as a global issue, and in order to attain this goal it is necessary to minimise the environmental load of all products and services that we are currently using. Within the current market economy system, it is important that consumers, corporations and government organisations place priority on the purchase of products that have less impact on the environment. This is called 'green purchasing'. The promotion of green purchasing will influence corporate activities in the market and encourage businesses to develop products that reduce the environmental load.

A series of 'Meetings Regarding the New Movement toward Environmentally Conscious Products' were held by the Environment Agency of Japan between 1994 and 1995, in which it was suggested that green purchasing should be actively promoted. In response, preparations for setting up a network to promote green purchasing were begun in the spring of 1995, primarily by the Environment Agency.

In February 1996, a number of organisations and individuals gathered in Tokyo to set up the Green Purchasing Network (GPN): forty major Japanese companies, including NEC, Matsushita Electric Industrial, Sony, Fuji Xerox, Suntory, Tokyo Gas, Marubeni, Shimizu Corp. and Mitsubishi Estate; the Environment Agency and nineteen local government bodies, including Saitama Prefecture, Shiga Prefecture, Yokohama City, Kobe City and Nagoya City; thirteen consumer groups and environmental NGOs, including World Wide Fund for Nature Japan Committee (WWF-J); Japanese Consumers' Co-operative Union; and eight academics and experts.

Purpose and Structure of the GPN

The GPN consists of member organisations that have decided to support green purchasing. The purpose of the GPN is to disseminate the concept and practice of green purchasing among all organisations and consumers. Established with 73 member organisations, the GPN has received much attention from various fields, and the number of member organisations has been continually increasing, rising up to over 1,300, including 820 corporations, 210 government organisations and 170 consumer groups and environmental NGOs, as of April 1998. These member corporations encompass all types of business and range from major companies with tens of thousands of employees to small and medium-sized enterprises.

The GPN is managed by a board of directors composed of 24 directors selected from the original member organisations, including corporations, government organisations, consumer groups and environmental NGOs, and academics and experts. The secretariat office is located at Japan Environment Association (JEA) in Tokyo. The GPN receives financial support from the government and various foundations, and collect fees that members pay to receive reference materials and to attend seminars.

Activities of the GPN

Establishment of the 'Principles of Green Purchasing'

One of the GPN's first activities after its establishment was to summarise the basic ideas of green purchasing into principles. In order to accomplish this, a study group was set up under the board of directors and a proposal was presented to members on two occasions, in order to collect various opinions and suggestions. The principles were officially established in November 1996.

The first principle presented was to 'note the environmental impact of a product at all stages of its life-cycle'. It was followed by eight detailed proposals including: (1) reducing harmful substances and chemicals; (2) resource and energy conservation; (3) the use of component materials that can be obtained on a sustainable basis; (4) selecting products that have long service lives; (5) selecting re-usable products; (6) selecting recyclable products; (7) promoting the use of recycled materials; and (8) low-impact disposal and treatment. Principle 2 is aimed at corporations' and distributors' environmental conservation efforts, while Principle 3 promotes the gathering and application of environmental information when purchasing products. (The 'Principles of Green Purchasing' are outlined in Appendix 1.)

These principles were established as matters to be considered when purchasing all kinds of product. To promote green purchasing, the GPN distributes easy-to-understand pamphlets that explain these principles, which are actually reflected in the green purchasing policies drawn up by many member companies and government bodies.

⫼ *Drawing up 'Purchasing Guidelines' for Each Type of Product*

The GPN has been drawing up specific purchasing guidelines for each type of product, based on the basic principles of green purchasing. In November 1996, the guidelines for purchasing 'paper for printers and other office machines' and 'copying machines, printers and facsimile machines' was completed. The guidelines for purchasing 'personal computers', 'toilet paper' and 'tissue paper' were established in November 1997, and guidelines for 'refrigerators' were completed in February 1998. The guidelines list considerations that should be addressed when making purchases, and encourage buyers to select products with less environmental impact.

The guidelines for purchasing 'paper for printers and other office machines' highlights four criteria: (1) high recycled content; (2) low level of whiteness; (3) low level of surface coating; and (4) lack of special coating, such as plastic (see Appendix 2).

The guidelines for purchasing 'copying machines, printers and facsimile machines' addresses energy conservation, two-sided copy functions, emission of ozone, recyclable designs, collection and recycling of used products and cartridges, use of re-usable parts and recycled materials, and avoiding the use of selenium (see Appendix 3).

The GPN is currently developing guidelines for the purchase of stationery and office supplies, washing machines, and light bulbs and lighting equipment. There are also plans to draw up as soon as possible guidelines for the purchase of cars, TV sets, air conditioners, office furniture and clothes, as well as considerations for the use of various services. These guidelines will be revised as needed in accordance with changes in social conditions and the development of new technologies.

Characteristics and Principles of the Guidelines. Guidelines are set up in accordance with 'Principle 1' and with consideration for a product's entire life-cycle. It should be noted that GPN guidelines do not set standards for products with reduced environmental impact, but rather propose desirable approaches to purchasing in terms of environmental preservation, and encourage buyers to follow the guidelines to every extent possible in order to select superior products. For example, the guidelines for paper suggest the use of products that 'contain as much recycled paper as possible', but do not specify criteria to indicate the desirable minimum percentage. Also, the guidelines for copying machines address low electricity consumption, but do not specify the maximum number of watts.

Setting criteria may be helpful for buyers and producers. However, unless these values are continually revised, producers or buyers will not be motivated to make the extra effort to produce or purchase better products. Also, if the criterion for electric consumption is set at 100 W, a product that consumes 102 W will be eliminated from the list of recommended products, despite the fact that the 2 W difference may be within an acceptable range when considering differences in the functions and quality among products.

For this reason, the GPN does not intend to include specific criteria in its guidelines, except for cases in which distinct, recommendable criteria can be set up.

Method Used to Draw up Guidelines. A special task group is organised for each type of product in order to draw up guidelines. Any member is free to join the task group. Companies producing or using the product, government organisations, consumer groups, environmental NGOs and experts also join the task groups to discuss the issue over a six-month period.

There have not been many opportunities in Japan for people with different viewpoints or opinions—companies, consumers and environmental NGOs in particular—to discuss the issues at the same table in a frank and practical manner in order to reach consensus. This has created unnecessary confrontations and distance between the parties. In this sense, the GPN provides an important opportunity for people involved in the same issues to understand each other's positions and technical developments, and reach mutual consensus.

Drafts made by task groups are widely distributed via fax and the Internet. After receiving the various inputs, the board of directors officially establishes guidelines.

▐▐ *Publishing Environmental Data Books to Assist in Comparing and Selecting Products*

In June 1997, the GPN published two guides under the title *Environmental Data Book for Appropriate Product Selection* (hereinafter referred to as the *Data Book*): one for 'paper for printers and other office machines' and the other for 'copying machines, printers and facsimile machines'. These *Data Books* compare specific environmental data on each product in accordance with the purchasing guidelines; they serve as important tools for the GPN in the dissemination of green purchasing information.

In the 'paper for printers and other office machines' version, data such as the recycled content, whiteness level, volume of surface coating and the use of special coatings, etc. are presented for about 200 products, covering the majority of products of this kind available in the Japanese market. In the 'copying machines, printers and facsimile machines' version, information on about 300 products is presented regarding the efficiency of energy consumption, compliance with international 'Energy Star' standards, two-sided copying functions, recyclable designs, the use of re-usable parts and recycled plastic, etc. The book covers most products of its kind currently in use in most offices (see Fig. 1).

The GPN is planning to publish *Data Books* on all types of product for which guidelines have been established. For 1998, *Data Books* are planned on the subjects of 'personal computers', 'toilet paper and tissue paper', 'refrigerators', 'washing machines', 'stationery and office supplies' and 'light bulbs and lighting equipment'.

Characteristics and Principles of the *Data Books*. The products presented in GPN *Data Books* are not being *recommended* by the GPN. The *Data Books* simply compare and analyse environmental data for each product, with the final decision to be made by each buyer. By comparing the data, readers can discover for themselves which products are superior, but of course products may often perform well under one criterion (for example, electricity consumption) but not under another (for example, recyclability). Therefore, it is necessary to consider all aspects in order to make an overall evaluation, and the choice is not always straightforward.

It is here that the GPN's method of providing information differs from eco-label systems, such as Japan's 'Eco Mark' or Germany's 'Blue Angel'. The eco-label system sets up quantitative criteria and provides labels for products that comply, making it a very easy-to-understand system. Broadly speaking, eco-labels are more useful for individual consumers, while the GPN *Data Books* may be more suitable for organisational buyers

	Company	#2	#3	#4	#5	#6	#7	#8		#9	#10	#11
Product A	W											
Product B	X											
Product C	Y											
Product D	Y											
Product E	Z											
Product F	X											
Product G	W											
...												

#2 Copy speed (sheets/minute)	#7 Use of recycled plastic
#3 Energy consumption efficiency (Wh)	#8 Recyclability of toner cartridges
#4 Compliance with the 'Energy Star' standards	#9 Special note (brief description)
#5 Off-mode consumption of electricity (W)	#10 Standard retail price (¥)
#6 Two-sided copy function	#11 Telephone number for enquiries

Figure 1: Descriptions of Copying Machines, as Presented in the *Environmental Data Book*

looking for guidance. The GPN is interested in feedback from *Data Book* users in order to maintain as effective a service as possible.

Method Used to Compile the *Data Books*. In compiling *Data Books*, the GPN uses data acquired directly from the manufacturers themselves; it does not attempt to verify the information. However, if any information is found to be false or exaggerated, it is likely that the company that provided the information will be punished by the market. Companies that provide information are also obliged to respond to further inquiries from *Data Book* users, enabling purchasers to gain a complete understanding of the product before making a decision. In addition, some products are rapidly replaced with new models (information on products such as computer goods may be obsolete within only six months) so the *Data Books* are revised annually.

Effect of the *Data Books*. Although the range of products presented is still limited, the *Data Books* are already being widely used. Although it may be too early to decide conclusively, it appears that they are already exerting an influence on manufacturers. Since they are setting a precedent in comparing the environmental performance of products from different companies, the *Data Books* are receiving attention from these companies and industry sectors in general, and provide a spur for improvement. Enquiries are being made—and orders being placed—on the basis of information presented in the *Data Books*, so their influence in the market is already apparent.

⫼ *Using the Internet*

The GPN has opened a home page on the Internet,[1] which presents current activities, a list of members, guidelines, and product information available in the *Data Books*.

The *Data Books* are scheduled to be published annually, while product information on the home page is updated several times each year. Once a manufacturer is registered, it can input its latest product information onto the GPN database via the Internet. Also, users can customise the search criteria when scanning the database.

⫼ *Promotion and Dissemination of Green Purchasing*

Green purchasing must guide corporate activities throughout the market, so it is essential to promote green purchasing principles among influential organisations as well as end-customers. Promotion and dissemination of green purchasing principles is key to GPN activities, along with provision of detailed information, as described above.

A large-scale nationwide forum is held annually in Tokyo. In addition, many forums and exhibitions of environmentally friendly products are held in Osaka, Kyushu, Kyoto, Sendai and various other places in order to promote the idea of green purchasing throughout Japan. The GPN is also engaged in the following activities to promote green purchasing:

- Present cases showing the implementation of green purchasing
- Award commendations to GPN members that participate in green purchasing activities
- Draw up guidelines for the introduction of green purchasing policies in corporations and government organisations
- Publish newsletters (four times a year)
- Produce and distribute promotional posters
- Produce illustrated pamphlets to explain green purchasing
- Use questionnaires to conduct a survey on the current status of green purchasing and related problems, and to elicit requests for GPN participation
- Send instructors to seminars
- Survey overseas conditions
- Conduct public relations activities focused on the mass media, etc.

⫼ **Dissemination of Green Purchasing in Japan**

Concurrent with the establishment of the GPN, there is a growing interest in green purchasing issues in Japan generally. Local autonomous bodies and major companies in particular are demonstrating a move towards implementing green purchasing. Green purchasing as an issue is often featured on TV or in the press, and it is often chosen as a theme for seminars sponsored by companies or the government.

---

1. The address is *http://www.wnn.or.jp/wnn-eco/gpn/* (at present, only in Japanese).

▌▌ Government Activities

Since the current market for certain environmentally preferable goods, such as recycled products or low-pollution vehicles, is limited, they are difficult to obtain and their prices are high in some cases. However, these products may be purchased in bulk by local autonomous bodies implementing public policies. If a government organisation provides the initial demand, the market will grow and the products will become more competitive.

The local government body in Shiga Prefecture, home to Lake Biwa, Japan's largest freshwater lake, has been addressing the issue of green purchasing for some time. In 1994, Shiga Prefecture established 'guidelines for purchasing environmentally friendly products' with the idea of compiling a unique list of recommended environmentally friendly products, in order to promote green purchasing as a prefecture-wide project.

Out of 59 prefectures and designated large cities, including Shiga Prefecture, forty have joined the GPN. More than fifty organisations are implementing or planning some sort of green purchasing activity, including promoting the use of recycled paper. The largest governmental body is the Tokyo Metropolitan Office, which has established guidelines for the use of recycled goods in order to promote the use of recycled paper and reconditioned tyres. Osaka Prefecture promotes green purchasing through its 'Eco Action Plan' and has announced its objective of using 100% recycled paper for all copy paper by 2001. Kyoto, Japan's ancient capital city, has been designating environmentally friendly paper and office supplies since 1997, and these have already replaced existing products in half of the areas. Also, small and medium-sized government bodies, such as Musashino City and Kamakura City, are also actively supporting green purchasing.

In the initial activity plan approved by the cabinet council meeting in June 1995, the national government also discussed green purchasing. Objective values were established for recycled paper in the plan. Currently, guidelines for each type of product and a list of recommended products are being created mainly by the Environment Agency. If green purchasing is promoted by the national government, it will probably encourage local autonomous bodies to tackle the issue.

▌▌ Company Activities

Many corporations—electrical and electronic equipment manufacturers in particular—that have been actively supporting environmental management are implementing the principles of green purchasing. Many of them buy greener parts and materials to enable them to produce and market environmentally conscious products themselves.

NEC, a company well known for its advanced environmental management activities, decided to implement the principles of green purchasing in September 1996. It organised a working group to discuss ways of implementing green purchasing for office supplies and production materials, and started fully-fledged green purchasing activities from June 1997. The green purchasing standard for supplies defines designs for energy conservation, recyclability, etc. in relation to contents of harmful substances and chemicals in products, and also defines criteria for suppliers' management policy in terms of environmental considerations. NEC also surveys its business suppliers using questionnaires in order to develop a database for environmental information and establish a system for using such information in the design and materials purchasing divisions.

Cannon also set up standards for green purchasing in August 1997, and informed its business partners of its decision to tackle green purchasing on a global scale for all items, including materials and office supplies. In its standards, Cannon mentions that it evaluates the corporate structures of its business partners as well as their products, and presents a list of harmful substances and chemicals that the company believes should be prohibited or reduced.

In addition, many companies in different industries, including Tokyo Gas, Fuji Xerox, Sony, Matsushita Electric Industrial, NKK, JDC Corp. (construction company), Japan Tobacco, etc. are setting up green purchasing policies beginning with paper and office supplies, and production materials.

▌▌ Utilisation of GPN information

The government bodies and companies mentioned above utilise GPN's 'Principle 1', purchasing guidelines and *Data Books* in order to set up basic policies and guidelines, or to select products. Autonomous bodies and GPN-member companies are looking to the GPN to create more guidelines and *Data Books* for office suppliers, etc.

▌▌ Obstacles to Implementing Green Purchasing

According to a summer 1997 questionnaire-based survey of members conducted by the GPN, the most serious obstacle to green purchasing was that 'environmentally conscious products are expensive'. To overcome this, it is necessary to expand the market and bring prices down, and to provide some sorts of tax benefit. The second most frequently mentioned problem was that 'companies and government bodies have not established appropriate systems within their own organisations'. Green purchasing is usually initiated by an organisation's environmental section. To address green purchasing throughout the organisation, however, an extensive horizontal network must be set up that involves the purchasing section, for example. The GPN plans to study cases in which such a network has been developed, and summarise the expertise gained from these cases as the basis of implementation guidelines.

▌▌ Outlook

Green purchasing is currently being disseminated among government bodies and companies throughout Japan. Although the green purchasing movement is currently exerting influence on manufacturers via the market for copy paper and office supplies, it is expected that green purchasing will disseminate more extensively in the future. Although comparatively large autonomous bodies and corporations have initiated green purchasing initiatives in the past, the key to future success depends on the dissemination of green purchasing widely among small and medium-sized companies and individual consumers.

The Green Purchasing Network will continue to provide information by drawing up guidelines and guidebooks for each type of product, while expanding its activities to promote green purchasing among the 120 million consumers and various kinds of organisations in Japan.

Appendix 1: *Principles of Green Purchasing*

As environmental problems have become increasingly serious worldwide, achieving a sustainable society has emerged as a global issue. In order to make this goal a reality, consumers should recognise that all the products and services (which, along with any containers and packaging, are referred to commonly as 'products' in these guidelines) we consider indispensable to our lives and economic activities entail a certain environmental impact, and that the concerted efforts of all can do much to help minimise this impact.

As consumers, we should carefully evaluate our need for a product before we purchase it. Once committed to a purchase, however, we should then try to implement the principles of green purchasing; that is, we should give priority to buying products that entail the lowest environmental impact. At the same time, we should remain aware of ways of reducing the adverse environmental impact of products both during and after their use.

The following are some of the basic tenets of green purchasing. They have been formulated to inform individuals and organisations who are energetically and voluntarily attempting to follow the principles of green purchasing.

1. Note the environmental impact of a product at all stages of its life-cycle. Buy a product only after considering its cumulative environmental impact, from the processing of its raw materials to its disposal.
Consumers should gain a full understanding of the various aspects of a product's environmental impact, including emission of greenhouse gases and ozone-depleting substances; pollution of the air, water and soil; and waste generation. We should also consider the seriousness and geographical extent of the environmental effects and the length of time required for the effects to be remedied.

In some cases, even though the environmental impact at one stage of a product's life-cycle may be small, the impact at other stages may be so large that, over the entire life-cycle of the product, the environmental impact is serious. As a result, it is essential that we examine the environmental impact of a product over its entire life-cycle—including the gathering of raw materials, production, distribution, use, disposal and recycling.

The following are some concrete examples of the factors that should be considered when purchasing a product.

Reducing harmful substances and chemicals. Select products that use and emit fewer substances that damage the environment or human health. Consumers should prefer products that use or emit fewer or no substances that may be harmful to the environment or human health, such as ozone-depleting substances, heavy metals and organochlorine compounds. Moreover, consumers should determine whether the emission of substances such as greenhouse gases and nitrogen oxides are limited as much as possible during various stages of the product's life-cycle.

Resource and energy conservation. Select resource-efficient and energy-conserving products. At their present rate of consumption, some metal resources and fossil fuels may be exhausted within several decades. Excessive use of fossil fuels such as oil and coal produce atmospheric emissions of carbon dioxide, a greenhouse gas, and accelerate global warming. Accordingly, we should select products that are made from and consume fewer resources and less energy during their use or distribution.

Avoiding depletion of resource. Select products whose component materials were obtained in a sustainable manner and used effectively. Some natural resources, such as forest resources, can be obtained on a sustainable basis if properly managed. If such resources are used in production, confirm that they are obtained on a sustainable basis, that the influence on the ecological system is minimised, and that the resources are used effectively.

Product serviceability. Select products that provide a long service life. Before purchasing consumer durables, note the ease of repair and parts replacement, the length of the maintenance and repair period, and the extendibility of functions. Model changes that promote frequent replacement should be avoided.

Re-usability. Select re-usable products. For containers, packaging and parts of consumer durables, products are considered to be re-usable as part of an environmentally sound system when they are used repeatedly in the same form for the same application following separation, washing and refilling processes. Consequently, one should determine whether a product is designed as re-usable or confirm the existence of recovery and recycling systems that can be easily used by consumers.

Recyclability. Select recyclable products. When re-use is impossible, a valid alternative is recycling, in which non-re-usable goods are decommissioned, disassembled and separated into elements that are then recycled as materials for various applications. Accordingly, consumers should check whether easily recyclable materials are used, whether the product is designed for easy decommissioning and disassembly, and whether consumer-accessible recovery and recycling systems are available.

Promoting recycling and re-use. Select products containing a high percentage of recycled materials or re-used parts. Buying products containing a high percentage of recovered and recycled materials and parts from homes, offices and factories contributes to resource recovery and reduced consumption of natural resources. Some consumer durables can be re-used following the simple replacement of supplies or damaged parts, and without specialised processing. The purchase of these reconditioned products is therefore essential.

Low-impact disposal and treatment. Select products that ensure trouble-free disposal and treatment. In spite of great efforts to re-use and recycle, some products inevitably end up incinerated or buried. Consumers should carefully note the design of products and choose those that minimise the impact on incineration facilities or landfill sites.

2. Assess corporate policies and activities. Select products manufactured and distributed by corporations with an active interest in environmental conservation.

In addition to assessing the products themselves, consumers should assess the environmental attitudes of businesses themselves when determining which products to buy. In other words, one must determine whether the company has adopted environmentally sound business policies and systems, has implemented proper environmental management and auditing, discloses environmental information, is actively committed to environmental conservation, and conforms to laws and regulations concerning the environment.

3. Gather and apply environmental information. Evaluate products by collecting environmental information on the products, manufacturers and distributors.

In determining which products to buy, consumers should actively gather environmental information from a wide range of sources, including: product labels; information disclosed in company promotional material; product purchasing guidelines (i.e. those that propose approaches to the purchase of particular types of product) and consumer guides (i.e. those that evaluate products comparatively by their performance and convenience), both of which are provided by the Green Purchasing Network; and eco-label certifications and assessments by third parties. Where information is insufficient, requesting the disclosure of environmental information from manufacturers and distributors is essential.[2]

2.   The principles listed in the appendices were established on 7 November 1996. They may be revised as necessary according to changes in social conditions and new information.

Appendix 2:

Guidelines for Purchasing Paper for Office Machines and Printing Paper (GPN-GL1)

1. *Scope*

This document lists important guidelines that should be considered from environmental points of view when purchasing paper for office machines (plain paper for copiers, printers and faxes) or printing paper.

2. *Guidelines*

When purchasing paper for office machines (plain paper for copiers, printers and faxes) or printing paper, the following guidelines should be considered to reduce their impact on the environment.

Both paper for office machines and printing paper will:

1. Be blended with a maximum of waste paper
2. Have low brightness

Printing paper will:

3. Have less surface coating
4. Not have any plastic coating that prevents ease of recycling

Appendix 3: *Guidelines for Purchasing Copiers, Laser Printers, Laser Faxes and Multifunctional Machines (GPN-GL2)*

1. *Scope*

This document lists important guidelines that should be considered from environmental points of view when purchasing copiers (using plain paper), laser printers, laser faxes or multifunctional devices. The guidelines cover those machines that are used mainly in offices, not including ink-jet printers, thermal faxes and colour copiers.

2. *Guidelines*

When purchasing a copier (plain paper), laser printer, laser fax or multifunctional device (all hereafter referred to as 'the machine'), the following guidelines should be considered to reduce their impacts on the environment:

1. The machine will consume as little power as possible during operation. The copier will have a low 'energy consumption rate' as stipulated in the Law Concerning the Rational Use of Energy.

2. The machine will include a function for automatically switching it into low-power or power-off mode a certain time after it has become inactive. (For all machines except multifunctional devices, the 'Energy Star' logo indicates the machine has such a function.)

3. The machine will have a two-sided copying/printing function.

4. The machine will emit low amounts of ozone during operation.

5. The machine will be designed to ensure that, at the end of its life, it can be easily disassembled and its parts or materials can easily be recycled.

6. The machine, at the end of its life, will be recovered; many of its parts will be re-used for new products; and others will be recycled as materials.

7. The machine will incorporate recycled parts and/or materials.

8. Regarding any machine that uses harmful selenium in its photo-sensitive drum, that substance will be properly recovered and recycled.

9. The used toner cartridge of the machine will be properly recovered and recycled.

15 The European Green Purchasing Network
Addressing Purchasers across Sectors and Boundaries

Raymond van Ermen and Arndt Mielisch

‖ Introduction

How do we in society currently attempt to achieve sustainable production and consumption? Businesses seek certification for their environmental management activities and develop models of product stewardship; different tiers of government use their purchasing power as a means of stimulating life-cycle analysis and innovative markets; consumer and other non-governmental organisations work with retailers to promote the availability of greener products.

However, so far, most of these activities are carried out in isolation. In response, the European Green Purchasing Network was launched on 3rd December 1997 to facilitate a joint purchasing initiative involving various stakeholders, including the public and private sector and governmental and non-governmental organisations. It follows the example set by the Japanese Green Purchasing Network which was formed in 1996 to promote the supply and the purchase of green products (see Chapter 14).

‖ Green Purchasing and Sustainable Consumerism

While it is true that budgeting of resources must take into account all phases of the product life-cycle, the link between suppliers and consumers is pivotal to the emergence of greener economies. It is at the point where production and consumption meet that appropriate signals for eco-innovative products must be given. Purchasers—domestic, public or corporate—can help decrease the environmental burden by carefully reviewing their consumption patterns; by opting for alternative, ecologically intelligent solutions to satisfy their organisations' needs; by selecting alternative environmentally preferable products; and by making a point of using them.

Purchasers can play a substantial role in creating a market for eco-innovative products and promoting eco-design of products. Recycled paper, for instance, has become the standard choice for offices in some European countries owing to the cumulative demand from public authorities. Their initiative has affected domestic as well as industrial consumers, which has given recycled paper a significant competitive lead. One important spin-off was that the electronics industry began to develop a new generation of office equipment adjusted to the use of recycled paper. In most

European countries recycled paper is now cheaper than virgin paper. In addition, recycled material can become marketable in new product areas once the negative stigma of recycled products is removed.

The European Green Purchasing Network focuses on purchasers' roles in implementing greener production and consumption policies. Purchasers are broadly defined as individuals having responsibilities as purchasing officers, marketing managers, or staff otherwise responsible for purchasing decisions, public or private.

III *Professional Characteristics*

Professional purchasers act on behalf of an organisational entity within which they fulfil several functions; in particular:

▶ Managing existing stock and assessing its cost

▶ Managing the flow of incoming products

▶ Specifying products, services and the organisation's potential suppliers

▶ Selecting those suppliers that offer the most favourable conditions for large purchasing transactions

▶ Co-operating with various departments in formulating their product needs and expectations

▶ Co-ordinating action with financial controllers and obtaining authorisation for purchases

▶ Undertaking the actual purchasing or contract transaction

▶ Working with suppliers to create solid business relationships

The mechanics of the purchaser's job depends on the way purchasing is arranged within the organisation as a whole. In central purchasing units, the purchaser acts as a kind of facilitator between the organisation's needs and the (potential) suppliers. In local authorities especially, the gamut of product and contract transactions handled is wide and includes the purchase of tangible and capital goods, as well as awarding service, maintenance and work contracts. In other organisations, purchasing competencies are assigned to already existing structures (departments). In this case, purchasing cannot be seen as the sole professional task of designated staff members. Some organisations distinguish between product 'specifiers', who assess and select goods, and purchasers, who manage the actual purchase. In the European Green Purchasing Network, the same term is used for both.

Professional purchasers are trained to understand how they can best serve their organisation or company (internal role). At the same time, in public organisations, their work relates to the public interest (external role). The latter aspect is reflected in public procurement legislation that requires efficient use of taxpayers' money. Another public interest issue is environmental protection, which concerns all institutions and households, private or public.

III *The Purchaser's Position: Bridging Purchasing and the Environment*

Implementing green purchasing requires the bridging of two separate worlds: purchasing and the environment (Consultancy and Research for Environmental Management 1997: 2). Clearly, purchasers cannot be expected to be environmental experts. Moreover, they work under time constraints and usually cannot afford to research environmental issues. Nevertheless, purchasers occupy a strategically important position regarding environmental concerns both within their organisation and towards other organisations.

III *Within the Organisation*

Purchasers are key personnel for advancing environmentally preferable patterns of behaviour within their organisation. Their position means that they are best placed and best qualified within an organisation to argue for the adoption of greener products and more environmentally friendly purchasing practices. This is relevant, as prejudices about the performance of 'green' products continue to exist among many organisations' management and staff. Purchasers have a superior vantage point as regards new product information, including products marketed with green credentials, but in order to adopt an influential and credible position within their own organisation, purchasers need to understand the issues.

III *Outside the Organisation*

As purchasers are in constant contact with supplier organisations' sales departments, they contribute to the perception of their organisation's environmental credibility. They verify suppliers' environmental standards and practices, and make other organisations aware of green purchasing-related issues. 'You do have a responsibility to use your position to help shape the environmental behaviour of others—namely the many thousands of businesses you are in contract with.'[1]

Yet how much responsibility should purchasers take? Ideally, green purchasing requires purchasers to combine their existing professional expertise with:

▶ Knowledge about the environmental impacts of products, materials and services

▶ An understanding of tools for the sourcing of environmentally relevant information

▶ Accumulating and disseminating practical experiences of alternative products

III *Supporting Purchasers and Policy-Makers*

The European Green Purchasing Network aims to support purchasers in their specialised tasks relating to the organisation and implementation of green purchasing; and to facilitate a professional information exchange network on green purchasing across national boundaries and business sectors. The network is also designed to

---

1. Patrick Mallon, Deputy Director of Business in the Environment, at a green purchasing conference held by the British Department of the Environment in July 1997 (*www.open.gov.uk/doe/envir/greening/greenpro/qe2*).

raise awareness among management of the importance of green purchasing in the organisational structure. One reason for this is that, ideally, any green purchasing policy is embedded in a larger environmental policy framework. Another important management aspect of green purchasing relates to the need to monitor and anticipate future issues that could affect supply and purchasing activities as well as production practices (e.g. new scientific developments, changes in public perception of the environment or emerging government policies, laws and regulations).

Drawing together private and public enterprises, the European Green Purchasing Network allows capacity-building and transfer of expertise in two main dimensions:[2]

▶ **Horizontally:** i.e. across various sectors (industry, trade, government, non-governmental, environmental pressure groups). This involves businesses integrating green purchasing into their environmental management schemes and their product-related activities (known as 'product stewardship', 'expanded producer responsibility', etc.). Public authorities, meanwhile, may glean valuable insights from the principle of continuous improvement as laid out by environmental management systems (EMSs). The increasing popularity of eco-auditing with local authorities in Europe and the rising commitment to supply chain management in industry are favourable signs that things are moving in the right direction.

▶ **Vertically:** i.e. along different phases of the product life-cycle. Industry, in particular, purchases a huge range of 'products', from raw materials to semi-finished and end-consumer goods. However, the allocation of work or service contracts should not be ignored. From a wider perspective, the contracting of services should be considered as an alternative to the purchase of tangible products.

It has been decided to launch a series of pilot initiatives, each involving businesses, local authorities and consumer organisations. At least two projects are to be started in the second half of 1998 in the fields of 'green' cleaning products and IT products, but further projects covering other areas of concern (packaging, agrifood, water treatment, tourism and transport) will follow.

▌ *The Municipal Group within the Network*

The Municipal Green Purchasing Group, launched and facilitated by the International Council for Local Environmental Initiatives (ICLEI), serves as a clearing-house for local authorities within the European Green Purchasing Network. So far, some 275 municipalities and regions/counties have indicated their interest in contributing to the exchange of green purchasing experience. There is a significant overlap between these local authorities and the signatories of the Aalborg Charter, many of which consider green purchasing a key element of their Local Agenda 21. The Municipal Group can therefore be described as the green purchasing campaign within the European Local Agenda 21 movement.

---

2. Terminology adopted from Oosterhuis, Rubik and Scholl (1996: ch. 4).

Mainly across northern and western Europe, a number of local governments have introduced their own green purchasing policies, developed purchasing checklists and applied standardised forms for bidders. As the OECD Environmental Directorate reports, 'greening of government and purchasing initiatives are mushrooming' at the local level (OECD 1997: 5). This phenomenon is the realisation of the long-standing expectations of environmentalists and policy-makers regarding public purchasing. Public administrations are focal points of public life and therefore receive particular attention. Consequently, they would lose credibility if they were seen to display environmentally unsound behaviour. Finally, as has often been stated, governments are usually the largest single buyers in their respective countries and thus can influence the market on a larger scale than private-sector enterprises.

Nevertheless, public purchasers operate within a particular legal, political and economic framework which leaves them comparatively little leeway to pursue green purchasing. In fact, European legislation on public procurement has spurred a lively debate as to how compatible are environmental considerations with the free trade principle. While the Maastricht Treaty of 1992 emphasised the need to combine single-market objectives with other European Community policies, especially environmental protection, the Public Procurement Directives of the same and the following year[3] clearly emphasise the Single Market over any other policy principle; environmental concerns are implicitly admissible where they do not interfere with the free trade principle.

As a consequence, many political actors and purchasers in public administrations have become insecure about their freedom to build environmental criteria into their calls for tenders and the decision-making process. A recent study on public procurement practices in Spain and the Netherlands found that public purchasers in both countries regard potential legal conflicts with manufacturers and suppliers an important barrier to greener purchasing (van der Grijp 1995). A study conducted in Denmark in the early 1990s reported the same findings (Pedersen 1992).

Through its Green Paper on Public Procurement, published in 1996, the European Commission included the amendments that environmental protection considerations could be incorporated into the technical requirements relating to the characteristics of the works, supplies or services; and that 'the Directives allow, under certain conditions that environmental protection objectives to be included among the criteria for selecting candidates' (CEC 1996b: 41). These amendments, however, appear too general to tackle the most fundamental question regarding the role of voluntary environmental commitments for which companies seek certification. Should a company's sound environmental management practices have any relevance when it comes to the purchase of a tangible product? Should eco-labelled products win a competitive edge over conventional or non-certified products? If so, what would be the role of the European Eco-label as opposed to other awards serving national or regional markets as in Germany, Austria, France, the Netherlands and the Nordic countries?

---

3. The Council Directives 92/50 on Service Contracts; 93/36 on Public Supplies; and 93/37 on Public Works.

A Council Communication of March 1998 in fact recognises that an additional document needs to be provided to clarify the relationship between public procurement, the Single Market and the environment:

> In the context of this exercise, the Commission will examine in particular the extent to which it is possible to make reference in technical specifications to the European Eco-label and, moreover, to national eco-labels. At the same time, it will analyse whether purchasing bodies can demand of suppliers that they have in place an eco-audit system such as EMAS or the ISO 14001 standard (CEC 1998).

In this context, the Network's pilot projects may allow additional insights. The Directorate General XV, concerned with the Single Market, has indicated its interest in supporting and being involved with the first of the pilot initiatives described above.

Another issue for the European Green Purchasing Network and its Municipal Group is political support for greener consumption patterns. Clearly, political will is a very important component of green purchasing. As a British purchasing guidebook for local authorities put it:

> . . . an authority can insist upon products, or equipment of a specific make or source, if it is necessary to meet the council's environmental policies . . . A local authority must therefore hold a corporate environmental policy covering purchasing, if certain environmental considerations are to be built into specifications (Groundwork 1996: 37).

There are a number of fine examples available from within the Municipal Purchasing Group as to how green purchasing can be embedded in a larger political context. The Austrian city of Graz, recipient of the European Sustainable City Award 1996, issued a progress plan that shifts the onus for green procurement onto each department. For any purchase transacted or contract awarded by a department, evidence has to be provided as to why the most environmentally favourable option was *not* chosen. This serves to invalidate persistent prejudices and assumptions about recycled or secondary products. In Gothenburg, Sweden, the City Council reached an unanimous decision that the local government committees, boards and companies should introduce environmental auditing as part of every purchasing decision. The City Council, moreover, has issued a ban on certain products and chemical substances and has issued general recommendations for purchasing.

However, local policies promoting green purchasing may not always be beyond reproach. Last year, the European Commission approached the Swedish government, expressing concern about a clause in the City of Stockholm's public procurement policy that requires sustainable transport as a technical requirement for the awarding of procurement contracts. The Commission apparently has doubts as to whether or not this requirement implies favouritism for local business and thus anti-competitive behaviour.

As mentioned above, many local authorities consider green purchasing as a key element of their Local Agenda 21. Interestingly, there is a potential for conflict between the idea of local self-reliance, as some commentators infer from Agenda 21 and the Aalborg Charter on the one hand, and the quest for greater market transparency on the other. To many environmentalists, the notion of building a local agenda with all relevant actors includes increased co-operation also between local businesses and local administration. When local authorities start contracting competing firms from outside the city limits, local firms may be inclined to withdraw from Local Agenda 21 activities.

With respect to such potential incongruencies between local policy-making and European legislation, the European Green Purchasing Network and its Municipal Group have pledged to work together with its members and the European Commission to reach clarification for all parties involved.

▌ *European Green Purchasing Network Membership Information*

The launch of the European Green Purchasing Network on 3rd December 1997, which was attended by some 65 participants, represented a promising start. The Network's first milestone event will be the *EcoProcura 98* congress and exhibition, hosted by ICLEI on 24–25 June 1998 in Hannover, Germany. On the occasion of this event, representatives from the cleaning products industry will meet with purchasers, environmentalists and policy-makers from local and the European level. Following *EcoProcura 98*, a series of conferences and exhibitions is planned to provide a forum for environmentally aware purchasers and suppliers and to carry on the Network's activities.

Membership of the European Green Purchasing Network is open to all organisations that procure goods and services. Local authorities should preferably approach ICLEI; all other organisations, including national governments, may address their applications to EPE.

The European Green Purchasing Network provides easy access to relevant green purchasing information on the Internet through its own server and offers its members a permanent forum for continuous information-sharing and networking. It makes available information on existing green purchasing instruments such as eco-labels, LCA (life-cycle assessment), EIA (environmental impact assessment of products) and EMS (environmental management systems) to all its members.

Over the next few years, the Network will gradually draw up purchasing guidelines for various types of product to assist purchasers in their daily work.

Appendix 1: *Principles of Green Purchasing and Guidelines for the Implementation of the Principle of Continuous Improvement within Environmental Management Systems*

The principle of 'continuous improvement of environmental performance' in relation to green purchasing should be viewed as follows:

1. General Principle
A green purchasing strategy should be developed by all public authorities, private and public enterprises. It should be part of any environmental management system

Actions should be identified to incorporate environmental considerations into the requirements related to the characteristics of the

▶ Works

▶ Supplies

▶ Services

Technical considerations should promote eco-efficiency and, where appropriate:

▶ Reduce the material intensity of goods and services

▶ Reduce the energy intensity of goods and services

▶ Reduce toxic dispersion

▶ Enhance material recyclability

▶ Maximise the sustainable use of renewable resources

▶ Extend product durability

▶ Increase the service intensity of goods and services

The green purchasing strategy should promote:

▶ Product and service stewardship

▶ Extended producer responsibility/shared responsibility

2. Organisational Policies for Public Procurement
The environmental performance improvement of all European national, regional and local governments in relation to green purchasing should consider, based on existing best practices, the following organisational policies:

▶ An overall strategy for the promotion of a sustainable product procurement policy

▶ An action plan

▶ An inter-departmental commission that brings together all the departments and agencies involved in the ongoing reform of purchasing codes

▶ Clear allocation of responsibilities leading up to the nomination of accountable officials responsible for the plan's implementation

▶ Precise rules for private purchasing agencies acting on behalf of public authorities

▶ Precise rules in relation to the decentralisation of purchasing decision-making

▶ Development of an information technology strategy (electronic market, dialogue between suppliers and purchasers, access to green purchasing guidelines, transparency and openness)

Technical requirements should no longer include the rejection of tenders on the grounds that goods incorporate reconditioned components or recycled materials.

Criteria are designed to test candidates' economic, financial and technical capacity. Environmental protection objectives should be included among the criteria for selecting candidates. They will be non-discriminatory and open to all tenders. Such environmental criteria should address:

- ▶ Performance conditions imposed contractually on successful tenders to perform the contract in accordance with certain constraints aimed at protecting the environment

- ▶ The existence of an environmental management scheme and of product stewardship practices of the bidders which should become a requirement after a certain period of time, which is to be fixed

3. Implementation of the Principle of Continuous Improvement with regard to Businesses

Environmental performance improvement with regard to businesses (transnational corporations and major companies) requires:

- ▶ An overall strategy for the promotion of a sustainable product purchasing policy

- ▶ An action plan, ideally as part of an environmental management system

- ▶ Organisational developments leading up to the nomination of accountable managers responsible for the plan's implementation

- ▶ Development of an information technology strategy (electronic market, dialogue between suppliers and purchasers, access to green purchasing guidelines, transparency and openness)

Retailers should implement customisation strategies based on own-brand products offering the best quality–cost ratios. Environment should stand among the qualitative issues that are integrated in the product.

Appendix 2: *The European Green Purchasing Network Pilot Initiative*
Launched with the Support of the European Commission
and the French Ministry of the Environment

Combine your Purchasing Power

The Network aims to develop a 'community of buying organisations' as a 'voluntary approach through excellence'. It should be a means of pushing towards a systemic approach where shared producer responsibility, environmental management systems and eco- and social labelling are addressed in an integrated way.

The Network invites companies, cities and consumer organisations to participate in a pan-European initiative, involving suppliers, purchasers, retailers and consumers.

The participants in the pilot initiative seek to:

▶ Develop a 'community of buying organisations' at pan-European level involving purchasers, suppliers, retailers and consumers who share common principles of green purchasing

▶ Design a process that is open to non-EU countries' comments, and which is transparent and participatory

▶ Maximise the opportunity for green purchasing within the limits of the present EU Single Market regulations related to procurement

▶ Identify meaningful approaches if EU and WTO rules relating to procurement need to be changed, proposing solutions that address not only environmental but also social concerns

▶ Identify recommendations that can be promoted in line with Commission initiatives and draft regulations/directives related to the environment

▶ Working with suppliers, focus on the implementation of a synergy strategy between instruments such as EMS and eco-labelling

▶ Examine the importance of contributing to the implementation of international conventions by developing specific guidelines related to raw material and energy

16 Putting the Green into Greener Purchasing
Protecting Nature Consciously[1]

Philip Sutton and Kathy Preece

▌▌ Introduction

Corporate environmentalism is taking off in leaps and bounds in many parts of the world, and at the same time there is a growing rhetorical recognition that biodiversity conservation is a central pillar of ecologically sustainable development. However, it is usually only the direct impacts of business decisions on biodiversity (e.g. the clearance of bushland for resource extraction or facility development) that are considered, and indirect effects are largely ignored. Despite purchasing being the key way of dealing with indirect effects of corporate activity on biodiversity, there is a notable absence of tools for doing so, and this is preventing businesses from effectively contributing to ecologically sustainable development.

This chapter develops a methodology to enable every organisation, no matter how small or large, to begin to take nature consciously into account. There are four main elements to the chapter. The first is an intellectual foundation for the guidelines that follow. The second—guidelines for choosing materials with least impact on biodiversity—is the heart of the chapter. The third part is a decision-making procedure which is intended to help purchasers find the best solutions in the short and longer term. The final section outlines a biodiversity-aware approach to life-cycle assessment: an innovation that is critical if we are ever to have the ability to make truly green purchasing decisions.

▌▌ Most Greener Purchasing is not Very Green

More and more organisations are improving their environmental performance, usually starting with their operations and then often moving on to look at their product design and purchasing. They are increasingly applying life-cycle thinking as a way of maximising the environmental benefit of product design and purchasing decisions.

1. We would like to thank Joe Pickin for his collaboration with us in early discussions about the chapter, and for commentary on the first draft. We would also like to acknowledge the financial contribution made by The Body Shop Australia to the project that led to this chapter.

The issues typically considered when making green purchasing decisions are whether the product:

▶ Is recyclable.

▶ Causes pollution or impacts on the atmosphere—during production, use or disposal.

▶ Requires large amounts of energy and materials during manufacture or use.

However, products that meet these criteria could still have quite serious impacts on nature.

Some firms do try to address biodiversity issues directly by:

▶ Avoiding products that contain rainforest timber or material from endangered species (e.g. where trade has been banned under the CITES convention).

▶ Using environmentally certified timber.[2]

However, most purchases that firms make do not involve these kinds of material. People who want to make green purchasing decisions are therefore usually limited to considering recyclability (as opposed to recycled content), pollution, energy and water issues—with no idea of how valuable those actions will be for the protection of biodiversity. This means that most purchasing decisions are made in a policy vacuum when it comes to biodiversity. **Greener purchasing, as it stands, contributes almost nothing to nature conservation in most environments.**

III *Specifying Ecological Sustainability*

In the spirit of continual improvement, we must ask: is this approach to greener purchasing as good as things can or should get? Figure 1 illustrates, using Australian examples, how product choices could have a highly targeted impact on biodiversity. The examples of alternatives show that better purchasing choices are possible. But what principles should guide the generation and selection of options if we are to maximise the benefit for biodiversity? What is our ultimate objective?

It is now widely accepted that the most fundamental environmental goal is ecological sustainability. This is not just a matter of minimising the negative effects of firms' own operations and products; it also requires an effort to boost society's ability to achieve ecological sustainability through the products that firms offer and through the influence that they exercise.

There are two possible broad justifications for pursuing ecological sustainability. One is to support human well-being through maintaining life-support systems and biologically based economic resources. The other is to support the viability of other life-forms for their own sake.[3] Around the world, it is increasingly common to find environmental programmes motivated by both objectives simultaneously. Each objective

---

2. Among the few companies that try to take their indirect impacts on biodiversity into account are the British firms Sainsbury's, B&Q Hardware and The Body Shop. These firms subscribe to the certification process of the Forest Stewardship Council. The FSC certifies forest operations that comply with their principles as being 'well managed' (see Chapters 9 and 24).

3. The UN Charter for Nature explicitly recognises this second objective.

PRODUCT INDUCING THE THREAT	THREATENED BIODIVERSITY	PROBLEMATIC MATERIAL OR PROCESS	ALTERNATIVES
Aluminium	Jarrah forests	Bauxite mining	❑ Recycled aluminium ❑ Bauxite from farmland ❑ Other materials
Canned tuna	Blue fin tuna fish	Fishing	❑ Tuna grown in fish farms ❑ Non-threatened fish species
Cars	Alpine environments (Mountain Pygmy-Possum)	CO_2 release/global warming	❑ Hypercars ❑ Compact city ❑ Public transport ❑ Bicycle/walking ❑ E-mail
Cheese	West Gipsland volcanic-soils eucalyptus forest (ecological community virtually extinct)	Cleared for dairy farms	❑ Reduced dairy diet ❑ Non-dairy substitutes
Fish fillets	Orange Roughy fish	Fishing	❑ Non-threatened fish species
Gold	Box-Ironbark forests (e.g. Regent Honeyeater and Swift Parrot)	Clearing native vegetation for mining	❑ Other metals ❑ End to the use of gold by central banks
Office copy paper	Cool temperate rainforest (Leadbeater's possum)	Timber harvesting	❑ E-mail ❑ Recycled paper ❑ Paper sourced from farm-based plantations
Paint	Bushland on coastal dunes	Titanium oxide from mineral sands mining	❑ Titanium oxide from farmland ❑ Surfaces not requiring paint
Steaks	Australian tropical woodlands (under pressure)	Cattle grazing on native pasture and cleared land sown with improved pasture	❑ Exports of services and manufactures rather than beef ❑ Low beef diet ❑ Other meats ❑ Vegetarian substitutes
Sugar products	Swamp forest (Mahogany Glider possum)	Sugar cane production	❑ Sugar from long-cleared land ❑ Reduced sugar use ❑ Beet sugar
Woodchip exports	East Gippsland mixed-species eucalyptus forest (Sooty and Powerful owls)	Timber harvesting	❑ Exports of farm-based plantation products ❑ Exports of services and manufactures rather than woodchips
Woollen clothing	Grassy woodlands (30 threatened species; 0.5% of 3 million hectares remains)	Sheep grazing	❑ Longer life products ❑ Synthetic fibre

Figure 1: Some Links between Products and Biodiversity

independently requires that life-support systems and biodiversity are protected. Given the irreversibility of extinctions and the very slow creation of new biological diversity through the process of evolution, the precautionary principle would suggest that we should not allow biodiversity or life-support system functions to be systematically lost.

In Figure 2, some of the policy implications of pursuing ecological sustainability are drawn out using the familiar structure of an environmental management system (policy→objectives→targets→actions). If we are to specify effective actions to achieve ecological sustainability, we must recognise that society is profoundly ignorant about the detail of how the earth operates as an ecosystem. Furthermore, much of the damage that we seek to avoid will only become apparent long after the causes have had their initial effects. So we need to adopt robust preventative strategies that can still work in these circumstances. The Natural Step programme has pioneered the development of such cybernetic rules for the achievement of ecological sustainability in a social context (Holmberg and Robert 1997). The objectives in Figure 2 have been developed from the Natural Step's four system conditions.

It is useful to develop targets to give decision-makers an idea of 'how far' we need to go to achieve ecological sustainability. Seven inspirational stretch goals are used as the targets, and these are based on the approach popularised by the Du Pont corporation.[4] However, before we can act effectively on objectives and targets, we must identify some high-level strategies. The 'actions' section of Figure 2 contains a comprehensive set of high-order strategies.

A chapter on green purchasing is not the place to debate fully all the details of how ecological sustainability should be specified. However, some of the sub-objectives (system conditions 1 and 2) and some of the targets (stretch goals 1 and 7) go so far beyond what many people are used to that they deserve some justification, and this is supplied in the appendix.

When all the objectives, targets and actions in Figure 2 are considered in the context of biodiversity conservation, a number of additional strategic guidelines can be derived. These are set out in Figure 3.

Where purchasers lack the time, expertise or information to fully apply these guidelines in Figures 3 and 4, they can apply the following six principles, which rather crudely condense the logic of the guidelines and pick up on the dematerialisation objective in the earlier section on specifying ecological sustainability.

▸ **Benefit biodiversity.** Material production systems should be managed where at all possible to provide benefits to biodiversity, either through changes to land management practices related to material production, or through unrelated 'offset' (compensatory) projects.

▸ **Dematerialisation.** It is preferable to meet human needs in ways that greatly reduce the use of materials and energy. This strategy has the least possible impact on natural habitat and reduces the demand for land to the greatest

---

4. In the light of the Japanese success with the stretch goal of 'zero defects', Du Pont repackaged its 190-year philosophy that all accidents are preventable as a goal of 'zero accidents'. They have now extended the idea into the environmental domain with the addition of the goals of 'zero waste' and 'zero emissions' (Krol 1996).

POLICY	OBJECTIVES (7 system conditions)	TARGETS (7 stretch goals)	ACTIONS (12 generic strategies)
Society should be **ecologically sustainable.**	**Ecological sustainability** must not be undermined by systematic: **1.** Increases in concentrations in nature of **substances that come from the earth's crust** **2.** Increases in concentrations in nature of **substances produced by society** **3.** Increases in the **manipulation** or **harvesting** of nature **4.** Failure to **restore the ecological basis** for biodiversity and ecological productivity Society must make it easy to achieve system conditions 1–4 by ensuring that: **5.** Society has the capability and resilience to **solve its major problems** in a timely fashion. **6.** Society's **aggregate use** of resources and land is **ultra-frugal,** and **material flows** into and out of society **do not increase systematically.** **7.** The human **population does not increase systematically**.	Society should aim for: **1.** 'Zero' **extinctions** **2.** 'Zero' **climate damage**[†] **3.** 'Zero' **soil** degradation **4.** 'Zero' **waste** **5.** 'Zero' **pollution** **6.** A 90% improvement in **resource use efficiency** (Factor 10)[‡] **7.** 'Zero' net **greenhouse gas emissions**	Society should take action to: **1. Contain** human activity (for nature) **2. Tread lightly** (for nature) **3. Restore** (for nature) **4. Dematerialise** **5.** Create a **closed-cycle economy** **6.** Use **renewable** resources **7.** Design for **no toxicity** **8.** Aim for sustainable **population** **9.** Green up **business** **10.** Green up **lifestyles** **11.** Green up **culture** **12.** Boost **social and economic capability**

[†] *Given the huge injection of greenhouse gases into the atmosphere over the last half-century and the enormous lead times for correction, this stretch goal becomes a long-term recovery target rather than a preventative goal.*

[‡] *See the International Factor 10 Club 1997.*

Figure 2: Policy Implications of Pursuing Ecological Sustainability

If, in order to achieve ecological sustainability, it is necessary to . . .	*then*	We need to . . .
❏ stop systematically increasing the manipulation of nature (bearing in mind the already massive loss of native habitat)		stop further clearance or loss of natural habitat.
❏ stop systematically increasing the concentration in the environment of substances from the earth's crust and from society		use organic agriculture.
❏ stop systematically increasing the concentration in the environment of substances from the earth's crust and from society, *and* ❏ acknowledge that no containment system can be 100% effective		avoid the use of containment systems to prevent the spread of ecotoxic substances by using, as far as possible, materials and substances that are common in the environment.
❏ restore habitat for depleted species and ecological communities, *and* ❏ achieve 'zero' climate damage		meet human needs using production systems that are less land-intensive
❏ aim for zero net emission of greenhouse gases		switch from fossil fuels to renewable fuels that do not require encroachment on native habitat.
❏ stop systematically increasing the manipulation of nature, *and* ❏ acknowledge that, if products compete in the marketplace on the basis of minimising cost (commodities), *or* firms are economically vulnerable during downswings or recessions, there may be a strong incentive not to pay for necessary ecological management		avoid using natural systems for production if they require expensive management to ensure sustainability and the product is a commodity or the environmental management systems cannot be guaranteed during economic downswings.
❏ acknowledge that there is great ignorance about how natural ecosystems operate, and that many effects of human activity on ecosystems do not show up until well after the triggering activities have occurred, *and* ❏ apply the precautionary principle		ensure that production occurs, as far as possible, outside natural ecosystems.
❏ stop further clearance or loss of natural habitat, *and* ❏ meet human needs using production systems that are less land-intensive		switch to recycled (re-used/reprocessed) materials to the maximum extent that is thermodynamically possible
❏ use recycled materials to the maximum extent that is thermodynamically possible, *and* ❏ use renewable fuels that do not require encroachment on native habitat, *and* ❏ acknowledge that there are limits to how much of such energy can be produced		maximise the dematerialisation of the economy.

Figure 3: Deriving Additional Strategic Guidelines

extent, thus making it easier to take land out of production for habitat restoration purposes.

▶ **Recycled materials.** Where materials must be used, it is preferable to use recycled materials, because this method of production has the least impact on natural habitats and the least land demand of all the materials production methods.

▶ **Farm-based production.** If recycled materials are not available, then materials produced on long-cleared farmland are preferable, as their production does not place great pressure on natural habitats.

▶ **Caution over commodities.** Materials from natural habitats should not be used if the producers are under intense pressure to cut their costs of production. There is tremendous pressure on commodity producers to cut corners on environmental management in order to be competitive, and this can apply to most producers during recessions, even if they do not produce commodity products.

▶ **No blockage of necessary habitat restoration.** Materials from farmland should not be used where the land should be restored to ensure the survival of threatened ecological communities and species.

▮▮ *Creating a Strategic Framework for Green Purchasing*

These strategic guidelines can be developed into a four-level hierarchy to guide decision-making towards the best options for green purchasing. The idea of the hierarchy is to make it easier to discriminate between options on the basis of their likely contribution to the achievement of ecological sustainability. Figure 4 shows a detailed categorisation of materials using the hierarchy. The green purchaser, ideally, would try to buy products made from category A materials. If options from the higher categories are not available, or are beyond the financial reach of the purchaser, a product with materials from a lower category might have to be chosen. The four levels of the hierarchy are:

A **Best options.** Sustainability achieved by reducing demand for land, avoiding degradation of native species and ecosystems, and, if at all possible, providing benefits to biodiversity.

B **Second-best options.** Sustainable outcomes possible, provided that environmental management is excellent. However, a precautionary approach would suggest that these options should be avoided because it is hard to achieve and hard to prove that a sustainable outcome has resulted.

C **Dubious options.** Will most likely be ecologically *un*sustainable, because, while these options involve no new clearing or new introductions, *either* they cause degradation through the removal of significant amounts of biomass or a key element of the ecosystem, or through the maintenance of a disruptive element such as a pest plant or animal; *or* they block restoration required in area biodiversity plan.

MATERIAL	**SOURCE**
A: *Best options.* Sustainability achieved by reducing demand for land, avoiding degradation of native species and ecosystems, and, if at all possible, providing benefits to biodiversity.	
Paper and wood	❑ Sourced from re-used material (i.e. not reconstituted).
	❑ Sourced from reprocessed material (i.e. reconstituted) and post-consumer content maximised to ensure that all post-consumer waste is recycled.
Biological products (wood, paper, food, etc.)	❑ Sourced from organic production system on land cleared in earlier times and, where at all possible, managed to provide benefits to native species and ecosystems. (This option drops to level C if it meets the criteria in Note 2, p. 219).
	❑ Sourced in very low quantities from the wild where ecologically sustainable indigenous management regimes apply.
	❑ Sourced from introduced species (e.g. pests) harvested from the wild to assist native species and ecosystem conservation by reducing or eliminating stocks.
Water	❑ Sourced from roofs and other existing structures or from waste-water.
	❑ Purified technologically, or purified and stored in artificial wetlands or lakes established on land cleared in earlier times and, where at all possible, managed to provide benefits to native species and ecosystems. (This option drops to level C if it meets criterion [b] in Note 2, p. 219)
Energy resources	❑ Drawn from renewable resources using urban or farmland (e.g. solar thermal power plants, wind generators and solar photovoltaic systems and biomass-to-energy conversion based on organic waste material). (This option drops to level C if it meets criterion [b] in Note 2, p. 219)
Non-biological, non-fossil fuel materials (minerals, stone, etc.)	❑ Sourced from re-used material.
	❑ Sourced from reprocessed material.
	❑ Sourced as a by-product of another production process that meets the option A criteria.
	❑ Extracted from land cleared in earlier times with no damage to the hydrology of the area and no potential for toxic seepage, and, where at all possible, managed to provide benefits to native species and ecosystems, provided the extraction doesn't contribute to a systematic increase in the concentration of substances in nature (i.e. all the materials extracted [not just the target substance] are made up of substances that are common in nature or in the soils). (This option drops to level C if it meets the criteria in Note 2, p. 219).
Substances generally	❑ In processing, use and reprocessing, the escape into the wider environment of small quantities of the substances (or their breakdown products) does not matter because they are not ecotoxic and are not contributing to a systematic increase in the environmental concentration (either because the substances and their breakdown products are not persistent or because they are already naturally common in the environment).
B: *Second-best options.* Sustainable outcomes possible, provided that environmental management is excellent. However, a precautionary approach would suggest that these options should be avoided because it is hard to achieve and hard to prove that a sustainable outcome has resulted.	
Biological products (wood, paper, food, etc.)	❑ Non-commodity-driven production from native habitat (e.g. native forest, grasslands, marine ecosystems) where green management is attempted and environmental management standards can be guaranteed to be maintained during economic down-swings (e.g. for wood, small-scale production of specialist timbers using small-patch harvesting; for paper, woodchips are a genuine by-product of non-commodity wood production).

MATERIAL	SOURCE
B: *Second-best options (continued)*	
Water	❑ Non-commodity-driven production from catchments covered with native habitat (e.g. native forest, grasslands, heathlands), extracted from ecologically degraded waterways and the waterways managed to avoid further disruption to the aquatic and riparian habitats, provided that environmental management standards can be guaranteed to be maintained during economic down-swings.
	❑ Drawn at a sustainable rate from deep aquifers.
	❑ Stored in depleted aquifers without groundwater contamination.
Energy resources	❑ Biomass-to-energy conversion from purpose-grown organic crops on land cleared in earlier times where a sustainable production system is used. (This option drops to level C if it meets the criteria in Note 2, p. 219).
Non-biological, non-fossil fuel materials (minerals, stone, etc.)	❑ Non-commodity-driven production involves locating extraction operations, facilities or wastes on native habitat (e.g. native forest, grasslands, marine ecosystems) where there is no potential for toxic seepage, and where affected ecosystems are highly tolerant of disturbance to biota and soils/geology/hydrology. Restoration of entire native species suite possible and undertaken. Green management is attempted and environmental management standards can be guaranteed to be maintained during economic down-swings.
Substances generally	❑ Non-commodity-driven production of substances that, although potentially ecotoxic, are to be contained to a very high degree during processing, use and reprocessing (substances are recycled) so that no more than traces enter the environment and these traces will not contribute to a systematic increase in the substance's concentration in the environment. Environmental management standards can be guaranteed to be maintained during economic down-swings.
C: *Dubious options.* Will most likely be ecologically *un*sustainable, because, while these options involve no new clearing or new introductions, *either* they cause degradation through the removal of significant amounts of biomass or a key element of the ecosystem, or through the maintenance of a disruptive element such as a pest plant or animal; *or* they block restoration required in area biodiversity plan.	
Biological products (wood, paper, food, etc.)	❑ Sourced from native habitat (e.g. native forest, grasslands, marine ecosystems) and attempting green management; *but either* commodity products produced *or* environmental management standards cannot be guaranteed to be maintained during economic down-swings.
	❑ Sourced from native habitat—using introduced species that are restocked or managed to maintain their commercial yield.
	❑ Sourced from land cleared in earlier times but not acceptable because it conflicts with the area biodiversity plan's requirements for native ecosystem restoration.
	❑ Sourced from irrigated agriculture that draws water from 'surface' systems (e.g. rivers, lakes, wetlands and near-surface groundwater) which support natural ecosystems.
Water	❑ Extracted from ecologically degraded waterways and the waterways managed to avoid further disruption to the aquatic and riparian habitats; *but either* commodity products produced *or* environmental management standards cannot be guaranteed to be maintained during economic down-swings *or* the use of the waterways is not acceptable because it conflicts with the area biodiversity plan's requirements for native ecosystem restoration.

MATERIAL	SOURCE
C: *Dubious options (continued)*	
Non-biological materials (minerals, stone, coal, oil and gas, etc.)	❑ Commodity-driven production involves locating extraction operations, facilities or wastes on native habitat. There is no potential for toxic seepage, affected ecosystems are highly tolerant of disturbance to biota and soils/geology/hydrology, and restoration of entire native species suite possible and undertaken. Green management is attempted, *but* environmental management standards cannot be guaranteed to be maintained during economic down-swings.
	❑ Sourced from land cleared in earlier times but not acceptable because it conflicts with the area biodiversity plan's requirements for native ecosystem restoration.
Substances generally	❑ Substances, although potentially ecotoxic, are meant to be contained to a very high degree during processing, use and reprocessing (substances are recycled) so that no more than traces enter the environment and these traces will not contribute to a systematic increase in the substance's concentration in the environment; *but either* commodity products are produced *or* environmental management standards cannot be guaranteed to be maintained during economic down-swings.
D: *Worst options.* Ecologically unsustainable, because *either* they involve permanent clearing or serious degradation through the removal of significant amounts of biomass or a key element of the ecosystem without considering biodiversity impacts, or the introduction of a disruptive element such as a pest plant or animal; *or* they provide support through significant commercial relationships with companies that in other aspects of their operations have major negative impacts on the environment.	
Biological products (wood, paper, food, etc.)	❑ Sourced from native habitat (e.g. native forest, grasslands, marine ecosystems) with no consideration of biodiversity.
	❑ Sourced from plantations, crops or introduced pasture on land that is cleared of native vegetation for the purpose.
	❑ Involves the introduction of non-local species to native habitat where those species do not currently occur there (e.g. replanting with non-local timber species in native forest, introducing or re-introducing non-local fish to natural aquatic systems).
	❑ Production processes result in genetic pollution of wild stocks of native species.
Water	❑ Extracted from natural surface drainage systems or from shallow aquifers that support native habitat (e.g. native forest, grasslands, aquatic ecosystems) with no consideration of biodiversity.
	❑ Stored on inundated terrestrial native habitat (e.g. native forest, grasslands, heathlands).
Energy resources	❑ Based on fossil fuels.
Non-biological, non-fossil fuel materials (minerals, stone, etc.)	❑ Extracted by strip mining or open cut from native habitat (e.g. native forest, grasslands, marine ecosystems) with no consideration of biodiversity.
	❑ Extracted by underground mining, but the overlying native habitat (e.g. native forest, grasslands, marine ecosystems) at risk from disruption and carried out with no consideration of biodiversity.
	❑ Extraction facilities and wastes located on native habitat with no consideration of biodiversity.
Substances generally	❑ Substances that are normally released (intentionally or not) to the environment during processing, use or disposal are persistent and contribute to a systematic increase in concentrations in the environment.

Note: *In aquatic environments, the term 'land' includes submerged land.*

Figure 4: Rules of Thumb to Guide Materials Choice

D **Worst options.** Ecologically unsustainable, because *either* they involve permanent clearing or serious degradation through the removal of significant amounts of biomass or a key element of the ecosystem, or the introduction of a disruptive element such as a pest plant or animal; *or* they provide support through significant commercial relationships with companies that in other aspects of their operations have major negative impacts on the environment.

Figure 4 classifies materials and energy sources produced under a wide range of circumstances using the four-level hierarchy.

The detailed guidelines in Figure 4 would be easier to use if they were embedded in a user-friendly software package that could hide the technical complexity and guide a purchaser to a decision with an automatically customised set of questions.

Note 1. The capacity to restore habitat is essential if the objective of conserving biodiversity (i.e. reversing its decline) is to be achieved. 'Area biodiversity plans' will need to be prepared to indicate, as far as possible, which parts of the area are to be restored as part of the recovery effort for threatened species or to prevent other species from becoming threatened with extinction. However, the restoration of naturally diverse communities and ecological processes is extremely difficult, if not impossible, especially in degraded areas.

Note 2. Some products will drop from category A or B to category C if they either: (a) involve irrigation that draws water from 'surface' systems (e.g. rivers, lakes, wetlands and near-surface groundwater) that support natural ecosystems; or (b) conflict with the area biodiversity plan's requirements for native ecosystems restoration.

▐▐ *Making Green Purchasing Decisions*

Ideally, a green purchasing decision should involve more than just the avoidance of the most damaging materials. Dematerialisation and life-cycle assessment should be considered, as should the adequacy of the decision-making process itself. The relevance of outside assistance should also be determined. All these considerations need to be choreographed. Figure 5 sets out an appropriate decision-making procedure to accomplish this. As with the Figure 4 guidelines, this purchasing procedure would be easier to use if it were incorporated into a user-friendly software package.

▐▐ *Biodiversity Life-Cycle Assessment*

After examining the procedure for making a green purchasing decision, it is clear that life-cycle thinking is critical to its full effectiveness. However, to date, most life-cycle assessment techniques have dealt poorly, if at all, with biodiversity issues. So this section sets out a basic framework on which a practical biodiversity life-cycle assessment methodology can be built.

It is suggested that the assessment methodology have two parts:

▶ **Firm-centred assessment**, covering: (a) inputs, intended effects and side-effects, and outputs; (b) direct impacts; and (c) management systems.

▶ **Product life-cycle assessment**, covering: full organisational or product life-cycle effects, including all direct and indirect impacts.

STAGES OF DECISION-MAKING	GUIDING QUESTIONS (*Things to be purchased are referred to as 'items'*)	COMMENTS
Getting oriented	**1.** What is proposed to be purchased?	Has the item been identified (e.g. a photocopier, a tonne of fertiliser) or is the request more like 'Could you get me something that does . . .'?
	2. What are the needs that the purchase is meant to satisfy?	To find win–win creative solutions, it is often necessary to understand the underlying needs if the conventional purchasing choice is not the best for biodiversity.
	3. Are you purchasing for yourself or someone else?	If the purchase is for someone else, good communications will be vital for non-routine purchases.
	4. Is it a one-off or repeat purchase? Will the purchase commit a large amount of money?	Repeat or expensive purchases will warrant more effort to get the purchasing decision right. In the case of repeat purchases, given the lead times in getting and considering good information, it might be acceptable if the earliest purchasing decisions are not as well based as later purchases.
	5. Is the item a good or a service?	Services use materials for their delivery, but the associated materials may not be as obvious as with goods.
	6. Is the item: **a** Something to be used in the firm? **b** Something for resale? **c** Something to be incorporated as part of a new product (good or service)?	These different circumstances may alter: ❑ The environmental implications ❑ The strategies for managing life-cycle impacts/the product stewardship requirements
	7. Are the performance criteria for the item: **a** Specified? **b** Assumed? **c** To be determined?	The performance criteria for a routine request such as 'Get me a box of fine-point blue pens' are probably assumed.
	8. If the performance criteria are specified or assumed, are they changeable: **a** Easily? **b** With difficulty? **c** Not at all?	The scope for finding the best purchasing choice may be constrained if the performance criteria are rigidly specified.
How well are you set up now and for the future? You will need to revisit this bracket of questions as you work through the questionnaire.	**9.** Do you have the **expertise** to make a good green purchasing decision in this case?	If the answer is 'no': ❑ Consider using a guidebook or software package. ❑ Consider being trained. ❑ Consider buying from a pre-assessed catalogue. ❑ Consider delegating the environmental assessment to an expert agent (a specialist in the firm or a consultant).

STAGES OF DECISION-MAKING	GUIDING QUESTIONS (*Things to be purchased are referred to as 'items'*)	COMMENTS
	10. Do you have access to the necessary **information** to make a good green purchasing decision in this case? Do you have access to good information about available options or their environmental implications?	If the answer is 'no': ❑ Consider using a guidebook or software package. ❑ Consider buying from a pre-assessed catalogue. ❑ Consider getting the information from an outside supplier. ❑ Consider requiring suppliers to provide the information (your firm might need to band together with other purchasers to appoint an advocate to push for this if you are to create sufficient leverage on suppliers).
	11. Do you have the **time** to make a good green purchasing decision in this case? **12.** Do you have time to absorb advice from others?	If the answer is 'no' to either question: ❑ Consider buying from a pre-assessed catalogue. ❑ Consider delegating the investigation stage to an expert agent (a specialist in the firm or a consultant). ❑ Consider delegating the actual purchasing decision to an expert agent. If you don't already have someone you can trust with these decisions, consider investing resources in developing such a relationship.
	13. Do you have enough **money** to make a good green purchasing decision?	Extra money might be needed to buy advice or advocacy or to pay a premium for green products.
	14. Are you easily able to make the value judgements necessary to make a green purchasing decision?	For example, how strongly do you want to apply the precautionary principle (i.e. how much are you prepared to put biodiversity at risk)?
	15. If the answer to 14 is 'no', have you got access to a set of value judgements that you or your organisation are prepared to use?	Will you use the value judgements from an industry body or a mainstream or radical environment group?
	16. If assistance from outside consultants or values groups is not available, can you take steps to see that such help is available in the future?	If you are too busy or not confident enough to do this catalyst work yourself, can you delegate it to a green purchasing advocacy group?

Stages of Decision-making	Guiding questions *(Things to be purchased are referred to as 'items')*	Comments
Pinning down the performance criteria	**17.** If the performance criteria for the item to be purchased have not been specified, specify them now.	❏ This also applies where criteria are assumed. ❏ Make sure that all the important non-environmental performance criteria are included too. ❏ The performance criteria should include the basic environmental standard to be sought. Will you aim for the best options as specified in Figure 4? How much of a dollar premium will you pay for a superior green product?
Dematerialisation	**18.** Is the new item really needed? Can the purchase be avoided?	❏ Ask the user. ❏ Think of other options. ❏ Seek other advice.
	19. If the item is a physical thing, can its service value be purchased instead? (Can the firm buy lawn-mowing or a pleasant outdoor surface instead of a lawnmower?)	❏ Consider case studies. ❏ Consider getting the advice of an expert to see what is possible.
	20. Will the purchase replace other items? **21.** Can they be upgraded or refurbished and retained? **22.** If the old items to be replaced are surplus to requirements, can they be re-used outside the firm or can they be recycled?	Who would have the technical competence to answer these questions?
Generating options in a whole system context	**23.** Read the section of this chapter on specifying ecological sustainability and look at Figure 4 to see how the ideas in them might influence the choice of materials and products.	In addition: ❏ Consider doing self-training using published materials. ❏ Consider doing formal training on biodiversity-oriented green purchasing and whole-systems thinking.
	24. If the user has asked for a particular item, generate variations on the theme and, if it can be negotiated, look at options that go beyond what the user originally had in mind.	❏ Consider options with a better suite of materials, better whole-system performance. ❏ Consider options where the physical activities or influence of the provider and any downstream users are superior.
	25. If the user has asked for 'something that will do x or y', develop a range of good options for meeting the user's needs that will have the best biodiversity outcome.	

STAGES OF DECISION-MAKING	GUIDING QUESTIONS (*Things to be purchased are referred to as 'items'*)	COMMENTS
Assessing options in a whole system context	**26.** Can you identify the main or obvious materials that are used to make each option (or deliver each option in the case of services)? If you can, do it now.	Seek information from: ❑ Published case studies ❑ The suppliers ❑ Assessment software packages ❑ Expert advisers Consider limits on time and money.
	27. Can you roughly map out the life-cycle of the options under consideration? (Do not worry about identifying impacts at this stage.) If you can map the life-cycle, do it now.	Seek information from: ❑ Published case studies ❑ The suppliers ❑ Assessment software packages ❑ Expert advisers
	28. What are the biodiversity and other environmental implications of the materials and the activities and influence exerted by the firms involved in their production?	Use Figure 4 to do a strategic impact assessment. Fine-tune this with specific impact knowledge if this can be found.
	29. What are the biodiversity and other environmental implications of each option when considered as a whole system?	❑ Sometimes it is better to use a material that has a higher negative biodiversity impact than an alternative material, if the performance of the product in use or when recycled is markedly improved—e.g. cars with recycled aluminium frames may be better than those with steel frames because of the reduced energy demand in operation. ❑ Consider documented case studies. ❑ Consider expert advice. ❑ Consider specific hot spots (− or +) anywhere in the life-cycle for biodiversity and other environmental or social issues (e.g. greenhouse and ozone, water systems, soil systems, clean air and water, materials conservation, energy conservation, amenity, human health, heritage, animal welfare, and social issues).
	30. Have you done the best assessment you can within your limits of information, money and time (bearing in mind the magnitude of the purchasing decision)?	More effort should be put into the assessment of options where the proposed purchase represents a large proportion of the firm's total material inputs or expenditures.

STAGES OF DECISION-MAKING	GUIDING QUESTIONS (*Things to be purchased are referred to as 'items'*)	COMMENTS
	31. If the assessment could have been much better with more information or greater access to assessment models, what can you do to improve the situation in the future?	Consider: ❑ Pressuring the suppliers to provide better information. ❑ Urging third-party information suppliers to provide needed information. ❑ Enlisting the support of a green purchasing advocate to press for a better system for decision-making.
Choosing the best option	*32.* Which option appears to be best after considering user needs and the needs of biodiversity conservation? *33.* Will the preferred option improve the environmental position of the firm or the society? *34.* Will there be a big-leap improvement? **a** In relative terms (e.g. compared to current practice) **b** In absolute terms (e.g. compared to the firm's other big impacts)	❑ Be prepared to make a decision despite information gaps if you have done the best you can within your time and money limits. ❑ Consult with the user (and possibly with other stakeholders) about what the best option would be. ❑ Consider what premium you can pay to get a better option (given the size of the purchase relative to the firm's total budget).
Avoiding premature lock-in	*35.* Is the best option an ideal choice?	
	36. How long will the preferred purchasing option lock in a particular level of environmental performance?	
	37. If the best option is far from ideal, would it be sensible to defer the purchase until a better option is available?	

Figure 5: How to Make a Purchasing Decision with Biodiversity Explicitly in Mind

It is worth noting that, for the vast majority of organisations, the *indirect* effects on biodiversity will be greater than the *direct* effects. Where this is the case, it is especially important that the organisations undertake a life-cycle assessment.

⦀ Firm-Centred Assessment

Through a firm-centred assessment, a firm will:

1. **Identify the firm's impact drivers** that may give rise to direct or indirect biodiversity impacts, for example:

    a Its own activities (both commercial and non-commercial)

   b Its production inputs

   c Its outputs: products (goods or services), discards (pollution, waste, etc.) and influence

2. **Assess the *direct* biodiversity impacts** arising from a firm's *own* activities.

   a Identify the intended effects and side-effects of the firm's own activities.

   b Determine the actual impacts or estimate the likely impacts (negative or positive) on biodiversity arising from the intended effects and side-effects.

3. **Assess the adequacy of the firm's environmental management system** for ensuring that biodiversity issues are dealt with well, including its capacity for handling indirect effects and for making positive contributions to biodiversity conservation.

Step 1 needs to be carried out for most other types of environmental assessment (pollution, energy, waste or water). This presents an opportunity to integrate some aspects of all the different types of assessment. Step 2 is a complex process of linking cause and effect, which eventually requires some sort of value judgement to be made about how significant or good or bad the impacts are. The organisation undertaking the assessment will need to determine explicitly the value system that it will use (see the section on assessment standards). The first two steps of the firm-centred biodiversity assessment process are illustrated graphically in Figure 6.

Unlike a product life-cycle assessment (see next section), a firm-centred assessment does not go as far as including the cumulative indirect impact of all the preceding and consequential activities and influences to which the firm's activities give rise.

The information produced in a firm-centred assessment could be generated for the whole firm or just for specific operating units, e.g. specific sites or divisions. The

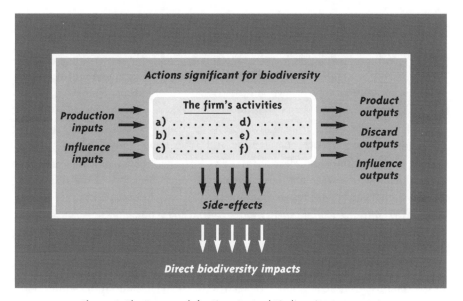

Figure 6: The Framework for Firm-Centred Biodiversity Assessment

information, however, will need to be reformatted and assigned at a later stage to apply to particular products.

Firms' activities can generate a variety of intended effects and side-effects that can affect biodiversity. For example, they can give rise to:

▶ Gross habitat loss (e.g. permanent clearing, draining, dredging, etc.)

▶ Direct and deliberate removal or destruction (e.g. as a result of land-forming, construction, pest-control or nuisance-abatement activities)

▶ Invasion by non-indigenous species (e.g. pest plants, animals and micro-organisms such as rabbits, foxes, exotic grasses, boneseed, blackberries, dieback disease, genetically engineered organisms, etc.)

▶ Inappropriate fire regime (i.e. too frequent, not enough, wrong time of year, wrong intensity, wrong spatial pattern, etc.)

▶ Habitat fragmentation

▶ Grazing

▶ Loss of tree hollows

▶ Inappropriate vegetation or ecological community structure

▶ Soil degradation (e.g. erosion, compaction, salinity, acidification, etc.)

▶ Inappropriate water regime (e.g. changed drainage patterns)

▶ Pollution

▶ Biomass removal (e.g. harvesting of trees, wild flowers, fish and other animals from the wild)

▶ Climate/atmosphere change (e.g. enhanced greenhouse, hole in the ozone layer, etc.).

Certain industrial activities, through their subsidiary activities listed in the brackets, frequently give rise to these effects. For example:

▶ Agriculture, plantation forestry, agroforestry, aquaculture (clearing, pasture improvement, grazing, use of chemicals, salinisation, changed fire and water regimes, introduction of environmental pest plants, animals and micro-organisms, discharges of organic material into waterways)

▶ Timber harvesting from native forests (clearing, roading, intensification of silvicultural practices, changed fire and water regimes, use of chemicals)

▶ Urban development (clearing, roading, spread of pest plants and animals, discharge of sewage and other chemicals, water diversion, changed fire and water regimes, burning of fossil fuels)

▶ Fishing in the wild (biomass removal, trawling damage)

▶ Mining (clearing, roading and trenching, soil moving, mixing and compaction, use of chemicals, seepage of tailings)

▶ Transport (roading, etc., clearing, changed fire regimes, discharges of oils, combustion products, etc., changed water regime, induced urban development, greenhouse gas production)

▶ Tourism and recreation (roading, trampling, soil compaction and erosion, spread of pest plants and animals, infrastructure impacts, induced urban development)

▶ Minerals/chemical processing and power generation (chemicals/pollution, habitat loss, use of fossil fuels)

▶ Horticulture (weed escapes, wild-harvesting of native plants, chemicals, soil degradation)

The various environmental effects can be aggregated into three strategically significant categories of direct ecological significance that might provide useful data for eco-labelling schemes or corporate environmental reports:

▶ Ecosystem **displacement/conversion** (e.g. permanent clearance or drainage, or permanent revegetation/restocking with non-indigenous species)

▶ **Degradation** of ecosystems and habitats (e.g. spread of non-indigenous species, modified fire regimes, habitat fragmentation, pollution, compaction, etc.)

▶ **Blockage of the necessary restoration of the habitats** of threatened ecological communities or threatened species (e.g. allocation of land for uses that are incompatible with the recreation of suitable habitat).

All the effects discussed above will, in the particular circumstances that they occur, have very specific significance for the species and ecological communities they affect. The assessment system should be able to infer typical links or track the actual links between a firm's activities, inputs and outputs and the specific effects on particular species and ecological communities.

⦀ Product Life-Cycle Assessment
To get the full picture of a firm's total effects or a product's total impact, it is necessary to add the impacts of the firm's activities (inputs, intended effects and side-effects, and outputs) and the consequential impacts of a product throughout its entire life-cycle of production. This will require the assessor to trace back through the complete cause–effect chain of activities undertaken to date, and also forward through the expected cause–effect chain to anticipate likely effects. Figure 7 sets out the basic framework for product life-cycle assessment.

To carry out a product life-cycle assessment, it will be necessary to add related information from associated organisations to build up the required information. Only after this has been done for each product can the total impact of a firm (both direct and indirect) be determined. Therefore, a fully documented life-cycle assessment can only be done if the relevant firm-centred assessments have been completed. In the absence of the complete suite of firm-centred assessments, rules of thumb would have to be used to infer the probable impacts.

The environmental histories of products should travel with the products as they move down the supply chain. In many cases, the information systems necessary to do this have already been put in place by firms as part of their quality management system. It is then just a matter of adding environmental data to the production data that these systems already handle.

Firms create five broad classes of industrial effects that can generate impacts on biodiversity:

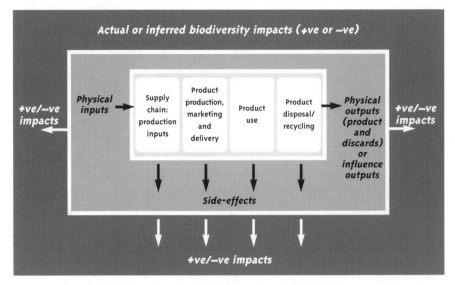

Figure 7: The Basic Framework for Product Life-Cycle Assessment

▶ **Process effects**

    a *In the case of primary industries:* the effects of growing resources in sensitive environments or extracting them from such environments

    b *In the case of manufacturing industries:* the process-related impacts, such as the effect of pollution discharged from production sites; the impact of siting development projects on natural areas or species' habitats (e.g. displacement or degradation effects); and the triggering of other threats such as the spread of non-indigenous species and the imposition of inappropriate fire regimes

▶ **Resource 'pull-through' effects:** those arising as a result of the induced demand or 'pull-through' of resources (e.g. the demand for timber from native forests, or the use of bauxite or mineral sands located beneath natural ecosystems).

▶ **Secondary development effects:** where the establishment of infrastructure is induced to service production activities (e.g. quarries, roads, power lines, water supplies, housing developments, waste disposal sites, etc.).

▶ **Market 'pull-through' effects.** Most enterprises are active in expanding the market for their products. Any success they have will expand the total impact of the whole process of producing, using and processing their products. These impacts will have a net negative effect on biodiversity unless the products: (a) substitute for more damaging products and do not retard the introduction of even better products; (b) are offset by activities or other products that compensate for their impacts; or (c) are used directly to conserve biodiversity.

❱ **Product 'push-through' effects**

    a Where products are designed for **purposeful use** in environments where there will be significant effects on biodiversity (e.g. fertilisers and pesticides, stocking with non-indigenous species, wild area tourism and recreation, etc.)

    b Where pollution or other unintended effects are generated **incidentally** during the use of products: for example, as a result of the release of gases, volatile liquids and other substances (there is speculation that the worldwide decline in frogs is due to the release of such substances which subsequently enter the global water cycle), or as a result of the unintended spread of non-indigenous species

    c Where **final disposal** of manufactured products presents problems of finding waste dumping sites and of controlling the pollution discharges from these sites

⫼ Assessment Standards

In drawing conclusions from both firm-centred assessments and product life-cycle assessments, it will be necessary to make value judgements about what is:

❱ The final state of the environment that is being aimed for

❱ The degree of risk that the organisation is prepared to tolerate

❱ The standard of the management systems to which the organisation aspires

Organisations may wish to create their own standards or they might like to adopt standards developed by other parties. Conservation agencies, scientific bodies and environmental groups might all like to develop their own standards. It will then be up to organisations doing an assessment, either individually or as co-operating groups, to select the standard or standards that seems right for them. As public awareness and knowledge improves, a general community consensus might emerge about which standard is preferable.

⫼ Comments on both Firm-Centred Assessments and Product Life-Cycle Assessments

The results of biodiversity assessments will often have to be qualitative and the information generated is unlikely to lend itself to high levels of aggregation if its full usefulness is to be retained. It will not be possible or useful to aggregate biodiversity impacts into one numerical grading.

Where an organisation undertakes activities that are not directly linked to a product (e.g. lobbying or good works), the assignment of a share of positive or negative impacts to a product will need to be carefully thought about. Also, a judgement about *organisational* biodiversity impact needs to be carefully distinguished from *product* impacts. For example, a firm might produce a niche product that is very good from a biodiversity point of view while continuing to market other products, the majority of which have high biodiversity impacts. In this case, the green niche product would show up better than the organisation as a whole.

||| The Outputs of Assessments

The data and judgements generated by biodiversity assessments might be made available in a number of different ways:

- **Internal assessment reports.** These might be kept for internal use only.
- **Public assessment reports.** These would be made available publicly.
- **Annual report summaries.** A condensation of the internal assessments might be made available through the annual report or a special environment report.
- **Product data sheets.** Special data sheets for products could be made available to the public routinely or on request.
- **On-line data sources.** The data and judgements might be made available on-line so that suppliers or customers can access the material when they are undertaking life-cycle assessments.
- **Label data or ratings.** The data and judgements could be summarised in corporate reports or on product labels through ratings for a select group of indicators. In the same way that energy-using appliances have a star rating system, products might have a 'green leaf' rating, reflecting factors such as hectares of habitat lost or gained or intensity of habitat damage or improvement per product dollar.

||| The Levels of Sophistication of Biodiversity Assessments

Assessments might be conducted at various levels of sophistication. The basic level would be based on very general rules of thumb and representative (or average) impact information. This type of assessment would be effectively a scoping exercise using information and rules of thumb taken from a simple manual. The green purchasing methodology in first half of this chapter illustrates this approach. The next level of sophistication could involve the use of a stand-alone computer package containing more detailed generic information and using a simple geographic information system (GIS) database. The highest level of sophistication would probably be an information-intensive on-line system connected with detailed regional, national and international databases.

||| Assessment Software

Because of the potential complexity of biodiversity assessment, there is a strong argument for creating software packages to assist organisations being assessed. A software package might operate as follows. Users would feed in information on:

- Activities (what sorts of things the organisation does)
- The scale of the organisation's activities
- Inputs (materials, energy, water, chemicals, etc., together with information on the sources of the information)
- Physical outputs (products, services, wastes, pollution)
- Influence outputs (contracts, legal controls, strategic alliances, lobbying, education campaigns, advertising, etc.)

> Current measures taken to reduce biodiversity impact or create positive benefit (in effect, the action elements of the organisation's environmental management system)

Each of these steps would be prompted by the computer. Locational information would be fed in too, where it was available. The computer software would contain checklists like those above and would also contain logical linkages between options on the checklists. In this way, the software would be able to trace a probable path between the assessment input information and the assessment information output described below.

Since a lot of the required information overlaps with information needed to do assessments for pollution, energy, waste, etc., it may be that the software could be developed by adapting one of the existing decision-support systems used for the well-established classes of environmental assessment. The computer might produce:

> A list of the most likely biodiversity impact trouble spots (which need to be investigated further and about which strategic decisions need to be made)

> Some possible strategic options for reducing the identified negative impacts

> A list of possible ways of benefiting biodiversity

> A list of possible actions to repay the 'ecological debt' incurred by past damage to biodiversity

> A rating of the adequacy of the organisation's environmental management system from a biodiversity conservation point of view

Biodiversity assessments would inevitably be primarily qualitative and strategic until the decision-support software can link to very detailed GIS data (from bioregional planning, etc.) and extensive libraries of life-cycle data, and until conservation management is able to draw on highly reliable predictive models. Even in the early stages, however, the system would still be useful at the qualitative and strategic level.

As the application of biodiversity assessment spreads (and provided there are data protocols so that assessment information from different organisations can be integrated meaningfully), it will become possible to conduct full life-cycle assessments based on case-specific data rather then inferred or average data.

In the longer term, a firm doing its own biodiversity assessment would create a detailed inventory of the activities it directly controls. To complete the life-cycle picture, it would either access standard libraries of information typical of its upstream or downstream activities, or it would simply download detailed assessment data from the specific firms it buys from or sells to.

To be most meaningful, the assessment technology should link with information and policies generated through bioregional planning and state-of-the-environment reporting. If people become accustomed to using a software package as a decision-support system, it is a small step eventually to link this software to the site-specific data in bioregional databases. The assessment software could also be used to test product designs before proceeding to manufacture or service delivery.

▐ Conclusions and Future Directions

How can we move most rapidly to a situation where green purchasing routinely considers the broad spectrum of biodiversity issues? The most critical thing to do is to fill the methodological gap. If people don't know how to take biodiversity directly into account in the purchasing decisions, then they won't do it. The most urgently needed method is at the entry level so that a large number of people can get involved and can start demanding that more sophisticated methods and supporting databases and other infrastructure are developed.

There are many points at which a green purchaser—whether a 'front-line' purchaser, specialist purchaser or major buying group—might benefit from outside assistance. This suggests that there is a need for a green purchasing support system of product developers, manufacturers and service providers. There is a need for technical information, guidebooks, decision-support software systems and catalogues of pre-assessed green products. Services are needed from trainers, product assessors, organisations that can offer decision rules based on distinctive sets of value judgements, environmental agencies and conservation groups.

These people and organisations need to play a role if an effective green purchasing system that deals with biodiversity issues is to be brought into existence as soon as possible. But probably the most critically important role of all is that of the green purchasing advocacy group. It will be groups of this sort that will galvanise the other players into action.

Green Innovations will continue to develop these ideas and the organisation looks forward to collaborating with others on the issue.

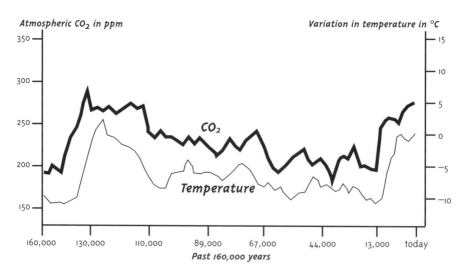

Figure 8: The Vostok Data: A surprisingly close correlation during the last 160,000 years between CO_2 concentrations and average temperatures on earth as established by chemical analysis of 'fossil air' enclosed in Antarctic ice

Source: Global Commons Institute, London, after Jouzel et al. 1987

Appendix:
Information Used to Specify Ecological Sustainability Objectives and Targets in Figure 2

While there is huge uncertainty about the likely ecological effects of particular materials in the environment, there is a high degree of certainty that, if substances of any sort increase systematically in the environment, especially if their concentrations rise, that there will, eventually, be significant environmental effects. One hundred years ago, it would have been difficult to imagine that industrial emissions of a natural and apparently innocuous substance such as CO_2 could cause ecological problems.

There are two classes of substance that are particularly prone to causing ecological problems. The first category is composed of substances that have been deposited in the earth's crust over the aeons and which are now rare in the environment. And the other category is made up of persistent substances that humans create that are not normally found in nature. Hence the first two system conditions in Figure 2.

The 'zero extinctions' stretch goal in Figure 2 is an approximation. Since extinctions are natural, and indeed are inevitable if evolution is to continue, they should not be prevented totally. The extinction rate, however, should not be excessive. The 'natural' rate of extinction that we should emulate is that experienced *between* the mass extinction events caused by natural disasters such as major meteor strikes and ice ages.

The Institute for Global Futures Research (1998) argues that the natural extinction rate that applied between the catastrophic mass extinction events that have occurred roughly every 100 million years is 0.0000182% per annum compared with the figure proposed by Swanson (1997: 9) of about 0.000009% per annum. Regardless of whichever figure is thought to be the more accurate, from a practical business management point of view, the scientifically defined target extinction rate is so low that it equates to a 'zero' extinctions stretch goal. Society's ability to manage global ecosystems is never likely to be effective enough to prevent all extinctions, so the pursuit of this goal will not cause evolutionary problems.

The stretch goal of 'zero' net greenhouse gas emissions also deserves comment, since it is so much higher than the reduction target negotiated at the 1997 Kyoto conference. The international Framework Convention on Climate Change signed in 1992 binds member countries to stabilise greenhouse gas 'concentrations at levels preventing a dangerous human interaction with the climate'. Past environmental conditions might give us some guide as to what level of atmospheric CO_2 can be regarded as 'dangerous'.

At no time in the last 160,000 years have atmospheric CO_2 concentrations been anywhere near as high as they are today. The current level of atmospheric CO_2 is 358 parts per million by volume (ppmv), whereas the pre-industrial level was 280 ppmv. And the massive industrial and agricultural emissions around the world mean that CO_2 concentrations in the atmosphere will not stop at 358 ppmv, but will continue to rise by about 1.5 ppmv per annum. In contrast, for most of the last 160,000 years, the CO_2 concentrations have been below even the immediate pre-industrial level. Only once in all that time have CO_2 concentrations exceeded the immediate pre-industrial level and that was 135,000 years ago when they peaked at about 300 ppmv, a whole 58 ppmv less than now (von Weizsäcker, Lovins and Lovins 1997) (see Fig. 8)

So what CO_2 concentration might be dangerous? Since we have little idea of what the ecological effects will be of pushing the levels beyond the natural range for a lengthy period, the precautionary principle suggests that it would probably be sensible to stabilise eventually at something close to or just under the 280 ppmv level if we are to have the greatest chance of conserving biodiversity.

What are the implications for industry and society of trying to stabilise the atmosphere at around 280 ppmv? Computer simulations are not publicly available for this level; however, the CSIRO[5] has published information about a scenario where the atmosphere is stabilised at 350 ppmv (Enting, Wigley and Heimann 1994) (see Figs. 9 and 10).

Even to achieve this unnaturally high level, it would be necessary, over the next sixty years, to keep reducing world industrial and agricultural CO_2 emissions until they reached zero (net), and then, for the following eighty years, it would actually be necessary to pull CO_2 out of the atmosphere on a net basis. This suggests that a 'zero' net greenhouse gas emissions stretch goal is much closer to what is needed than the reductions targets negotiated at the 1997 Kyoto climate conference (5.2% below the 1990 levels in developed countries [as a whole] achieved somewhere between 2008 and 2012). It also suggests that very large carbon sinks will need to be created to soak up excess CO_2 from the atmosphere. The best way to do this from a biodiversity conservation point of view will be to restore native vegetation cover, as part of a native habitat restoration programme, rather than committing vast areas to exotic monocultural plantations.[6]

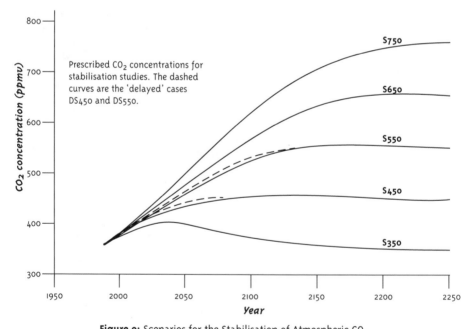

Figure 9: Scenarios for the Stabilisation of Atmospheric CO_2

5. Australia's largest public scientific research organisation.
6. Plantations do have an important role to play, but they should not be established without regard to the need to restore native habitat on a significant scale.

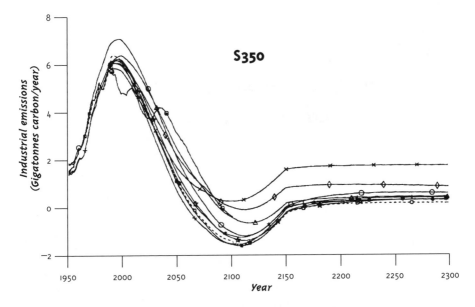

Figure 10: Industrial Emissions Profile for a Stabilisation of Atmospheric CO_2 at 350 ppmv, Generated by Ten Different Climate Models Used around the World
Source: Enting, Wigley and Heimann 1994

© 1998 Green Innovations, Inc.

17
The Role of Independent Eco-labelling in Environmental Purchasing

Michael Jones

▮▮ Introduction

Approaches to greener purchasing can focus on the environmental management system (EMS) that the supplier has in place, or on the features of the product itself. The shortcoming of reference to the EMS is that it may be sound, and followed religiously, but may not necessarily equate to best practice. In any event, the existence of even an excellent EMS does not have a full bearing on the environmental properties of the product.

A focus on the product, on the other hand, might simply take account of its inherent environmental features—recyclability or re-usability, energy or resource consumption (for example, electricity, water and detergent in the case of a washing machine), and its impact on disposal. But such an approach may not be relevant in every case. Paper is a good example where the major impacts lie in its manufacture rather than in its use or disposal. This all points to the need to look at the whole life-cycle of the product from cradle to grave, an approach that eco-labelling provides.

Eco-labelling schemes were set up in response to the rapid growth in green consumerism in the late 1980s. This led to a proliferation of products on the market that carried a variety of claims to be environmentally 'friendly'. In many cases, the claims were of doubtful validity, and the result was a high level of confusion and cynicism among buyers. More recently, the UK government has published a code of practice for green claims which should further help reduce the number of false or misleading claims. However, the role of the eco-label will remain as before, to set a benchmark for products with a high overall level of environmental performance.

Increasingly, the independent eco-label is being regarded by manufacturers as one measure of excellence in their products that differentiates them from others on the market. For corporate buyers of goods, the eco-label provides a ready means of meeting the requirements of environmental purchasing policies.

▮▮ The EU Eco-label Scheme

The European Union voluntary eco-label scheme, launched in 1992, is expanding to cover a wide range of products, other than food, drink and pharmaceuticals.

The scheme is intended to:

▶ Promote the design, production, marketing and use of products that have a reduced environmental impact during their entire life-cycle

▶ Provide consumers and other buyers with a simple and credible way of identifying products that overall cause less harm to the environment than others in the same category

The conditions for awarding an eco-label are defined by product group. Such groups, the specific ecological criteria for each group, and for how long they are valid, are set through a process involving the European Commission, member states and interest groups.

▋ *Life-Cycle Assessment*

Beginning with extraction of the raw materials and ending with final disposal, no human activity or product is completely environmentally benign. Resources in the form of energy as well as raw materials will be consumed and wastes will be emitted into the environment. Most eco-labelling schemes, including the EU scheme, use life-cycle assessment (LCA) as a basis for developing criteria for products. If a product meets the criteria, it can be awarded an eco-label.

LCA provides a scientific and transparent basis for establishing ecological criteria for the EU eco-label scheme. Its main characteristics are:

▶ To compare products on the basis of their function

▶ To relate environmental impacts throughout all stages of the product's life, from cradle to grave, to both market changes and technological improvements

▶ To minimise the data required when an application is made, by identifying well-founded ecological criteria

LCA is often described as a 'cradle-to-grave' approach. The product's life-cycle starts with raw materials, goes through the manufacturing process, distribution (including packaging), use, and ends with the final disposal—the 'grave'. It takes into account the following (see also Fig. 1):

▶ Use of natural resources and energy

▶ Emissions to air, water and soil

▶ Disposal of waste

▶ Noise

▶ Effects on ecosystems.

Investigating every aspect of a product's life-cycle requires a great deal of detailed research. The main environmental impacts sometimes occur during just one phase—an example of this is given in the case study at the end of this chapter. The eco-labelling scheme aims to identify where the product harms the environment the most, and develops criteria to reduce the impact on the environment for those parts of its life-cycle. Assessment of the general environmental impacts includes consideration of issues such as global warming, ozone depletion, human toxicity and acidification (i.e. acid rain).

Production	Use	Disposal
❑ Are the raw materials renewable or non-renewable?	❑ How much energy is involved during the use of the product?	❑ What kind of impact will the product have when it is disposed of?
❑ How much energy is used during manufacture?	❑ What kinds of pollutant does the product emit to air, water or land?	

Figure 1: Typical Questions Asked during a Life-Cycle Assessment

LCA is only a tool for decision-making, which cannot replace the actual decision-making itself. In line with this, a clear distinction should be made between the procedure for drawing up ecological criteria (which for the EU eco-label scheme is the responsibility of the European Commission), and the life-cycle assessment itself (which is the responsibility of the LCA practitioners). Both are included in the phases detailed in the following section.

III *The Phases of Decision-Making*

III *The Feasibility Study*

The initiative to select a group of products for possible inclusion in the scheme is taken by the European Commission. The main stakeholders, i.e. industry, commerce, consumer organisations, environmental protection organisations and trade unions, are consulted on the choice of product groups.

The first stage of the process is to carry out a feasibility study. This will seek to identify the likely key issues and explore whether it is worthwhile to set criteria. The study report will include an indication of what is available, the nature of the market, including industrial and economic interests and structures, the perceived environmental issues, what needs to be done, the relevance and potential benefits of the label for the environment, the risks of distortion between the various national segments of the internal market and, finally, international aspects.

This information is presented in a way that facilitates decisions about product group definition, fitness for use and visibility (the last in terms of market share and/or other relevant considerations). The way in which the market for the product varies across Europe is also an important consideration. Technically, Europe is well on the way to becoming a single market, but, in terms of actual products that consumers buy in the shops, there are often important differences in design and performance. If there is too much variation, it may be impracticable to set common criteria.

An ad hoc workshop composed of experts from the member states and representatives of all the parties concerned evaluates the feasibility study.

III *Inventory and Environmental Impact Assessment*

This is the core part of the LCA. The first stage is to prepare an inventory of the different environmental impacts at each stage in the life-cycle. This is followed by an assessment of the impacts on the environment, using internationally recognised methods, in an objective, qualified and representative manner, using LCA. LCA mainly focuses on quantifiable information. In those cases where environmental impacts cannot be quantified, qualitative aspects have to be taken into account in the final decision-making process.

▌▌ Setting of Criteria

The main elements of this phase are to:

▶ Determine the most important environmental impacts, based on the results of the LCA, and identify the accessible areas of economic and technical development that are the most relevant to the environmental impacts

▶ Determine the applicable criteria and define the level required for each criterion

▶ Determine the necessary test methods and certification procedures, and consider solutions for qualitative and other related issues

The ecological criteria have to be precise, clear and objective so as to ensure uniform application by the member states. They are designed to ensure a high level of environmental protection, are based as far as possible on the use of clean technology and, where appropriate, reflect the desirability of maximising product life.

The proposal for ecological criteria is officially presented to a forum set up under the EU regulation (the legal instrument setting up the eco-label scheme) for consultations with interest groups. The proposal is discussed and voted on in a regulatory committee composed of member state representatives. The final stage is formal adoption by the Commission and publication of the criteria in the *Official Journal of the European Communities*.

Given the nature of the eco-label, which involves a range of responsibilities, and the internal procedural rules of the Commission's departments, those departments collaborate closely in the various stages of the process of drawing up the criteria. In particular, the draft decision to be presented to the regulatory committee is the subject of prior inter-departmental consultation. Consideration is given to the text that accompanies the decision, which will explain, in particular, the reasons why the product group was selected for development, the criteria set and the expected environmental benefits.

▌▌ *Operating the EU Eco-label Scheme*

The EU scheme for the award of the eco-label consists of three main activities: establishing and revising criteria, awarding the label to products, and promoting the scheme to consumers and suppliers. Whereas responsibility for establishing and revising the criteria lies mainly with the Commission, awarding the label to products is a matter for the national bodies. These bodies, which are independent and neutral, have been designated by the member states of the EU to implement the eco-label scheme at national level. In the UK, the scheme is operated by the UK Eco-labelling Board.

Operating the EU eco-label scheme in the UK primarily involves promoting the scheme to industry, retailers and consumers, contributing to the development of product criteria, receiving and assessing applications from manufacturers for the award of the eco-label, and making awards if appropriate. Eligible products are those manufactured or first marketed in the UK, or imported into the UK from a country outside the European Union. Applications are assessed against the agreed criteria for the product group by an independent third party, the results being used to decide whether to award an eco-label. A summary of each application is circulated to all the national bodies, with the complete dossier on the evaluation of the product being sent only on request. Successful applicants enter into a contract with the board, and pay a licence fee to use the label for a specified period of up to three years.

▌▌ *Progress So Far*

Ecological criteria are now available for ten product groups:

▶ Washing machines

▶ Tissue paper (for example: toilet paper, kitchen rolls, napkins, facial tissues)

▶ Laundry detergents

▶ Single-ended light bulbs

▶ Double-ended light bulbs

▶ Paints and varnishes

▶ Bed linen and t-shirts

▶ Copier paper

▶ Refrigerators

▶ Soil improvers

In addition to these, criteria are under consideration for:

▶ Rubbish bags

▶ Floor-cleaning products

▶ Dishwasher detergents

▶ Shampoos

▶ Personal computers

▶ Growing media

▶ Batteries for consumer goods

▶ Sanitary cleaning products

▶ Bed mattresses

▶ Textile products

These criteria are likely to emerge over the next year or so.

Eco-labels have already been awarded to washing machines, kitchen rolls, toilet paper, paints and varnishes, bed-linen and washing powder.

III *Corporate and Public Purchasing*

At the launch of the EU eco-label scheme, the target was seen to be individual consumers rather than corporate or public purchasers. This is reflected in many of the product groups for which criteria are now available, and indeed in the clutch of products that carry the eco-label. There is some degree of overlap—light bulbs, paints and varnishes and copier paper representing the few good examples. However, it is recognised that the scale of corporate and public-sector purchases dwarfs those in the domestic sector. Given that the scheme is intended to major on those products with the greatest impact on the environment overall, the emphasis on consumer products is certain to shift.

Although no services are currently covered by the scheme, it is expected that these will be included in the future. The Canadian 'Environmental Choice Program' has been successful in developing criteria for services, in response to demand. The approach to developing criteria for services would be to seek to achieve a significant reduction in the input of resources (energy, raw materials) when compared with others in the market.

Although a green purchasing policy can be pursued by buying goods that already carry the label, procurement might also be made using the established criteria as part of the specification. This approach has the benefit of minimising the effort otherwise expended in developing specifications for goods that have a reduced impact on the environment, yet at the same time using criteria that have sound credentials.

III *Revision of the EU Eco-label Scheme*

As for many other European initiatives, the EU eco-label scheme is being reviewed five years after it came into effect, and the European Commission has published proposals to improve its effectiveness. These would involve streamlining the decision-making procedures and focusing more sharply on products that are most important in terms of the volume of trade in the Community, and their impact on the environment. Following voting by the Environment Committee of the European Parliament, they will be put to the Council of EU Environment Ministers.

III *Case Study: Environmental Impacts of a Washing Machine*

A wide range of sources of information was used in the life-cycle assessment for washing machines (see Fig. 2). The following main phases were covered.

- **Cradle production:** use of raw materials and the manufacture of washing machines
- **Distribution:** transporting and packaging
- **Use:** including the generation of the electricity used by the machine, use of water resources and treatment of waste-water
- **Grave disposal** transport to disposal site, energy used to recycle useful materials, amount of solid waste produced

ENVIRONMENTAL FIELDS	PRODUCT LIFE-CYCLE				
	Pre-production	Production	Distribution	Utilisation	Disposal
Waste relevance	✓	✓	✓	✓	✓
Soil pollution and degradation					
Water contamination				✓	
Air contamination		✓	✓	✓	
Noise		✓		✓	
Consumption of energy	✓	✓	✓	✓	✓
Consumption of natural resources	✓	✓	✓	✓	
Effects on ecosystems	✓			✓	✓

Figure 2: Life-Cycle Assessment Indicative Matrix: Case Study: Washing Machines

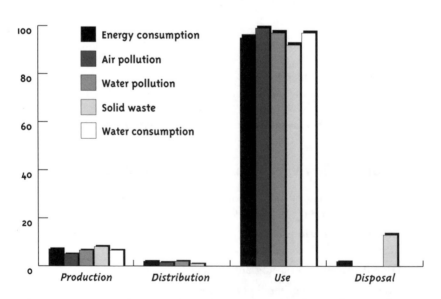

Figure 3: Environmental Impacts of a Washing Machine According to Phases in Life-Cycle

The results of the study are shown in Figure 3. This clearly shows that it is when a washing machine is being used that it has the greatest impact on the environment. This led to the setting of the key criteria shown below.

⫴ Key Criteria

▶ **Energy consumption:** must use less than 0.23 kWh of electricity per kg of washing at 60°C.

▶ **Water consumption:** must use less than 15 litres of water per kg of washing at any temperature.

▶ **Detergent consumption:** the machine must lose less than 5% in a wash.

18
Ethical Purchasing
Developing the Supply Chain beyond the Environment

Rita Godfrey

||| Introduction

The practice of monitoring and improving environmental performance in the supply chain is fast becoming a requirement of responsible business practice. It is also accepted that the ecological performance of a company may depend on that of its suppliers. The reluctance of companies to tackle this facet of business practice reflects the complexity involved in designing a system that will be robust enough to withstand the future changes in demands of business reporting and supplier–customer partnerships.

Add to that the increasing need to expand the scope of supplier 'greening' to include social issues, labour conditions and animal welfare, and the task becomes even more difficult. However, expand the scope we must. Truly 'sustainable' products cannot be judged purely on their environmental impacts, but must embrace all aspects of ethical performance.

This chapter focuses on the challenge to business of producing meaningful supply-chain improvement systems that reflect real business needs and embrace social change.

||| A Brief History of Supplier Ecological Performance Rating

Supplier evaluation began life as mostly financial checking via commercial referees for potential suppliers, in order to protect businesses from financially risky contracts with unreliable suppliers. The development of this evaluation to include quality was a logical next step, again protecting the company against unreliable suppliers.

As environmental pressures forced organisations to take stock of the way they operated, the environmental impact of the supply chain came under scrutiny. Supplier quality evaluation systems have been adapted to cover environmental issues, and supporting this a number of guidelines have been developed which include systems for measurement of and working with suppliers on environmental performance (Business in the Environment 1993). Although research has shown that this element of environmental business management is not well supported (Business in the Environment 1996), its place in environmental management has nonetheless been established. The principles of the 1991 ICC Business Charter for Sustainable Development have been incorporated into European Union Eco-Management and Audit Scheme (EMAS), including the purchasing and sourcing of raw materials. Today there are many practical examples of companies taking steps towards responsible supplier stewardship.

In recent years there has been growing interest in the ethics of the supply chain and pressure for businesses to guarantee the social pedigree of their products—ensuring, for example, that acceptable working conditions are in place. Pressure for users of animal-derived products to ensure the safe history of production has increased supply-chain investigation within related industries. In the United States, considerable pressure has been exerted on retailers of footwear, toys and garments to ensure that abuses of human rights in the workplace are avoided: for example, the Oxfam 'Clean Clothes' campaign. As a result, companies such as Levi-Strauss, The Gap and Reebok have developed in-house monitoring and auditing systems for verifying the standards of their suppliers with regards to workers' conditions. In effect, they are checking that the values of their suppliers are consistent with the expectations of their customers.

This pressure has increased the requirements of supplier investigation and has left businesses fearful of designing systems that will be outmoded rapidly due to the ever-changing demands of society. Recent research confirmed concerns that progress in this area was being constrained by a shortage of information, terminological confusion and a lack of clarity as to what approaches might satisfy the stakeholder groups.

Indeed the question is no longer should we involve our suppliers in improvement programmes but how will we do that and what will be the limits of our scope.

▐ *Expanding the Scope of Supply-Chain Evaluation*

The arena of supplier improvement should and can be expanded to encompass other ethical issues using the same methods and approach as environmental management. Questions of priorities, resources and weighting of these 'values' areas become more focused, but they are only extensions of the same thought processes. This natural progression is the way forward in ethical business management moving the whole process toward holistic sustainability evaluation. 'Sustainability', not just with reference to environmental impacts but in a holistic sense, must include:

▶ Social issues of human rights, workers' conditions and the rights of indigenous communities

▶ Environmental viability

▶ Animal welfare issues including endangered species, biodiversity and farming methods in addition to environmental issues

▶ Economic viability

▶ Quality

These issues, which are wider than the traditional view of 'environment', are slowly but surely breaking their way into the arena of 'sustainability'. Examples of this are the recent inclusion of the fate of calves into the requirements for certification of milk sources as 'organic' and the recent view that the treatment of animals farmed for food is an 'environmental' issue (Nicholson-Lord 1997).

The very complex issues of sustainability in its wider sense bind all these aspects of supplier performance. All are seen by consumers as equally important and we therefore need to avoid the danger of having separate approaches for each issue, with the associated risk that information will become fragmented. The 'values' areas of people, animals and environment cannot always be separated and many issues impact on more than one area, either as complementary or conflicting pressures. The weighting of these separate impacts on an individual business or industry provides a basis for risk assessment as the first step to designing a supplier evaluation and improvement strategy.

This expansion of ethical audit has been championed by progressive businesses and follows the goal of 'sustainable business' in its broadest sense. The emergence of ecological auditing into both internal and supply-chain management highlights a clear change in the perspective of product sustainability. Parallel to expanding the scope of sustainability, a methodology for measurement of these factors must be developed. Combining clear ecologically sustainable goals with evaluation systems provides business with the means to measure improvement in the supply chain in addition to commercial supply-chain performance.

There is a need therefore to pioneer management systems based on a wider perspective of how environmental protection and conservation relate to business obligations. If we are to avoid the kind of crisis foreseen by some and move towards a more genuinely 'eco-centric' approach to business, new techniques are needed. These techniques may borrow from existing management theory and practice, including techniques used in environmental, health and safety, or quality management and auditing. But business will need a broader and more holistic set of values together with systems for implementing those values if it is to make a genuine commitment to sustainable development. A paradigm shift is needed, complete with methodological underpinning. Integrated ethical auditing that takes into account social, animal welfare and environmental protection issues is one technique that may help.

▌ *Risk versus Resource*

Of course, the practicalities of business require that these guarantees of sustainability must also be included without a large increase in product cost. Customers are committed to sustainability until they have to dig too far into their pockets. The screening of suppliers has already expanded from a financial basis to include quality; this is acceptable as risk reduction. However, the inclusion of environmental and other issues related to sustainability must not add any further to the growing overheads of supplier assurance.

In addition, any system must provide the basis for informed purchasing choices. The inevitable trade-offs and incompatibilities, both within ethical areas and as a conflict between commercial and ethical benefits, require difficult decisions. Given that many companies are still struggling with the implementation of environmental management systems within their own organisations, it is not surprising that smaller businesses are wary to attempt supplier evaluation. However, as a basis for defensible purchasing decisions, evaluation systems prove a benefit rather than a drawback.

One hurdle for business, particularly small and medium-sized enterprises (SMEs), is the need for a level of expertise in setting supplier codes of practice or evaluation tools, requiring businesses to become experts not only in their particular business sphere, but also in the complex issues of the environment. While large organisations have been leading the way in experimenting and developing innovative methods of supplier partnership, this has been possible because they can afford the necessary resources. This highlights the issue of companies who are smaller or have lesser capabilities than their suppliers, and the need for evaluation systems that allow the supplier to make improvement recommendations for the customer companies.

Undertaking supplier evaluation and involvement with such a wide remit does require commitment. Indeed, any level of supplier partnership with regard to ecological performance improvement requires certain prerequisite discussion within the company. There is a need therefore to evaluate:

▶ The company's business aspirations and the desired outcome of the supplier involvement/evaluation

▶ The level of potential ethical risks within the supply chain

▶ The existing skills and capabilities for the company to design its own evaluation system

▶ The potential risk of non-involvement, including competitive advantage

▶ The level of assistance the company is prepared to give to suppliers who fall short of requirements and what will be the consequence of grave non-compliance

The results of this evaluation will form the basis of the company attitude toward supplier evaluation and therefore the level of commitment versus the need for action—thus bringing resource needs into the equation. It is essential, therefore, that discussion is carried out at the top of the organisation and involves representatives of all areas of the company. These discussions should also involve external expertise and stakeholder groups where relevant or necessary.

On the practical level, there are two facets of risk: the risk of not carrying out supplier evaluation versus the ethical risks inherent in the supply chain and their ultimate effect on the sustainability of the business. In common with existing environmental and health and safety management systems, risk assessment of supply-chain impacts is vital to assess the priority for and the depth of investigation required.

▌▌ *Developing Evaluation Options*

Having highlighted the inherent business risks in the supply chain and committed to carrying out supply-chain evaluation and improvement, businesses are faced with a long list of optional approaches supported by little detailed practical guidance in any area other than quality and the basic elements of environmental supplier engagement. This leaves businesses with three main options: (1) engage external certification standards; (2) work with outside agencies to develop a suitable system; or (3) design their own systems using elements gleaned from outside sources. These three options are discussed as follows.

1. *External Certification Standards*

While health and safety and environmental audit standards have been established for some time, the external certification of supplier ethical performance is still in development—largely in the context of sustainable agriculture and forestry and recently with labour conditions and fair trade. Certification ensures independent endorsement of standards by both quality agencies and pressure groups—individual company standards, however high, are not measurable by the customer. It also provides an off-the-peg answer for smaller companies to use, assuring them that the standards are adequate, realistic, constructive and defensible. They can also be sure that many of the problems have been ironed out during development.

The results of experimentation by leaders in the field have highlighted a need for industry and NGOs (non-governmental organisations) to work together in standard-setting and problem-solving and in doing so not only achieve a means of ensuring the quality of the supplier but achieve a real improvement in practice. In these circumstances, NGOs can offer specialist knowledge, consumer perspective and advice on strategic and policy issues. Successful examples of this approach include, for instance, the World Wide Fund for Nature (WWF) 1995 Group initiative to ensure sustainability of wood supplies. Schemes such as this have highlighted the benefits of certification to agreed standards developed by these industry–NGO partnerships (Murphy and Bendell 1997). Currently there are many groups, also comprising of industry and stakeholder representatives, working together on industry standards within the scope of ethical behaviour and best practice. Examples in the UK are the Ethical Trading Initiative and the Global Sourcing Working Group, who are both developing standards in the area of labour conditions in the supply chain.

The processes of verification supporting these standards are likely to follow existing quality and environmental verification processes and the basic certification can be underpinned with specific standard requirements: for example, certified Forest Stewardship Council sustainable wood or health and safety audits where high risk is assessed in any particular area.

The main drawback of this option is cost, which may limit smaller business to working with only a small number of suppliers.

2. *Employing Outside Agencies*

It is to be hoped that the current work being undertaken by these leaders will provide a package of evaluation tools and standards for smaller businesses to use. Certainly, this must be one of the main aims of such developmental work. Equally important is the adaptability of the engagement methods to allow for all levels of technology and capability.

Until this time, companies who do not have the advantage of in-house expertise in these extended 'values' areas will have a need for outside assistance and advice. At present, this is limited and those businesses looking for assistance in developing a rounded system will find that they have to work with individual organisations for advice in the separate areas and combine the results themselves into a working model that will be compatible with their current working methods. This option is therefore at present very limited. However, the growth in the number of business ethics forums allows companies more access to relevant partners and other businesses with whom they can collaborate.

3. Designing a System In-House

There are many examples of workable methodologies for supplier prioritisation which have been developed for environmental and health and safety evaluation. These principles can be adapted to include human rights and animal welfare impacts.

The basic rules for businesses that opt to develop their own systems are simplicity and adaptability. It is more effective initially to employ a modest system that works well and is supported than to be too ambitious. An overview of such a system may take the following lines:

1. A set of criteria including indicators encompassing all ethical and commercial risks. Examples of these would be: amount of business placed with the supplier; type of product and process; geographic/geopolitical location. These should be weighted to allow clear decisions to be made on the number of suppliers to be included in further evaluation and to what level.

2. Initial screening at a low level using key indicator questions to signal high risk and facilitate decision-making on the requirement for further investigation, with the minimum of effort. These can be developed for either in-house or external judgement. Many companies consider the inclusion of external expertise at this point as the most economical use of external resources.

3. A variety of investigation options from comprehensive site audit to self-certification/questionnaire, depending on company resources, capabilities and risk. Whichever option is used, it should follow the principle of gathering information only in a format that is usable and appropriate. The level of investigation should also take into account the level of technology and capabilities of suppliers.

4. A method of harnessing the knowledge and experience of those suppliers who have a higher technology or a more advanced ethical management system than the customer company. Evaluation is not carried out in a vacuum and the exchange of experience may be the most effective means of improving supply-chain performance.

5. Continuous improvement is an element of all management systems and, based on supplier capabilities, is the most important element of supplier evaluation. This element must also prompt the discussion within the company concerning action to be taken when non-compliance and high-risk problems are highlighted (as they surely will be).

The most critical element of supplier evaluation, and probably the area that causes the most difficulty, is that of traceability. The inability to trace the source of products or materials purchased on a company's behalf can signify the highest risk to the business. This prompts another grave difficulty faced by many businesses who are considering supplier investigation for the first time, i.e. the decision concerning how far down the supply chain one should investigate. An in-depth investigation of a product manufacturer is hardly worth it if the risks are connected with the production of product ingredients. For this reason the pedigree of materials purchased on the commodities market or from collectives should be of special concern.

This brings into play the option of life-cycle analysis (LCA) in the form of ethical impact assessment as a tool for investigation of the salient elements of the production processes. Its use both in a quantitative role and as an indicator of ecological negative impact is useful. Developed in partnership with ecological groups and industry associations, supplier practice can be measured against industry norm and/or best practice. Issues of lack of traceability can also be partially overcome by using industry LCA information to fill the gaps in knowledge. However, this brings with it the obvious drawbacks of industry partiality.

At its best, this type of process investigation can give not only guidance on probable negative impacts, but even in a shallow form can provide a basis for decisions regarding how far down the supply chain investigation should be carried by examining production processes.

▌ *Feedback and Improvement*

Set against codes of conduct (internal or external) and company targets, audits and investigations can be conducted to acquire feedback from and agree improvement recommendation with suppliers. Every tool in the supplier evaluation portfolio must result in the provision of recommendations for improvement. These must be made on a basis of supplier capability and level of requirement, versus risk. Improvement recommendations based on the level of supplier capability rather than a standard level of performance (e.g. attainment of ISO 14000) require a broader knowledge of the company's business, including commercial status and industry factors. Obviously, this impacts on the resources needed, both in time demands and the level of expertise of auditors.

Demands on the performance of suppliers are high and buyers have to ensure that they are honouring their side of this relationship. As with most supply-and-demand relationships, there can be a tendency to ignore the needs of those who supply. Pressure placed on any one level of the supply chain will have a ripple effect all along, and so the pressure for improvement must be shared. Any evaluation/performance improvement scheme needs to include elements of assistance and co-operation as well as making demands.

The depth of investigation is dependent on many factors, e.g. industry type, level of technology of industry, resources available, access to expertise. At a more basic level where a full audit is not deemed necessary, this can be fed back to the supplier following questionnaires or across-the-board requirements.

With the expansion of the scope of supply-chain improvement, the requirement for a complete cycle of audit–feedback–development is even more important. Without this, a basis of continuous improvement cannot be guaranteed and the evaluation will be ineffective and inefficient. This highlights the need for measuring, reporting on and improving ethical performance. As a means of ensuring full involvement of stakeholders, the implementation of social audit is a very important and useful tool. It is also becoming a familiar term both in and outside the business framework. In this context, 'social audit' refers to the process whereby an organisation can account for, report on and improve its social performance. It assesses the social impact and behaviour of an organisation in relation both to its own aims and to those of its stakeholders (Sillanpaa and Wheeler 1997).

In terms of the supplier–customer relationship, social audit gives an opportunity for feedback and helps answer the questions concerning the type of ethical improvement needed in the supply chain and how that can be achieved in a manner that is acceptable and achievable by all parties. As such, it can also act as a major tool in the risk assessment of the supply chain. This option is not solely aimed at larger corporations: to ensure that this does not become the privilege of these larger organisations, guidelines have been produced for smaller organisations. Although this form of audit is comparatively new, the concept has rapidly become accepted and its usefulness as a strategic tool for total improvement has been recognised.

▌▌ *Ethical Screening: The Future*

Accountability up and down the supply chain will become a more important facet of business strategy in the future; however, it is likely to remain a tool for large organisations for some time. The broadening of the scope of investigation, screening and reporting, along with the expansion of communication and a sharpening of responsibilities for both manufacturer/customer and supplier will breed a better quality of relationship leading to better 'quality' products.

Supplier evaluation will be more structured and standardised due to the need for common expertise, not generally available to smaller businesses, requiring collaboration between businesses and NGOs. Expanding on this, future supply verification will be based on a widely approved set of criteria agreed by the customer and industry, endorsed by relevant stakeholders, e.g. NGOs, and assessed and verified by external agencies.

From this, individual businesses or industries will have 'add-on' investigation levels to reflect either the higher resources available or particular areas of concern. The gradual improvement in practice in all areas of ethical business practice will be seen as a means by which businesses can work together to gain a competitive edge and as a means of improving national business profile and raising business standards. Underlying this, a closer relationship between suppliers and customer companies will improve general performance on a more day-to-day level.

▌▌ *Conclusion*

The need for business to take on the responsibility for improvement of ethical performance in the supply chain is patent. However, in order for this to become mainstream practice and not just the responsibility of larger organisations or those with a sympathetic company culture, there must be more support and encouragement for smaller companies to adopt supply-chain improvement systems and more pressure for larger organisations to work in liaison with them.

For ethical evaluation to become a part of mainstream supplier evaluation alongside commercial and quality evaluation, there is a need for packages to guide businesses at all levels of capability and resource, considering not only the capabilities of the supplier but that of the customer company.

Section 4

Case Studies

19
The Practicalities of Greener Purchasing
A Guide with Examples from Washington State

Sandra Cannon

‖ *Introduction*

This chapter sets forth recommendations for the establishment and maintenance of a greener purchasing initiative. It discusses the practical issues that most organisations, regardless of size, will have to address, particularly, as is often the case, when purchasing responsibilities are decentralised. The three principles of greener purchasing—reduce purchases and packaging; re-use products; and purchase recycled products—are examined. In the final section, examples are drawn from two organisations in Washington State that are confronting the problems of improving suppliers' performance, overcoming internal opposition and capturing reliable statistics.

‖ *First Step for a Greener Purchasing Initiative: Who to Involve*

By analogy with 'one is what one eats', a budget is what one buys. A greener purchasing initiative will begin simply with an analysis of what is being bought, and this applies to all organisations, from small family businesses to multinationals. This analysis must involve the personnel actually responsible for purchasing, on whatever scale, as well as those within the organisation who will actually be using what is purchased.

Whether the impetus for the initiative has stemmed from the purchasing department, the end-user or upper management, the purchasers and users must be involved in the entire process—analysis, decision-making and implementation—because it is the purchasers and users who will either successfully or unsuccessfully implement the results. The purchasers know the suppliers, performance and prices of many products the company purchases. The users of the products typically have ideas about how the cost of a product could be saved by changing a process or re-using the product. Sometimes the first challenge is to convert the purchasers and users to thinking green. Involving them in the analysis can open a floodgate of information and good ideas and encourages green thinking in those who are reticent to change.

In companies with centralised purchasing departments, identifying the purchasers is easy. However, many companies have replaced their purchasing departments with decentralised systems, where responsibility is devolved throughout the organisation and employees are issued credit cards. Greening the purchasing of a company with decentralised purchasing is a greater challenge because of the shear number of employees involved. A company of 3,000 employees might have as many as 1,000 of them purchasing products. Each of those 1,000 needs to be invited, if not actively to analyse and decide on the company's purchasing practices, at least to contribute ideas to the analysis and decision-making.

A side-note to those companies considering decentralising their purchasing: in tallying up the cost savings of eliminating the purchasing department, managers need to take into account the increased cost of having numerous non-experts purchase the same product. Under the centralised system, typically one person always purchases certain products. That person keeps up to date on suppliers, best quality and best prices of her/his suite of products. Under a decentralised system, the same product may be purchased by 100 different employees. To find the supplier with the best-quality product at the best price, each of those employees must spend at least fifteen minutes checking catalogues and calling suppliers. An employee might purchase up to fifty products for her/his organisation. Fifty products times 100 employees times fifteen minutes' worth of their salaries can add up to a large sum of money.

‖ *Second Step: Identifying Products and Regulations*

Arriving at a list of what products a company purchases is fairly straightforward. It may be time-consuming because the list is enormous. If that is the case, hopefully the list is electronic so it can be quickly sorted by quantities and values. When gathering the list, knowing the quantities and values of the products a company purchases is important. The products on which the company spends the most money each year will be the ones the company wants to analyse first because they have the potential to provide the greatest savings.

In addition to knowing the products, a company also needs to identify any regulations governing its purchases. In the United States, for instance, certain purchases with federal money are governed by the Resource Conservation and Recovery Act (RCRA)[1] and Executive Order 12873[2] signed by President Clinton in October 1993. Because federal money infiltrates even local governments, the smallest of city governments in the United States comes under RCRA and Executive Order 12873.

The basic premise of RCRA and Executive Order 12873 is to reduce purchases to whatever extent possible, to re-use products whenever possible, and to purchase products with recycled content wherever possible. These tenets also apply to product packaging. RCRA and Executive Order 12873 also establish a framework for ensuring recycled products are purchased. The US Environmental Protection Agency (EPA) is given authority continually to designate products that must be purchased with a

---

1. 42 USC 6901 *et seq.* (as amended). 21 October 1976. 'Resource Conservation and Recovery Act of 1976'. Public Law 94-580.
2. 58 FR 54911 *et seq.* (as amended). 20 October 1993. 'Federal Acquisition, Recycling, and Waste Prevention'. Executive Order 12873.

specific amount of recycled content. President Clinton also established the Office of the Federal Environmental Executive to stimulate government 'to lead the way by buying products manufactured from the raw materials it recovers' (McPoland 1995: 2).

The designation process takes several years because: first, EPA identifies a recycled product that seems to be available for purchase. Then, EPA works with federal agencies, state and local governments, product manufacturers, key trade associations and standards development organisations to determine whether the product meets performance standards and is available throughout the nation. Next, EPA proposes the product be designated and asks for public comment on the designation and proposed recycled content. If the product passes muster, it is placed on the list of designated products. All government entities and contractors using federal money then have one year to establish programmes to ensure that the designated products they purchase contain the specified recycled content. The designated products do not have to be purchased if they are too costly, not available, or do not meet performance standards. To date, 36 products have been designated in a variety of categories, such as construction, landscaping, transportation, office and janitorial (see Fig. 4 in Chapter 3, page 50).

III *Third Step: Identifying Greener Purchasing Opportunities*

Once the products for which the company spends the most money and the products governed by regulations have been identified, the company will then want to analyse which purchases could possibly be reduced. If a product cannot be reduced, can it be re-used? For those products that can be neither reduced nor re-used, the company will want to discover whether the product can be economically purchased with recycled content. This involves surveying suppliers and comparing the recycled content with the performance and the price of each product, both in its recycled and virgin form.

To compare prices, a company should assess the life-cycle costs of the products in question. Not only should the recycled content, capital cost, installation cost, operating and maintenance costs be taken into account, but the environmental cost of producing the product as well as the environmental cost of disposing of it.

After the analysis, the company will want to implement greener purchasing initiatives. Specific techniques for reducing, re-using and buying recycled are discussed in the following sections, but all these methods require the establishment of a system that keeps employees up to date on how to reduce, re-use and purchase recycled products. For companies whose employees have access to the Internet, the most readily updatable and easily accessible source of information is a guide on the Internet. Next most accessible, economical and updatable would be to issue a guide either as an attached document to an e-mail message, on a diskette, or on a CD to all employees who purchase products. Such a guide would provide up-to-date information so employees know (1) how to reduce the purchase of products or find less toxic substitutes; (2) how to ensure re-use of products where feasible; (3) which products

---

3. For an example of such a guide, see the *GreenGuide* on the Internet at *http://www.pnl.gov/esp/greenguide/*.

are affected by any regulations for purchase with recycled content; (4) the percentage of recycled content required; and (5) which suppliers have recycled products available and, if possible, with a link to the suppliers' price information on the Internet.[3]

To purchase recycled products efficiently in a decentralised purchasing system, a company also needs to establish a communication network among all purchasers to share up-to-the-minute CAP (cost, availability, performance) information. Companies with electronic communication systems can use electronic mail to convey such information quickly with a pre-established mailing list of the company's purchasers. Should an employee become aware of a product, for example with 100% recycled content, which outperforms the parallel virgin products and has a lower price, that person can electronically alert the other purchasers to this opportunity.

Also necessary for a company with a decentralised purchasing system is to make green purchasing as easy as possible. Many suppliers of green products offer electronic purchasing on the Internet. It is worthwhile for a company to work with these suppliers to adapt their systems to the company's needs and train the company's employees on how to purchase green products on the Internet or at least how to find product information quickly.

Most important to the success of greener purchasing is for management to be a driving force and to fund both the establishment of the initiative as well as its maintenance and development once it is established. No matter how efficient the system is, it will need someone continually to encourage employees to find new ways to reduce and re-use, someone to discover new recycled products or at least recycled products with better performance and prices, someone to keep suppliers informed of the type of recycled product a company seeks, and someone to keep employees informed of the latest 'reduce', 're-use' and 'purchase recycled' information. Management's green purchasing motto should be 'spend enough to save a lot'.

▐ Fourth Step: Keeping the System Running

Green purchasing is not limited to the obvious products a company purchases. A company should also think green when purchasing services and products that are out of its normal line of purchases. For instance, it should build green purchasing into its subcontracts, or, when organising a conference, for example, a company will typically allocate money for hotels, shuttle services, name tags, handouts, food and waste disposal. Thinking green for each expenditure brings up the following questions. Can the conference be held at a 'green' hotel (one that has shown itself to be environmentally oriented)? Are public transport systems sufficient rather than renting individual automobiles? Are alternative-fuel vehicles available? Were plastic name tag covers collected at the end of a prior conference and now available for re-use, or are recycled plastic name tag covers at least available for purchase and then re-use at the next conference? Can speakers at the conference give their presentations electronically instead of with viewgraphs, or can the viewgraphs at least be printed on recycled viewgraph sheets? Do the attendees really want handouts? By having the attendees sign up at the conference for the handouts they desire, often the speaker can send the information electronically. If hard copy is needed, the quantity is limited to only the amount necessary. Can hard copies be printed double-sided with at least four viewgraphs to a side on chlorine-free, recycled paper with the highest post-consumer content? Has the company and environmental expense of disposable food containers been avoided by requiring all food to be served in durable containers? Are recycling containers available for those products that must be disposed of but can be recycled?

As soon as the word 'purchase' comes to mind, the questions of how to reduce, re-use and purchase recycled should immediately follow.

Reduce

Reducing means trying to eliminate the need for the product or service or replacing it with a less environmentally detrimental substitute, as well as reducing or eliminating product packaging. Questions to ask to help reduce are:

- Is there an alternative to the purchase? For example, could chemical purchases be eliminated by conducting the laboratory test electronically? Could paper purchases be reduced by sending messages, routing memorandums and publishing documents electronically?

- Is an environmentally benign substitute available that is less toxic or hazardous than the product being purchased? For example, could chlorine, phosphates and other harmful materials be reduced by purchasing cleaning products free of them?

- Is the quantity ordered only the amount needed? If ordering more than necessary, will the product go to waste in the future because the quantity will outlast its shelf-life?

- Can the product be purchased in bulk to reduce packaging?

Re-use

Re-using means using the product in its present form. Questions to ask to help re-use are:

- Has my company set up a system to encourage re-use by returning commodities (manila file folders and unused chemicals, for example) to supply cabinets when no longer needed or advertising their availability to other organisations instead of disposing of them?

- Does another department or organisation already have what is needed? If so, is it a commodity they will be willing to share or donate?

- Is the product to be purchased refillable or durable rather than disposable? What costs can be saved by purchasing durable rather than disposable products?

- Is the product repairable rather than replaceable? What costs can be saved by repairing rather than replacing?

- Can the product packaging be returned to the vendor (pallets, containers, etc.)?

Purchase Recycled

Purchasing recycled means buying products that are made of pre-consumer and post-consumer waste. Pre-consumer waste is material resulting from a production process, such as sawdust at a timber mill. Post-consumer waste is material that has served its intended purpose but instead of being disposed of is processed and used to make another product, such as copy paper being made into newspaper. Questions to ask to help purchase recycled products are:

▶ Is this product available with recycled content or in a remanufactured form?

▶ What is the highest recycled content available for the product, taking price into consideration?

▶ What is the energy-efficiency or water-conservation rating of the product? Is the same product available from another manufacturer with a better rating?

▶ How will the purchased product be disposed of when the end-user is done with it? Can it be re-used by others? Can it be recycled?

▶ Is there a threshold quantity beyond which the supplier will reduce the price of the recycled product? Can that quantity be reached by ordering in conjunction with others?

▶ Will the supplier accept the returned packaging? If not, is the packaging minimal, of recycled content, and recyclable?

▶ What is the life-cycle cost of the product: amortised annual cost of a product, taking into account the environmental cost of its production, the capital cost to the company as well as installation, operating, maintenance and disposal costs over the lifetime of the product?

▌▌ *Case Studies*

Once a company has established its greener purchasing programme, its employees are enthusiastic buyers of recycled products, and it has found suppliers for most of the recycled products needed, it will still be faced with the problems of CAPS:

▶ **C**ost

▶ **A**vailability

▶ **P**erformance

▶ **S**tatistics

Case examples of two organisations in Washington State, Walla Walla government offices and the Pacific Northwest National Laboratory, will be used to discuss each of these issues.

▌▌ *Cost: Pushing Prices Down*

A town in a sparsely populated area of the state of Washington tackled the problem of the cost of recycled products, in particular copy paper, being too high. Walla Walla has a population of 29,000 and is located three hours from the nearest metropolitan area. The government offices are small, typically purchasing quantities of copy paper in the area of fifty reams per year—not exactly an amount that makes paper companies desperate to compete for their business. The result was that these government offices were not purchasing recycled copy paper because the price in 1992–93, for example, was 17% higher than the price of virgin copy paper.

One solution seemed to be to form a co-operative to negotiate bulk prices. The Walla Walla County Recycling Committee (a volunteer group) invited the purchasing agents for the government offices in Walla Walla to a fact-finding meeting. They discovered all of the government offices were affected by Executive Order 12873 and that only one of them, the school district, ordered quantities of copy paper large enough to comprise a lorry-load—the minimum required for discount. By forming a co-op and thereby pooling their purchases, the government offices pushed the price of recycled copy paper down by almost $2.00 per ream and so were able to afford to purchase recycled.

The Pacific Northwest National Laboratory (PNNL) operated by Battelle for the US Department of Energy in Richland, Washington, also tackled the problem of the high cost of recycled products. The problem was that PNNL had switched from a centralised purchasing system to one where each organisation purchased products with a credit card. As in Walla Walla, the result was that none of the organisations ordered quantities large enough to have any price leverage. In addition, PNNL had approximately 100 staff members individually purchasing roughly the same products.

The solution was to establish preferred customer agreements with suppliers. PNNL went out with requests for proposal and selected the suppliers with the most recycled products that met the federal guidelines at the best prices. However, to keep those suppliers competitive with whom PNNL had agreements, PNNL still allowed its employees to purchase from any supplier. The advantages of purchasing from suppliers with whom PNNL had agreements were that the suppliers had greatly reduced their prices for PNNL because of the potential quantity of purchases and had set up electronic ordering systems which save employees' time. An example of the savings is the price of recycled diskettes, which went from $7.00 (well over the price of virgin diskettes) to $4.60 (still higher than virgin but within a reasonable price range).

Closed-loop agreements can push prices even lower by eliminating disposal costs. A company should seek to purchase recycled products from manufacturers who will take the used products back as parts for remanufacturing. Recycled toner cartridges and retread tyres are two examples of products that lend themselves to closed-loop contracts.

▌ Availability: Pressing Suppliers to Produce

Usually keeping suppliers apprised of what products a company needs is sufficient to ensure the availability of recycled products. Sometimes, however, encouragement is needed.

Avoiding single-supplier contracts can help a company ensure the availability of the recycled products it wants to buy. The supplier with whom PNNL had the office product agreement had no plastic envelopes with recycled content available but a competitor did. Sharing that information pressed the preferred supplier to start carrying the product as well.

Closed-loop contracts can also help ensure availability. The supplier with whom PNNL had a toner cartridge agreement had no recycled ink-jet cartridges. However, PNNL had established a closed-loop contract with that supplier. By returning spent ink-jet cartridges to the supplier, it soon was able to manufacture recycled ink-jet cartridges.

||| Performance: Appealing to Pride

Poor performance is a third problem companies need to address. An example is the initial poor performance of recycled toner cartridges. When recycled toner cartridges first came on the market in the United States, no specifications were available to define quality. Many sold were of poor quality, giving them a bad reputation which is hard to reverse.

PNNL tackled the problem by first testing a variety of recycled toner cartridges and defining specifications for them. With the specifications in hand, PNNL then established agreements with suppliers, which included guarantees that their recycled toner cartridges would meet the specifications, any defective cartridges would either be replaced or the money refunded, and any damage to printers as a result of a defective cartridge would be paid for. For those employees who refused to use recycled cartridges because of bad experiences in the past, PNNL solicited free recycled cartridges from the preferred suppliers for doubting staff to test. The tests were 100% successful and turned the negative attitudes around.

||| Statistics: Capturing the Successes

To continually improve its green purchasing programme, a company needs to track its purchases of recycled products. Purchasing recycled products is typically not as difficult as how to measure the success in purchasing them, especially for companies with decentralised purchasing systems. How can a company capture the purchases from numerous suppliers by 1,000 employees?

PNNL first tried having staff report their purchases directly. While 33% of the purchasing staff responded, that still did not capture PNNL's actual success rate. The reason for the low response rate was that not all staff had systems set up where they could easily pull such information together. Because purchasing is only a minimal component of these staff members' work, there was a question as to the appropriateness of funding an extensive amount of time to set up information collection systems tailored to each staff member's situation.

Next PNNL tried having the suppliers provide statistics. However, only six of the suppliers had the capability. These six were for the most part national companies with electronic systems from which they could readily pull the statistics needed. The positive component of gathering statistics from the suppliers is that it affords a regular opportunity to review the results with the suppliers, applaud them when they have worked hard to provide the recycled products needed, and encourage them to add those recycled products to their inventory that are lacking. These discussions should focus on the CAP (cost, availability and performance) and thereby make suppliers aware that providing quality recycled products at reasonable prices is in their companies' best interest. However, as only six suppliers provided statistics, this still did not capture PNNL's success rate.

So PNNL incorporated a recycled statistics component into its purchasing card and purchase request software programmes. When staff reconcile their purchasing card bills or make a purchase request, they indicate which of their purchases are recycled products. The programme then generates a report, denoting the quantity of the designated products purchased with and without recycled content.

The one drawback seems to be the need to rely on input from staff because the purchasing software programme does not capture enough information from the supplier to recognise which products are recycled. While this appears to be a retreat to PNNL's initial system of asking staff to supply the statistics, it is an organised retreat. Staff already have to reconcile their purchasing card bills. By allowing them to indicate in the course of that reconciliation which products have recycled content, PNNL was offering them an organised way to report without costing them much additional time.

The ability to capture statistics through PNNL's purchasing software programmes was a learning process. For example, the programmes at first did not allow staff to indicate the reason for not purchasing the designated products with recycled content. An ability to indicate that the product was not purchased with recycled content because of the CAP has now been incorporated.

Another example is that the default for the purchasing card software programme was set so staff had to remember to denote 'recycled' for such products. The results of the first purchasing card report showed staff purchased only 13% of the designated products in contrast to the supplier statistics for the same period which showed staff purchased 68%. (However, for that period, even the supplier statistics were questionable since the statistics from the first two quarters of 1997 showed staff to be purchasing over 80% of the designated products.) The default is now being changed so that staff must select whether the product had recycled content or not. As the purchasing card and purchase request software programmes are fine-tuned, PNNL will continue to compare the resulting statistics with those from the suppliers until it is sure it is capturing as accurately as possible its recycled product purchasing success.

Recommendation. The most accurate way to capture recycled product purchasing success would be for the manufacturers to agree on a set of common codes for like products. The codes would indicate whether a product was recycled and what recycled content it contained. This would be comparable to what the plastics industry did by placing a number on the bottom of plastic containers to indicate the type of plastic. If recycled products had a similar system, then any company's software could identify which recycled products its staff had purchased and which were not being purchased. The company could then work to solve the reasons why particular recycled products were not being purchased and turn that around—a goal for the future of greener purchasing and a goal for the future of a greener company.

20 Enabling Environmentally Conscious Decision-Making in Supply Chains
The Xerox Example

Kirstie McIntyre

Ill Introduction

It is suggested that it is the supply chains of the future that will bring true com-petitive advantage to companies (Christopher 1993). Currently, supply chain organ-isations have to compete in rapidly changing circumstances, not least legal, but also customer requirements, performance measurements, data provision and labour mar-kets, to name a few. Information is a key factor in the continuing development of supply chain operations. Measurement is a quality management tool enabling the monitoring and subsequent better understanding of processes and operations. Mea-suring performance is not just about how well a company is doing, it is also a means of demonstrating its recognition of its obligation to the future. The environment in which supply chains operate is changing rapidly. In order to accommodate this change, those managing the firm need adaptable and accurate performance metrics (Caplice and Sheffi 1994). The Integrated Supply Chain at Xerox Ltd is a large, complex organisation which has many potential impacts on the environment. In order to better understand and reduce those impacts, an environmental bias has been intro-duced into the decision-making process which allows more environmentally con-scious decisions to be made. This chapter details some of the issues concerning the measurement of environmental performance in supply chains and how Xerox has developed its own environmental performance matrix to provide a measure of envi-ronmental performance for the whole supply chain, for each functional element within the chain and for different product delivery scenarios.

Ill Greening the Supply Chain

A review of current measurement techniques in the supply chain discusses the appar-ent divergence between two developing schools of thought on measuring supply chain performance and greening supply chains (McIntyre *et al.* 1998a). Although there has been considerable effort placed on measuring supply chains in order to assess their performance, these techniques have been found to be time- and cost-focused, aimed at coping with rapid change. This approach tends to have a short-term outlook. Work on 'greening' supply chains is much longer term in outlook, is information-intensive and biased towards the supply side. These two mindsets appear to be developing in conflicting directions. This is an alarming prospect for the environment, which has no place in future supply chain performance measurements, thus running the risk of being increasingly sidelined; and for performance measurement, which is unconcerned with longer-term sustainability in terms of the environment.

The study of logistics is a developing subject area, but practitioners are realising that the environment is important for supply chain organisations too. There have been considerable environmental developments within certain discrete elements of the supply chain, but the danger lies in viewing any of the aspects in isolation (Penman 1994). There is a need to look strategically beyond the immediate environmentally driven aspects of supply chain management. The logistics discipline is well qualified to deal with cradle-to-grave issues because of logistics' focus on supply chain management, which emphasises the control of materials from suppliers, through value-added processes and on to the customer. The interface between logistics and the environment is embedded in the value-adding functions a firm performs (Wu and Dunn 1995). To minimise total environmental impact, it must be evaluated from the total-system perspective.

However, there are still many advocates of concentrating on one or two aspects of supply chain operations and functions in order to improve overall environmental performance. While there is nothing wrong with taking this approach to begin with, it is difficult to see where the most environmental impact is realised in the supply chain and whether it is being reduced by acting on one part of the whole chain. Functional units within a supply chain that are recommended for environmental action are the transport and storage of goods. Cooper, Browne and Peters (1992: 270-92) suggest that, as this is at the centre of any logistics activity, these are where a company should concentrate its efforts to reduce its environmental impacts. Transport is viewed as an activity with a negative environmental impact, yet the transport sector represents 7% of the GDP of Western Europe and employs 7% of the workforce. On the other hand, the cost to society in terms of congestion, pollution and accidents has been estimated to be 5% of the GDP (Howie 1994). Reverse logistics management is also recommended as the answer to improving the environmental impact of the supply chain by improving material use. Lamming and Hampson (1996) mention that 'environmental pressures may be expected to increase in the future' and suggest that 'an effective means of dealing with them must be implemented through the purchasing function'. The supplier base of a company can act as the focus for supply chain environmental performance, but environmental performance criteria need to be attached to the whole supply chain function to encompass the whole, not just the upstream, effects.

The accounting function of a supply chain is proposed as the ideal environmental performance measurement tool. 'Life-cycle costing' encompasses every conceivable direct and indirect cost associated with the acquisition, operation, support and disposal of the system. It should be capable of providing comparisons, identifying risks and establishing baseline data for sensitivity analysis (Jones 1995: 18.1-9). Accountancy can act as a scorekeeper, but it has not yet achieved this role for the environment. The incorporation of the environment into accountancy may help managers to decide whether they are moving away from or towards sustainability (Bebbington, Gray and Thomson 1994). However, formal decision analysis and traditional management accounting neglect the social costs and benefits of corporate activities. Management is under pressure to provide this type of information to stakeholders, but specialist information on the environment is unfamiliar to accounting systems. Conventional accounting and traditional economics consider preference indicated by willingness to pay, but this is a rather exploitative approach to natural resources.

Stakeholders are also taken as the focus for environmental performance (Azzone *et al.* 1996; IBM 1995). IBM asked its stakeholders—employees, customers, investors, decision-makers, etc.—what they considered to be the most important aspects of IBM's environmental performance. The results were quite interesting and showed that proof of concern and action for the future was foremost in the stakeholders' minds. Cahan and Schweiger (1994) stress the importance of integrating environmental considerations into corporate decision-making in order to reduce impacts through the product's life-cycle. This a very useful point, but neither takeback nor the transport element of the life-cycle are considered. James and Bennett (1993) aim to show companies why they should be measuring environmental performance. While this is the most comprehensive of the environmental performance measurement systems reviewed, it is too generic and would require a vast amount of information to make it work. What the outcomes of such a huge database would be are not clear.

Corbett and van Wassenhove (1991) remind us that the disastrous effects of an incorrect performance measurement system is illustrated by the poor environmental state of Eastern Europe. Eastern European governments found a fixed relationship between input and output of plants. The input used by a plant was taken as the measure of a plant's performance, as it was easier to measure than output. This provided plant managers with a very strong incentive to maximise input per unit output, leading to highly inefficient manufacturing practices currently encountered in Eastern Europe: the amount of energy and other inputs required by a plant per unit value of output is 2–3 times higher than that of the West.

▌▌ *The Role of Logistics*

Logistics is not just about lifting and shifting, but has an important contribution to make to competitive advantage. Logistics has the advantage of cutting across traditional functional boundaries and being able to provide an integrated concept. There is a debate currently under way as to whether it is better to take a vertical (or functional) focus in the firm or a horizontal (or process) orientation (Christopher 1993). Cooper (1994) proposes that planning and forecasting will be very important to supply chains in the future, if somewhat difficult. Until the 1970s, products were pushed down distribution channels to the customer; during the 1980s, systems became driven by customer needs and this demand-pull logistics continues into the 1990s. For the new millennium, logistics will move into flexible fulfilment, customising to the exact terms of product configuration and service. As Cooper highlights, uncertainty can lead to the inefficient use of time in logistics, which becomes especially important when companies start competing through time in order fulfilment. Therefore 'smarter systems are needed to simulate modelling approaches to test new designs thoroughly at the conceptual stage' (Cooper 1994: 11). This is particularly pertinent in terms of the environment where it is important to identify the impacts resulting from a course of action before damage has occurred.

▌ *Xerox's Integrated Supply Chain*

From the comments summarised above, it is apparent that there is a need for a top-level decision-making tool for the supply chain, one that considers every part of the supply chain and which can be related back to the metrics that are used to plan better supply chains. At Xerox Ltd, such a tool has been designed and is aimed at senior managers to enable more environmentally conscious decisions to be made about manufacturing and supply chain strategy at any point in a product's life-cycle. As suggested, the environment is of increasing importance to the Integrated Supply Chain and will form part of the new generation of more externally focused logistics metrics. Information is seen as being key to the future competitiveness of Integrated Supply Chains and the management and dissemination of this information is vitally important. The metric has to be designed to represent all sections of the Integrated Supply Chain. However, as can be appreciated, there are many different functions within a supply chain, all of which have distinct performance measurements and different effects on the environment.

All of these impacts and measurements make it hard to encapsulate the overall picture of environmental performance throughout the organisation. The many different processes result in many different impacts on the environment and, while all of these could be recorded and indeed many are, they cannot be added together or be compared to give an overall performance view. Until the environment becomes represented by an easily understood, top-level metric, it will be difficult to achieve the level of environmental integration that will be required to make the leap into long-term sustainability. In order to tackle this problem, an 'environmental common denominator' approach has been adopted. All processes and operations have environmental themes running through them: the amount of energy they consume, their materials intensity or the pollutants produced. It is these on which the Xerox Environmental Performance Matrix has concentrated, as demonstrated in Figure 1.

In this way, it is possible to identify 'hot spots' of environmental impact within the Integrated Supply Chain which can be targeted and improved. This matrix approach is readily expanded to incorporate other factors such as financial cost and time to represent the business case. Values such as corporate priorities can be added to reflect changing attitudes and situations. The actual data contained within the model is useful to identify the 'hot spots' of high energy consumption or low materials intensity. However, the real strength of this decision-making tool comes when planning future strategies or assessing different manufacturing or product delivery scenarios. In this way, different scenarios can be run that highlight changes in the 'hot spots' of environmental impact or affect overall values. For example, a decision can be made regarding currently ambiguous situations—e.g. the environmental impacts of different servicing strategies. Decisions such as these are currently being made at Xerox without the ability to consider the whole picture. This in no way suggests that current decisions are the wrong ones, but that this is uncertain from an environmental perspective owing to the lack of effective measurement tools.

FUNCTIONAL ELEMENTS OF THE XEROX INTEGRATED SUPPLY CHAIN

ENVIRONMENTAL COMMON DENOMINATOR	Acquire	Assemble	Distribute	Install	Working life	Remove	Asset recovery
Energy consumption	E_{aq}	$+E_{as}$	$+E_d$	$+E_i$	$+E_{wl}$	$+E_r$	$+E_{ar}$
Materials intensity	M_{aq}	$+M_{as}$	$+M_d$	$+M_i$	$+M_{wl}$	$+M_r$	$+M_{ar}$
Pollutants emitted	P_{aq}	$+P_{as}$	$+P_d$	$+P_i$	$+P_{wl}$	$+P_r$	$+P_{ar}$

Figure 1: The Xerox Environmental Performance Matrix

The model seen above is constructed using data readily available at Xerox. By taking the standard elements of the supply chain—e.g. 'acquire'—this means that the model, although measuring a different aspect, is familiar to those who are intended to use it. It is important to present a recognisable format to potential practitioners—in a familiar language using customary terms and formats. Each element of the supply chain is broken down into its component parts. This is achieved by taking one product delivered through the Xerox Integrated Supply Chain and interviewing those managers responsible for that element of the supply chain. This yielded a list of sub-processes for which specific data could be gathered. This makes data-gathering a more straightforward process as specific environmental information is sought from those particular parts of the organisation. It then becomes a matter of standardising the data across the supply chain to provide a measure of environmental performance capable of being compared both across the supply chain in different scenarios and within the distinct functional elements. For energy consumption, this is a matter of converting electricity and gas consumption by manufacturing plants presented in kWh (kilowatt hours) into MJ (megajoules) and similarly converting the fuel energy consumed by transport elements in litres of diesel to MJ. The conversion factors for these are standard terms of reference and can be found in Boustead and Hancock 1981, for example. This gives a total energy consumption for each element within the supply chain and, by totalling across the matrix, for that particular supply chain scenario. As mentioned above, this work has concentrated on one supply chain scenario to simplify the amount of data required to populate the model and demonstrate its use.

Although somewhat crude, the model as described above provides a method for comparing different supply chain scenarios and for understanding where in a supply chain the environmental hot spots are. This in turn provides indicators for where to concentrate effort in managing and reducing environmental impacts. In effect, it acts as a root cause analysis for identifying and prioritising environmental impacts within a very large and complex organisation. Once all the data have been collected, the functional unit then has to be established. This is important so that the terms of reference for the subsequent results are confirmed. As mentioned above, one product has been used for clarity when collecting data. This is a new product which represents the future of products for Xerox Ltd. The geographical area is restricted to the UK—again for ease of data collection, but this can be readily expanded for the whole of Europe. The average lifetime of these products is assumed to be approximately five years, although this is difficult to predict as the products are designed to be upgradable within the customer's premises. Therefore the functional unit is one year's service from a digital copier/printer. This 'discounts' the environmental impact of acquiring the components, assembling the machine, delivering and installing it by five, as this 'cost' is, in effect, spread over the five years of lifetime.

Preliminary results show that it is the working life of the machine that consumes the most energy relative to the other parts of its supply chain. The acquisition of the materials and components is also an important factor in the overall picture. These results are not unexpected. Full life-cycle analysis (LCA) of another Xerox product and washing machines have shown that it is the working life of the machine that creates the biggest environmental impact (Xerox Corp. 1997; Jonson 1997). This is certainly the case in terms of energy. The energy consumption represented here includes the direct electricity consumption of the machine, the manufacture and delivery of spare parts, including toner cartridges, and the transport energy used by the service engineer when travelling to service the machine. However, results also show that the delivery of components within the 'acquire' function is also very important. This suggests that the sourcing of raw materials can have a great impact on the environmental performance of a product.

However, there is more than one environmental common denominator that has been identified to describe usefully the environmental impacts arising from the supply chain of a Xerox product. Another common denominator that has been mapped is the pollutants that are emitted from each stage in the supply chain of this Xerox product. Pollutants emitted were chosen because all stages in the life of a product cause airborne pollutants to be emitted to the atmosphere whether directly or indirectly. There are diesel emissions from freight trucks delivering components to the manufacturing site or finished goods to the customer, and also indirect air emissions from power stations generating electricity used to run the product or operate machinery that manufactures the product. Although all stages in the life-cycle of the product result in air emissions, there are many different types, and again the problem of comparing like with like throughout the supply chain arises. Recently, ICI plc in the UK put together their 'Environmental Burden Approach' to measuring pollutants emitted from their operations in the UK (ICI 1997). The approach ranks different chemical emissions in order of their potential to cause environmental damage. Chemicals are compared and given a 'global warming potential' which indicates how effective that chemical is in adding to global warming. Carbon dioxide is given a global warming potential of 1 and carbon monoxide a potential of 3. ICI has generated these indices (see ICI 1997 for details) using external experts to validate the methodology and data. The formula, which enables the evaluation of the relative potential environmental impacts of ICI's emissions, reflects both the weight (in tonnes) and the potency of each emission to exert its possible impact. This gives an overall global warming potential for that emission.

The rationale for applying this methodology to the Xerox Integrated Supply Chain is that it too has many different functional elements, all of which produce a range of chemical emissions. Simply adding these together would not give a readily understandable metric that would indicate whether or not that supply chain scenario caused less environmental impacts than another. Of course, there are orders of magnitude difference between the air emissions produced by an ICI chemical plant and the 'install' function of the Xerox supply chain, for example, but the comparability across functions in still valid. Using the same sub-processes as identified in the energy consumption model, air emissions are allocated to the functional elements of the supply chain. The data used are taken from a variety of published sources and also from the *Eco-bilan* life-cycle analysis software databases that Xerox Corporation uses for full product life-cycle studies (Xerox Corp. 1997). These data are not claimed to be irrefutable, but the best that are available at the current time. When more accurate data become available, they will be inserted into the model. Air emissions arising from power generation are taken from the UK Electricity Industry's website[1] and uses data from 1995, and are those attributed to power generation from fossil fuel. In the UK, this accounts for 64% of the total power generated, but for this study 100% of electricity is assumed to be generated from fossil-fuel-fired power stations. This makes the air emissions from electricity consumption higher than they are actually but, for comparison's sake, this does not distort the figures disproportionately. The results indicate that again it is the working life of the product that causes the most environmental impact due, in the main, to the direct energy consumption of the machine and manufacture and delivery of spare parts.

III **Summary**

The methodology described above has shown that environmental impacts can be modelled for a complex, dynamic, multifunction organisation such as the Xerox Ltd Integrated Supply Chain. The results generated are enabling relationships to be established between current measures of performance within the supply chain, such as stocking levels in warehouses, and the environment. In this way, managers will be able to see what impact on the environment will result from their decisions made concerning the supply chain. This work continues to expand this level of understanding within Xerox Ltd and is now being incorporated into standard supply chain modelling at Xerox. The next steps with this project are to develop the materials intensity common denominator and to further establish the relationships between environmental impacts and current supply chain measures. This will result in more environmentally conscious decision-making in the Xerox Ltd Integrated Supply Chain.[2]

1. UK Electricity Industry website: *http://www.electricity.org.uk:80/uk_inds/environ/brochure97_gen.html*.
2. For a more in-depth discussion on the development and results of this model, see McIntyre *et al.* 1998b.

21
Purchasing Operations at Digital's Computer Asset Recovery Facility

Joseph Sarkis, Mark Liffers and Susan Malette

||| Introduction

Green purchasing is critical to a green supply chain. The elements of the green supply chain include both forward and reverse logistics. To move product and material through an industrial eco-system, the purchasing and logistics functions of an organisation form the most important inter-enterprise linkages. Purchasing green materials is not necessary for operations of a forward logistics chain, but is required for reverse logistics operations to exist. Reverse logistics has a number of elements, including operations of disassembler, demanufacturing, or remanufacturing organisations. These organisations and their customers have both typical and special purchasing requirements. The purchasing and logistics function within a demanufacturing or disassembly organisation has special requirements and characteristics that make it unique from a natural environment perspective.

This chapter investigates the purchasing relationships between a demanufacturing operation, its customers, and suppliers. Digital Equipment Corporation (Digital)'s America's Material Recovery Organisation (AMRO) will be the specific demanufacturing operation where various green purchasing and logistics practices are described. Not only is this organisation not a typical production, warehousing and service facility, it is unique in that it is also one of the first organisations in Digital (and the US) to be ISO 14001 certified. Even though many of the practices detailed here are specific to this particular organisation, there are clear factors that can be applied to industry practice in general. In addition, the processes and operations that are performed at this facility contribute to making supply chains more green. This facility completes the green supply chain by providing processes and services to remanufacture, re-use and recycle equipment, components and parts. By definition, most material purchased by this organisation (or all supplies that flow into the manufacturing system) could be considered a 'green' purchasing arrangement. Also, this organisation may serve as a supplier for other companies that wish to practise green purchasing.

A number of characteristics of a disassembly and demanufacturing organisation are identified in this chapter. These corporate environmental and operational characteristics have implications for both the purchasing and logistics functions. The

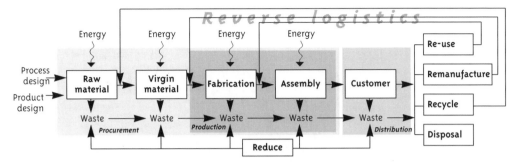

Figure 1: Functional Model of an Organisational Operational Life-Cycle with Environmentally Influential Practices

discussion will focus not only on material purchasing operations, but also how customers' purchasing practices may be influenced by AMRO. Evidence will show that multifunctional input is critical to the green purchasing and logistics dimensions of the organisation. Initially, some general background on green supply chain management and purchasing will be introduced. A brief description of the organisational background and environment of the AMRO facility will begin the case study. General operating practices and policies are reviewed. A summary of the issues and practices completes this chapter.

‖ *Purchasing and Green Supply Chains*

Competitive pressures have recently begun to force organisations to incorporate natural environmental dimensions into their strategic plans and operational execution. These dimensions have been felt not only in traditionally environmentally sensitive industries such as chemicals and petroleum, but have effected the planning and practices of other manufacturing and service-based industries. From a core operational perspective, environmental influences range from inbound logistics (where purchasing and procurement play a large role), to manufacturing and operations, to outbound logistics and distribution. Supporting functions such as engineering, finance and information systems have also been profoundly influenced by these greening pressures.

Purchasing and logistics functions are the engines that allow materials to flow through an organisation. Purchasing includes not only the movement of materials, but relates to the selection of vendors, design of products and processes, packaging, outsourcing, strategic partnership formation and inventory management, among other organisational activities. The relationship of procurement and logistics within a general operational life-cycle framework is shown in Figure 1. Within Figure 1 we see a material flow that is influenced by the process and product design. Waste, and thus environmental influences, can be seen throughout this framework (in addition to wastes that may occur within the reverse logistics flow portion of the cycle, which is not detailed in this diagram). Three general practices for reintroducing materials back into a manufacturing system—re-use, remanufacturing and recycling—

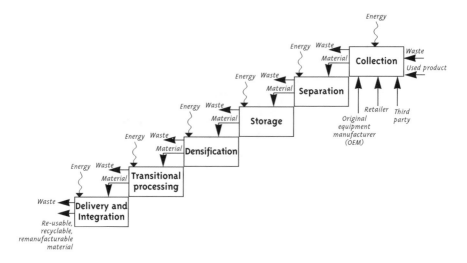

Figure 2: Functional Components of a Reverse Logistics Chain

are shown in Figure 1. The further 'upstream' that a material is introduced into this operational cycle, the larger the potential energy used and waste generated before the product flows back out of the system. The range of potential negative environmental impacts moves (most to least) from disposal to recycling to remanufacturing to re-use and finally reduction. This relationship also holds true for the reverse logistics chain, where potential profit margins of material that flows through the phases of reverse logistics are greatest for re-usable material since they would typically require less energy and processing.

A typical set of reverse logistics activities and processes are shown in Figure 2. This reverse logistics cycle requires wastes or used products as a major input. Purchasing or procurement's primary activities are to locate and acquire the necessary material from 'vendors' who supply the necessary material that will be re-integrated into the forward logistics stream. Unfortunately, sales and marketing for vendors of material that needs to flow into the reverse logistics activities is not as well established as those for materials and supplies for forward logistics. This purchasing and marketing relationship in the reverse logistics cycle is the primary area of our case study. Each of the activities shown in Figure 2 is also completed by the AMRO facility. It is not the goal of this chapter to detail the efforts in each of these activities, which are interesting more from a general operations perspective.

▌▌ *The America's Materials Recovery Operation (AMRO) at Digital*

Digital is one of the world's leaders in open client–server computing solutions, from personal computers to integrated worldwide information systems. The corporation does business in 100 countries, deriving more than 65% of its revenue from outside of the United States, developing and manufacturing products in North and South America, Europe, and the Pacific Rim. Digital, a Massachusetts corporation founded in 1957, is a world leader in implementing and supporting networked business solutions in multi-vendor environments based on high-performance platforms and global service and support. Digital provides a complete range of information-processing solutions from personal computers to integrated worldwide information systems.

Digital's organisational structure is composed of three major divisions or groups: Manufacturing; Sales and Marketing; and Field Services. It is within the Field Services group that its facilities for recovery of material and products are controlled. There are two facilities within Digital that carry out recovery of materials from products manufactured by Digital and other organisations within the computer electronics industry. One facility, located in the Netherlands, is the European Materials Recovery Operation. The second facility, which this case study will examine, is located in Contoocook, New Hampshire, in the United States. This facility is called the America's Materials Recovery Operation (AMRO).

Initially, in the 1970s and early 1980s, the AMRO site was just a distribution and warehouse facility. In 1986 the product disassembly centre was added and eventually became AMRO. Its sole purpose was to serve as an end-of-life facility for Digital products and components. The origination of this facility and its operations was to provide Digital with an avenue to maintain control over its waste stream. Initially formed under a reactive policy of responding to environmental regulations, these operations soon evolved into a strategic element of Digital services offered to its customer base. Much of the material that Digital sent through its operations cycle had a number of potentially hazardous by-products. To minimise the environmental damage caused by these end-of-life materials, Digital decided to disassemble the components and direct its waste stream in the most efficient and environmentally benign direction. Part of the motivation for maintaining its own disassembly facility was that many of the products offered by Digital at that time were leased products.

Eventually, Digital realised that many of the products that were either returned, obsolete or beyond repair had components and elements that could be re-used, remanufactured or recycled. These characteristics of the material and products allowed Digital to benefit from the reintroduction or resale of components and materials. What was viewed as a cost centre had the capability to provide a cash flow stream that could be profitable. The AMRO facility demanufactures between 25–30 million pounds of discarded electronic equipment every year. It is currently self-sufficient and even generating positive revenue for Digital. The Contoocook facility is also one of the first twenty organisations in the US to gain ISO 14001 certification.

Operations at the AMRO Facility

The AMRO facility serves two major functions: as a warehouse for returned and excess equipment, and also as a materials recovery facility. The operations in this portion of the plant typically involve the acquisition and receipt of products and materials. Two inbound flows of material make up over 25 million pounds per year that is processed at the AMRO facility. The first flow of material goes directly to the disassembly portion of the facility, the second to a sorting section to determine the category of material. The material may be (1) stored as-is in the warehouse facility or (2) tested. Testing determines whether it is working, needs some simple 'remanufacturing', or needs to be disassembled for recovery of re-usable parts or recyclable material. Clearly, depending on the material inflow, some materials will require little processing, while others will require a significant amount of processing. Thus, the AMRO facility is geared to operate through the spectrum of practices defined above.

Computer and electronics components form the overwhelming proportion of material that is processed within AMRO. However, office furniture and other office-related products and materials also arrive for processing. Typically, intact parts are removed, tested and stocked as spares. Precious metals (gold, platinum and silver) are extracted and resold. Plastic, glass and other materials are recycled. Less than 0.1% of the material ends up in landfills.

Long-term purchasing and policy decisions for the AMRO facility are primarily controlled through the corporate headquarters. The determination of which vendors are acceptable and the criteria that need to be met for materials and supplies are determined by the corporate acquisition group. As part of the general environmental and corporate standards set by this group, a restricted materials list is published. It is part of corporate policy not to purchase materials from this 'laundry list' of hazardous material, nor can that material occur in any products. These are the primary environmental factors that are explicitly considered in any vendor selection or contract agreement.

▌▌▌ Demanufacturing Materials Suppliers for the AMRO Facility

Purchasing, marketing and customer service at the AMRO facility are intertwined. Purchasing and the remaining functions within AMRO are primarily focused on managing a reverse logistics function. The reverse logistics system causes a fuzzy relationship to exist between marketing and purchasing, including the roles of marketing agents as purchasers and customers as suppliers.

One of the unique purchasing characteristics of the AMRO facility is the dual role of the supplier of material also serving as a customer. The suppliers of the 'raw material' that flows into the AMRO facility for processing are divided into internal and external suppliers. The internal materials supplies include equipment and materials from other groups and divisions within Digital. Some of the external suppliers include organisations that have various Digital and brand-name electronic components that they no longer require, are obsolete, scraps, etc. Internal suppliers of material to AMRO include the manufacturing plants, physical plants and any other facilities owned or operated by Digital. To do business with AMRO, internal suppliers compose a service-level agreement or internal contract. The materials from internal suppliers include inventories that may have been stored in manufacturing or service parts warehouses. External suppliers include a number of *Fortune 500* and small companies, as well as various governmental and municipal agencies. The external suppliers are divided into the following five categories:

1. Original equipment manufacturers
2. Brokers
3. Assemblers
4. Financial and institutional businesses
5. Government agencies

These suppliers of material to AMRO come from all stages within a supply chain. The original equipment manufacturers may deliver material right from their processes (from scrap) or inventory (obsolete material). Brokers serve a collection role and serve as an intermediary for disposal or resale of products. Assemblers are similar to manufacturing in that scrap and obsolete material may be sent to the AMRO facility, while financial institutions and government agencies dispose of their equipment after use usually due to upgrading or equipment that is beyond repair.

Some municipal government relationships go even further into the post-disposal stage of a supply chain. One example is an innovative pilot study with some local government agencies to locate electronics equipment for recycling. This initiative does not look at the agencies' offices, but is investigating the possibility of exploring local landfills for computer and electronic components. At present, this project is only at the planning and feasibility stages of investigation.

Currently, there are less than 100 external suppliers of material for processing at AMRO. Since locating external suppliers is a relatively recent (within the previous two years) strategic focus of AMRO, the number of materials suppliers is expected to grow substantially. An important part of the marketing strategy to increase these external suppliers is to offer computer assets recovery as part Digital's service portfolio. When corporate marketers and salespersons seek out potential customers, this after-sales service has become an important and creative dimension to the life-cycle product and service portfolio offered by Digital. Within Digital, it is termed the 'reverse logistics' service offering.

As stated above, the suppliers of the raw materials are also customers. Whether a supplier could be considered a customer depends on whether there is an inflow or outflow of income. That is, some suppliers of material get paid if the value of the material that arrives at the AMRO facility is capable of generating more revenue than transportation and processing costs. If the material does not generate more revenue than the cost of transport and processing, it is expected that the supplier of the material will pay for the additional costs, thus a supplier becoming a customer.

▌▌▌ Purchasing Agents as Account Managers

In Digital, the external suppliers of the material for processing within the AMRO facility are called customers whether or not they are paid for the material, and they are managed by account managers. It is up to these account managers, who are physically located at the AMRO facility, to locate potential suppliers of material and negotiate contractual agreements. The process for determining the value of the material is also completed by these managers. This estimation and forecast of the potential value of the material is critical in determining the expected revenue and proceeds of the various deliveries.

These account managers, who are business managers with a fair amount of experience at mid-management level, have to be multi-skilled, since they serve as both purchasing agents and sales personnel. Negotiation skills, products, legal and environmental knowledge are essential. Of the four account managers, the background of one is as a former remediation manager from the environmental health and safety

(EHS) support function. Each of the managers has also been trained in various programmes offered by EHS.

The product life-cycle issues regarding computer and electronic components have a profound impact on the roles of the account managers and how they complete their jobs. The volatility in the computer and electronics component industry is due to the speed of innovation of most products, components and even processes. As product life-cycles continue to decrease, it is expected that the market for remanufacturing and demanufacturing operations will increase. Yet a difficulty arises in being able to forecast what the market will become. Account managers are faced with having to predict how long certain products will remain on the market and when the potential suppliers of AMRO materials will be available. In addition, they have to rely on the flexibility of the processes to handle whatever new advances will be encountered.

Locating Suppliers of Material. Finding organisations that want the service is another duty of the account managers. Materials suppliers receive a number of benefits from the AMRO facility, one being that these organisations no longer have to worry about where and who will take old equipment off their hands. Instead of paying a waste haulier to remove the equipment and pay for waste management costs, they may actually receive some potential income from this service. In addition, some organisations experience lowered environmental risks because products that they once owned would be managed within a set of environmentally conscious organisational processes. They are made more aware of the environmental performance and process management available at AMRO because of this facility's ISO 14001 certification, making the account manager's job much easier.

Selection of materials suppliers is not just a one-way street. Some material suppliers, viewing AMRO as a vendor that supplies a service to them, will complete a vendor certification process. One of the primary reasons that suppliers come to AMRO is for environmental reasons: they wish to dispose of their product in an environmentally sound manner (similar to the reason Digital established AMRO as an internal service group). Maximising financial recovery also plays a role. These materials suppliers come in and inspect the operations and processes from an environmental perspective. This certification process will, in the future, be less cumbersome for both internal and external environmental auditors due to the ISO 14001 certification of the facility. When internal materials suppliers come in to inspect the facility, the inspection is usually carried out by the corporate environmental staff. In a way, this serves as a self-audit of the facility.

▌ The Negotiation, Bidding and Pricing Process

Once potential customers are identified, a bidding process for the supplies may ensue. Even though this is a relatively new business environment, a number of large competitors do exist. Some of the larger competitors are the manufacturers of electronic components such as Lucent Technologies and Sun Microsystems. There are also specialised companies for electronics components materials recovery, such as ECS Refining, Inc. and BDI. The bids and the bidding process can range from simple bids sent by fax to long-term partnerships and alliances, which require a prolonged and detailed bid process. This process requires estimation of revenue and value of products. The prices and costs are negotiated for larger deals. Smaller bids are completed from a standardised price list that would be sent to potential suppliers of materials.

Pricing and Bidding by Account Managers. Since they are central to the negotiation and bid process, the account managers need to be able to estimate the worth of products and materials that flow into the disassembly system. Thus, awareness of the product, its components and recovery value is necessary. This knowledge helps them to determine the potential revenue that could be generated from the product or component once it has either been disassembled, repaired or stored for future re-use. Required knowledge includes market prices for various computer equipment, components, and various recyclable materials such as precious metals, metals, plastics, glass, etc. Sources of information would include commodities markets, computer markets (e.g. the Boston Computer group), and from customers for end-of-process (outputs) materials.

Knowing the potential revenue generation is only half the equation. The account managers also need to be aware of potential transportation, processing, handling and inventory costs for the various products that arrive. This will help them determine potential margins for the material from a supplier. Knowing the processing costs requires each account manager to be aware of the necessary process steps whether it is for re-use (e.g. storage costs), remanufacture (e.g. skilled labour, disassembly and assembly costs) or recycling and reclamation (disassembly, sorting, transportation). To acquire and maintain knowledge about the processes, account managers are usually out on the plant floor observing the various operations and keeping track of any changes in the process.

There is no standard contract or margin/price negotiation for materials. In fact, most contracts require a determination of the market price for various materials that flow out of the system before final revenue sharing or cost is determined. Every contract is unique. Furthermore, every computer system and its components delivered for evaluation by AMRO may also differ. For example, the differences in market price for a nine-year-old VAX system versus a ten-year-old system may depend on the value of any working components, the material within the components, and whether various components are still used in the current technology. To aid the account managers in estimating costs, a design-for-disassembly tool, from Boothroyd & Dewhurst, is currently being evaluated by AMRO management. This tool helps to determine what costs will be encountered in a disassembly process given a set of components. One rule of thumb that the account managers do use in their evaluation is that prices and margins decrease as product characteristics range from re-usable (remarketable), repairable, remanufacturable, recyclable materials to disposal.

Difficulties in Delivery Scheduling. Managing the delivery of supplies in this environment is also a difficult proposition. Thus far, other than general contractual relationships with the organisations (unless the contract is for a one-time delivery), no long-term scheduling of material deliveries is completed. A few days' notice is usually provided. There is some electronic tracking of the material as it is delivered, but this only occurs when actual delivery is taking place. Part of the reason for this type of situation is the difficulty (or lack) of forecasting when, what and why materials will be delivered to AMRO. This situation is true for both the supplier of the material and AMRO. The service-level agreement helps to define some of these issues from an internal customer perspective but, similar to external organisation contracts, delivery schedules are left open.

||| Outgoing Materials Management Suppliers

Similar to inbound materials suppliers that are considered customers, 'customers' for the outgoing processed materials from the AMRO facility are considered vendors. There are a number of outgoing materials vendors for the AMRO facility. These vendors may be grouped into:

▶ **Recyclers (basic materials)**

1. Copper smelters

2. Precious metal recovery

3. Scrap paper

4. Scrap metal recyclers

5. Hazardous waste disposal

▶ **Re-users and remanufacturers (parts and components)**

6. Brokers

7. Secondary parts suppliers (large and small)

8. Digital service parts stream

9. Repairable or directly re-usable material (may be stored in warehouse)

Again, similar to the relationship of the inflow materials suppliers, most of these groups of outflow materials vendors or customers may either charge AMRO for removing the material or pay AMRO for these same materials. That is, AMRO may either receive revenue or increase costs depending on the value of the material that is to be shipped out. Most of these vendors are approved and certified by Digital corporate headquarters. These vendors (from a corporate-headquarters-approved list by commodity) are asked to submit bids on a weekly or bi-weekly basis.

The outflow material suppliers and vendor base has shifted over the life of AMRO. Initially, AMRO's major processes focused on complete destruction and disposal of the equipment and components that flowed through it. Much of these destructive characteristics were due to the proprietary nature of the products owned by Digital. The products were smaller and lighter with less precious metal content, which made reclamation a less profitable enterprise. What wasn't recycled or reintroduced into other products was disposed of. With the focus on only Digital equipment and components, the remarketers and brokers were less interested in the outflow of materials. The new strategy of disassembly and processing of brand-name components and equipment provides opportunities to increase the numbers of brokers and remarketers. Now that computer components and products have become more mature (evolving through the product life-cycle), the amount of components and parts that have proprietary characteristics has decreased. This more mature product environment allows for easier resale and marketing of materials. Yet, even in a multi-vendor environment, many suppliers of material to AMRO will require full destruction of products, thus limiting the re-usability and remanufacturing markets. Reintroducing re-usable components to the market is slowed for competitive reasons. Thus, we see that maturing product life-cycles (and strategic proprietary reasons) have an impact on the types of operation that an asset recovery facility may pursue. The types of process requirement are typically included in any contractual agreements.

Over the years a few 'test' relationships have existed between Digital and its outflow materials vendors. One of the best-known examples of customer–supplier co-operation in a green supply chain context was a demonstration project operated jointly by Digital, General Electric Plastics and Nailite, Inc. of Miami, Florida. Obsolete Digital computer products are recovered from customers and dismantled in AMRO. The computer housings were shredded and the plastic is reprocessed and delivered to Nailite, where it is used to manufacture roofing products for McDonald's restaurants. The final result of this pilot study was that is wasn't economically viable. The total cost of the plastic tile was determined to be equal to that of new ones, and few markets were available for this product. Aesthetically, they couldn't compare to new tiles.

The second green supply pilot project focused on the glass material from cathode ray tubes (CRTs). This project was in response to the US EPA's efforts to limit more stringently the amount of lead allowed in the environment. Leaded glass, a major part of CRTs, has been considered hazardous and requires disposal in hazardous waste landfills. In 1989, before these restrictions became law, Digital sent one load of old CRTs to a hazardous waste landfill. With the transportation cost and manifesting requirements, the cost was around $200,000—about ten times their normal disposal fees. Envirocycle joined with Digital to begin developing a process for the leaded glass. Envirocycle approached Corning Asahi Video (a partnership between Corning and Asahi Glass in Japan) about the possibility of testing and ultimately using the recycled glass to manufacture new monitors and televisions. Development of a recycling process took about a year. Four different types of leaded glass are used by makers of CRTs and a way had to be found to keep each kind separate. Hazardous wastes now make up less than 0.5% of the waste generated from this facility.

These types of pilot relationship have been part of Digital's strategy to find new markets for materials that flow from the AMRO system. Of course, this requires close vendor, purchasing and logistics relationships to develop. Innovative environments such as this are a requirement for developing and building potentially lucrative supply chains of materials.

Improvement of Relationships between AMRO and Suppliers/Customers

Partnering with suppliers and customers is one of the critical roles of any procurement and purchasing function. The focus on partnering in this case is to improve product and processes within the partner organisations. One of the more important services offered by Digital and AMRO personnel to their materials suppliers is in the design of products and components. A service is offered where review of existing and proposed product designs and their environmental influences are to be completed. Both internal and external materials suppliers are charged for this service. Currently, many organisations take advantage of this service but future possibilities may allow for it to become fee-free if long-term relationships over the product's life-cycle are formed. With input from AMRO, the designs may allow for easier and more efficient disassembly and processing. AMRO needs to consider these savings.

Part of this design improvement process and service includes development of capability images. Photographs, component materials, man-hours, tools, options and alternatives are presented to material suppliers. This analysis can be carried out with either current products or with prototypes. Design-for-disassembly software from Boothroyd & Dewhurst (which was used by account managers for pricing) is useful for these activities. Some of these efforts within Digital have led to a number of changes as the products and components mature, and more recent material has clearly enjoyed the benefit of better design for disassembly. At the AMRO facility, engineers work with the corporate office and Maynard office's EHS personnel. This 'product stewardship' group is part of how EHS communicates with AMRO. Thus far, only the engineering group within AMRO is actively involved with the product stewardship groups, but potential involvement for account managers is also possible.

The intra- and inter-organisational roles of the AMRO personnel and facility are still evolving, as management continue to determine the various potentials that this facility and its operations entail.

||| *General ISO 14001 Certification Implications at AMRO*

As mentioned, the AMRO facility is ISO 14001 certified. Nonetheless, ISO 14001 certification and the registration process did not greatly impact on the practices between AMRO and its suppliers/customers. However, there were some clear advantages that did occur from receiving the certification. It showed a commitment to environmental issues in AMRO and at Digital in general, which made it more likely that those organisations (outside of Digital) seeking a green supply chain would consider AMRO as a reverse logistics service. Customers who previously performed their own materials recovery have seen this certification as a catalyst for going outside their organisation. ISO 14001 certification essentially provides these customers with a relatively safe reason to outsource their material recovery operations. With ISO 14001 certification, processing costs have remained stable, and, overall, ISO 14001 certification has had a positive impact on other customers that buy Digital products (not just the services offered by AMRO, but the overall company), as the environmental commitment of the whole organisation becomes apparent. And where better to implement it than an area whose primary operations are to aid in environmental management of materials?

ISO 14001 requires that suppliers be evaluated on environmental performance, and meeting this requirement was not a problem for the AMRO facility. Vendors who provided services to AMRO are required to have quality and environmental programmes, but this requirement was part of the Digital policies before ISO 14001 certification, so no new requirements were necessary. The vendor qualification process has also remained unchanged. AMRO and Digital personnel regularly go out to vendors and complete regulatory and process reviews and ask them to make appropriate changes. Also, many suppliers and vendors come in and evaluate them. With ISO 14001 certification, this process is shortened and made easier for both AMRO and its suppliers/customers. They have never been rejected due to environmental reasons, and ISO 14001 will help them maintain that record.

Thus far, with environmental operations at AMRO more stringently controlled than is called for by ISO 14001, management has viewed ISO 14001 more as a good marketing tool than as a way of improving purchasing and other functional improvements with respect to environmental performance.

▍ *Summary and Conclusions*

Issues relevant to purchasing at a demanufacturing and disassembly facility, which, by definition, is a 'green' enterprise, have been rarely investigated by researchers. We have presented a number of practices from an actual facility that completes this function for a major computer and electronics organisation (Digital). Considering only the purchasing and logistics functions, we see that there are a number of characteristics that make this environment unique. One of the major characteristics is the varying relationships between suppliers as customers and customers as suppliers. The fuzziness of this relationship makes the standard functions of a purchasing manager into a relatively unique juggling act, not present in standard forward logistics environments. Issues relevant to forecasting, negotiations, bidding and materials management are all evident from the case study. A call for more research and investigation into this environment may provide managerial paradigms that can be useful to all organisations. Treating the supplier as customer is one of the immediate practices that may help most organisations.

Purchasing managers will need to build up their skills in this environment, where knowledgeable and multi-skilled purchasing managers may need to be the norm.

22
Integrating Environmental Considerations into Purchasing Programmes at Procter & Gamble

Robert J. Shimp and Henri de Henau

▌▌ Introduction

Since its beginnings in 1837, Procter & Gamble (P&G) has grown into a multinational corporation of over 110,000 employees. Today, the company has total worldwide sales of over $35 billion, with over 300 different brands in more than 150 countries. P&G brands include: Tide and Ariel laundry detergents; Charmin toilet tissue; Pampers nappies; Pringles potato snacks; Pert and Pantene shampoos; Dawn, Dreft and Fairy washing-up liquids; Always, Whisper and Tampax feminine hygiene products; and Hawaiian Punch and Punica beverages.

The company's statement of purpose is to 'provide products of superior quality and value that improve the lives of the world's consumers'. This statement clearly recognises the need to provide products that have superior performance, quality and value. In addition, the company recognises that there are at least four key requirements for 'improving the lives of the world's consumers'. All of its products, packages and operations must:

1. Be safe for workers, consumers and the environment.

2. Meet the letter and spirit of the law.

3. Use resources wisely and minimise waste.

4. Address the needs and concerns of external stakeholders, especially for information.

In order to fulfil these responsibilities, especially given the global scope and diversity of its business, P&G must focus on understanding and managing the environmental aspects of its products across their entire life-cycle. This includes the purchase of raw materials, manufacturing operations, the use of the product, and the product's final disposal. Over 95% of the raw materials P&G purchases are transformed into products that are sold to consumers. Of the remaining 5%, 3% is recycled and 2% is waste, with most being non-hazardous solid waste.

Once used by consumers, P&G's products generally reach the environment in one of two ways: either 'out with the rubbish' or 'down the drain'. As a result, the company must ensure that its products are safe and compatible with disposal in virtually every possible environmental circumstance.

▌ *Environmental Policies and Organisations*

Prior to describing how the company's purchasing practices are integrated with its environmental programmes, it will be useful to understand the company's overall environmental policy and organisational structure.

In the late 1980s, P&G published a formal *Environmental Quality Policy*. Its purpose was to bring together the key elements of organisational responsibilities that had been in place for several decades, building from the company's statement of purpose. The policy has seven key principles, which build on the requirements noted in the previous section:

- Ensure our products, packages, and operations are safe for our employees, consumers, and the environment.

- Reduce or prevent the environmental impact of our products and packaging in their design, manufacture, distribution, use, and disposal, whenever possible.

- Meet or exceed the requirements of all environmental laws and regulations.

- Continually assess our environmental technology and programs, and monitor progress toward environmental goals.

- Provide our consumers, customers, employees, communities, public interest groups, and others with relevant and appropriate factual information about the environmental quality of P&G products, packaging, and operations.

- Ensure every employee understands and is responsible and accountable for incorporating environmental quality considerations in daily business activities.

- Have operating policies, programs, and resources in place to implement our environmental quality policy.

Organisationally, P&G's environmental responsibilities are divided across four key functions. These have some overlap in responsibilities, but in general address the following areas:

- ▌ **Professional & Regulatory Services (P&RS)** concerns itself with products and packages. P&RS is responsible for ensuring that these are safe for consumers, safe for the environment and in compliance with all laws and regulations where they are sold. They also address any external questions or concerns that arise about the safety or environmental aspects of products and packages.

- ▌ **Health, Safety and the Environment (HS&E)** focuses on manufacturing operations, especially employee safety, site environmental protection, waste management, regulatory/legal compliance and relations with local communities.

- ▌ **Environmental Quality (EQ)** co-ordinates issues related to P&G's overall environmental policy, goals and reporting. It also publishes the company's *Environmental Progress Update*—a public report on the company's environmental goals, progress and activities.[1]

1. Copies of P&G's most recent *Environmental Progress Update* can be obtained by writing to Dr Deborah D. Anderson, Vice-President, Environmental Quality, Worldwide, The Procter & Gamble Company, 2 Procter & Gamble Plaza, Cincinnati, OH 45202, USA; or send an e-mail request to environmentrep.im@pg.com.

▶ **Public Affairs (PA)** manages external communications and government relations as they are related to consumer safety and the environment.

In addition to their core responsibilities, each of P&G's environmental functions is responsible for ensuring that the company monitors and anticipates future issues that could affect its business. These include new scientific developments, changes in public attitudes about the environment and emerging government policies, laws and regulations.

P&G's business is divided into four geographic regions: Asia, Europe (including Central and Eastern Europe, the Middle East and Africa), Latin America and North America. Each of the four organisations described above exists in one form or another at a regional or national level. Altogether, P&G has approximately 1,500 people spending most of their time managing the environmental affairs of the company. In addition, as a matter of the company's fundamental values, every employee is viewed as having some basic responsibility for considering the environmental implications of his/her decisions and actions.

▮ *A Global Environmental Management System*

Last year, as part of a continuous improvement process, P&G assessed how the company's environmental systems could be restructured to work more effectively on a global basis, especially on issues that cross geographic, organisational or product boundaries. As a result of this review, the company created a framework called the 'Global Environmental Management System' (GEMS; see Fig. 1).

Figure 1: Procter & Gamble's Global Environmental Management System

The GEMS is not a formal organisation. Rather it is a work process that integrates the four organisations responsible for the company's environmental matters. A small council of senior managers representing each organisation and region of the world oversees the activities of the GEMS. The GEMS Council is a forum for discussing how the company should respond to emerging environmental issues, devising integrated global approaches, and enabling the different organisations to work together more effectively.

The GEMS makes the management of environmental issues across regions and businesses more effective in a variety of ways. For example, it allows the company to learn about new issues more quickly; it enables the re-application of successful projects worldwide; it permits organisations in different parts of the world to share resources and expertise more efficiently; moreover, it helps ensure consistency of purpose in P&G's worldwide environmental programmes.

||| Purchasing and the Environment

||| Organisational Relationships

With global sales of over $35 billion and more than 300 brands, P&G purchases literally thousands of different ingredients, from surfactants for laundry detergents and shampoos, to wood pulp for paper products, to peanuts for peanut butter. Thus, it has literally hundreds of different suppliers around the world. Some are small speciality chemical companies; others are large multinational firms that sell the company high-volume 'commodity' materials. P&G's purchasing organisations are generally decentralised, with each business sector and region having its own organisation. Materials are generally purchased regionally, as well as imported from abroad. A few, very large-volume items are acquired by a centrally located purchasing organisation.

P&G's purchasing people rely on various organisations to help define what materials to purchase. These include: Product Development to define specifications for each raw material from a product performance standpoint; Product Supply to define specifications for manufacturing; and Quality Assurance to establish quality-related needs. Each of these organisations draws upon its respective safety and environmental organisations (especially P&RS and HS&E) for knowledge and decisions that relate to human safety and the environment.

||| Environmental Considerations

The selection of a supplier for any given raw material is a complex task, with many considerations. These include the material's technical performance, its price, availability, quality, as well as safety and the environment. P&G does not have a separate 'green' purchasing policy. Rather, the company's purchasing organisations operate in a manner that is consistent with the corporate *Environmental Quality Policy*.

As a matter of fundamental values and policy, P&G's first and foremost need is to establish that a raw material is going to be safe for consumers, employees and the environment. The key to establishing safety is collecting the right data. P&G's purchasing groups, product development and manufacturing organisations, the company's safety experts, and a supplier work together to identify what specific environmental and toxicological information is required to evaluate an individual raw material.

The company makes use of tools such as questionnaires, site audits and 'think-lists' to help identify and collect the appropriate information for decision-making. However, much of it is collected via personal contacts and dialogue between experts at P&G and their counterparts at a supplier. The company's toxicologists and environmental scientists also routinely utilise the scientific literature and government databases to collect information. If a supplier or the literature does not have sufficient information to evaluate a material's safety, the company conducts the necessary research using its own laboratories, contractors or academic institutions. Often, such programmes are conducted in co-operation with a supplier. Once sufficient knowledge is collected, the company's environmental experts use tools such as human and ecological risk assessment to analyse the data, and ensure that a material is safe for its use in a specific product or package.

Ultimately, P&G develops specifications for each raw material and 'formula cards' for each product. Most of these specifications focus on material performance and quality. However, in some cases, where it is deemed necessary by the company's scientists, environmental or safety specifications may be developed as well (e.g. threshold limits for a particular contaminant). Regardless, all raw material specifications and product formula cards must be approved by P&RS and HS&E prior to the purchase of a material or the manufacture of a product.

In addition to safety information, P&G also frequently asks for information about a supplier's overall environmental management system, as well as any environmental 'issues' that could be relevant to P&G's business. Increasingly, the company is finding that public interest groups and people generally may query it about issues that are associated with the environmental performance of suppliers (e.g. forest management). P&G needs to be prepared for such issues, and ensure that any concerns are being adequately addressed. Where such discussions with suppliers occur, it is done in the spirit of mutual trust and support, where the intent is to encourage continuous improvement, not prescribe solutions in areas for which P&G is not directly responsible.

▌▌ Promoting Environmental Improvement via Supplier Partnerships

As noted above, P&G seeks to integrate the safety and environmental aspects of raw material purchases into its everyday relationships with suppliers. The company has also established programmes with suppliers to improve one or more aspects of a raw material's environmental profile, or to help address new environmental concerns. The following examples illustrate such programmes.

1. Since the mid-1980s, P&G has sought to improve the biodegradability of various ingredients in its laundry and cleaning products. This programme has been led by company researchers. However, suppliers have been an integral part of the work, since they have access to both fundamental chemical technology and manufacturing expertise. Suppliers have also helped P&G establish biodegradability success criteria, conduct basic environmental testing, and study the effectiveness of new materials in products or packages. As a result of these co-operative efforts, the company has introduced a variety of new, even more biodegradable ingredients, including detergent builders, surfactants and soil release polymers.

2. In the late 1980s, concerns arose in the scientific community about newly discovered chlorinated organic chemicals, especially dioxins, in effluents and pulps from pulp mills that used traditional chlorine gas bleaching processes. As a result of these findings, P&G implemented a global policy to phase out its purchase of chlorine-gas-bleached pulp for all the company's paper products. Over the course of approximately 3–5 years, P&G worked with a number of suppliers around the world to develop alternative processes for making pulp. Today, the company uses only pulp manufactured with 'Elemental Chlorine Free' or 'Totally Chlorine Free' bleaching processes. These processes have virtually eliminated potentially harmful chlorinated organic materials.

3. As recycling and composting have become increasingly widespread tools for managing solid waste, P&G has needed to ensure that its products and packages are compatible with these new systems. In co-operation with raw material suppliers and trade associations, the company has supported both fundamental laboratory research, pilot studies and full-scale evaluations of various raw materials in both products and packages. The company has also worked closely with suppliers to increase the level of recycled material in packages, whenever it makes economic, technical and environmental sense.

4. Recently, there has been a growing interest in forestry management practices in the pulp and paper industry. While P&G manages only a few forests of its own (in the US), the company is also accountable for ensuring that it is purchasing wood pulp from responsible suppliers. Over the past several years, P&G has conducted forestry audits at most of its key suppliers. The company has worked with industry trade associations on forest management programmes such as the American Forest & Paper Association's 'Sustainable Forestry Initiative'. P&G has also sponsored forestry management research, such as a wildlife management field studies programme with the Audubon Society in north-eastern Pennsylvania. Each of these initiatives is aimed at improving the forest management practices of the industry, via co-operative and mutually beneficial partnerships.

▌▌ General Principles for 'Green Purchasing'

In recent years, both private and public enterprises have increased their interest in 'green purchasing'. Based on its experience, P&G believes that such programmes must be based on mutual co-operation between a purchaser and its suppliers. In general, the company believes that the following principles are important for *any* organisation that seeks to improve its environmental performance via its purchasing practices.

1. Organisations should seek to *integrate* environmental considerations with performance, cost, safety and other factors. No single aspect can, or should, dictate decision-making.

2. Both purchasers and suppliers should recognise that there is no methodology that has broad scientific credibility and acceptance for identifying materials

or products that are *overall* 'environmentally preferable'. Therefore, decisions should reflect a product purchaser's specific needs, using *factual* environmental information from a variety of sources that:

   a. Are based on sound scientific methodology, data and interpretation.

   b. Identify attributes that are meaningful and relevant to environmental protection, reflecting regional or local priorities when appropriate.

   c. Are derived from consideration of the entire life-cycle of the product.

3. Environmental considerations in purchase decisions should be based on data provided by suppliers or gathered by purchasers, in co-operation and dialogue. Environmental information should be communicated in a clear, understandable manner, along with appropriate background knowledge that can help facilitate balanced, information-based decisions.

4. Decisions should not be delegated to the judgements of third parties. Rather, regular communications and analysis by suppliers and purchasers should form the basis for individual choices. Third parties *can* be an important source of information, and can help verify data. However, they rarely have the detailed knowledge of either a supplier's product or a purchaser's needs to qualify them to be responsible for decisions.

5. Environmental improvement programmes should be flexible enough to accommodate and encourage innovations that offer the opportunity for future performance and environmental improvement. The ability to innovate is key for any institution's environmental improvement programme.

P&G believes these considerations are especially important for public organisations, such as local, national and regional governments. Since government organisations use public resources (tax monies) for their purchases, there is a special need for them to base decisions on the best available scientific information and analysis.

ⅡⅠ *Summary*

P&G views 'green purchasing' not as a distinct programme, but rather as an integral part of its overall business. Environmental considerations and safety are inherent elements in all decision-making. The key to success is a focus on co-operatively identifying critical issues, collecting factual information, and making decisions based on the best scientific analysis available. The company views these as absolutely vital for continuous environmental improvement and business success.

23 *Environmental Purchasing*
Some Thoughts and an IBM Case Study

Brian Whitaker

▌▌ *Introduction*

Few would dispute that the supply chain is potentially one of the most effective means of promulgating environmental improvement. This analysis of the situation will start with that well-known trio: What?, Why? and How?, and these will be used to frame a number of questions which this chapter will attempt to answer.

▶ **What** are we trying to achieve?

▶ **What** are the incentives for the various players in the supply chain?

▶ **What** is being done today?

▶ **What** are the goals?

▶ **Why** should any of the players do anything to improve the environmental performance of others in the supply chain?

▶ **How** important is it?

▶ **How** can performance and effectiveness be measured?

▶ **How** should it best be done?

These questions can be grouped into a set of four main topics.

▶ Motivation

▶ Measurement

▶ Current practice

▶ Best practice

Each of these topics will be considered in the light of the author's experience, and the chapter concludes with an appendix that outlines IBM's environmental purchasing policies and methods.

▌▌ *Motivation*

It goes virtually without saying that any organisation will use the supply chain to improve the environmental performance of other players if it is clearly in the best interests, however defined, of that organisation. But what influences the perceived best interests of that organisation? What is the source of those influences and how can they be best understood?

One key source of such influences is a body that has received a significant amount of attention lately, namely the stakeholders. When IBM in the UK undertook a project to better understand the views of its stakeholders, it commissioned independent consultants, ECOTEC Ltd, to interview a sample of those who influence or are influenced by IBM's operations in the UK and who were defined as belonging to one of the following categories of key stakeholders.

▶ Customers

▶ Employees

▶ Opinion-formers

▶ Government and regulators

▶ The City

▶ Neighbours

These stakeholders were asked to define and to prioritise those issues that were of major concern to them regarding IBM's environmental performance in the UK. Of the eleven identified, it is significant that the fourth-highest priority was defined as helping to improve the environmental performance of IBM's customers, while the fifth-highest was to improve the performance of IBM's suppliers. This clearly showed that the use of the supply chain to promote the improvement of environmental performance is important to IBM's stakeholders. It also serves as a timely reminder that the supply chain is a two-way street and that, if a business wishes to take the supply chain seriously, it must consider how to help its customers improve their environmental performance.

Another significant influence on organisations is legislation. It is clear that the European Commission is going to produce a wide range of environmental legislation over the next few years. It has to be said that much of this proposed legislation would appear to owe more to single-market considerations than to real environmental concerns. A classic example of this is the current legislation concerning the recovery and recycling of packaging waste. Current calculations suggest that these regulations will cost British business approximately £1 billion a year, and that much of this expenditure will be on data collection and on the demonstration of legal compliance rather than on actual environmental improvements. It is to be hoped that future legislation does not have such an serious impact on business while apparently doing so little for the environment.

Clearly, the ultimate determinant of the effectiveness of the supply chain is the attitude of customers, for it is, of course, from them that a business derives its revenue. While there is plenty of evidence that a company can affect the environmental performance of its suppliers, there is, unfortunately, less evidence to suggest that consumers are having a powerful effect on retailers, despite the many opinion polls that suggest that consumers are environmentally aware and are prepared to use their purchasing power in pursuit of improved environmental performance. Certainly, the IT industry has produced very few cases over the last ten years where environmental considerations have been a major factor in a purchasing decision. The most casual read of any PC magazine will show that the major features advertised are all about price and performance.

Finally, no business can afford to ignore its competitors. Where a business gains commercial advantage from improved environmental performance, its competitors will be obliged to improve their environmental performance. No company claiming to be green can afford to be seen to be using 'ungreen' suppliers.

▮ *Measurement*

When Company A decides to initiate a supply chain programme with its suppliers, Companies B and C, it is important to know how effective these programmes are, not only in terms of their effects on the supplying companies but also how well Company A is actually using the supply chain. Despite the evidence of the IBM consultation exercise that customers are more important than suppliers, there is very little evidence to suggest that the various UK equivalents of Company A are successfully using the supply chain to help their customers. We see many examples of exhortation, but are they working?

The second phase of IBM's stakeholder consultation project involved the use of independent consultants to measure IBM's actual performance on each of the issues identified by its stakeholders. Since most of the issues were essentially non-quantifiable, it was necessary to devise a methodology that could measure and demonstrate IBM's performance on each. ECOTEC, with IBM's help, developed a questionnaire consisting of 307 questions with a minimum of 25 for each issue. There are four possible scores for each question which can be summarised as follows:

o   Nothing is being done and there is no plan.

1   There is a plan and some action has been taken.

2   There is a plan and significant action has been taken.

3   The performance represents the best practicable.

Using this methodology, ECOTEC scored every question and summarised the results in an environmental performance index. The approach has a number of important advantages.

▮ The index scores are a function not only of the actual performance, but also of stakeholder priority. This prioritises issues in a different order from that which would result from the use of the raw scores alone and is therefore valuable when it comes to the allocation of scarce resources.

▮ The questionnaire approach enables the development of targets that are fully relevant to a company's environmental performance.

▮ The index is an excellent graphical representation of the environmental performance of a company. Further, it enables a company to demonstrate continuous improvement and to be able to compare graphically its performance with peer companies in a benchmarking exercise.

Approximately sixty questions were devised in order to measure IBM's performance in respect of supply chain management for both customers and suppliers.

By using these, it is possible to measure the effectiveness of a company's use of the supply chain. It is suggested that this is a more meaningful measure of supply chain management than the use of questionnaires by purchasing departments to attempt to measure the environmental credentials of either a company or its products, as the following section indicates.

▌▌ *Current Practice*

Current practice on supply chain management can, unfortunately, be summed up by the word 'questionnaire'! It is probably true to say that the vast majority of environmental managers are heartily sick of environmental questionnaires from customers! Very few have any problems with the principle that customers are entitled to ask questions of their suppliers regarding their environmental performance, even if multiple incompatible formats are a significant irritant.

The real problem relates to the use to which the answers are put. Many are in pursuit of the 'tick in the box' philosophy because company policies often require that suppliers should be evaluated as to their environmental policies and practices. Therefore, purchasing departments need to be able to demonstrate that they have carried out an appropriate audit. Clearly the existence of a completed questionnaire from a supplier is proof that such an evaluation has been carried out.

In the early days of the focus on the environmental performance of business, such questionnaires had some use in that they brought the attention of suppliers to environmental considerations. As the pursuit of environmental improvement has become more sophisticated, it is perhaps regrettable that the way in which the supply chain is managed has not kept pace. Whenever I was obliged to fill in a supplier questioner, I would always ask what would be done with the information and how it would contribute to any purchasing decision. I have to report that I never received a satisfactory answer.

One might also question whether or not it is for the best to make a company's purchasing department responsible for managing the environmental performance of the supply chain. Many would suggest that they are already heavily engaged in the pursuit of price, quality and delivery. A solution would be for companies' policies to seek to improve the environmental performance of their suppliers rather than to evaluate it. This would be a proactive stance on the environment rather than a defence mechanism to contain a company's exposures and certainly more in line with the priorities of IBM's stakeholders.

▌▌ *Best Practice*

In the author's experience, the most effective way of using the supply chain to improve environmental performance has been through products and through the transfer of technology—what might be referred to as the 'clean technology' approach as opposed to the 'end-of-pipe' approach represented by questionnaires.

This approach will work both ways along the supply chain. For instance, as far as the consumer is concerned, it is possible to deliver a wide range of products whose environmental impacts are much lower than their predecessors. If these improved products are made the default option, then by definition the environmental performance of households will be made that much better. Examples of products that offer improved environmental performance without necessarily being demanded by the customer include cars, white goods, electrical and electronic products and detergents. In these cases, technological improvements are delivered to households without the consumer necessarily being aware of it.

As far as the other direction of the supply chain is concerned, a company can ensure that its suppliers improve their environmental performance by demanding products of a higher environmental specification. This means that supply chain management must start in the design office and requires that companies commit to product stewardship. By having a policy that demands constant improvement of the environmental impact of both products and manufacturing processes, a company will be able to achieve a high degree of leverage on the environmental performance of both customers and suppliers. For instance, IBM's product stewardship programme (see appendix) has been able to help its suppliers develop new technologies and manufacturing processes. An example of this is a closed-loop process which was developed with two suppliers to recycle the PVC used in keyboards and monitor housing. As a result, less PVC has to be manufactured and less has to be disposed of. Since both these activities can involve unpleasant chemicals, the environment is a clear winner. Furthermore, recycled PVC costs less than virgin, so there is a business benefit as well. Truly a win–win situation!

||| *In Conclusion*

The author would like to sum up by listing the five key points that he has attempted to bring out in this paper.

1. The overall objective of any supply chain programme must be to improve environmental performance. In order that this can be made to happen, there has to be some motivation for the company initiating such a programme and the various players in the supply chain must play a partnership role, and this includes customers.

2. It must be remembered that the supply chain is a two-way street and that environmental demands and environmental improvements can flow in both directions. Consumers are particularly important. Not only must their purchasing power be harnessed, but business must deliver the technology that enables them, consciously or unconsciously, to acquire a means of reducing household environmental impacts.

3. Environmental questionnaires are not the most effective means of promoting environmental improvements. Technology transfer is much more effective. This means that the process must start in the design office.

4. 'If you can't measure it you can't manage it!' How can the supply chain be managed if there is not a suitable methodology for measuring all aspects of performance? The methodology developed by ECOTEC for IBM's stakeholder consultation project would seem to be a good starting point for this.

5. Finally, is the purchasing office really the right place upon which to impose the goal to improve the environmental performance of suppliers and customers? It does not seem right that the buyer, in addition to all other responsibilities, should be required to evaluate the environmental performance of companies and products.

Appendix: *Environmental Purchasing at IBM*

The IBM management system is based on a set of Corporate Instruction Letters (CILs) which cover all aspects of the company's business. Responsibility for compliance rests with local management. This compliance is monitored by means of twice-yearly self-assessments and by both internal and external audits.

The instruction letter setting out IBM's policy for the environmental evaluation of suppliers covers the following points.

1. The objectives of the policy are to use environmentally responsible suppliers and to contain IBM's liability.

2. There is a graduated requirement for the evaluation of suppliers. This characterises suppliers according to the following criteria.

   ▶ Chemicals used

   ▶ The uniqueness of the product

   ▶ The environmental impact of the product, the manufacturing process and the supplier

   ▶ The percentage of the supplier's output that is represented by IBM's business

   The evaluation should cover the following points.

   ▶ Legal compliance

   ▶ The supplier's financial ability to remediate any environmental damage

3. IBM auditors should visit the supplier's site and review all aspects of their environmental performance. However, environmental advice must not be given by IBM.

4. The health, safety and environment department is responsible for providing advice to the purchasing department, who are responsible for the implementation of the policy.

In the UK, IBM's major purchasing activity is at its factory in Greenock where all IBM PCs are made for Europe, the Middle East and Africa. Their total purchasing bill amounts to a figure in the region of £1 billion a year. To implement the Corporate Instruction Letter, the Greenock purchasing office applied the selection criteria described above to their suppliers. Including new ones, some sixty suppliers were identified. All were sent a questionnaire and the answers were used to evaluate the environmental credentials of these suppliers, with special emphasis on the overall policy objectives: namely, the use of environmentally responsible suppliers and the need to contain IBM's liability.

While this process completely fulfils the objectives of IBM's environmental procurement policy and ensures that IBM does not do business with environmentally irresponsible suppliers, it does not necessarily help to improve the performance of those who already meet IBM's criteria. This is best achieved by a process that can be described as 'technology transfer'. By specifying product and manufacturing processes with a reduced environmental impact, IBM is able to help to ensure that its suppliers improve their performance.

This places major responsibility on the product designers who are required to implement IBM's product stewardship objectives. These are:

- Upgradability
- Re-use and recycle
- Safe disposal
- The use of recycled materials
- Energy efficiency and conservation

The IBM Engineering Centre for Environmentally Conscious Products in Raleigh, North Carolina, has been established to provide guidance to designers to help them to design products and processes with improved environmental performance. To ensure that these product stewardship objectives are met, the IBM management process includes an Environmental Impact Assessment (EIA). This is mandatory for all new and changed products and processes and ensures that all applicable IBM standards are met. The EIA information is summarised in a Product Environmental Profile (PEP) in the following categories.

- Energy data
- Noise data
- Radiation levels
- Hazardous parts and assemblies
- Materials table
- Chemical emissions
- Banned or restricted chemicals
- Parts containing precious metals
- Environmentally conscious attributes
- Disposal plan

In its turn, the environmentally conscious attributes section covers the following topics.

- The product is easy to disassemble.
- Plastic parts are coded.
- Major plastic parts are the same material and colour.
- Plastic parts are not painted or coated.
- Metal components are easily sorted.
- Recycled material should be used where possible.
- The product should meet the criteria of the 'Energy Star' award.

In pursuing its product stewardship objectives, IBM is able to ensure that its products and processes meet ever higher environmental standards. This means that IBM's suppliers have to raise their environmental performance in order to be able to continue to do business with IBM. This is seen as a really effective means of ensuring that the supply chain is an efficient vehicle for improving the environmental performance of all the relevant players.

24

How Effective is B&Q's Timber Purchasing Policy in Encouraging Sustainable Forest Management?

Liz Humphrey

||| Introduction

Forests are now understood to have a direct role in global environmental problems such as climate change and loss of biodiversity. The acknowledgement of this connection in the 1980s turned public attention in industrialised countries towards the high rate of deforestation in tropical regions, and the destructive logging practices of both local and multinational companies. Quick financial returns on forest concessions are a stimulus for rapid economic growth in timber-producing countries and can be a disincentive to maintaining long-term yields. In the hope of reversing this trend, northern pressure groups have previously called for the outright ban of tropical timber. However, environmentalists now generally emphasise that timber trading itself is not harmful as long as the management of forests is conducted on a sustainable basis. Furthermore, this principle also applies to temperate and boreal forests, where degradation in forest quality is a major problem, bringing under scrutiny the practices of logging companies and timber processors in both developed and developing nations.

B&Q is the largest Do-It-Yourself (DIY) retailer in the UK, whose products include a high proportion of raw timber and wood-based items. In 1991, the company was targeted in NGO campaigns to boycott tropical timber. Concerned that connections of their timber stock to rainforest destruction would deter customers, B&Q embarked on an elaborate scheme to trace their timber sources and de-list suppliers if their products were found to originate from unsustainable forests.

This paper examines B&Q's timber purchasing policy and the role of this and other similar corporate initiatives in the move towards the goal of sustainable forest management. The Forest Stewardship Council's *Principles and Criteria for Natural Forest Management* are used as a benchmark for the debate. Timber certification is then introduced as a market-driven method of instigating the application of the principles, and the roles of the World Wide Fund for Nature '1995 Group' and the Forest Stewardship Council are outlined. Against this background, B&Q's unique corporate process of supplier auditing is described and the results of their work presented. Finally, B&Q's work is set against the wider implications of a voluntary certification system so that the effectiveness of their purchasing policy can be assessed in relation to the adoption of sustainable forestry practices.

The paper will argue that B&Q's policy of independent certification improves forestry management along the supply chain to UK stores because the conditions required for certification to be effective are satisfied in the UK market. However, the large majority of the company's timber sources are located in temperate or boreal regions; there will be a limited effect on tropical timber growers, the original focus of the movement for better forestry, because other business opportunities are open to tropical producers both for domestic consumption and for entry into markets where there is no demand for 'environmentally friendly' products. The existence of such market imperfections implies that certification should be used in combination with other methods if sustainable forest management is to be more widely practised.

Ill *What is 'Sustainable Forest Management'?*

Sustainable forest management is now widely recognised as a key issue in tackling the worldwide problems of deforestation and forest degradation, but its precise meaning is unclear. A parallel can be drawn with the definition of the popular phrase 'sustainable development', in that it attempts to combine the objectives of development and conservation, and is open to interpretation by groups of actors with different interests (Humphreys 1996: 68).

Various bodies have published guidelines on what they believe constitutes sustainable forest management, a detailed comparison of which is beyond the scope of this paper. In brief, the International Tropical Timber Organisation (ITTO) *Guidelines* were developed and agreed in May 1990, while the 1992 United Nations Conference on Environment and Development (UNCED) resulted in 120 participating countries agreeing to the *Statement of Forest Principles*. The latter are a non-legally binding global consensus on the management, conservation and sustainable development of all forest types, but Humphreys (1996: 69) believes they compare somewhat unfavourably with ITTO guidelines. Additionally, the *Smartwood Programme* run by the Rainforest Alliance is based on the latter's own definitions which are applied in the USA.

This lack of cohesion inevitably causes confusion in any scheme that aims to implement more sustainable forestry. The Forest Stewardship Council (FSC) *Principles and Criteria for Natural Forest Management* were devised in 1993 to clarify the situation, and are a comprehensive guide to forestry management applicable to all types of forest (see Chapter 9, page 123). These guidelines have been adopted by B&Q as the objective of their timber policy, and as such are used here as a definition of sustainable forest management. Each principle is supported by a set of criteria that explicitly state what is required to achieve compliance.

Meanwhile, the International Organisation for Standardisation (ISO) is also developing a certification scheme to integrate with their ISO 14000 environmental management series. The ISO scheme is not as stringent as the FSC because it does not deal with the quality of forestry practice on the ground, but focuses instead on a company's management systems. There have been suggestions of converging the two schemes to avoid further confusion, a call that has won the support of the FSC itself (*Forestry and British Timber* 1996: 4).

▮ *From Definitions to Action*

Translating written principles into practical projects that meet the criteria is a crucial step in reaching the goal of sustainable forest management. Dudley, Jeanrenaud and Sullivan (1995: 108-54) identify three approaches to the problem: forest-based, policy-based and market-based solutions. Forest-based methods involve low-impact management systems devised from local ecological knowledge, while policy-based initiatives cover national- and international-level projects such as forestry standards legislation in individual producer countries, and the ITTO and UNCED processes. The success of market-based solutions is built on consumer demand for timber that is specifically from a sustainably managed source. This is achieved through certifying the forest accordingly and labelling its products so that they are differentiated from items from non-certified sources throughout the supply chain; customers can then choose their preferred purchase.

The World Wide Fund for Nature (WWF) has been instrumental in encouraging a market-based certification strategy. Frustrated at the inertia of ITTO (Elliott and Sullivan 1991: 1), coupled with the political deadlock of northern versus southern interests which diluted the UNCED *Forest Principles* to a 'wish list' of should-dos (Sullivan and Jeanrenaud 1993: 1), WWF decided to work directly with traders in the UK through the formation in 1991 of the '1995 Group' (a full members' list is shown in the appendix). The main objective was that, by the end of 1995, members were to purchase all timber products from well-managed sources, covering temperate, boreal and tropical forests. The lack of a definition of sustainable management to include all forest types prompted the establishment of The Forest Stewardship Council in 1993, as described above and, consequently, the 1995 Group evolved into a buyers' group committed to the FSC and its *Principles and Criteria* (Bendell and Sullivan 1996: 6). The group trades over £1 billion of wood and wood products every year, almost 10% of total wood consumption in the UK (Dudley, Jeanrenaud and Sullivan 1995: 153), and each member is given a one-, two- or three-star rating to correspond with their environmental performance.

▮ *The B&Q Story*

B&Q hold a 15% share of the British DIY market (B&Q 1995: 120), and achieve annual profits in excess of £97 million through their 283 stores.[1] They are the second largest timber retailer behind the furniture chain store MFI, and estimate that one in four of their products contain timber.[2] The company was one of the ten founder members of the 1995 Group and has been a key force in maintaining the momentum of the initiative. It also played a prominent role in pushing for the formation of the FSC, and has become a company that many environmentalists feel they can trust (Murphy 1996b: 57).

---

1. Personal communication with Alan Knight, 2 April 1997. See also the B&Q website at *http://www.diy.uk.*
2. Personal communication with Alan Knight, 2 April 1997.

It should be noted that, while this paper focuses on its timber policy, B&Q has an extensive environmental programme which audits suppliers of all product ranges, and have now established a similar system to monitor the environmental performance of their stores. Its achievements are documented in the detailed environmental reviews *How Green is My Hammer?* (B&Q 1993) and *How Green is My Front Door?* (B&Q 1995). A third edition, *How Green is My Patio?* (B&Q 1998b) will be available in summer 1998

▌ Greening the Timber Supply Chain

Initially, B&Q's interest in environmental problems was sparked by Rainforest Action Group and, later, Friends of the Earth protests which were launched in early 1991 to highlight the problem of tropical deforestation (see Chapter 9). Demonstrators moved into the company's supercentre car parks wielding giant inflatable chainsaws to attract attention to the stock of hardwood, assumed to be from tropical forests. Meanwhile, a *Sunday Times* enquiry revealed that a director of the company was unable to confirm the source of B&Q timber (House of Commons Environment Committee 1996: xcviii; Knight 1995: 32). The adverse publicity and its potential effect on sales prompted a company initiative to identify the origin of its wood products, beginning with the appointment of environmental specialist, Dr Alan Knight.

Consultation with organisations ranging from Friends of the Earth to the Timber Trade Association brought inconclusive results; B&Q felt there was too much emphasis on tropical timber when forests in other regions were not necessarily managed sustainably, while trade groups denied there was a connection between deforestation and the timber trade. Under this pretext, Dr Knight and a team of consultants undertook their own forest study tours in 1991 and set the first target in September of that year: By the end of 1993, B&Q would only buy timber of which the precise sources were known, moving towards the 1995 Group target two years later. A formal timber policy was published in 1992:

> B&Q will only buy timber whose harvesting has not caused destruction of or severe damage to a forest anywhere in the world. Indigenous people and forest inhabitants must not be harmed and ideally should benefit from the forest management (cited in B&Q 1995: 21).

The policy corresponds to the Forest Stewardship Council Principles 3, 5 and 6 (see Chapter 9, page 123), and was used as an interim definition before the FSC was established. Indeed, prior to the existence of a formal certification body, a fundamental problem in the project was ensuring the criteria were being met in reality. While over half of suppliers claimed that their sources were 'definitely sustainable', 90% were unable to identify which country their timber was from (B&Q 1996: 2). Since 'self-certification' was not working, the company requested suppliers to stop describing their timber-based products as 'sustainable' or 'environmentally friendly'. As an alternative, B&Q began to develop its own internal scrutiny process which is summarised in Figure 1. The procedure is integrated with the FSC independent certification scheme as advocated by the 1995 Group; however, it is designed to include non-certified suppliers so that they can work in partnership with B&Q towards the goal of certification. The procedure culminated in a full supplier audit in December 1994, with the pass mark set at 50% (B&Q 1995: 25).

(i) SUPPLIER COMMITMENT

Three-star 1995 Group members	30%
Two-star 1995 Group members	25%
One-star 1995 Group members	20%

OR (if not a 1995 Group member)

Existence of written policy	5%
Written commitment of 1995 target date	5%
Written acknowledgement of value of independent certification	0%–5%
Overall quality of the policy	1%–10%
Maximum score without 1995 Group membership	*25%*

(ii) QUALITY OF INFORMATION

Excellent	25%
Good	20%
Moderate	15%
Basic	5%
Poor	0%
None	−10%
Maximum score possible for non-certified source	*25%*

(iii) EVALUATION OF INFORMATION

Certification very likely	25%
Certification likely	20%
Certification possible	15%
Certification marginal	5%
Insufficient information	0%
Certification unlikely	−10%
Certificability of a typical source (country rating)	−10% to 25%
Maximum score possible for non-certified source	*25%*

Figure 1: B&Q's Internal Scrutiny of Suppliers

Source: B&Q 1995: 23-24

III Audit Results

A perhaps surprising fact was revealed by tracing the supply chain back to the source; in 1994, only 8.4% of timber used by B&Q originated from tropical sources, while 91.6% was from temperate and boreal forests (B&Q 1995: 21). Also, 54% of the total timber used was from UK sources (B&Q 1995: 27). The distribution of the supply base forms the parameters of the sphere of influence of the policy; the implications of this are discussed in later sections.

But what of the results of the internal scrutiny process itself? At the beginning of 1996, 91.5% of suppliers had achieved the 50% pass mark, action had been taken on 8%, and 0.5% were unable to meet the target (Knight 1996: 37). In May 1995, 44 supply chains were judged to be critical failures—that is, the mark is unlikely to be improved—which constituted about 2.5% of the volume of timber used. Further orders on these products were put on hold until the problems could be resolved (B&Q 1995: 30).

Analysis of sales figures are revealing about the behaviour patterns of consumers. B&Q found that green consumerism can be irrational; for example, garden furniture is an environmentally sensitive product, while wallpaper—which has a high proportion of wood-product content—is chosen on the basis of price (House of Commons Environment Committee 1996: xcviii). This shows the importance of increasing consumer awareness in the success of certification schemes.

‖ Beyond 1995

In May 1995, B&Q declared their goal that, by the end of 1999, all timber will come from sources independently certified by the Forest Stewardship Council, with integrated targets for preceding years, as shown in Figure 2.

END OF YEAR	MINIMUM PASS MARK
1995	50%
1996	60%
1997	70%
1998	85%
1999	100%

Figure 2: B&Q Supplier Targets
Source: B&Q 1996a: 8

Several of the WWF companies have also committed to full certification by 1999, and have formed the '1995 Plus Group'. Dr David Murphy—who, with Jem Bendell, includes a chapter on B&Q and other DIY retailers in *In the Company of Partners* (Murphy and Bendell 1997), and whose discussion of the UK DIY sector can be found in Chapter 9 of this volume—believes that of the 1995 Plus group members, B&Q are the most open with information and are closer than anyone else to reaching the 1999 target.[3] Even so, recent progress reports by B&Q focus on the products that have achieved certification rather than on the number of FSC-approved suppliers. By the end of 1997, the company had almost 800 certified product lines accounting for 8% of total volume (B&Q 1998a: 2). The apparent shortfall in reaching their original targets is not through lack of commitment to environmental goals, but a reflection of the complex issues surrounding certification and its relation to sustainable forest management. This calls for a closer look at the potential effects of such a purchasing policy and the implications for the timber trade.

---

3. Personal communication, 7 March 1997.

II Timber Certification: The Wider Debate

There is much discussion about the effectiveness of timber certification to induce more sustainable management practices in forests. Although the scheme currently operates on a voluntary basis, it seems to be viewed as an inevitability (Sullivan and Jeanrenaud 1993: 1); retailers in industrialised countries are pushed to support certification to keep up with competitors and maintain their market share.

First, in addition to the long-term environmental and economic benefits brought about by sustainable forestry, certification can bring other advantages to businesses who support it; these positive points may further encourage companies to advocate certification. Figure 3 summarises these commercial benefits alongside the evidence for each point in the case of B&Q. However, incentives for the retail sector to work towards timber certification may not necessarily lead to sustainable forest management at the other end of the supply chain. There are a number of difficulties and tensions that accompany the concept of independent certification; the rest of this section highlights the main areas of contention and the effects of the concept with reference to B&Q's policy and the FSC.

BENEFIT	THE B&Q EXPERIENCE
Distinguishes companies making genuine efforts at reform from fraudulent claims.	Credibility to enter a specialised market niche which attracts a 'green' consumer base.
Provides clear idea of what is expected in terms of forest management.	The FSC principles/criteria give suppliers an explicit guide to what B&Q require.
Avoids confrontation with environmental NGOs.	No more giant chainsaws in the car park!
Provides open forum for discussion.	Increasing interest in B&Q and certification involves them in debates about the issue, e.g. business–environment partnership seminars.*
Gives positive incentives for change.	Has led to other environmental projects covering different product ranges.

* Dr Alan Knight was a key speaker at Environmentalist and Business Partnerships: A Sustainable Model?, the ninth Professional Environment Seminar held at the University of Cambridge, 25 January 1996.

Figure 3: The Commercial Benefits of Certification
Source: adapted from Dudley, Jeanrenaud and Sullivan 1995: 143-44

III Avoiding Bias in Accreditation

The credibility of any system of independent certification lies in its ability to remain impartial and objective. In the FSC procedure, six companies have been accredited to perform forest audits and award certification. There is also a dispute mechanism designed to allow others to challenge decisions, leading to a rigorous review process where all information is publicly available.[4] One recent accreditation will be a test case of the system: German logging company Isoroy/Leroy-Gabon was given FSC certification in 1996 by SGS-Forestry, but NGOs claim that the company does not practise sustainable forest management and has plans to start logging in a government-protected zone (Ngangoue 1996: 2). This would be a violation of FSC Principle 1, as listed earlier.

The FSC is funded by donations, membership dues and fees for accreditation services.[5] This is a delicate balance between non-profit and for-profit interests, and its success is dependent on the ability of the FSC to raise enough finance from its independent funding base. As more forests are certified, financial pressure will increase (Bendell and Sullivan 1996: 14); it is noted that donations from accredited companies are not accepted.

In 1996, representation of the 'economic sector' in the FSC general assembly was increased from one-quarter to one-third of the vote on decisions, with social and environmental interests sharing equally the other two-thirds (*Forestry and British Timber* 1996: 4). This shift in power highlights the possibility of 'regulatory capture', a process first described by Bernstein in 1955; his theory describes how regulatory commissions are sparked by a crisis (in this case, high rates of deforestation), engage in conflict to impose new regulations (fighting resistance to certification), but eventually are subordinated by the very groups they were designed to regulate (Bernstein 1955: 74-95). Business–environmentalist partnerships are often viewed with cynicism by environmental groups, but only time will tell whether the FSC can resist dominance by the business sector.

▌▌▌ The Costs of Certification

The main problem with investing in better forestry management is that the costs are borne by the producer while the benefits accrued are mostly external, even global in nature. Baharuddin (1995: 19) points out that these costs can essentially be divided into two categories:

▌ The cost of improving forest management practices to meet certification

▌ The cost of the accreditation procedure itself, including the forest audit and monitoring the 'chain of custody' to the final destination of the product

The above are applicable to all forest types, although the FSC principles are adapted to local criteria. However, the costs themselves vary enormously depending on the extent to which current practice matches the requirements for sustainability, whether the forest is tropical, temperate or boreal, or whether it is heterogeneous or homogenous, among other factors.

An estimated 10%–20% increase of current tropical log prices would result, with lower compliance costs over time because of improved forest management (Varangis, Crossley and Primo Brago 1995: 28). Meanwhile, the average extra cost of the actual certification process alone is thought to be US$0.30–0.60 per hectare to developed

---

4. Personal communication with Dr David Murphy, 7 March 1997.
5. See Forest Stewardship Council at *http://antequerrra.antequerra.com:80/FSC/index.html*, p. 4.

country producers (temperate/boreal forests), and 5%–10% of the total tropical logging costs in developing countries (Varangis, Crossley and Primo Brago 1995: 29).

The debate over who meets the costs incurred by the producer is central to the political deadlock that has typified the negotiation of timber policies at different levels. Discussions involving governments (such as at UNCED) and trade groups (such as ITTO) are consistently paralysed as northern countries assert the need to curb deforestation, and southern countries ask for financial assistance or concessions to help them achieve this. In the case of B&Q, the approach has been one of co-operation; the company is currently providing funding to some suppliers in developing countries to adopt sustainable forest management (B&Q 1995: 39). Other retailers with a more extensive tropical timber supply base may not be in a position to do so.

Although there is also a distinction in ability to pay for certification between growers in different regions, it should be stressed that bearing the costs of better practice is not just a problem for producers in developing countries. Small timber growers in rich countries are complaining that it is more costly for them to comply with guidelines on environmentally sound forestry than their larger rivals (*The Economist* 1996: 64). Meanwhile, the UK Forestry Commission is not fundamentally opposed to certification, but is concerned with the costs associated with it; it has asked the FSC not to impose any additional requirements if existing regulations are found to be compatible with the FSC principles and criteria (House of Commons Environment Committee 1996: lxiv).

ⅠⅠⅠ *Different Market, Different Signals*
The economic viability of timber certification is based on the assumptions that consumer purchasing patterns can be influenced by differentiating products' environmental attributes, and that consumers are willing to pay a premium for certified products (Baharuddin 1995: 19). Research by Haji-Gazali and Simula in 1994 showed that, on average, UK consumers are willing to pay approximately 13% more for a 'green' product (cited in Varangis, Crossley and Primo Brago 1995: 21). On paper, a higher price should compensate the producer for the investment in upgrading forest management.

However, the theory breaks down when there is no eco-sensitive consumer base and therefore no specific demand for certified timber. B&Q gained first-hand experience of this 'market imperfection' from a retail perspective when they opened their first international store in Taiwan in 1995.[6] The Taiwan Supercentre uses a different supply base to the UK operation, with more than 95% of stock being locally sourced (B&Q 1996b: 6). Yet the strict environmental criteria described earlier do not necessarily apply; the general manager of B&Q Taiwan admitted that, if the company rigorously imposed the same regulations, they 'would simply not have any suppliers'.[7] Meanwhile, Dr Knight asserts that B&Q are waiting to become more established in Taiwan so that they 'have more clout with suppliers', but did not say

---

6. The company has since opened a further store in Taiwan and plans another by the end of 1998 (personal communication, 17 March 1998).
7. Personal communication, 1 June 1996.

when that time would be.[8] The difficulties stem from the absence of consumer demand for certification or environmental friendliness in the Taiwan market, meaning there would be no 'green premium' and little incentive to invest in management structure without the promise of economic benefit.

From a producer perspective, the different signals coming from different consumer bases create opportunities for trade diversion, especially for tropical growers. It must be noted that the majority of non-coniferous tropical timber production is for domestic use—only 6% of tropical timber actually enters the international trade (Barbier 1993: 1); moreover, of this comparatively minute proportion that is exported, 70% is destined for developing countries and Japan (Varangis, Crossley and Primo Brago 1995: 16). Since Asian consumers do not show preference for certified timber, a new trade pattern could emerge: trade in uncertified products will go to East Asia, while certified wood will supply the European and US markets (Varangis, Primo Braga and Takeuchi 1993: 24).

In addition, the rejection of uncertified timber by markets in industrialised countries could depress its price; this would increase the appeal to 'non-eco-sensitive' consumers and decrease the incentive to work towards certification. In the light of all these arguments, Kiekens concludes that:

> Even where implemented, just a few accredited forest concessions would generally suffice to supply the market segments demanding certified timber. Domestic timber consumption, strongly increasing in many developing countries and particularly in Asia, would be unaffected by timber certification (Kiekens 1995: 27).

Furthermore, Environment Strategies Europe (1996: 1-2) argues that timber certification can only contribute to higher deforestation and biodiversity depletion since privatisation of forestry policy encourages deregulation of the forestry sector at a time when stronger regulation is needed. These assertions highlight the weakness of certification if it is the only strategy adopted to encourage more sustainable forestry. A more effective approach would be to use a combination of other policies and legislation to complement market-based methods.

⫼ Substitution for Other Materials
Another concern raised by the possible distortions to trade patterns if certification becomes more widespread is that, if certified timber in industrialised countries becomes too expensive, retailers may look for cheaper alternatives made from other materials. The overall environmental impact of wood substitutes may be higher than that of timber from a sustainably managed source. In this context, B&Q asserts that 'timber is arguably the only building material with the potential to be produced and consumed in a sustainable way' (B&Q 1996a: 3)

⫼ Certification and GATT
The adoption of any unilateral national requirement for timber imports to be from a sustainably managed source is in direct conflict with the GATT philosophy of trade liberalisation, since it constitutes a 'technical barrier to trade' under Article

---

8. Personal communication, 2 April 1997.

XX. The governments of Austria and the Netherlands have attempted to pass legislation of this type in 1992 and 1994 respectively (Varangis, Crossley and Primo Brago 1995: 3), but both initiatives were invoked.

However, the FSC certification and labelling system advocated by B&Q is essentially voluntary, and therefore is not expected to comply with free trade rules. Concern does exist about the degree of government involvement in the execution and funding of eco-labelling projects (West 1995: 20); although the FSC operates as an independent body, it has received funding from the governments of Mexico, Austria and the Netherlands.[9] Furthermore, the Timber Trade Federation considers the FSC to be illegal under EU and UK laws; the head of the Federation wrote to all members of the 1995 Plus Group last year warning that companies may face claims for damages and fines for entering a restrictive trading agreement. B&Q's Dr Knight angrily rejected the assertion, since the FSC is an optional scheme applicable across the whole world and is not a discriminatory restraint of trade (House of Commons Environment Committee 1996: lxiv).

⫼ Sovereignty

There is some evidence that UN bodies feel threatened by independent certification because it bypasses international law through its voluntary nature, and is therefore a market-driven infringement of sovereignty in the producer country.[10] Indeed, B&Q's Dr Knight has been surprised at the power of his company, and asserted that 'we are more powerful than small governments because we have enormous cheque books' (cited in Madden and Orton 1996: 26)! This is dubious ethical ground in the light of FSC Principle 3, which respects the rights of indigenous peoples to govern their own territory (see Chapter 9, page 123); how does this differ from the larger-scale national sovereignty issue?

⫼ B&Q: An Effective Policy?

In the light of the broader issues of the certification debate, a set of conditions can be identified that must be satisfied to enable a policy such as that of B&Q's to function effectively. Figure 4 depicts the major players in B&Q's policy where each circle represents a sub-set of a larger group—that is, sustainably managed forests as a section of the timber trade, DIY retailing as a part of the timber products trade and eco-sensitive consumers as a sector of the whole consumer base. The overlap of these circles illustrates a combination of different circumstances that occur as the actors from each group interact; for example, DIY traders deal with sustainably managed forests when they advocate timber certification, while 'green' consumers may specifically choose B&Q over their competitors because of the company's environmental reputation (although customers may not necessarily be product-discriminating once inside the store!). Only when the conditions required by the central sub-set are met will certification be effective: that is, where DIY customers who specifically demand timber from sustainably managed forests are willing to pay the price premium on certified products.

---

9. Forest Stewardship Council at *http://antequerrra.antequerra.com:80/FSC/index.html*, p. 4.
10. Personal communication with Dr David Murphy, 7 March 1997.

THE TIMBER TRADE

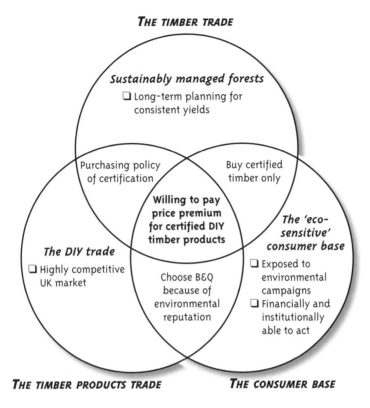

THE TIMBER PRODUCTS TRADE   **THE CONSUMER BASE**

Figure 4: The Major Players in B&Q's Timber Purchasing Policy

The opportunity for this combination exists in a small sector of the UK market, producing a win–win strategy that benefits the environment and the company culture while securing a specialised niche in the competitive DIY business. The B&Q policy has applied pressure to upgrade management practices, thereby encouraging sustainable forest management within the boundaries of its timber supply chain for UK stores.

However, as mentioned above, B&Q's research identified that most of its timber sources are located in temperate and boreal zones. While not denying the extent of forestry management problems that exist in these regions, consumer awareness in the North—which prompts the demand for certified timber—is generally focused on the global consequences of tropical deforestation. The purchasing policy will have a limited impact on the adoption of sustainable forest management in the tropics because of the small proportion of trade that is connected with these regions, and the existence of other business options open to tropical growers if the criteria prove too troublesome. As B&Q strives to meet its staggered targets leading to full certification, there is a danger that UK consumers will perceive that this market-driven approach is tackling the problems of deforestation and forest degradation globally when the benefits of the B&Q policy are otherwise distributed.

The absence of a significant eco-sensitive consumer base in the Taiwan market coupled with a higher proportion of tropical producers in the local supply base means that the conditions illustrated in the diagram cannot be satisfied, and therefore B&Q has difficulty in implementing such a rigorous policy as that applied in the UK. This is a major limitation of a market-based approach; in the wider picture, it is clear that other instruments are needed to encourage the adoption of sustainable practices when market-driven tools cannot be fully effective.

▌ *Conclusion*

This discussion began by defining sustainable forest management according to the Forest Stewardship Council, and introduced the World Wide Fund for Nature's 1995 Group and its support of the FSC in their independent certification scheme. As a key force behind the formation of both of these organisations, B&Q has come a long way in the environmental sphere since the days of inflatable chainsaws; its rigorous system of internal scrutiny, now extended to the objective of full product certification by the FSC, has earned it a reputation of environmental champion in the DIY and other trades.

However, the adoption of a certification process has wider implications. It is imperative that the accreditation body—as named by the FSC in this case—remains independent, a position that becomes increasingly difficult to maintain as the organisation matures. Furthermore, the debate over the costs of improving management practices is the same issue that paralyses political discussions at international level. Certification moves towards bypassing the deadlock but does not eradicate the problem; it may even exacerbate inter-governmental tension over issues such as GATT compliance and sovereignty.

Finally, a market-based solution in the quest for sustainable forestry is restrained by the market signals that induce its conception. B&Q is to be congratulated for the achievements of its timber programme; but where consumer demand for certified timber is negligible, as is the case in Taiwan and other Asian countries, the economic incentive for producers to improve management practices is diminished. Similarly, if retailers find the challenge of sourcing only certified timber too restrictive, substitute materials may be used with a potentially greater environmental impact.

The role of any private corporation in encouraging better forestry practices is limited. Independent certification as a market-based instrument should not be seen as an alternative to regulation, but a complement to forest-based and policy-based approaches. In this context, B&Q's work is a positive commercial initiative which forms a small step on the long road towards the objective of widespread sustainable forest management.

Appendix: *Members of the 1995 Group (July 1995)*

Source: Dudley, Jeanrenaud and Sullivan 1995: 154

- Acrimo Ltd
- John Laing Homes Ltd
- Akzo Nobel Decorative Coatings UK & Eire
- Magnet Ltd
- B&Q DIY Supercentres
- F.W. Mason and Sons Ltd
- BBC Magazines
- MFI
- Bernstein Group plc
- Milland Fine Timber
- Bioregional Charcoal Co. Ltd
- M&N Norman Timber
- Boots the Chemists
- Moores of Stalham (UK) Ltd
- Borden Decorative Products Ltd
- Premium Timber Products Ltd
- Bovis Construction Ltd
- Rectella International Ltd
- P.J. Bridgman and Co. Ltd
- Rothley Limited
- British Rail
- Sainsbury's Homebase
- Richard Burbidge Ltd
- J. Sainsbury plc
- Chindwell Co. Ltd
- F.R. Shadbolt and Sons Ltd
- Core Products Ltd
- Sherwood Promark
- Do It All Ltd
- Shireclose Housewares Ltd
- Douglas Kane Hardware
- WH Smith Business Supplies
- Dudley Stationery Ltd
- WH Smith Retail
- Ecological Trading Company
- Spur Shelving
- Ethan UK
- Swish Products Ltd
- Richard Graefe Ltd
- Tesco plc
- Greenlife Marketing Company
- Texas Homecare
- The Habitat Group
- Vymura plc
- Harrison Drape
- Wickes Building Supplies Ltd
- Hawk Developments plc
- John Wilman Ltd
- Helix Lighting Ltd
- Woodbridge Timber Ltd
- Hunter Douglas
- Woodlam Products
- John Dickinson Stationery Ltd

Bibliography

Aarne, M. (ed.) (1994) *Yearbook of Forest Statistics 1993–1994* (Helsinki: Finnish Forest Research Institute).

Apaiwongse, Tom Sorrowful (1991) 'Factors Affecting Attitudes among Buying Center Members towards Adoption of an Ecologically-Related Regulatory Alternative: A New Application of Organizational Theory to a Public Policy Issue', *Journal of Public Policy and Marketing* 10.2: 145-60.

Apaiwongse, Tom Sorrowful (1994) 'The Influence of Green Policies on a Dual Marketing Center', *Journal of Business and Industrial Marketing* 9.2: 41-50.

Azzone, G., G. Noci , R. Manzini, R. Welford and C. Young (1996) 'Defining Environmental Performance Indicators: An Integrated Framework', *Business Strategy and the Environment* 5: 69-80.

B&Q (1993) *How Green is My Hammer?* (Eastleigh, UK: B&Q).

B&Q (1994) *Environmental Policy Statement* (Eastleigh, UK: B&Q).

B&Q (1995) *How Green is My Front Door? B&Q's Second Environmental Review* (Eastleigh, UK: B&Q).

B&Q (1996a) *The B&Q World of Timber: A Report on B&Q's 1995 Timber Target* (Eastleigh, UK: B&Q).

B&Q (1996b) 'All you Wanted to Know about the Nankan Store in Taiwan', in *Talking Shop: The Magazine for Everyone at B&Q* 93 (March 1996).

B&Q (1998a) *Progress Report by B&Q on FSC Certification* (mimeo; Eastleigh, UK: B&Q).

B&Q (1998b) *How Green is My Patio?* (Eastleigh, UK: B&Q, forthcoming).

Baharuddin, H.G. (1995) 'Timber Certification: An Overview', *Unasylva* 183.46: 18-24.

Baily, P., and D. Farmer (1990) *Purchasing Principles and Management* (London: Pitman).

Barbier, E. (1993) *Policy Issues and Options Concerning Linkages between the Tropical Timber Trade and Sustainable Forest Management* (LEEC Paper, DP 93-02; London: London Environmental Economics Centre).

Barrett, S., and D. Murphy (1995) 'Implications of the Corporate Environmental Policy Process for Human Resource Management', *Greener Management International* 10 (April 1995): 49-69.

Barry, A. (1996) 'Buyers Start to Spread the Green Message', *Purchasing and Supply Management* February 1996: 21-23.

Bauer, Bjørn, and Bénet Hermind (1995) *Miljøaspekter af den europæiske standiseringsproces* (*Environmental Aspects of the European Process of Standardisation*) (Centre for Alternative Social Analysis [CASA] Working Report 21 for the Danish Environmental Protection Agency; Copenhagen: Miljøstyrelsen [Danish Environmental Protection Agency]).

Baylis, R.N., L.M. Connell and A.C. Flynn (1997) *Pollution and Waste Regulation Survey of Manufacturing and Processing Companies in Industrial South Wales: Preliminary Analysis* (Papers in Environmental Planning Research Working Paper; Cardiff: University of Wales).

Bebbington, J., R. Gray and I. Thomson (1994) 'Accountancy and Sustainability: Tentative Findings on the Meaning and Implementation of Sustainability', *Fourth Interdisciplinary Perspectives on Accounting* Conference, University of Manchester, 11–13 July 1994.

Bendell, J., and E. Warner (1996) 'If you can't Beat 'em Join 'em! Business–Environmental Group Partnerships for Sustainable Development: The Case of the WWF 1995 Plus Group', paper presented at the 1996 *ERP Business Strategy and the Environment Conference*, University of Leeds.

Bendell, J., and F. Sullivan (1996) 'Sleeping with the Enemy? Business–Environmentalist Partnerships for Sustainable Development: The Case of the WWF 1995 Group', in R. Aspinwall and J. Smith (eds.), *Environmentalist and Business Partnerships: A Sustainable Model?* (Cambridge: The White Horse Press): 3-33.

Bernstein, M.H. (1955) *Regulating Business by Independent Commission* (Prinnceton, NJ: Princeton University Press).

Boustead, I., and G.F. Hancock (1981) *Energy and Packaging* (London: Ellis Horwood).

British Telecommunications plc (BT) (1995) *Environmental Briefing: Purchasing and the Environment* (London: BT, May 1995).

Business in the Environment (BiE) (1993) *Buying into the Environment* (London: Business in the Environment).

Business in the Environment (1996) *The Index of Corporate Environmental Engagement* (London: Business in the Environment).

Bytheway, A. (1995) *Information in the Supply Chain: Measuring Supply Chain Performance* (Working Paper 1/95; Cranfield, UK: Cranfield School of Management).

Cahan, J., and M. Schweiger (1994) 'Product Life Cycle: The Key to Integrating EHS into Corporate Decision Making and Operations', *Total Quality Environmental Management* Winter 1994: 141-50.

Cahill, D.J. (1997) *Internal Marketing* (Boston, MA: Haworth Press).

Cairncross, F. (1990) 'Cleaning Up: A Survey of Industry and the Environment', *The Economist* 316.7671: 21-26.

Calahan Klein, Rebecca, Kathryn Gavaghan, Terry Pritchett and Jim Olsen (1997) *Greening the Supply Chain: Benchmarking Leadership Company Efforts to Improve Environmental Performance in the Supply Chain* (San Francisco: Business for Social Responsibility Education Fund).

Caplice, C., and Y. Sheffi (1994) 'A Review and Evaluation of Logistics Metrics', *International Journal of Logistics Management* 5.2: 11-28.

Carlson, Les, Stephen J. Grove and Norman Kangun (1993) 'A Content Analysis of Environmental Advertising Claims: A Matrix Approach', *Journal of Advertising* 22.3: 27-40.

Chartered Institute of Purchasing and Supply (in collaboration with Business in the Environment and KPMG) (1994) *Buying into the Environment: Guidelines for Integrating the Environment into Purchasing and Supply* (London: Business in the Environment).

Christie, I., H. Rolfe and R. Legard (1995) *Cleaner Production in Industry: Integrating Business Goals and Environmental Management* (London: Policy Studies Institute).

Christopher, M. (1993) 'Logistics and Competitive Strategy', *European Management Journal* 11.2: 258-61.

Clarke, K., and S. Fineman (1995) 'Greening Managers: The Stakeholder Influence', in *The 1995 Business Strategy and the Environment Conference, 20–21 September, The University of Leeds: Conference Proceedings* (Shipley, UK: ERP Environment): 43-48.

Clayton, J., and N. Rotheroe (1997) 'An Analysis of Supplier Environmental Assessment in the UK', in *The 1997 Eco-Management and Auditing Conference, 3–4 July, The Manchester Conference Centre: Conference Proceedings* (Shipley, UK: ERP Environment): 19-24.

Commission of the European Communities (CEC) (1993a) 'Towards Sustainability: A European Programme of Policy and Action in Relation to the Environment and Sustainable Development', *Official Journal of the European Communities* C138.17 (May 1993): 5-98.

Commission of the European Communities (CEC) (1993b) 'Council Regulation (EEC) No. 1836/93 of 29 June 1993 Allowing Voluntary Participation by Companies in the Industrial Sector in a Community Eco-Management and Audit Scheme', *Official Journal of the European Communities* L168.36 (July 1993): 1-18.

Commission of the European Communities (CEC) (1996a) *Progress Report from the Commission on the Implementation of the European Community Programme of Policy and Action in Relation to the Environment and Sustainable Development* (COM[95] 624 final; Brussels: CEC).

Commission of the European Communities (CEC) (1996b) *Public Procurement in the European Union: Exploring the Way Forward* (Green Paper; COM[96] 583 final; Brussels: CEC).

Commission of the European Communities (CEC) (1998) *Les marchés publics dans l'Union Euopéenne* (Communication 143/6; Brussels: CEC).

Commonwealth Environmental Protection Agency (1994) *The Development of Scientific Criteria for Commonwealth Government Purchases of Environmentally Preferred Paper Products* (Canberra: Commonwealth Environmental Protection Agency).

Confederation of British Industry (CBI) (1994) *Environment Costs: The Effects on Competitiveness of the Environment, Health and Safety* (London: CBI).

Confederation of British Industry (CBI) Small and Medium Enterprise Council (1993) *Generating Growth* (London: CBI).

Conrad, James Lee (1993) *Buying 'Green': Implementation of Environmentally-Sound Purchasing Requirements in Department of Defense Procurements* (unpublished paper; Washington, DC, December 1993).

Consultancy and Research for Environmental Management (ed.) (1997) *Green Procurement: Opportunities for Stichting Milieukeur* (CREM Report, 97.187; Amsterdam: Consultancy and Research for Environmental Management).

Cooper, J. (1994) 'The Professional Vision: Logistics in the 21st Century', *Institute of Logistics Annual Conference Proceedings*, Birmingham, Institute of Logistics.

Cooper, J., M. Browne and M. Peters (1992) *European Logistics: Markets, Management and Strategy* (London: Blackwell Business).

Corbett, C.J. and L. Van Wassenhove (1991) 'How Green is your Manufacturing Strategy? Exploring the Impact of Environmental Issues on Manufacturing Strategy' (INSEAD series paper; Fontainebleu, France: INSEAD).

Crewe, S. (1996) *Great Mills (Retail) Ltd and WWF 1995 Group: Achievements During 1995* (Paulton, UK: Great Mills [Retail] Ltd).

Danish Environmental Protection Agency (1995) 'Memorandum on the Authority to Impose Environmental Requirements under the EU Public Tender Rules', in Centre for Alternative Social Analysis (CASA) and I/S ØkoAnalyse, *Bedre miljø gennem indkøb: Håndbog til miljø- og energibevidst indkøbspolitik i det offentlige (Guidebook on Greener Public Purchasing)* (Copenhagen: Miljøstyrelsen).

Danish Environmental Protection Agency (1996) *Memo Presenting Proposals for Ways to Clarify and Further Develop EU Public Contracts Directives with a View to Integrating Environmental Considerations in Public Procurement Procedures* (Copenhagen: Miljøstyrelsen, August 1996).

Davis, Joel J. (1993) 'Strategies for Environmental Advertising', *The Journal of Consumer Marketing* 10.2: 19-36.

de Boer, M. (1997) Speaking Notes by the Minister of Housing, Spatial Planning and the Environment of the Netherlands, Mrs Margaretha de Boer, at the Press Conference of the Informal Council of Environment Ministers (19 April).

Delphi Group (1996) *Development of Criteria for Green Procurement: Summary Report* (Prepared by The Delphi Group for the National Round Table on the Environment and Economy, Canada; Ottawa: Delphi Group, March 1996).

Doyle, P., A.G. Woodside and P. Michell (1979) 'Organizations Buying in New Task and Rebuy Situations', *Industrial Marketing Management* 8: 7-11.

Drumwright, M.E. (1992) *Socially Responsible Organizational Buying* (Boston, MA: Marketing Science Institute).

Drumwright, M.E. (1994) 'Socially Responsible Organizational Buying: Environmental Concern as a Noneconomic Buying Criterion', *Journal of Marketing* 58.3: 1-19.

Dudley, N., J.-P. Jeanrenaud and F. Sullivan (1995) *Bad Harvest? The Timber Trade and the Degradation of the World's Forests* (London: Earthscan).

Elliot, C., and F. Sullivan (1991) *Incentives and Sustainability: Where is ITTO Going?* (World Wide Fund for Nature Position Paper; Godalming, UK: WWF, November 1991).

Elliott, D., D. Patton and C. Lenaghan (1996) 'UK Business and Environmental Strategy: A Survey and Analysis of East Midlands Firms' Approaches to Environmental Audit', *Greener Management International* 13 (January 1996): 30-49.

ENDS (1993) 'B&Q: Lessons Learned in Supplier Auditing', *ENDS Report* 221 (Company Report, 159; June).

ENDS (1994) 'Dairy Disaster Highlights Food Industry's Pollution Problems', *ENDS Report* 232 (May): 3-4.

ENDS (1995) 'BS 7750 Impedes the Greening of Supply Chain, Says B&Q', *ENDS Report* 246 (July): 24.

ENDS (1996) 'ISO 14001 Arrives but Uptake Stays at a Low Level', *ENDS Report* 271 (October): 7.

ENDS (1997a) 'Akzo Becomes Second BS 7750 Firm to be Fined for Pollution', *ENDS Report* 267 (April): 44.

ENDS (1997b) 'UK Slides down EMAS League', *ENDS Report* 272 (September): 4.

Enting, I., T. Wigley and M. Heimann (1994) *Future Emissions and Concentrations of Carbon Dioxide: Key Ocean/Atmosphere/Land Analyses* (Technical Paper, 31; Melbourne: CSIRO Division of Atmospheric Research).

Environment Canada (1997) *Environment Canada's Sustainable Development Strategy* (Hull, Ottawa: Environment Canada, April 1997).

Environment Canada and the Environment Agency of Japan (1996) *Final Report of the Canada–Japan Workshop on Greening Government Operations: Opportunities for Government and for Business* (Vancouver: Environment Canada, August 1996).

Environmental Strategies Europe (1996) *Timber Certification: An Ill-Conceived Approach for Saving the World's Forests* (unpublished).

Euro Info Centres in Utrecht, Berlin, Slough, Dijon, Turin, Venice, Athens, Herning, Taastrup, Zaventen, Liege, Luxembourg, Madrid, Toledo, Coimbra, Limerick, IMd Micon bv, uve GmbH (1995) *Eco-Management Guide: A practical Approach for Environmental Self-Analysis* (Slough, UK: Thames Valley European Information Centre).

Forest Stewardship Council (FSC) (1994) *Forest Stewardship Council Principles and Criteria for Natural Forest Management* (Oaxaca, Mexico: FSC).

Forestry and British Timber (1996) 'FSC and ISO Must Converge', *Forestry and British Timber* 13 August 1996: 4.

Gillett, J. (1993) 'Ensuring Supplier Performance', paper presented at *Purchasing Policy and the Environment Conference*, The Chartered Institute of Purchasing and Supply, London, 22 June 1993.

Gillies, M. (1995) 'Supply Side Rivalry Intensifies', *The Guardian* 27 June 1995.

Glover, G. (1994) 'New Concepts in Environmental Packaging: Meeting the Challenges and Opportunities', *Environmental Marketing: Critical Success Strategies for Reaching the Green Consumer. Proceedings of the 1994 Conference*, February 1994: 39-44.

Goldschmidt, L. (1995) 'Internationalt standardiseringsarbejde: En udfordring for miljøadministratio-nen' ('International Standardisation: A Challenge for Environmental Administration'), in P. Lübke (ed.), *Miljøet, markedet and velfærdsstaten* (Fremad).

Gouldson, A. (1995) 'Co-operative Advantages and Strategic Alliances in Life Cycle Environmental Man-agement', in *The 1995 Eco-Management and Auditing Conference, 3–4 July, The University of Leeds: Conference Proceedings* (Shipley, UK: ERP Environment, July): 182-94.

Government of Canada (1995a) *A Guide to Green Government* (Hull, Ottawa: Environment Canada).

Government of Canada (1995b) *Directions on Greening Government Operations* (Hull, Ottawa: Environment Canada).

Government of Canada (1996) *National Workshop on Greener Government Purchasing: Workshop Proceedings* (North York: Government of Canada, November 1996).

GRIP (1996) *Miljøeffektivitet: Styrket konkurransevene for norske virksomheter* (Oslo: GRIP).

Grønt Arbeidsliv (1994) *Grønt kontor in kommunene* (Oslo: Grønt Arbeidsliv).

Groundwork (1996) *Purchasing and Sustainability* (Birmingham: Groundwork).

Hamner, Burt (1996) *Waste Reduction: The Cost Effective Approach towards ISO 14000 Compliance* (Makati, Philippines: ASEAN Environmental Project).

Hansel Kampanjat (1996) *Tarjousuutiset Hanselin kanta-asiakkaille, Numerot 3, 4, 7, 8-9* (Helsinki: Hansel Kampanjat).

Harvard Business Review (1994) 'Going Green', *Harvard Business Review* 72.4 (July/August 1994), 37-50.

Helsingin kaupunki (1993) *Johtajistotoimikunta Pöytäkirjanote 22.9.1993, 407/93* (Helsinki: Helsingin kaupunki).

Helsingin kaupunki (1995) *Helsingin kaupungin ympäristönsuojelun tavoite- ja toimenpideohjelma 1994-98: Seurannan väliraportti 1995* (Helsinki: Ympäristökeskus, 13 November 1995).

Helsingin kaupunki (1996) *Kaupunginhallitus Pöytäkirjanote 3.6.1996* (Helsinki: Helsingin kaupunki).

Hepher, M. (1994) 'Don't Be Green on the Environment', *The Evening Standard* 7 December 1994.

Hill, J., I. Marshall and C. Priddey (1994) *Benefiting Business and the Environment* (London: Institute of Business Ethics).

Hill, K.E. (1997) 'Supply-Chain Dynamics, Environmental Issues, and Manufacturing Firms', *Environment and Planning A* 29: 1257-74.

Hillary, R. (1995) *Small Firms and the Environment: A Groundwork Status Report* (Birmingham: Groundwork).

Holland, L., and J. Gibbon (1996) 'SMEs in the Metal Manufacturing, Construction and Contracting Service Sectors: Environmental Awareness and Actions', *Eco-Management and Auditing* 4: 7-14.

Holmberg, J., and K.-H. Robert (1997) *The System Conditions for Sustainability: A Tool for Strategic Planning* (Author's working paper; e-mail: John Holmberg at frtjh@fy.chalmers.se).

House of Commons Environment Committee (1996) *World Trade and the Environment* (London: HMSO).

Howie, B. (1994) 'Environmental Impacts on Logistics', in G. Brace (ed.), *An International Review of Logistics Practice And Issues* (London: Logistics Technology International): 53-55.

Humphreys, D. (1996) *Forest Politics: The Evolution of Co-operation* (London: Earthscan).

Huovila, L. (1996) *Kestävä kehitys etenee kuntiin* (Helsinki: Helsingin Sanomat, 17 December 1996).

Hutchison, J. (1997) *Integrating Environmental Criteria into Purchasing and Supply Decisions* (MBA thesis; Leicester: University of Leicester, 1997).

IBM UK (1995) *Consulting the Stakeholder: A Profile of IBM UK's Environmental Performance* (London: IBM UK Ltd).

ICI plc (1997) *Environmental Burden: The ICI Approach* (London: ICI Public Affairs).

Industriförbundet (1996) *Yttrande över betänkandet Upphandling-en miljöfråga* (Stockholm: Industriförbundet, 15 May 1996).

Institute for Global Futures Research (1998) *Global Futures Bulletin* 57 (1 April 1998) (ISSN 1328-5157; e-mail publication at igfr@peg.apc.org).

International Factor 10 Club (1997) *Statement to Government and Business Leaders* (Carnoules, France: Factor 10 Institute).

Jackson, W.D., J.E. Keith and R.K. Burdick (1984) 'Purchasing Agents' Perceptions of Industrial Buying Center Influence: A Situational Approach', *Journal of Marketing* 48: 75-83.

James, P., and M. Bennett (1993) *Measuring the Environmental Performance of Business* (Ashridge, UK: Ashridge Research Group).

Janhager, Stefan (1995) *Procurement Profile: National Capital Region* (Hull, Ottawa: Administration Directorate, Environment Canada, 29 November 1995).

Jay, L. (1990) 'Green about the Tills: Markets Discover the Eco-Consumer', *Management Review* 79.6: 24-28.

Johannesen, R, (1996) *Miljøaspekter* (Mimeo; Oslo: Statskjøp, 18 September 1996).

Johnson, Wesley J., and Jeffery E. Lewin (1996) 'Organizational Buying Behaviour: Toward an Integrative Framework', *Journal of Business Research* 35.1: 1-15.

Jones, J.V. (1995) *Integrated Logistics Support Handbook* (New York: McGraw-Hill).

Jonson, G. (1997) *LCA: A Tool for Measuring Environmental Performance* (London: Pira International).

Jouzel, J., *et al.* (1987) 'Vostok Ice Core: A Continuous Isotope Temperature Record over the Last Climatic Cycle (160,000 Years)', *Nature* 329: 403-408.

Julkiset hankinnat (1994) *Painatuskeskus* (Helsinki: Julkiset hankinnat).

Kaas, K.P. (1992) 'Marketing für umweltfreundliche Producte', *Der Betriebwirtschaft* 52.4.

Kiekens, J.-P. (1995) 'Timber Certification: A Critique', *Unasylva* 183.46: 27-28.

Knight (1995) 'B&Q, its Suppliers and the Environment', in *UNEP Industry and Environment* April–September 1995: 32-34.

Knight, A. (1996) 'A Report on B&Q's 1995 Timber Target', in R. Aspinwall and J. Smith (eds.), *Environmentalist and Business Partnerships: A Sustainable Model?* (Cambridge: The White Horse Press): 34-44.

Knight, A.P., L. Coutts, L. Jamison, C. Cox, A. Ball and C. Ball (1995) *How Green is my Front Door?* (Eastleigh, UK: B&Q plc).

Krol, J. (1996) *Remarks by J. A. Krol, President and Chief Executive Officer, Du Pont, at the Yale School of Management, Newhaven, Connecticut.* (Du Pont working paper).

Kybert, M. (1993) 'Applying Life Cycle Analysis', paper presented at *Purchasing Policy and the Environment Conference*, The Chartered Institute of Purchasing and Supply, London, 22 June 1993.

Kyocera Electronics Australia (1994), *Kyocera Ecosys: The Printer that doesn't Cost the Earth* (Sydney: Kyocera Electronics Australia).

Kyocera Electronics Australia (1995) 'Kyocera Presents', *Time* 146.47 (27 November 1995): 5.

Kyocera Electronics Australia (1995–96) 'Kyocera: Presenting a Printer that Meets Tomorrow's Standards . . . Today', *Time* 146.51 (25 December 1995–1 January 1996): 8.

Lamming, R., and J. Hampson (1996) 'The Environment as a Supply Chain Management Issue', *British Journal of Management* special issue.

Langrehr, V.B., F.W. Langrehr and J. Tatreau (1992) 'Business Users' Attitudes toward Recycled Materials', *Industrial Marketing Management* 21: 361-67.

Lankiniemi, M., and K. Annala (1996) *Environmentally Acceptable Procurements: Review of the Situation 1996* (Pori, Finland: Working Party on the Sustainable Development of the City of Pori).

Laurent, Ann (1997) 'Sudden Impact', *Government Executive* September 1997.

Mackenzie, A. (1993) 'Green Offices Pay Dividends', *Asian Business* 29.10: 56-57.

Madden, P., and E. Orton (1996) *The Global Supermarket: Britain's Biggest Shops and Food from the Third World* (London: Christian Aid).

Magill, G. (1995) *WWF 1995 Group Final Report.* (Dudley, UK: Do It All, December 1995).

Maitland, A. (1996) 'Unilever in Fight to Save Global Fisheries', *The Financial Times* 22 February 1996: 4.

Mattson, M.R. (1988) 'How to Determine the Composition and Influence of a Buying Center', *Industrial Marketing Management* 17: 205-14.

McDaniel, S., and D. Rylander (1993) 'Strategic Green Marketing', *Journal of Consumer Marketing* 10.3: 4-10.

McIntyre, K., H. Smith, A. Henham and J. Prettore (1998a) 'Logistics Performance Measurement and Greening Supply Chains: Diverging Mindsets', *The International Journal of Logistics Management* in press.

McIntyre, K., H. Smith, A. Henham and J. Prettore (1998b) 'Environmental Performance Indicators for Integrated Supply Chains', *Supply Chain Management: An International Journal* in press.

McPoland, F. (1995) 'Notes from the Federal Environmental Executive, Fran McPoland', *Closing the Circle News* 1 (Fall): 2.

Meffert, H., and M. Kirchgeorg (1993) *Marktorientiertes Umweltmanagement* (Stuttgart: Schäffer-Pöschel Verlag).

Mendleson, N., and M.J. Polonsky (1995) 'Using Strategic Alliances to Develop Credible Green Marketing', *Journal of Consumer Marketing* 12.2: 4-18.

Menon, A., and A. Menon (1997) 'Enviropreneurial Marketing Strategy: The Emergence of Corporate Environmentalism as Market Strategy', *Journal of Marketing* 61.1: 51-67.

Miles, M., and I. Hubberman (1984) *Qualitative Data Analysis* (Lexington, MA: Lexington Books).

Milieukeur (1994) *Certification Schedule: Copier Paper, KPR.2, MK14* (Den Haag: Stichting Milieukeur, 1 June 1994).

MiljøKompetans (1992) Grønt kontor: Et pilotprosjekt in OL-regionen (Oslo: MiljøKompetans).

MiljøKompetans (1994) *Grønn statlig innkjøpspolitikk* (Oslo: MiljøKompetans).

Miljøverndepartementet (Norway) (1993) *Grønt Kontor in Miljøverndepartementet, Fase 1* (Oslo: Miljøverndepartementet).

Miljøverndepartmentet (Norway) (1994) *Grønt Kontor in Miljøverndepartementet, Fase 2* (Oslo: Miljøverndepartmentet).

Ministry of Environment and Ministry of Economic Affairs, Netherlands (1996) *Memorandum on Products and the Environment* (The Hague: Ministry of Environment and Ministry of Economic Affairs).

Ministry of Environment, Ministry of Economic Affairs, Ministry of Agriculture, Nature and Fisheries and Ministry of Transport and Water Management, Netherlands (1997) *Memorandum on Environment and Economy: Towards a Sustainable Economy* (The Hague: Ministry of Environment, Ministry of Economic Affairs, Ministry of Agriculture, Nature and Fisheries and Ministry of Transport and Water Management).

Ministry of the Interior, Netherlands (1997) *Environmental Clauses* (The Hague: Ministry of the Interior).

Moss, S.J., *et al.* (1994) *A Guide for Reviewing Environmental Policy Studies* (Sacramento, CA: California Environmental Protection Agency).

Murphy, D.F. (1996a) DIY–WWF Alliance: Doing it Together for the World's Forests (Research working paper series on corporate social responsibility; Bristol: School for Policy Studies, University of Bristol).

Murphy, D.F. (1996b) 'In the Company of Partners. Businesses, NGOs and Sustainable Development: Towards a Global Perspective', in R. Aspinwall and J. Smith (eds.), *Environmentalist and Business Partnerships: A Sustainable Model?* (Cambridge: The White Horse Press): 45-72. Cambridge Environmental Initiative.

Murphy, D.F. (1997) *The Partnership Paradox: Business–NGO Relations on Sustainable Development in the International Policy Arena* (Unpublished PhD thesis; School for Policy Studies, University of Bristol).

Murphy, D.F., and J. Bendell (1997) *In the Company of Partners: Business, Environmental Groups and Sustainable Development Post-Rio* (Bristol: The Policy Press).

National Round Table on the Environment and the Economy (NRTEE) (Canada) (1997) *Going for Green: Meeting Foreign Demand for Environmentally Preferable Products and Services through Federal Procurement: Backgrounder* (Ottawa: NRTEE).

National Round Table on the Environment and the Economy (NRTEE) (Canada) (1998) *Statement on Federal Green Procurement* (Ottawa: NRTEE, January 1998).

Naturvårdsverket (1995) *Offentlig upphandling med miljöhänsyn* (Rapport 4508; Stockholm: Kemikalieinspektionen, Nämnden för offentlig upphandling).

Naturvårdsverket (1996) *På miljöns sida: Vägledning om Miljöanpassad statlig upphandling* (Stockholm: Kemikalieinspektionen, Nämnden för offentlig upphandling).

Ngangoue, N.R. (1996) 'Gabon-Environment: NGOs Want Eco-label Stripped from German Firm', *Interpress Service*.

Nichols, M. (1993) 'The Green Office: Plastic Wood and Grainy Paper', *Harvard Business Review* 71.4: 9.

Nicholson-Lord, D. (1997) 'Good for the Planet Good for the Cow', *Green Futures Magazine* 5: 24-25.

Nordisk Miljømerking (1996) *Lisenser, Produkgruppe finpapir, 22-10-1996* (Oslo: Nordisk Miljømerking).

NPI (1997) *NPI Global Care Unit Trust Manager's Report* (London: NPI Investment Managers Ltd, May).

Oakland, J. (1993) *Total Quality Management: The Route to Improving Performance* (Oxford: Butterworth–Heinemann).

Oosterhuis, F., F. Rubik and G. Scholl (1996) *Product Policy in Europe: New Environmental Perspectives* (Dordrecht/Boston/London: Kluwer Academic Publishers).

Organisation for Economic Co-operation and Development (OECD) (1997) *Greener Public Purchasing* (Issues Paper prepared by the OECD Secretariat for the International Conference on Greener Public Purchasing [*Green Goods IV*], Biel-Bienne, Switzerland, 24–26 February 1997).

Ottman, Jacquelyn (1995) 'Mandate for the '90s: Green Corporate Image', *Marketing News* 29.29: 8.

Palmer, J., and R. van der Vorst (1996) 'Are "Standard" Systems Right for SMEs?', *Eco-Management and Auditing* 3: 91-96.

Peattie, K. (1995) *Environmental Marketing Management: Meeting the Green Challenge* (London: Pitman).

Peattie, K., and M. Ratnayaka (1992) 'Responding to the Green Movement', *Industrial Marketing Management* 21: 103-10.

Peattie, K., and Tony M. Ring (1993) 'Greener Strategies: The Role of the Strategic Planner', *Greener Management International* 3: 51-64.

Pedersen, A. (1992) *Ecological Practice of Public Bodies in Denmark, Germany and the Netherlands* (Copenhagen: Centre for Alternative Social Analysis).

Penman, I. (1994) 'Environmental Concern: Implications for Supply Chain Management', in J. Cooper (ed.), *Logistics and Distribution Planning: Strategies for Management* (London: Kogan Page, 2nd edn): 165-72.

Pento, T. (1997) *Environmentally Preferable Public Procurement of Paper* (Research report, draft; Paris: OECD).

Polonsky, Michael Jay (1995) 'A Stakeholder Theory Approach to Designing Environmental Marketing Strategy', *Journal of Business and Industrial Marketing* 10.3: 29-46.

Porter, M.E. (1985) *Competitive Advantage: Creating and Sustaining Superior Performance* (New York: Free Press).

Porter, M.E., and C. van der Linde (1995) 'Green *and* Competitive', *Harvard Business Review* 73.5: 120-38.

Price Waterhouse (1996) *Costs and Benefits of Greening Federal Government Operations* (Ottawa: Price Waterhouse, 15 May 1996).

Pulp and Paper International (1996) *International Fact and Price Book 1997* (Brussels: Pulp and Paper International).

Robinson, T. (1991) *Partners in Providing the Goods: The Changing Relationship between Large Companies and their Small Suppliers. A Study Commissioned by 3i* (London: 3i).

Sillanpaa, M., and D. Wheeler (1997) *The Stakeholder Corporation* (London: Pitman Publishing).

Silver, A. (1993) *Ympäristönäkökohdat kaupungin tavarahankinnoissa: Porin kaupungin 'KEKE' projektin loppuraportti* (Porin ympäristösuojelulautakunnan julkaisu 3/93; Pori, Finland: City of Pori).

SOU (Statens offentliga utredningar) (1996) *Kartläggning och analys av den offentliga sektorns upphandling av varor och tjänster med miljöpåverkan* (Stockholm: SOU).

Sørensen, S.Y. (1998) 'From Survival of the Fittest to Survival of the Cleanest' (Presentation by Stig Yding Sørensen, Research Director, Centre for Alternative Social Analysis [CASA], at the 9th International Public Procurement Association Conference, Copenhagen).

Stafford, E.R., and C.L. Hartman (1996) 'Green Alliances: Strategic Relations between Businesses and Environmental Groups', *Business Horizons* 39.2: 50-59.

Statens forvaltningstjeneste (1996a) *Statlig innkjøperforum* (Oslo: Statens forvaltningstjeneste).

Statistics Canada (1995) *Environment Industry 1995 Preliminary Data* (Ottawa: Statistics Canada).

Statskjøp (1996) *Prisbland: Kopieringsutstyr, papir og rekvisita, 01.01.96–31.12.96* (Oslo: Statskjøp).

Sullivan, F., and J.-P. Jeanrenaud (1993) *The Inevitability of Timber Certification* (Godalming, UK: World Wide Fund for Nature).

Sunderland, T., and M. Thomas (1997) 'Environmental Management Standards and Certification: Do they Add Value', in *The 1997 Eco-Management and Auditing Conference, 3–4 July, The Manchester Conference Centre: Conference Proceedings* (Shipley, UK: ERP Environment).

Swanson, T. (1997). *Global Action for Biodiversity* (London: Earthscan).

TerraChoice Environmental Services Inc. (1997) *Corporate Profile* (Ottawa: TerraChoice Environmental Services Inc., 7 October 1997).

Texas Homecare (1990) *Texas Environmental Statement* (Wellingborough, UK: Texas Homecare).

The Economist (1996) 'Turning a New Leaf', *The Economist* 340.7981 (31 August 1996): 64.

Toft, J., and O. Dall (1992a) *Grøn, statslig indkøbspolitik: Kortlægning of vurdering af insatsområder* (Oslo: Miljøstyrelsen).

Toft, J., and O. Dall (1992b) *Grøn, statslig indkøbspolitik: Erfaringer* (Oslo: Miljøstyrelsen).

Treasury Board of Canada Secretariat (1995) *Material, Risk and Common Services* (Ottawa: Canadian Treasury Board Manual).

Treasury Board of Canada Secretariat (1996) *Contracting Policy Notice 1996-6: Aboriginal Business Procurement Policy Performance Objectives* (Ottawa: Treasury Board of Canada Secretariat).

Umweltbundesamt (Germany) (1992) *Umweltfreundliche Beschaffung* (Wiesbaden: Bauverlag, 3rd edn).

Unipart Group of Companies (UGC) (1997) *TEN(D)-TO-ZERO. The Third Phase: Towards World Class* (internal publication; Oxford, UK: UGC).

US Environmental Protection Agency (EPA) (1995) *Guidance on Acquisition of Environmentally Preferable Products and Services: Solicitation of Comments and Meeting. Notices* (60 FR 50722; Washington, DC: EPA, 29 September 1995).

US Environmental Protection Agency (EPA) (1996) *Pollution Prevention through Procurement Practices* (EPA 430-F-96-046; Washington, DC: EPA, July 1996).

US Environmental Protection Agency (EPA) (1997a) *Paving the Road to Success* (EPA 742-R-97-007; Washington, DC: EPA, November 1997).

US Environmental Protection Agency (EPA) (1997b) *Leading by Example,* (EPA 742-R-97-006; Washington, DC: EPA, December 1997).

US Environmental Protection Agency (EPA) Office of Pollution Prevention and Toxics (1994) *Concept Paper for Development of Guidance for Determining 'Environmentally Preferable' Products and Services* (Washington, DC: EPA, 28 January 1994).

US Environmental Protection Agency (EPA) Office of Solid Waste and Emergency Response (1997) *Environmental Fact Sheet: EPA Expands Comprehensive Procurement Guideline (CPG)* (Washington, DC: EPA, November 1997).

US General Services Administration (GSA)/US Environmental Protection Agency (EPA) (1997) *Cleaning Products Pilot Project* (EPA 742-R97-002; Washington, DC: EPA, February 1997).

Väisänen, P.K., and A. Nissinen (1994) *Valtion materiaalihankinnot ja ympäristö*, 2. *painos* (Helsinki: Ympäristö-ministeriö).

van der Grijp, N.M. (1995) *Product Policy and the Environment: The Example of Public Procurement* (R-95/4; Amsterdam: VU University Press).

van Scheppingen, Y. (1995) *Milieugericht aanschaffingsbeleid bij provincies: Case studie kantoormeubilair* (*Environment-Oriented Public Procurement at the Provincial Level: Case Study Office Furniture*) (Amsterdam: Free University, Faculty of Economic Sciences and Econometries).

Vandermere, S., and M.D. Oliff (1991) 'Consumers Drive Corporations Green', *Long Range Planning* 23.6: 10-16.

Varangis, P.N., C.A. Primo Braga and K. Takeuchi (1993) *Tropical Timber Trade Policies: What Impact will Eco-Labelling Have?* (World Bank Policy Research Working Paper, WPS 1156; Washington, DC: World Bank, July 1993).

Varangis, P.N., R. Crossley and C.A. Primo Brago (1995) *Is there a Commercial Case for Tropical Timber Certification?* (World Bank Policy Research Working Paper, WPS 1479; Washington, DC: World Bank).

Vesi- ja ympäristöhallitus (1994) *Ympäristöä säästävä työyhteisö vesi- ja ympäristöhallituksessa ja Suomen ympäristö-keskuksessa* (Helsinki: VYH).

Von Weizsäcker, Ernst Ulrich, Amory Lovins and L. Hunter Lovins (1997) *Factor Four: Doubling Wealth, Halving Resource Use* (London: Earthscan; St Leonards, NSW, Australia: Allen & Unwin).

Walley, Noah, and Bradley Whitehead (1994) 'It's Not Easy Being Green', *Harvard Business Review*, 72.3 (May/June 1994): 46-52.

Webster, Cynthia (1993) 'Buyer Involvement in Purchasing Success', *Industrial Marketing Management* 22: 199-205.

Welford, R., and A. Gouldson (1993) *Environmental Management and Business Strategy* (London: Pitman).

Welford, R.J. (1994) 'Barriers to the Improvement of Environmental Performance: The Case of the SME Sector', in R.J. Welford (ed.), *Cases in Environmental Management and Business Strategy* (London: Pitman Publishing): 152-65.

West, K. (1995) 'Eco-labels: The Industrialisation of Environmental Standards', *The Ecologist* 25.1 (January/February 1995): 16-20.

Williams, H.E., J. Medhurst and K. Drew (1993) 'Corporate Strategies for a Sustainable Future', in K. Fisher and J. Schot (eds.), *Environmental Strategies for Industries: International Perspectives on Research Needs and Policy Implications* (Washington, DC: Island Press): 117-46.

Winter, L., and G. Ledgerwood (1994) 'Motivation and Compliance in Environmental Performance for Small and Medium-Sized Businesses', *Greener Management International* 7 (July 1994): 62-72.

World Wide Fund for Nature (WWF) (1991) 'Business and Environment: A Discussion Document', prepared for *WICEM II Second World Conference on Environmental Management*.

World Wide Fund for Nature (WWF) (1995) *Forests for Life: WWF's 1995 Forest Seminar Proceedings* (Godalming, UK: WWF UK).

World Wide Fund for Nature (WWF) (1996) *The WWF 1995 Group: The Full Story* (Godalming, UK: WWF UK).

World Wide Fund for Nature (WWF) 1995 Group (1994) *Joint Accord between Four DIY Retailers and WWF* (Godalming, UK: WWF 1995 Group).

Wu, H.-J., and S.C. Dunn (1995) 'Environmentally Responsible Logistics Systems', *The International Journal of Physical Distribution and Logistics Management* 25.2: 20-38.

Xerox (1994) *The Environment Comes First and That's Official* (Sydney: Xerox).

Xerox Corp. (1997) *Life Cycle Assessment at Xerox* (internal company report; New York: Xerox Corp.).

Zeffane, Rachid, Michael Jay Polonsky and Patrick Medley (1994) 'Corporate Environmental Commitment: Developing the Operational Concept', *Business Strategy and the Environment*. 3.4: 17-28.

Biographies

Robert Baylis

Department of City and Regional Planning, Cardiff University, PO Box 906, Cardiff CF1 3YN, Wales, UK. Tel: +44 (0)1222 874000 ext. 6243; fax: +44 (0)1222 874845; e-mail: baylis@cardiff.ac.uk; web page: http://www.cf.ac.uk/uwcc/cplan/pollwaste.html

Robert Baylis is employed by the University of Wales, Cardiff, as project manager of the Pollution and Waste Regulation project which is part-funded by the European Regional Development Fund (ERDF). This aims to help small and medium-sized enterprises in industrial South Wales comply with environmental legislation and improve environmental and economic performance. The project also explores the implementation of environmental management systems, environmental innovation and the impact of environmental regulation with specific reference to SMEs.

Jem Bendell

Researcher, School for Policy Studies, Rodney Lodge, Grange Road, Clifton, Bristol BS8 4EA, UK

Jem Bendell is a researcher, writer and consultant on social and environmental management and co-author of *In the Company of Partners: Business, Environmental Groups and Sustainable Development Post-Rio* (Bristol: Policy Press, 1997). He focused on forest certification issues while at WWF UK, before working on the establishment of the Marine Stewardship Council (MSC). He is also co-ordinator of The Values Network, which brings together business, NGOs, policymakers and researchers to discuss standards and certification for responsible business practice. He is currently researching for a PhD on international trade and sustainable development in Latin America.

Michael J. Birett

Regional Municipality of Waterloo, 925 Erb St W., Ontario, Canada, N2J 3Z4. Tel: (519) 883 5150 ext 233; fax: (519) 747 4944; e-mail: bmike@region.waterloo.on.ca

Specialising in hazardous and non-hazardous waste management, Mike Birett has provided environmental consulting services to local business for over twelve years. In various capacities with government and industry he has advised clients on matters ranging from regulatory and compliance issues to process improvement and business development. Previous experience includes responsibility for environmental, health and safety compliance for the regional government's waste management operations and development of the region's industrial waste reduction and household hazardous waste programmes. He has lectured extensively on the application of behavioural change theory to programme and market development. He is also actively involved on the board of several professional and business development organisations.

Harry Brooks

University of Newcastle, Newcastle NSW 2308, Australia

Harry B. Brooks has a Bachelor of Business degree, majoring in Marketing, from the University of Newcastle, Australia, and the material reported in Chapter 11 was undertaken as part of that degree. He is currently studying for a Masters of Commerce-Marketing at the University of Western Sydney. He is an account manager with Commercial Minerals Ltd, Australia's largest non-metallic minerals producer.

Sandra Cannon

Co-ordinator, Environmentally Preferable Purchasing, Pacific Northwest National Laboratory,
PO Box 999, Mailstop K9-13, Richland, WA 99352, USA. Tel: +1 509 372 6210;
fax: +1 509 375 5963; e-mail: sd_cannon@pnl.gov

Sandra Cannon is responsible for implementing environmentally preferable purchasing at the Pacific Northwest National Laboratory, a research laboratory operated by Battelle for the US Department of Energy in Richland, Washington. She began in 1992 by encouraging the publication of research results on the Internet and on recycled paper when hard copies were required. Since then she has been working with staff to reduce purchases, re-use products where possible and, if all else fails, to purchase recycled products.

Prior to working with Pacific Northwest National Laboratory, Ms Cannon lived in Karlsruhe, Germany, for fifteen years where she was instrumental in establishing a recycling system that earned money for a condominium complex of over 300 households.

Lianne Connell

Department of City and Regional Planning, Cardiff University, PO Box 906, Cardiff CF1 3YN,
Wales, UK. Tel: +44 (0)1222 874000 ext. 6243; fax: +44 (0)1222 874845;
e-mail: connelllm@cardiff.ac.uk; web page: http://www.cf.ac.uk/uwcc/cplan/pollwaste.html

Lianne Connell is the research assistant on the Pollution and Waste Regulation project of the University of Wales, Cardiff, UK.

Andrew Flynn

Department of City and Regional Planning, Cardiff University, PO Box 906, Cardiff CF1 3YN,
Wales, UK. Tel: +44 (0)1222 874000 ext. 6243; fax: +44 (0)1222 874845;
e-mail: flynnac@cardiff.ac.uk web page: http://www.cf.ac.uk/uwcc/cplan/pollwaste.html

Andrew Flynn is involved with the Pollution and Waste Regulation project of the University of Wales, Cardiff, UK, and is also a lecturer in environmental planning and policy.

Rita Godfrey

The Body Shop International plc, Watersmead Business Park, Littlehampton, West Sussex
BN17 6LS, UK. Tel: +44 (0)1903 731500; fax: +44 (0)1903 844020;
e-mail: rita_godfrey@bodyshop.co.uk

Rita Godfrey is head of Supplier Ethical Audit at The Body Shop. Her role focuses on the area of supplier improvement and evaluation. She works with the purchasing teams and supply companies and was instrumental in launching the Better Business Forum, a business club for Body Shop suppliers. She is also a corporate advisor on several external committees dealing with the development of supplier evaluation standards, including the Council on Economic Priorities Accreditation Agency Advisory Board. Her background is in product development, quality and technical information systems and she has used this experience in the design and implementation of the supplier evaluation strategy for The Body Shop.

Tito Gronow

Tito Gronow received an MSc in Business Administration from the Swedish School of Economics in Helsinki in 1995 and a LicSc in Environmental Management from the University of Jyväskylä, Finland, in 1998. He has worked for the OECD Environment Directorate and been an environmental management consultant for UNIDO. His current responsibilities with the Conference of European Paper Industries in Brussels include life-cycle assessment studies.

Julie M. Haines

Julie M. Haines is the Managing Director for the US–Asia Environmental Partnership's (US–AEP) Clean Technology and Environmental Management (CTEM) Programme. She is employed by Louis Berger as a Senior Project Manager and holds bachelor degrees in Geology and Political Science, and a Masters Degree in Business (MBA). As Managing Director for CTEM, Ms Haines leads the US–AEP partners in the conception, design and implementation of all industry-related pollution prevention and clean technology programmes in ten strategic countries in Asia.

Henri de Henau

Procter & Gamble, Brussels, Belgium

Henri de Henau has a Masters degree in Chemical Engineering for Agrochemical Industries. He graduated in Gembloux (Belgium) in 1961. Mr de Henau has been working for Procter & Gamble at the European Technical Center in Brussels for the past 25 years in environmental sciences and regulatory positions. He has contributed to designing a number of test methods in ISO, OECD and the EU, for the assessment of biodegradability and ecotoxicity of chemicals. He is an active member of several European Industry Associations co-operating with the EU Commission on Environmental and Chemical Control Legislation.

Philip Henry

University of Newcastle, Newcastle NSW 2308, Australia

Philip Henry has a Bachelor of Business degree, majoring in Marketing, from the University of Newcastle, Australia, and the material reported in Chapter 11 was undertaken as part of that degree. He also has a Certificate in Management from Deakin University. He currently works in Product Management for Iplex Pipelines, Australia's leading manufacturer of pipe systems.

Liz Humphrey

Liz Humphrey is a researcher at the Institute of Development Studies, University of Sussex, UK. She gained a BA in Chinese and Management Studies at Durham University, UK, and then moved to Taiwan where she worked first as a translator and later in the shoe trade. Her commercial experience in a highly polluted context led to an interest in wider environmental issues, in particular what the business sector could do. She returned to the UK in 1995 and holds an MA in Environment, Development and Policy from Sussex University.

Jim Hutchison

19 Peel Road, Wolverton, Milton Keynes MK12 5AX, UK. Tel and fax: +44 (0)1908 310 945.

Jim Hutchison is an advisor in environmental management, training and education. He is also a Research Associate and Senior Lecturer in Environmental Management at the University of Hertfordshire, UK, where he has developed two courses on 'environmental review' and 'environmental auditing for an MSc, Environmental Management, for Business (by distance learning). Prior to this he worked for ten years with the British Standards Institution where he became involved in the creation and implementation of EMS standards. He is currently running an environmental auditing course for the construction industry, a joint venture between the university and Kier Construction Ltd. He received an MBA from the University of Leicester in 1997 completing a research project on Integrating Environmental Criteria into Purchasing and Supply Decisions.

Michael Jones

UK Ecolabelling Board, 7th Floor, Eastbury House, 30–34 Albert Embankment, London SE1 7TL, UK. Tel: +44 (0)171 820 1199; fax: +44 (0)171 820 1104.

Michael Jones has a background in engineering and information management. Before joining the executive of the UK Ecolabelling Board on secondment from the Department of Trade and Industry, he was involved in the development of programmes to promote best management practice in business. At the Board, his responsibilities include policy and operations, international issues, and promoting the eco-label scheme through procurement. Michael is the UK delegate to the ISO working group developing the international standard for eco-label schemes, and a member of the working group of the European Green Purchasing Network. He holds a Master's degree in information management from City University, London.

Mark Liffers

Digital Equipment Corporation, 40 Old Bolton Rd, Stow, MA 10775, USA. Tel +1: 508 496 9220; fax: +1 508 486 9105; e-mail: Liffers@mail.dec.com

Mark Liffers is an environmental and operations manager in the logistics planning and modelling function within the Services Division of Digital. He has over twenty years of experience and has served as quality and environmental health and safety manager for a number of facilities within Digital. Recently, he was instrumental in obtaining the ISO 14000 certification for Digital's Material Recovery (reverse logistics) operation, one of the first twenty in the US. He has also been involved in designing and implementing more efficient reverse logistics operations in various Digital facilities worldwide. He has a BSc from the University of Massachusetts at Lowell and an MSc from Harvard University.

Susan Malette

Digital Equipment Corporation. E-mail: Malette@mail.dec.com

Susan Malette is a quality manager at Digital's Salem, Massachusetts, computer assembly facility. She has been with Digital for a number of years, and has been actively involved in various quality implementation efforts and programmes including corporate-wide quality strategies and ISO 9000 certification. While at the Contoocook AMRO facility, she led the effort to acquire ISO 14000 certification.

Kirstie McIntyre

Xerox Ltd. E-mail: kirstie mcintyre.rxl@eur.xerox.com

Kirstie McIntyre is currently engaged on the Engineering Doctorate programme in Environmental Technology, University of Surrey/Brunel University, UK. This is a four-year research degree, awarded for industrially relevant research, based in industry and supported by a programme of professional development courses. Kirstie's project involves the development and implementation of a decision-making model to incorporate the environment into business channel planning in the Xerox Ltd Integrated Supply Chain. The model is designed to complement existing business performance indicators and provide scenario-modelling capabilities from an environmental perspective.

Arndt Mielisch

Arndt Mielisch studied political science and mass communication at the University of Munich (1990–93), and at the University of Colorado at Boulder (1994–95) where he graduated with an MA in Journalism. Since January 1997, he has been a staff member of the International Council for Local Environmental Initiatives (ICLEI) at Freiburg, Germany, and is involved in ICLEI's municipal green procurement campaign. He is the author of the *Green Purchasing Workbook* which was distributed to all participants at the European Green Purchasing Network launch.

David F. Murphy

Senior Researcher, New Academy of Business, 3–4 Albion Place, Galena Rd, London W6 0LT, UK.
Tel: +44 (0)181 563 8780; fax: +44 (0)181 563 8618;
e-mail: dfmurphy_newacademy@compuserve.com

David F. Murphy is the senior researcher with the New Academy of Business, a London-based independent educational organisation. Prior to joining the New Academy, David did his doctoral research on business–NGO partnerships for sustainable development at the School for Policy Studies, University of Bristol. In recent years, he has undertaken assignments for the International Labour Organisation, the World Conservation Union, the UN Research Institute for Social Development, the European Commission and the UK Department for International Development. Before his arrival in Bristol, he was a programme manager for CUSO, a Canadian development NGO, in both West Africa and Canada. David is the co-author with Jem Bendell of *In the Company of Partners: Business, Environmental Groups and Sustainable Development Post-Rio* (Bristol: Policy Press, 1997).

Tapio Pento

Tapio Pento gained an MSc in Business Economics from the Helsinki School of Economics, an MS from Carnegie-Mellon University, and a PhD from the University of Michigan. He has been manager and officer for several international firms for over fifteen years, and was appointed professor at the University of Jyväskylä in 1993. His current teaching and research focuses on environmental management. Prof. Pento has been a consultant to the OECD Environment Directorate, and is the co-ordinator of the European Environmental Management network of over sixty universities.

Michael Jay Polonsky

Department of Management, University of Newcastle, Newcastle NSW 2308, Australia.
Tel: 61 49 215 013; fax: 61 49 216 911; e-mail: mgmjp@cc.newcastle.edu.au

Michael Jay Polonsky is a Senior Lecturer in Marketing within the University of Newcastle. He has taught in the US, South Africa, New Zealand and several universities in Australia. One of his main research interests is environmental marketing and management. He has co-edited a book dealing with environmental marketing and has published environmental works in such journals as *Business Strategy and the Environment*, *The International Journal of Advertising* and *The Journal of Business and Industrial Marketing*.

Kathy Preece

Kathy Preece has a degree in ecology and has worked with Australian State Governments for the past sixteen years, mainly on park asset management planning, wilderness quality assessment and biodiversity legislation and policy. She has a particular interest in the development of methods for addressing nature conservation in life-cycle assessments, having seen at first hand the power and speed with which new tools can change society's perspective and decision-making systems.

Alain Rajotte

Alain Rajotte has a Baccalaureate in Journalism and a Master's degree in Sociology from the University of Quebec at Montreal, and he is continuing toward his PhD at the University of Paris à Sorbonne. From 1989 to 1991, Rajotte was an International Co-ordinator for Greenpeace International and served at the OECD Environment Directorate's Pollution Prevention and Control Group from 1991 to 1997.

Trevor Russel

Trevor Russel is a journalist, writer and public relations consultant based in the UK. He reports on environmental issues and developments for publications in Europe and in the United States, and he has authored a recent book on environmentally sustainable technologies. He advises major companies and business organisations on environmental communications issues. He was Director of Communications for the Business Council for Sustainable Development from 1992–94.

William Sanders

Director, Office of Pollution Prevention and Toxics, US Environmental Protection Agency, 401 M Street SW, Washington, DC 20460, USA. Tel: +1 202 260 3810.

Dr William Sanders has been Director of OPPT since May 1995, with responsibilities including the overseeing of the Toxic Substances Control Act (TSCA), and the administration of the Toxic Release Inventory (TRI). Prior to this appointment, Dr Sanders served for fifteen years as the Director of EPA Region 5's Environmental Sciences Division. He holds a BSc degree in Civil Engineering from the University of Illinois at Chicago, an MSc in the Management of Public Service in Quantitative Methods from the De Paul University, Chicago, and a PhD in Environmental and Occupational Health Sciences from the University of Illinois at Chicago. He is the author of numerous articles and studies, including a series of lead reports conducted under the Lead Education and Abatement Programme (LEAP) project, and, among other awards, he received the Agency's Gold Medal Award for outstanding service on environmental equity in 1992, and the National EEO Award in 1994.

Joseph Sarkis

Clark University, Graduate School of Management, 950 Main Street, Worcester, MA 01610, USA. Tel: +1 508 793 7659; fax: +1 508 793 8822; e-mail: jsarkis@clarku.edu

Joseph Sarkis is currently an Associate Professor in The Graduate School of Management at Clark University. He earned his PhD from the State University of New York at Buffalo. His research interests include manufacturing strategy and management, with a specific emphasis on justification issues, enterprise modelling and environmentally conscious operations and logistics. He has published over seventy articles in a number of peer-reviewed academic journals and conferences. He is a member of the American Production and Inventory Control Society (APICS), the Institute for Operations Research and Management Sciences (INFORMS), the Decision Sciences Institute (DSI), and the Production and Operations Management Society (POMS). He is also a certified production and inventory manager (CPIM).

Hiroyuki Sato

Hiroyuki Sato has been Deputy Director General at the Green Purchasing Network (GPN), Japan, since 1996. Prior to that he was Vice-Secretary General of Japan's Eco-Life Centre (JELC). He is currently Head of the General Affairs Office of the Global Ecolabelling Network (GEN) and, since 1997, has been Manager of the Japanese Environment Association.

Craig Schweizer
University of Newcastle, Newcastle NSW 2308, Australia

Craig Schweizer has a Bachelor of Business degree, majoring in Marketing, from the University of Newcastle, Australia, and the material reported in Chapter 11 was undertaken as part of that degree. Since completing his degree has held several marketing positions, and now works as an Area Manager for Pure & Natural Beverages.

Robert J. Shimp
Associate Director, Environmental Quality Worldwide, The Procter & Gamble Company, 2 Procter & Gamble Plaza, Cincinnati, OH 45202, USA. E-mail: shimp.rj@pg.com.

Dr Shimp has been with Procter & Gamble for fourteen years, with past assignments in the company's Corporate Environmental Sciences Department, Paper Technology Division in Schwalbach, Germany, and the North American Paper Division. He holds a doctorate in Environmental Microbiology and Engineering from the University of North Carolina, and is the author or co-author of approximately 25 publications on various aspects of environmental science. Currently, Dr Shimp is responsible for helping to guide Procter & Gamble on ways of optimising the environmental aspects of its products, packages and operations, and of evaluating the impact of evolving global environmental policies on the consumer products industry.

Stig Yding Sørensen

Mr Stig Yding Sørensen works as Research Director for the environmental department at the Centre for Alternative Social Analysis (CASA) in Denmark. CASA, an interdisciplinary centre for consultancy and research, has been involved in a large number of projects on greener public purchasing since 1991. Before working for CASA, Mr Sørensen worked for more than three years on greener public purchasing as a head of section at the Danish Environmental Protection Agency. Mr Sørensen was also a member of the steering committee that organised the first international OECD conference on greener public purchasing in Biel, Switzerland, in 1997. Mr Sørensen has a masters degree in Political Science and has studied at the University of Aärhus, London School of Economics and Essex University.

Philip Sutton
Director, Policy and Strategy, Green Innovations Inc., 195 Wingrove Street, Fairfield (Melbourne) VIC 3078, Australia. Tel and fax: +61 (0)3 9486 4799; e-mail: psutton@pegasus.com.au; web page: http://www.peg.apc.org/~psutton/green-innovations.html

Philip Sutton is the Director of Policy and Strategy of Green Innovations Inc., a non-profit-making think-tank and consultancy organisation. He developed the Flora and Fauna Guarantee legislation for the Australian State of Victoria, and now works on the application of environmental management systems and other strategic tools by sustainability promoting organisations.

Nicolien van der Grijp
Institute for Environmental Studies (IVM), Vrije Universiteit, De Boelelaan 1115, 1081 HV Amsterdam, Netherlands. Tel: +31 20 4449 555; fax: +3 20 4449 553; e-mail: secr@ivm.vu.nl

Ms van der Grijp studied Dutch Law at the University of Amsterdam and afterwards completed Academic Professional Training in Environmental Management (UBM). She has worked at the Institute for Environmental Studies (IVM) of Vrije Universiteit in Amsterdam since

1989. For several years she has been conducting research on legal and policy issues with specific relevance to the Netherlands. Her current work includes research on the mechanisms influencing environmental performance within national and international product chains.

Raymond van Ermen
European Partners for the Environment (EPE)

With degrees in Social Sciences, Urbanism, and Town and Country Planning, Raymond Van Ermen started his professional career in 1978 as Delegate and later as Secretary General of Inter-environment Wallonie. In 1989 he was elected Secretary General by the European Environmental Bureau. In 1993, he launched a multi-stakeholders dialogue out of which European Partners for the Environment was born.

Wayne Wescott
Environs Australia

Wayne Wescott is currently the Director of Projects for Environs Australia. After experience as a Friends of the Earth activist and managing a depot at the former City of St Kilda, Wayne has been involved directly in many environmental issues in local government. These include such initiatives as Local Agenda 21, Cities for Climate Protection, waste management and CouncilNet (a website).

Brian Whitaker

On graduating from Cambridge University with an engineering degree, Brian spent five years in the automotive industry before joining IBM as a salesman. After some twenty years in IBM Public Sector Marketing with responsibility primarily for the academic sector, Brian was seconded to the DoE as a Business Advisor and was a member of the Secretariat of the first ACBE. On his return to IBM, he was appointed Environmental Affairs Manager for Northern Europe until his retirement at the end of 1996. He is Chairman of the FEI's (Federation of Electronic Industries) Environment Committee and undertakes freelance environmental consultancy work.